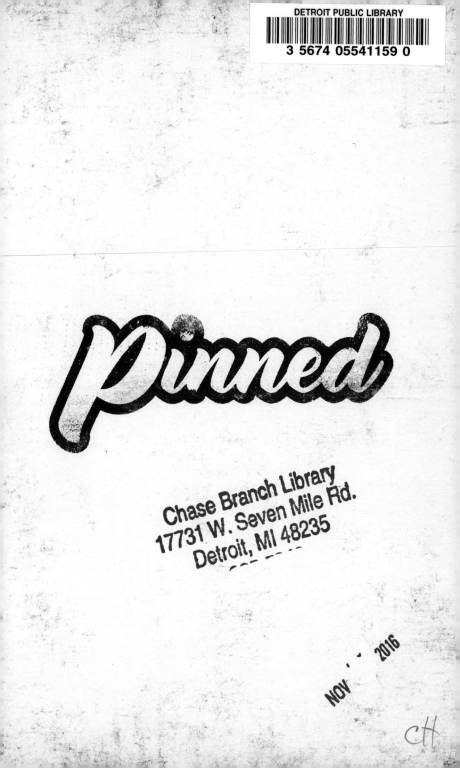

Pinned

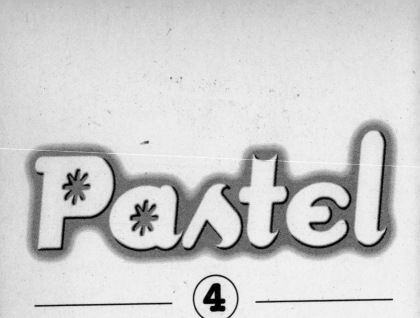

Pastel

4

TOSHIHIKO KOBAYASHI

Translated and adapted by David Ury

Lettered by Foltz Design

DEL REY

BALLANTINE BOOKS • NEW YORK

Pastel, volume 4 is a work of fiction. Names characters, places, and incidents are the products of the author's imagination or are used fictitiously. And resemblance to actual events, locales, or persons, living or dead, is entirely coincidental.

A Del Rey Trade Paperback Original

Published in the United States by Del Rey Books, an imprint of The Random House Publishing Group, a division of Random House, Inc., New York.

Del Rey is a registered trademark and the Del Rey colophon is a trademark of Random House, Inc.

Publication rights arranged through Kodansha Ltd.

First published in Japan in 2003 by Kodansha Ltd., Tokyo

ISBN 0-345-48690-0

Printed in the United States of America

www.delreymanga.com

1 2 3 4 5 6 7 8 9

Translator and Adapter—David Ury
Lettering—Foltz Design
Cover Design—David Stevenson

Pastel

CONTENTS

A Note from the Author

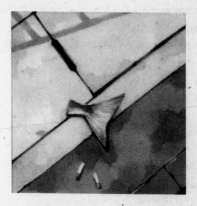

PASTEL GALLERY

I WENT TO ONOMICHI ON A
RESEARCH TRIP...FOR SOME
REASON THERE WAS A FISH TAIL
JUST SITTING THERE ON THE
SIDEWALK ALONG THE HIGHWAY.
IT'S NOT LIKE I WAS NEAR THE
OCEAN, SO WHAT WAS A FISH'S
TAIL DOING THERE? I DECIDED
I'D BETTER TAKE A PHOTO.

Honorifics Explained

Throughout the Del Rey Manga books, you will find Japanese honorifics left intact in the translations. For those not familiar with how the Japanese use honorifics, and, more important, how they differ from American honorifics, we present this brief overview.

Politeness has always been a critical facet of Japanese culture. Ever since the feudal era, when Japan was a highly stratified society, use of honorifics–which can be defined as polite speech that indicates relationship or status–has played an essential role in the Japanese language. When addressing someone in Japanese, an honorific usually takes the form of a suffix attached to one's name (example: "Asuna-san"), as a title at the end of one's name, or in place of the name itself (example: "Negi-sensei" or simply "Sensei!").

Honorifics can be expressions of respect or endearment. In the context of manga and anime, honorifics give insight into the nature of the relationship between characters. Many translations into English leave out these important honorifics, and therefore distort the feel of the original Japanese. Because Japanese honorifics contain nuances that English honorifics lack, it is our policy at Del Rey not to translate them. Here, instead, is a guide to some of the honorifics you may encounter in Del Rey Manga.

-san: This is the most common honorific and is equivalent to Mr., Miss, Ms., Mrs., etc. It is the all-purpose honorific and can be used in any situation where politeness is required.

-sama: This is one level higher than "-san." It is used to confer great respect.

-dono: This comes from the word "tono," which means "lord." It is an even higher level than "-sama" and confers utmost respect.

-kun: This suffix is used at the end of boys' names to express familiarity or endearment. It is also sometimes used by men among friends, or when addressing someone younger or of a lower station.

-chan: This is used to express endearment, mostly toward girls. It is also used for little boys, pets, and between lovers. It gives a sense of childish cuteness.

Bozu: This is an informal way to refer to a boy, similar to the English terms "kid" or "squirt."

Sempai/

Senpai: This title suggests that the addressee is one's senior in a group or organization. It is most often used in a school setting, where underclassmen refer to their upperclassmen as "sempai." It can also be used in the workplace, such as when a newer employee addresses an employee who has seniority in the company.

Kohai: This is the opposite of "-sempai," and is used toward underclassmen in school or newcomers in the workplace. It connotes that the addressee is of a lower station.

Sensei: Literally meaning "one who has come before," this title is used for teachers, doctors, or masters of any profession or art.

-[blank]: This is usually forgotten in these lists, but is perhaps the most significant difference between Japanese and English. The lack of honorific means that the speaker has permission to address the person in a very intimate way. Usually, only family, spouses, or very close friends have this kind of license. Known as *yobisute*, it can be gratifying when someone who has earned the intimacy starts to call one by one's name without an honorific. But when that intimacy hasn't been earned, it can also be insulting.

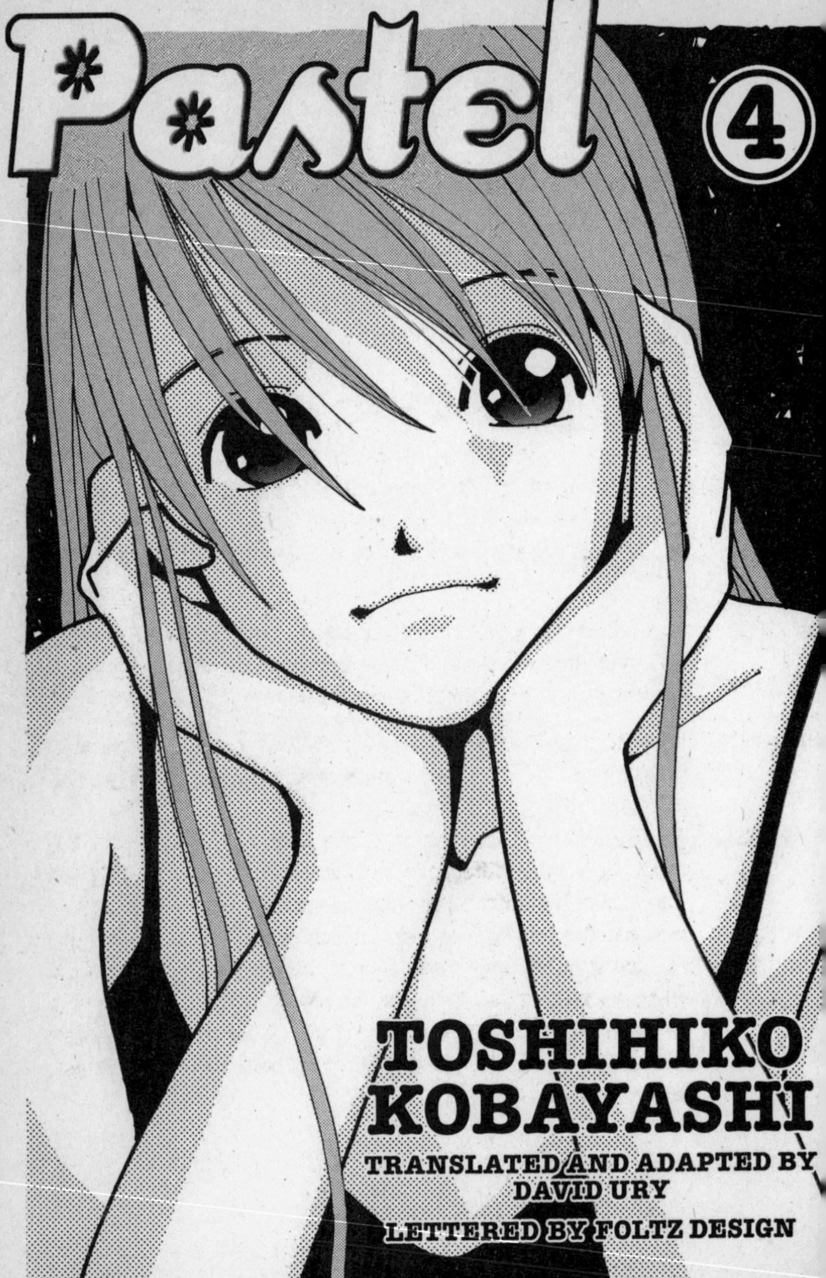
Pastel
4
TOSHIHIKO KOBAYASHI
TRANSLATED AND ADAPTED BY DAVID URY
LETTERED BY FOLTZ DESIGN

Pastel

CONTENTS

Pastel

MIRACLE 23:
THE INTERSECTION OF LOVE

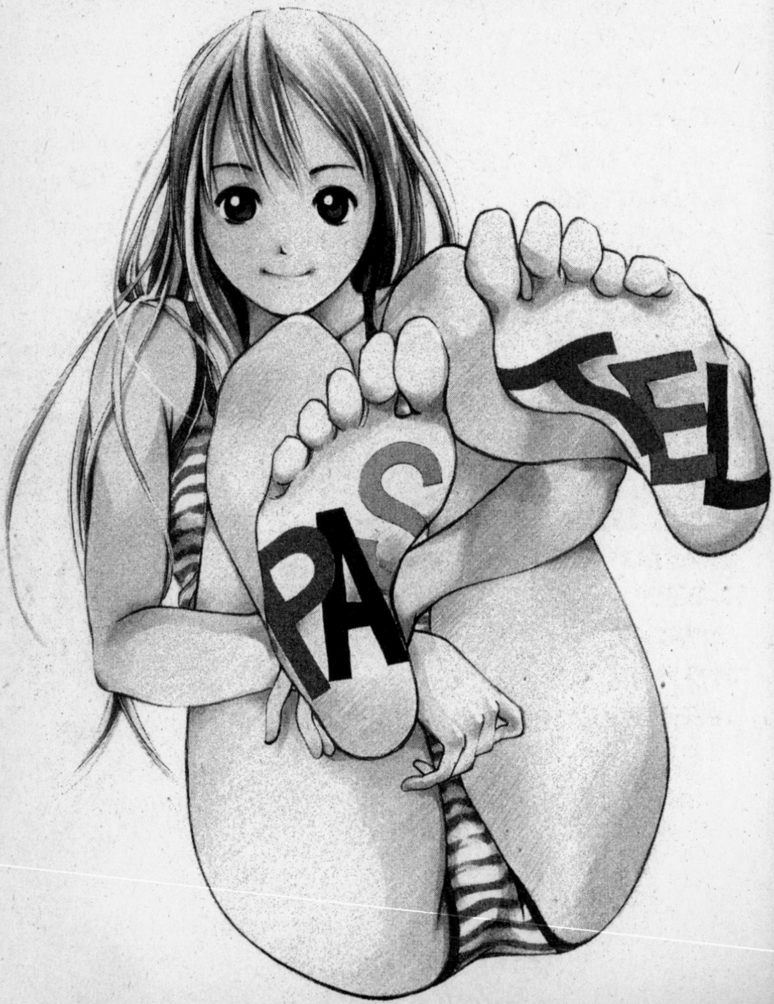
PAS
TEL

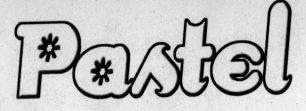

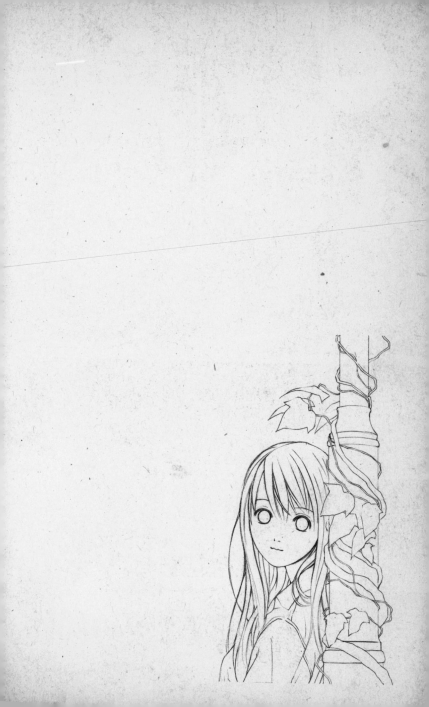

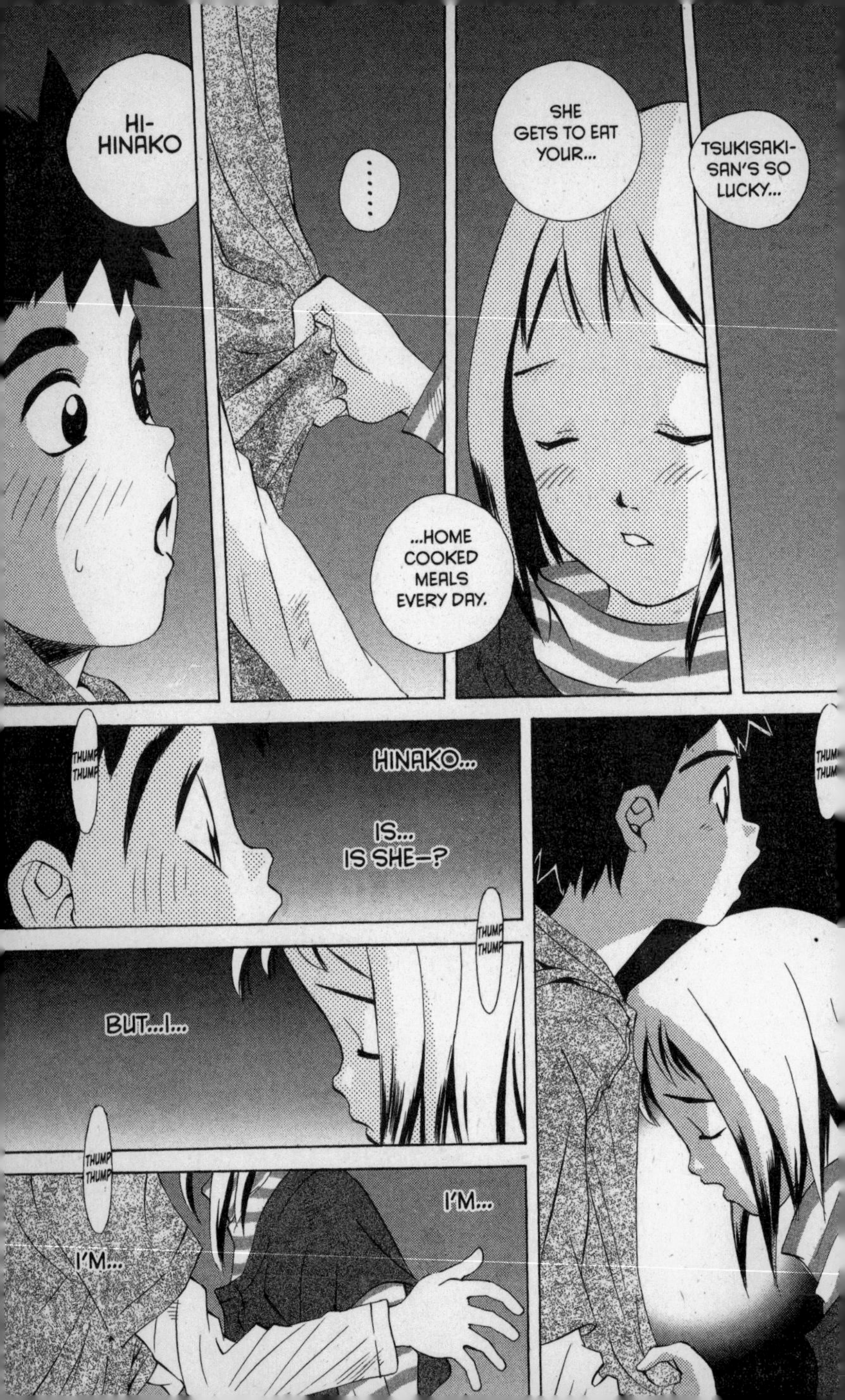
TSUKISAKI-SAN'S SO LUCKY...
SHE GETS TO EAT YOUR...
...HOME COOKED MEALS EVERY DAY.
......
HI-HINAKO
THUM THUM
THUMP THUMP
HINAKO...
IS... IS SHE—?
THUMP THUMP
BUT...I...
THUMP THUMP
I'M...
I'M...

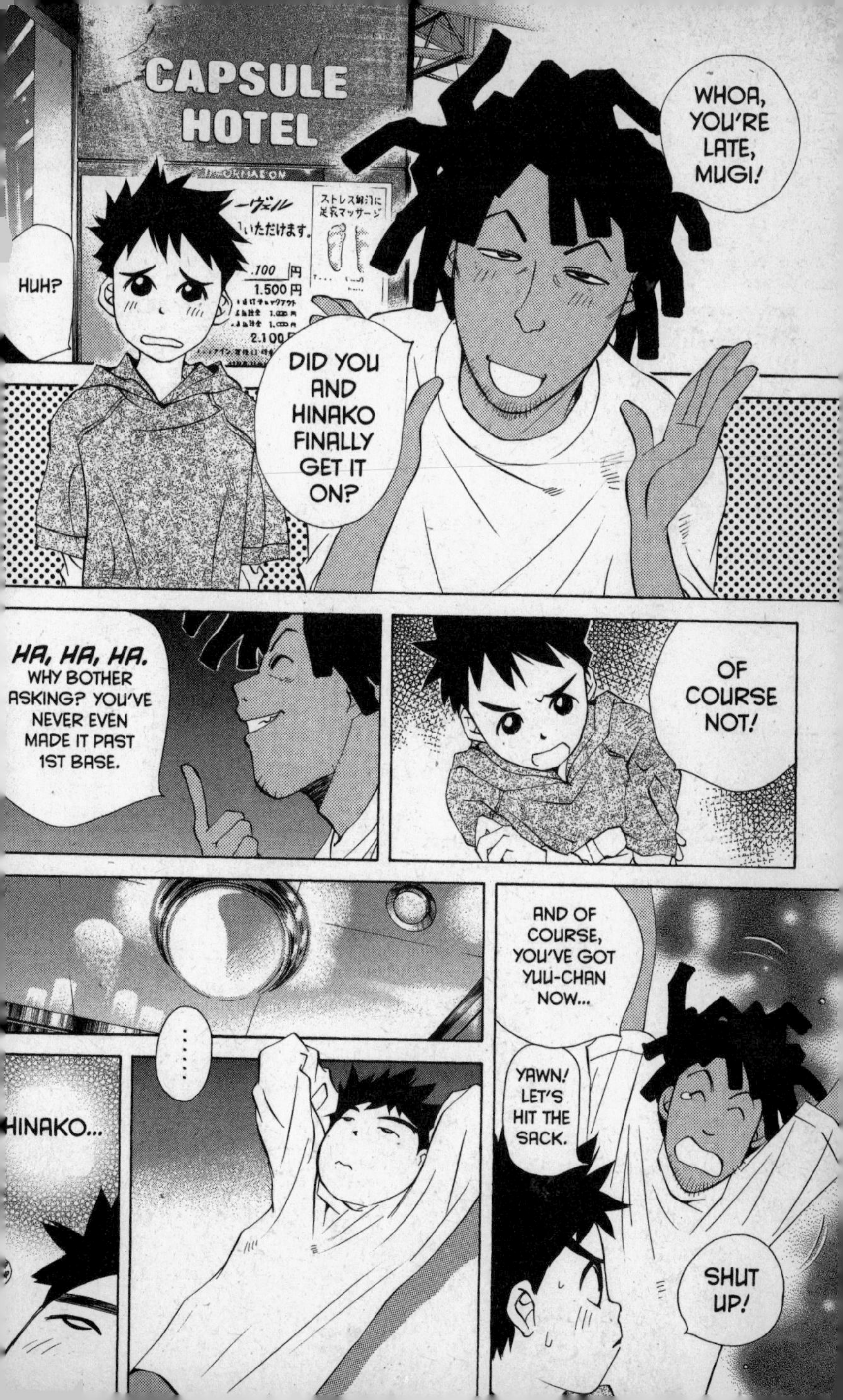
CAPSULE HOTEL
WHOA, YOU'RE LATE, MUGI!
DID YOU AND HINAKO FINALLY GET IT ON?
HUH?
OF COURSE NOT!
HA, HA, HA. WHY BOTHER ASKING? YOU'VE NEVER EVEN MADE IT PAST 1ST BASE.
AND OF COURSE, YOU'VE GOT YUU-CHAN NOW...
YAWN! LET'S HIT THE SACK.
SHUT UP!
......
HINAKO...

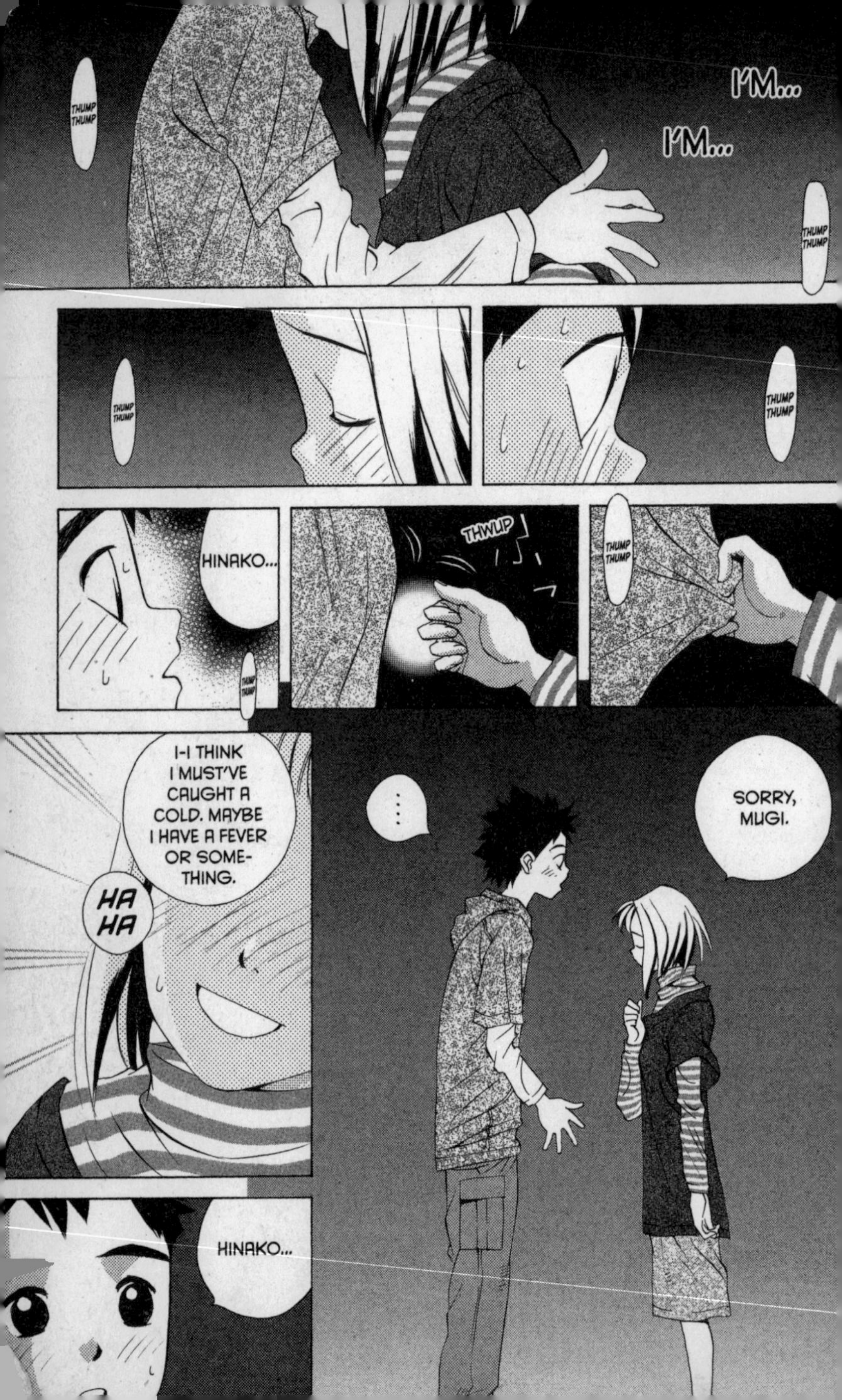
I'M...
I'M...
THUMP THUMP
THUMP THUMP
THUMP THUMP
THUMP THUMP
THUMP THUMP
THWUP
HINAKO...
THUMP THUMP
SORRY, MUGI.
...
I-I THINK I MUST'VE CAUGHT A COLD. MAYBE I HAVE A FEVER OR SOME-THING.
HA HA
HINAKO...

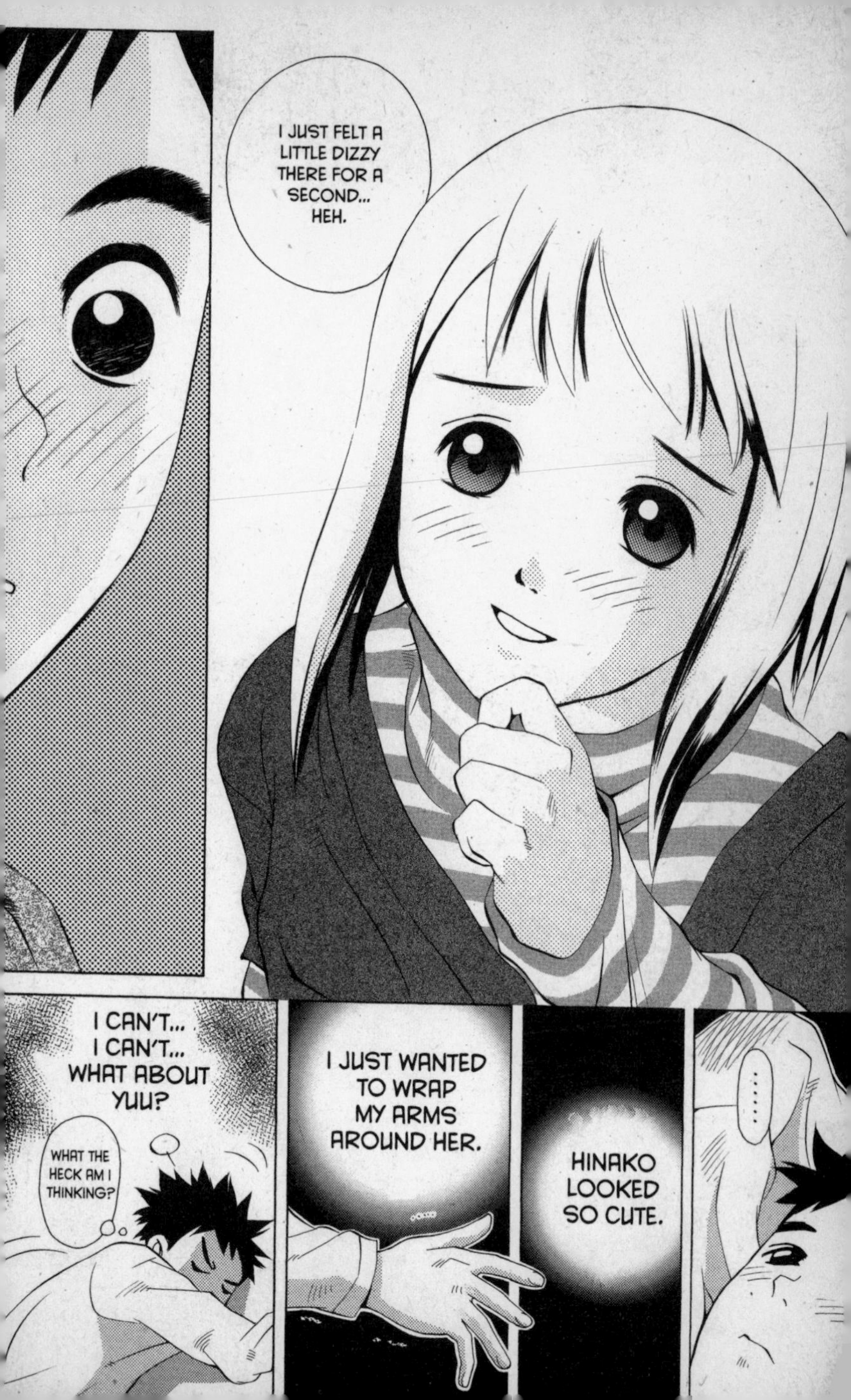
I JUST FELT A LITTLE DIZZY THERE FOR A SECOND... HEH.
......
HINAKO LOOKED SO CUTE.
I JUST WANTED TO WRAP MY ARMS AROUND HER.
I CAN'T... I CAN'T... WHAT ABOUT YUU?
WHAT THE HECK AM I THINKING?

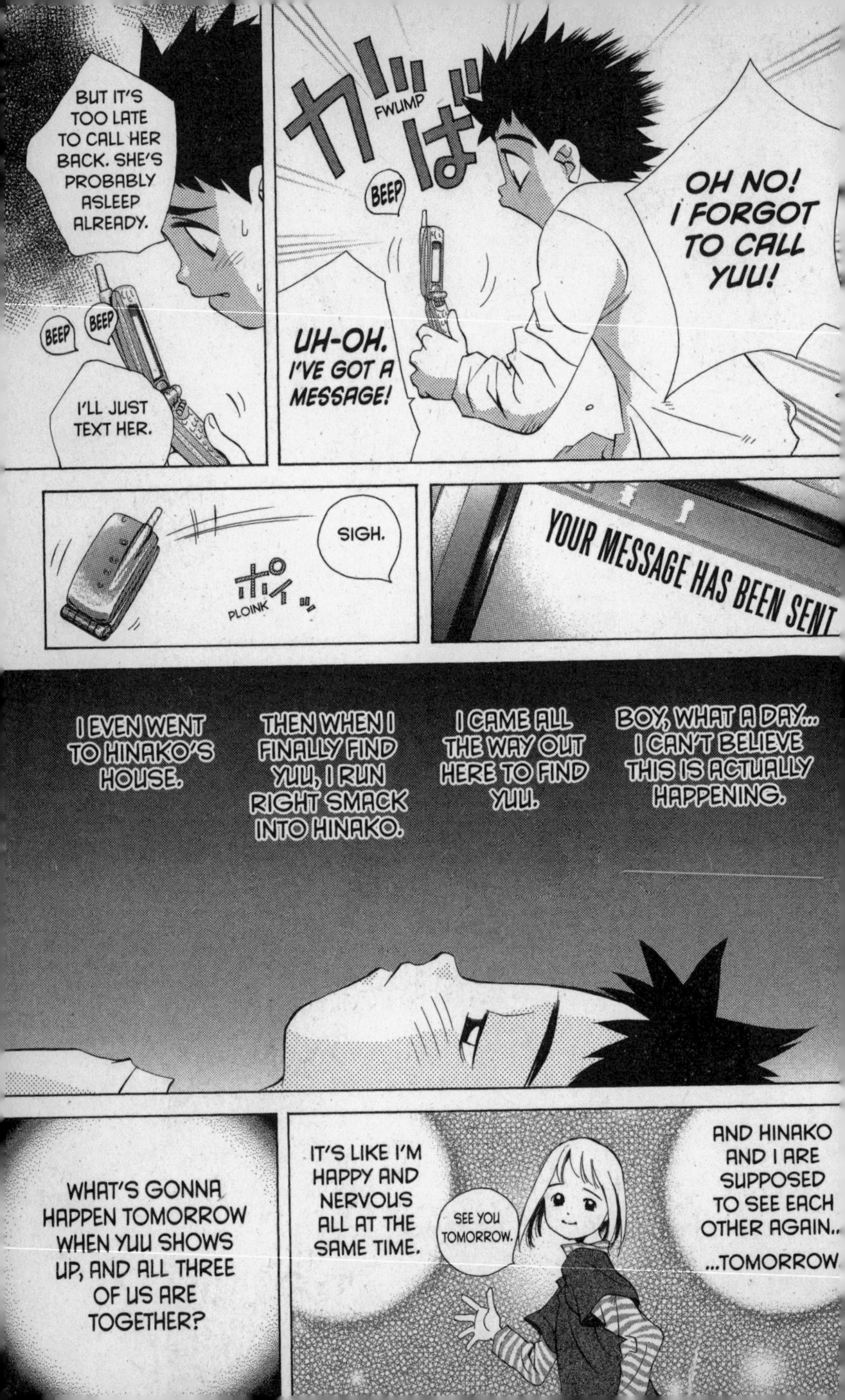
OH NO! I FORGOT TO CALL YUU!
FWUMP
BEEP
UH-OH. I'VE GOT A MESSAGE!
BUT IT'S TOO LATE TO CALL HER BACK. SHE'S PROBABLY ASLEEP ALREADY.
BEEP
BEEP
I'LL JUST TEXT HER.
YOUR MESSAGE HAS BEEN SENT
SIGH.
PLOINK
BOY, WHAT A DAY... I CAN'T BELIEVE THIS IS ACTUALLY HAPPENING.
I CAME ALL THE WAY OUT HERE TO FIND YUU.
THEN WHEN I FINALLY FIND YUU, I RUN RIGHT SMACK INTO HINAKO.
I EVEN WENT TO HINAKO'S HOUSE.
AND HINAKO AND I ARE SUPPOSED TO SEE EACH OTHER AGAIN..
...TOMORROW
SEE YOU TOMORROW.
IT'S LIKE I'M HAPPY AND NERVOUS ALL AT THE SAME TIME.
WHAT'S GONNA HAPPEN TOMORROW WHEN YUU SHOWS UP, AND ALL THREE OF US ARE TOGETHER?

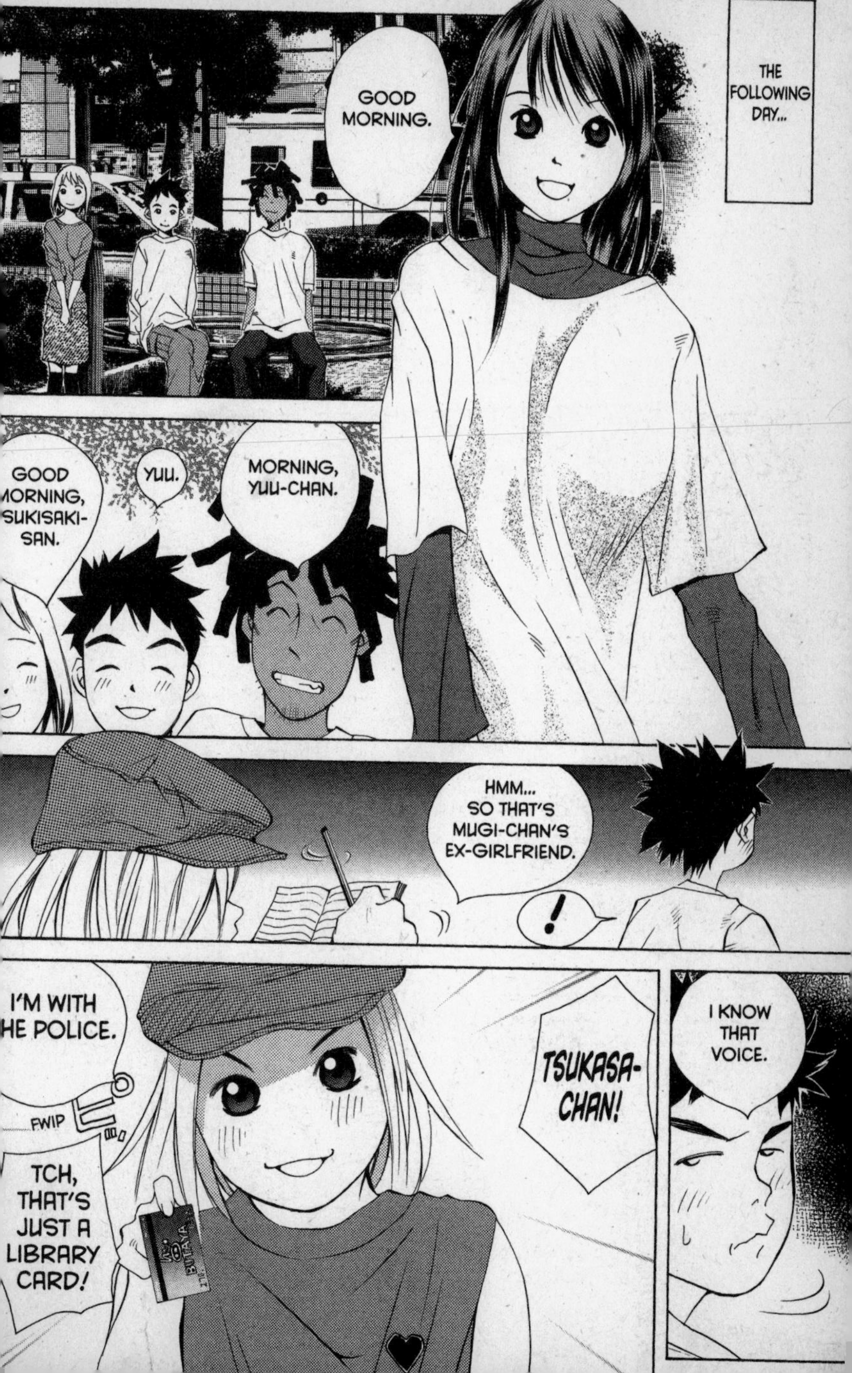
THE FOLLOWING DAY...
GOOD MORNING.
MORNING, YUU-CHAN.
YUU.
GOOD ORNING, SUKISAKI-SAN.
HMM... SO THAT'S MUGI-CHAN'S EX-GIRLFRIEND.
!
I KNOW THAT VOICE.
TSUKASA-CHAN!
I'M WITH HE POLICE.
FWIP
TCH, THAT'S JUST A LIBRARY CARD!
BUTAYA

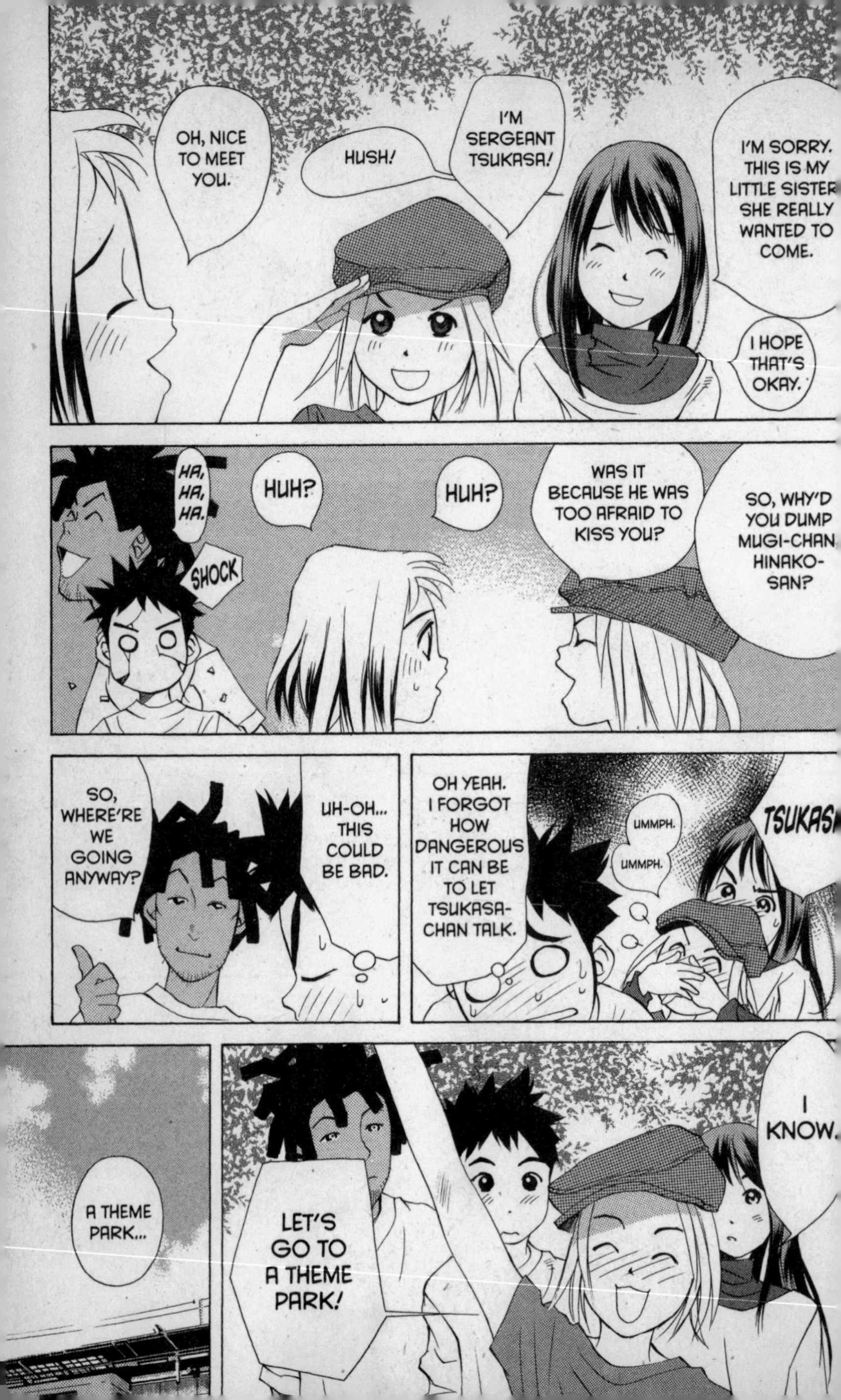
I'M SORRY. THIS IS MY LITTLE SISTER SHE REALLY WANTED TO COME.
I HOPE THAT'S OKAY.
I'M SERGEANT TSUKASA!
HUSH!
OH, NICE TO MEET YOU.
SO, WHY'D YOU DUMP MUGI-CHAN HINAKO-SAN?
WAS IT BECAUSE HE WAS TOO AFRAID TO KISS YOU?
HUH?
HUH?
HA, HA, HA.
SHOCK
TSUKAS
UMMPH.
UMMPH.
OH YEAH. I FORGOT HOW DANGEROUS IT CAN BE TO LET TSUKASA-CHAN TALK.
UH-OH... THIS COULD BE BAD.
SO, WHERE'RE WE GOING ANYWAY?
I KNOW.
LET'S GO TO A THEME PARK!
A THEME PARK...

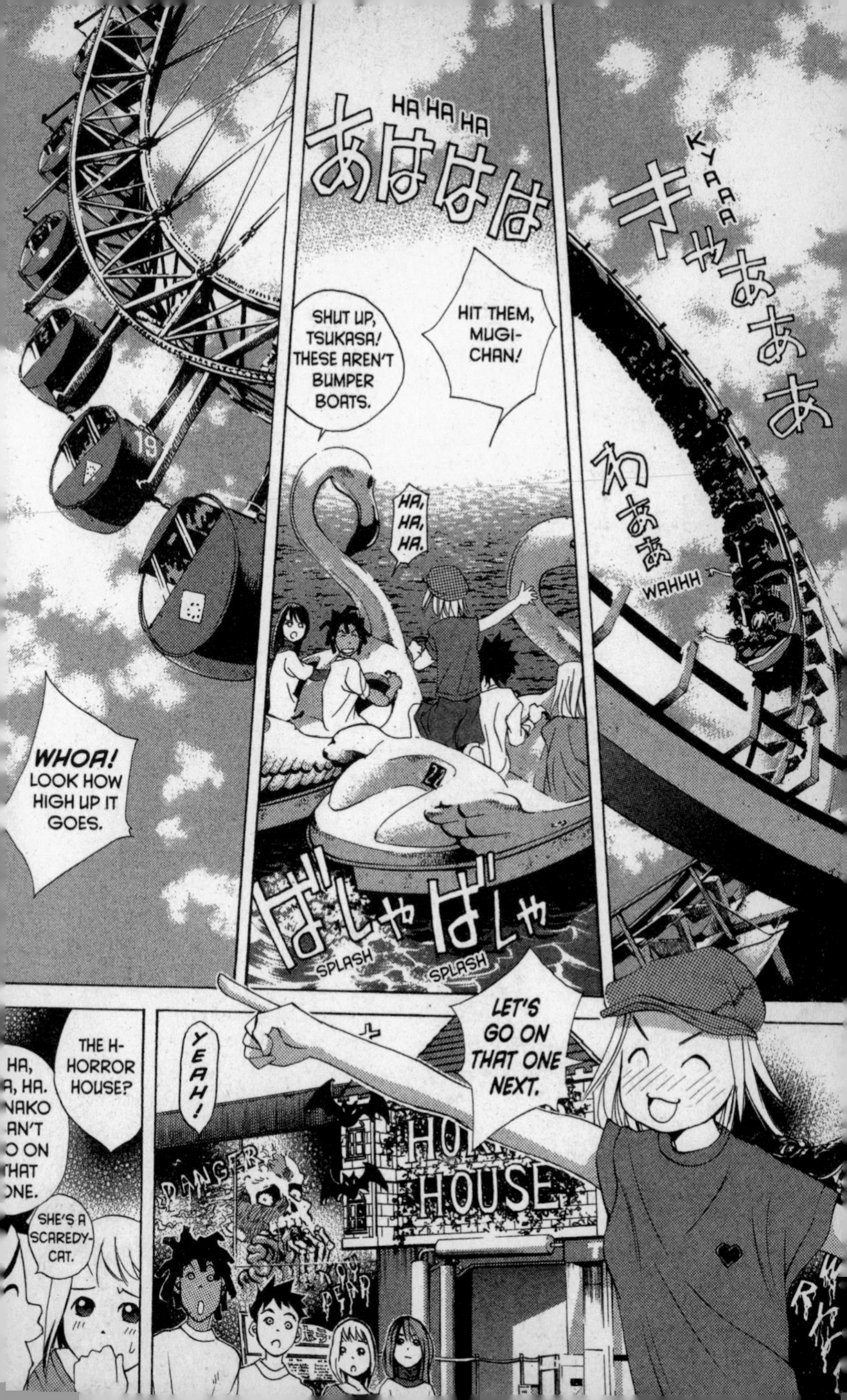

きゃあああ
KYAAAA
わあああ
WAHHH
あははは
HA HA HA
HIT THEM, MUGI-CHAN!
SHUT UP, TSUKASA! THESE AREN'T BUMPER BOATS.
HA, HA, HA.
ばしゃばしゃ
SPLASH SPLASH
WHOA! LOOK HOW HIGH UP IT GOES.
LET'S GO ON THAT ONE NEXT.
HOUSE
YEAH!
THE H-HORROR HOUSE?
HA, HA, HA. NAKO CAN'T GO ON THAT ONE.
SHE'S A SCAREDY-CAT.

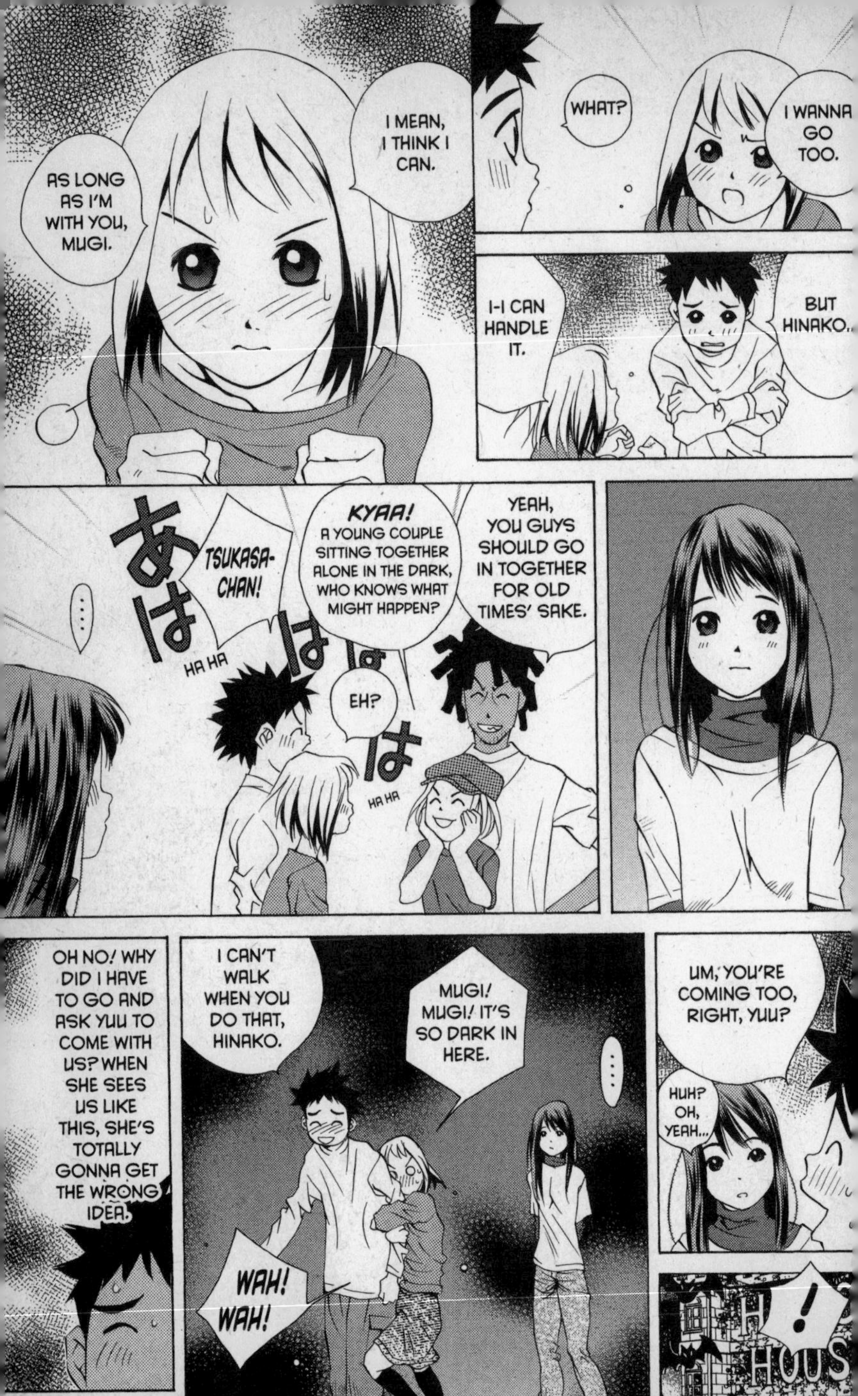

I WANNA GO TOO.
WHAT?
BUT HINAKO...
I-I CAN HANDLE IT.
I MEAN, I THINK I CAN.
AS LONG AS I'M WITH YOU, MUGI.
YEAH, YOU GUYS SHOULD GO IN TOGETHER FOR OLD TIMES' SAKE.
KYAA! A YOUNG COUPLE SITTING TOGETHER ALONE IN THE DARK, WHO KNOWS WHAT MIGHT HAPPEN?
TSUKASA-CHAN!
あは
HA HA
はは
HA HA
EH?
....
UM, YOU'RE COMING TOO, RIGHT, YUU?
HUH? OH, YEAH...
!
HOUS
MUGI! MUGI! IT'S SO DARK IN HERE.
I CAN'T WALK WHEN YOU DO THAT, HINAKO.
....
WAH! WAH!
OH NO! WHY DID I HAVE TO GO AND ASK YUU TO COME WITH US? WHEN SHE SEES US LIKE THIS, SHE'S TOTALLY GONNA GET THE WRONG IDEA.

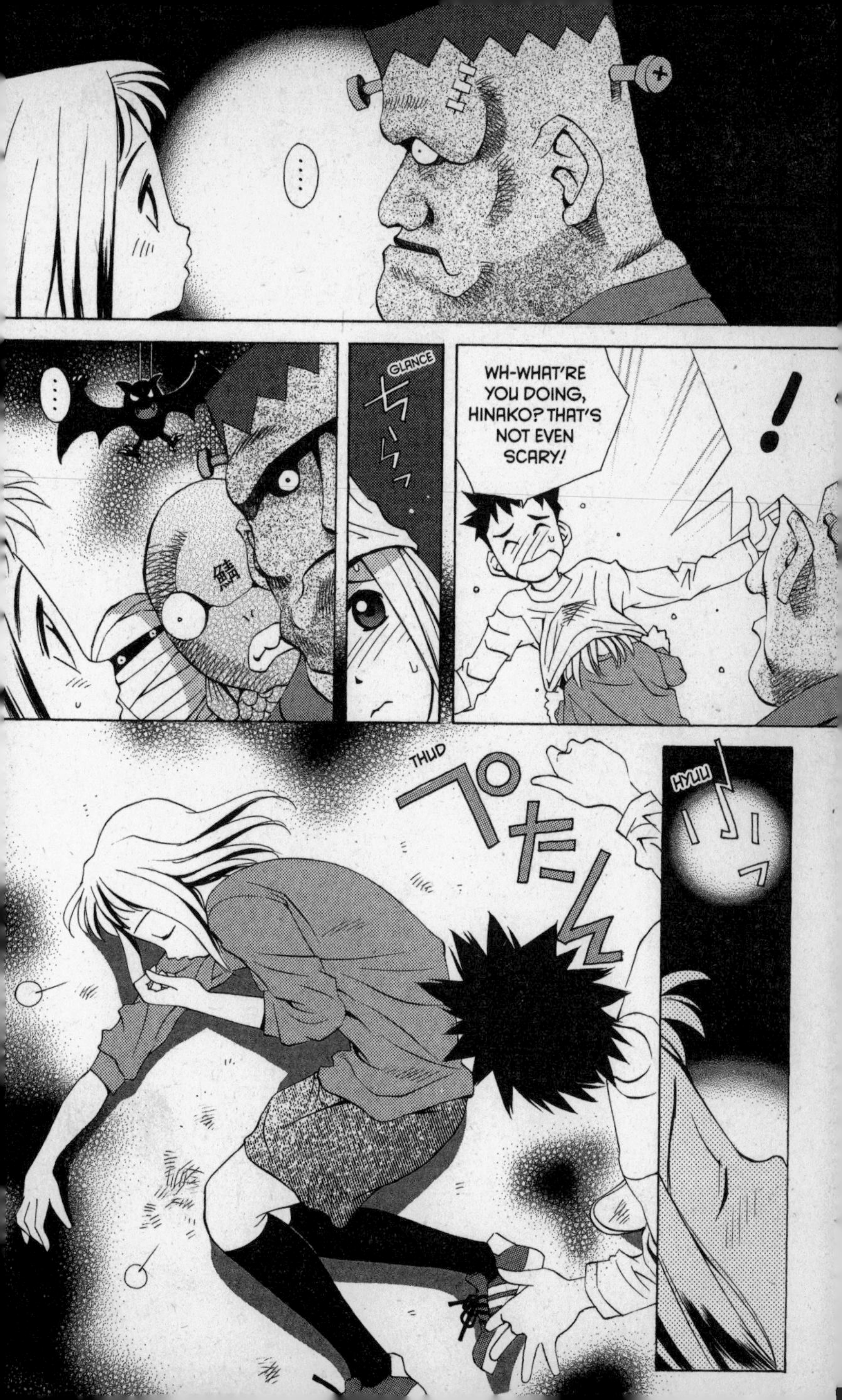
......
!
WH-WHAT'RE YOU DOING, HINAKO? THAT'S NOT EVEN SCARY!
GLANCE
......
HYUU
THUD
ぺたん

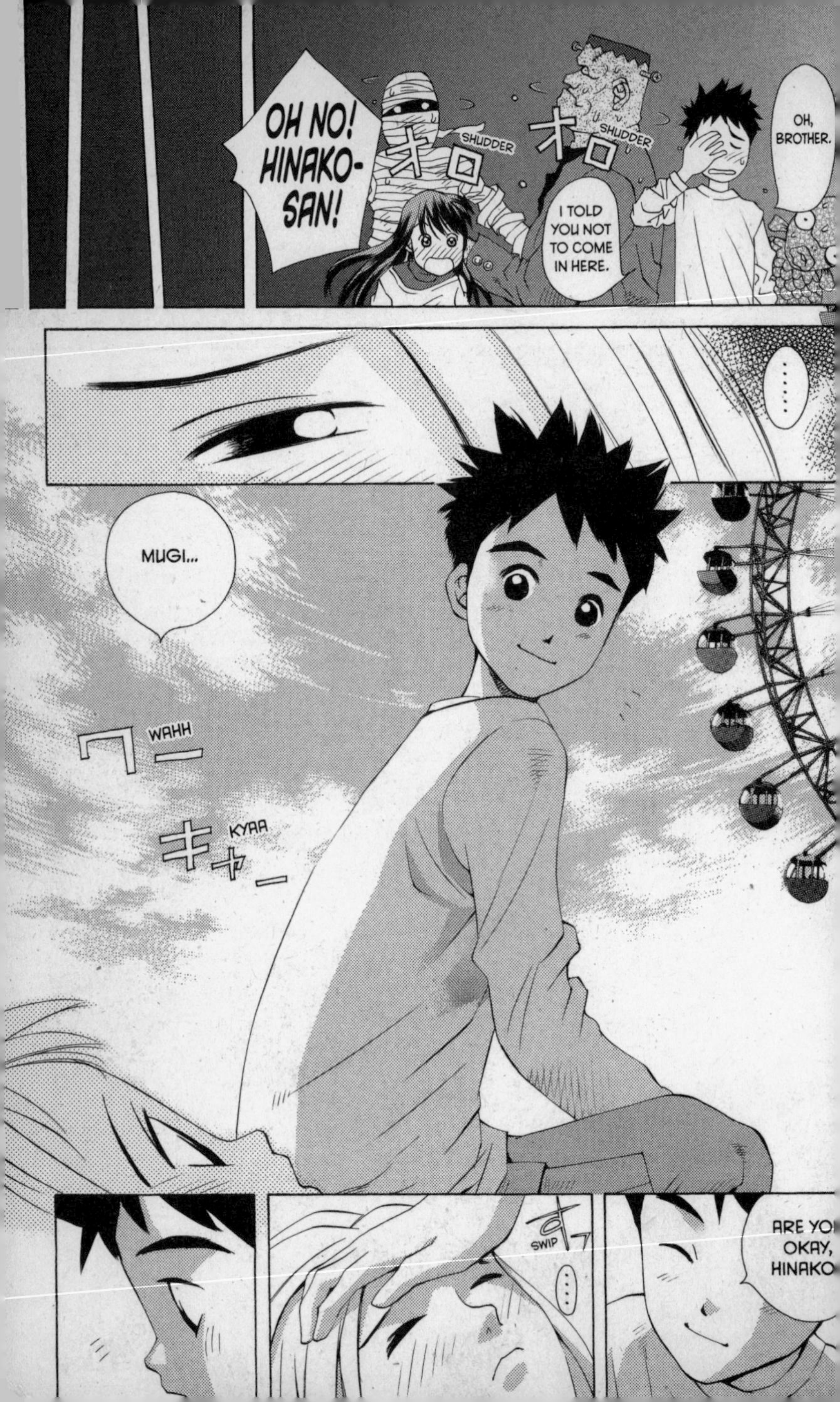
OH, BROTHER.
SHUDDER
オロ
I TOLD YOU NOT TO COME IN HERE.
SHUDDER
オロ
OH NO! HINAKO-SAN!
......
MUGI...
WAHH
ワー
KYAA
キャー
ARE YO OKAY, HINAKO
SWIP
すっ
...

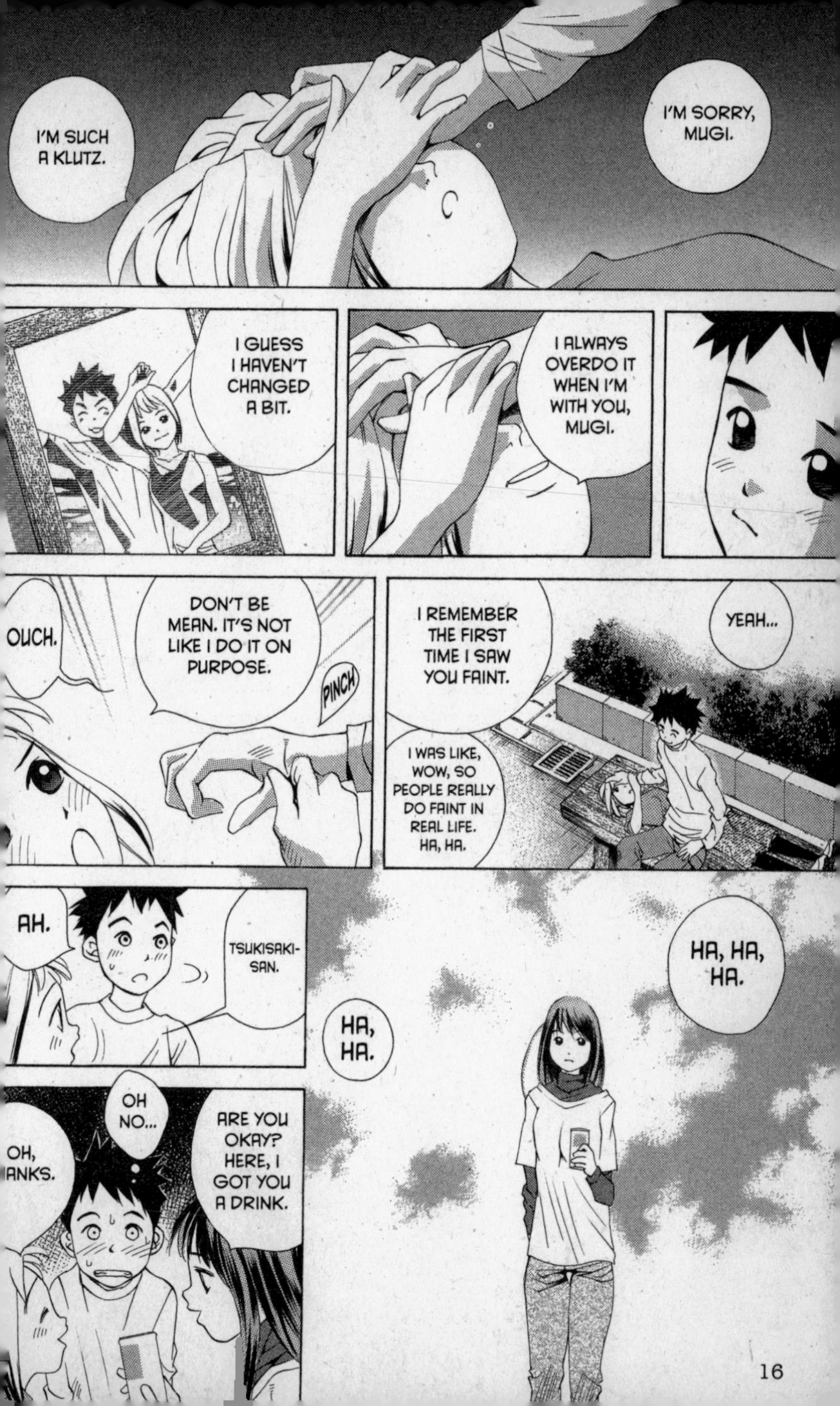

I'M SORRY, MUGI.
I'M SUCH A KLUTZ.
I ALWAYS OVERDO IT WHEN I'M WITH YOU, MUGI.
I GUESS I HAVEN'T CHANGED A BIT.
YEAH...
I REMEMBER THE FIRST TIME I SAW YOU FAINT.
I WAS LIKE, WOW, SO PEOPLE REALLY DO FAINT IN REAL LIFE. HA, HA.
PINCH
DON'T BE MEAN. IT'S NOT LIKE I DO IT ON PURPOSE.
OUCH.
HA, HA, HA.
HA, HA.
TSUKISAKI-SAN.
AH.
ARE YOU OKAY? HERE, I GOT YOU A DRINK.
OH NO...
OH, ANKS.

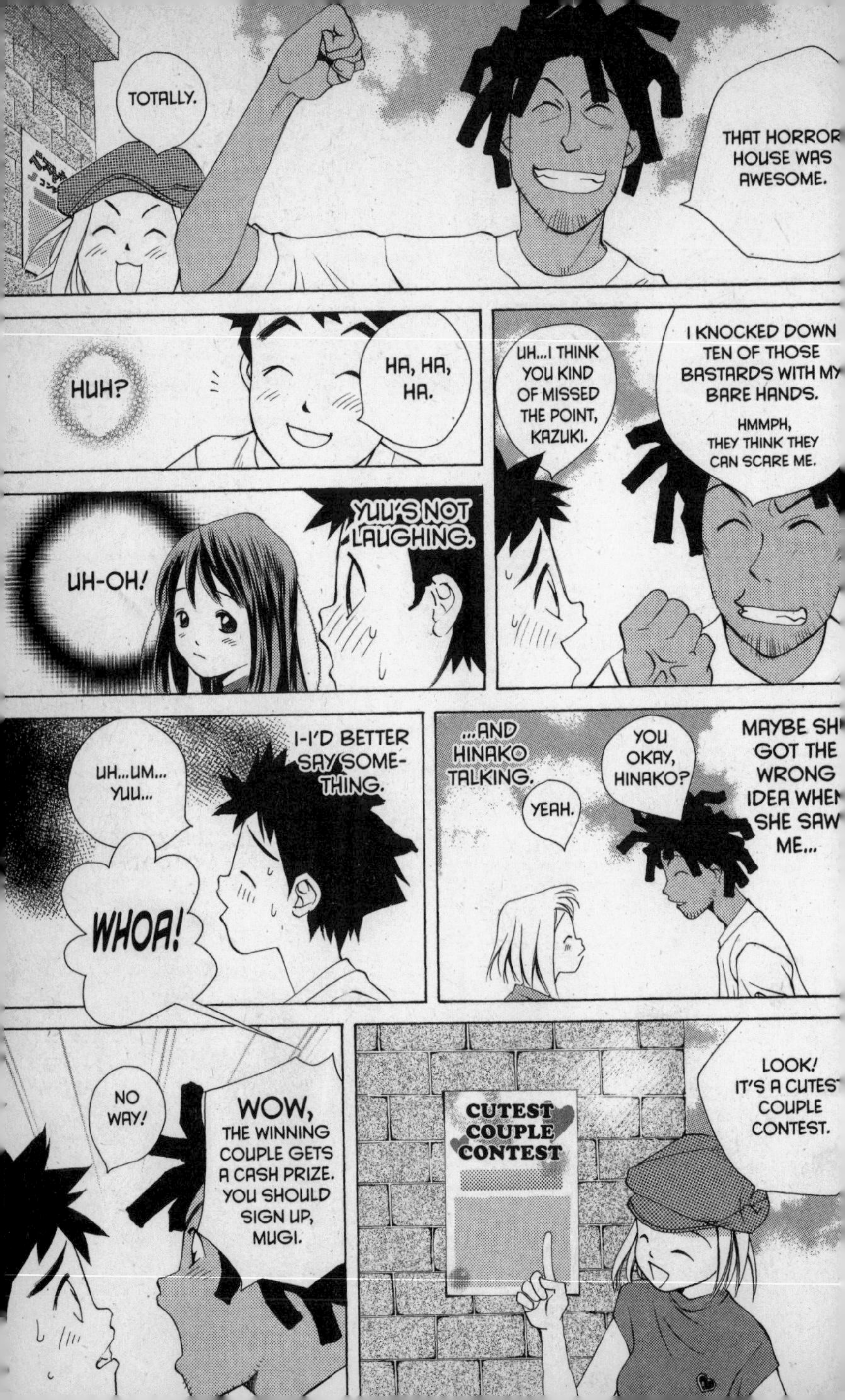
THAT HORROR HOUSE WAS AWESOME.
TOTALLY.
I KNOCKED DOWN TEN OF THOSE BASTARDS WITH MY BARE HANDS.
HMMPH, THEY THINK THEY CAN SCARE ME.
UH...I THINK YOU KIND OF MISSED THE POINT, KAZUKI.
HA, HA, HA.
HUH?
YUU'S NOT LAUGHING.
UH-OH!
MAYBE SHE GOT THE WRONG IDEA WHEN SHE SAW ME...
YOU OKAY, HINAKO?
YEAH.
...AND HINAKO TALKING.
I-I'D BETTER SAY SOME-THING.
UH...UM... YUU...
WHOA!
LOOK! IT'S A CUTEST COUPLE CONTEST.
CUTEST COUPLE CONTEST
WOW, THE WINNING COUPLE GETS A CASH PRIZE. YOU SHOULD SIGN UP, MUGI.
NO WAY!

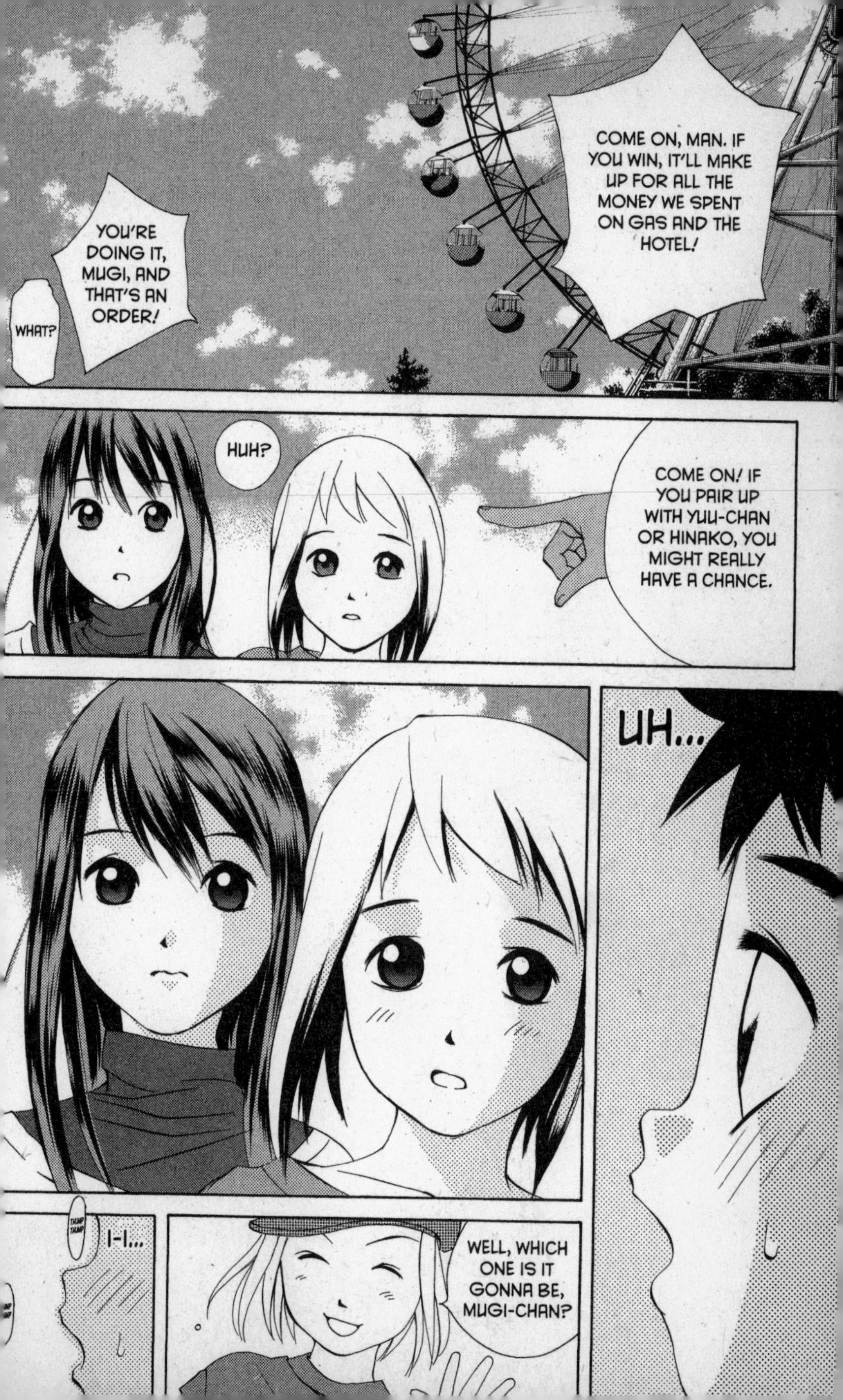
COME ON, MAN. IF YOU WIN, IT'LL MAKE UP FOR ALL THE MONEY WE SPENT ON GAS AND THE HOTEL!
YOU'RE DOING IT, MUGI, AND THAT'S AN ORDER!
WHAT?
COME ON! IF YOU PAIR UP WITH YUU-CHAN OR HINAKO, YOU MIGHT REALLY HAVE A CHANCE.
HUH?
UH...
WELL, WHICH ONE IS IT GONNA BE, MUGI-CHAN?
THUMP THUMP
I-I...

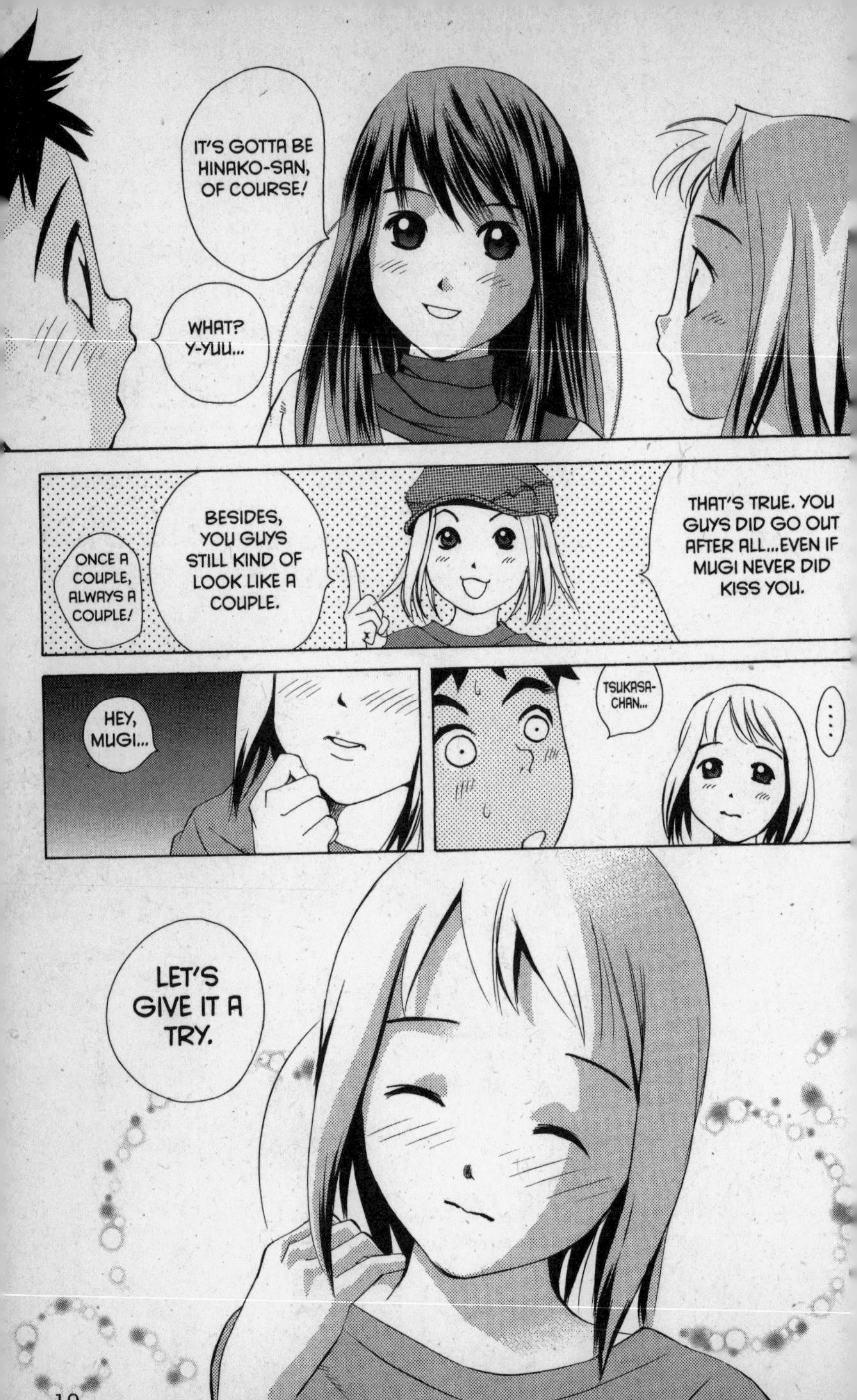
IT'S GOTTA BE HINAKO-SAN, OF COURSE!
WHAT? Y-YUU...
THAT'S TRUE. YOU GUYS DID GO OUT AFTER ALL...EVEN IF MUGI NEVER DID KISS YOU.
BESIDES, YOU GUYS STILL KIND OF LOOK LIKE A COUPLE.
ONCE A COUPLE, ALWAYS A COUPLE!
....
TSUKASA-CHAN...
HEY, MUGI...
LET'S GIVE IT A TRY.

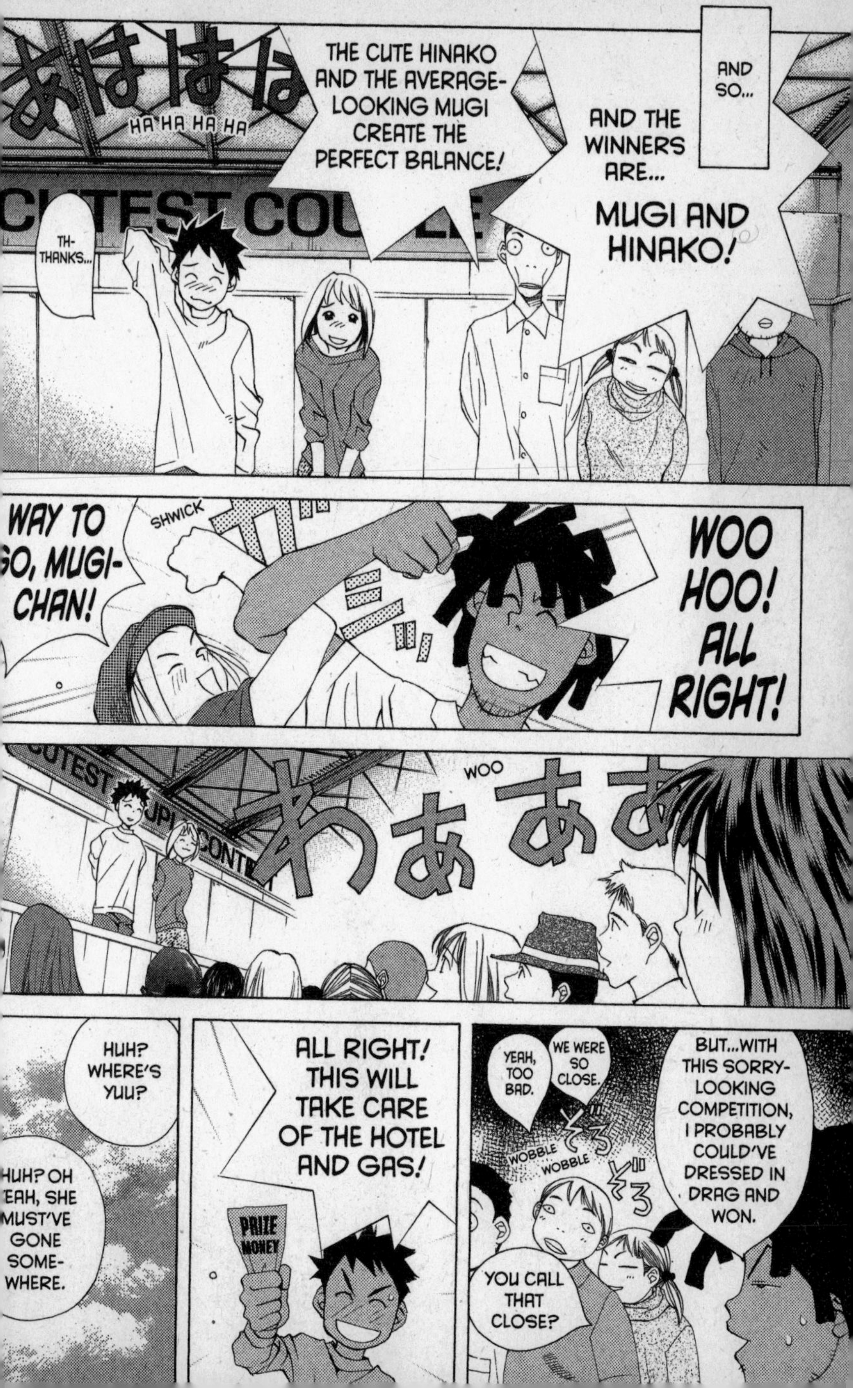
AND SO...
AND THE WINNERS ARE...
MUGI AND HINAKO!
THE CUTE HINAKO AND THE AVERAGE-LOOKING MUGI CREATE THE PERFECT BALANCE!
HA HA HA HA
CUTEST COU LE
TH-THANKS...
WOO HOO! ALL RIGHT!
SHWICK
WAY TO GO, MUGI-CHAN!
WOO
BUT...WITH THIS SORRY-LOOKING COMPETITION, I PROBABLY COULD'VE DRESSED IN DRAG AND WON.
WE WERE SO CLOSE.
YEAH, TOO BAD.
WOBBLE WOBBLE
YOU CALL THAT CLOSE?
ALL RIGHT! THIS WILL TAKE CARE OF THE HOTEL AND GAS!
PRIZE MONEY
HUH? WHERE'S YUU?
HUH? OH YEAH, SHE MUST'VE GONE SOME-WHERE.

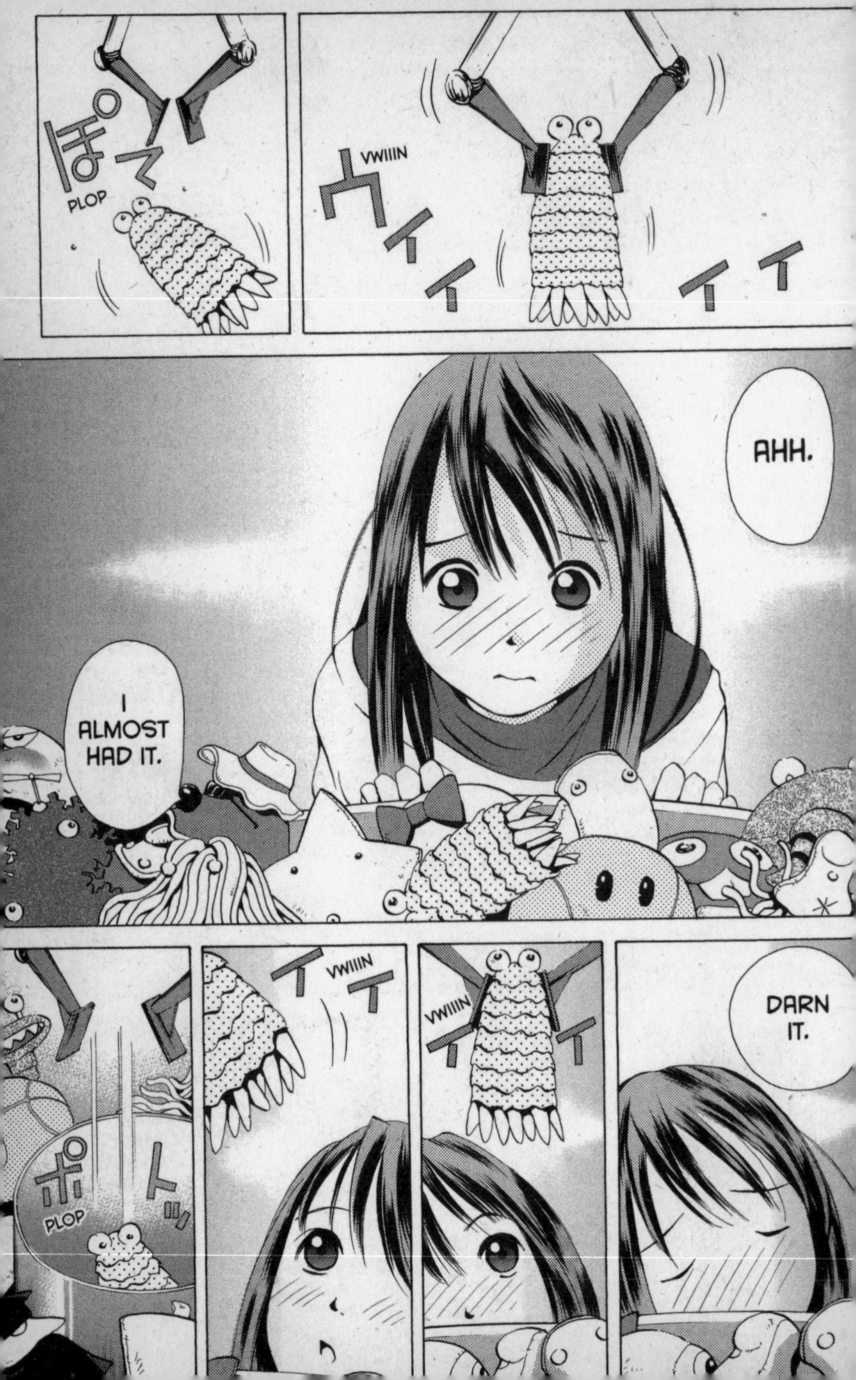
ウイイイ
VWIIIN
ぽて
PLOP
AHH.
I ALMOST HAD IT.
DARN IT.
イイ
VWIIIN
イイ
VWIIIN
ポトッ
PLOP

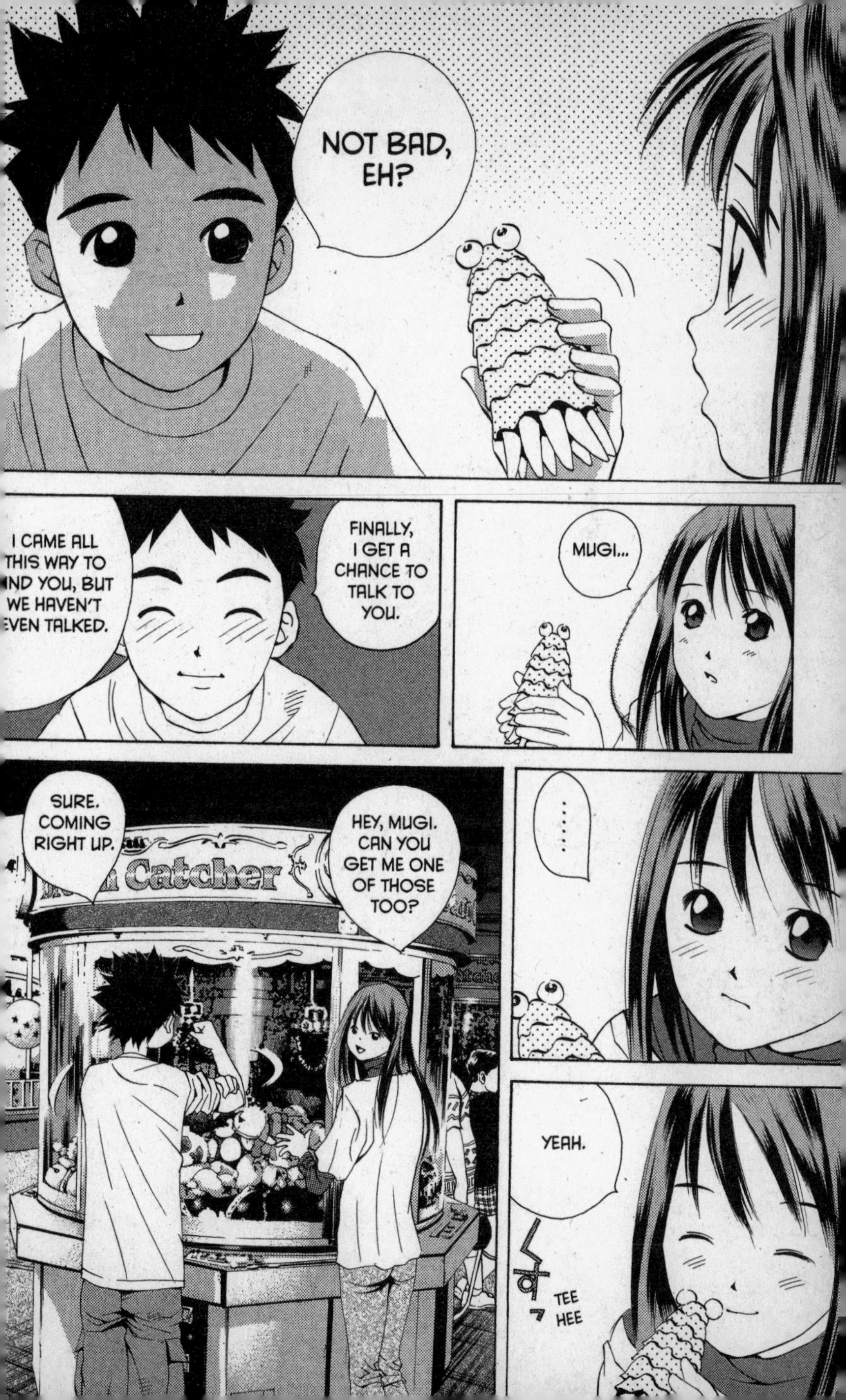
NOT BAD, EH?
MUGI...
FINALLY, I GET A CHANCE TO TALK TO YOU.
I CAME ALL THIS WAY TO ND YOU, BUT WE HAVEN'T EVEN TALKED.
......
YEAH.
くすっ
TEE HEE
HEY, MUGI. CAN YOU GET ME ONE OF THOSE TOO?
SURE. COMING RIGHT UP.
Catcher

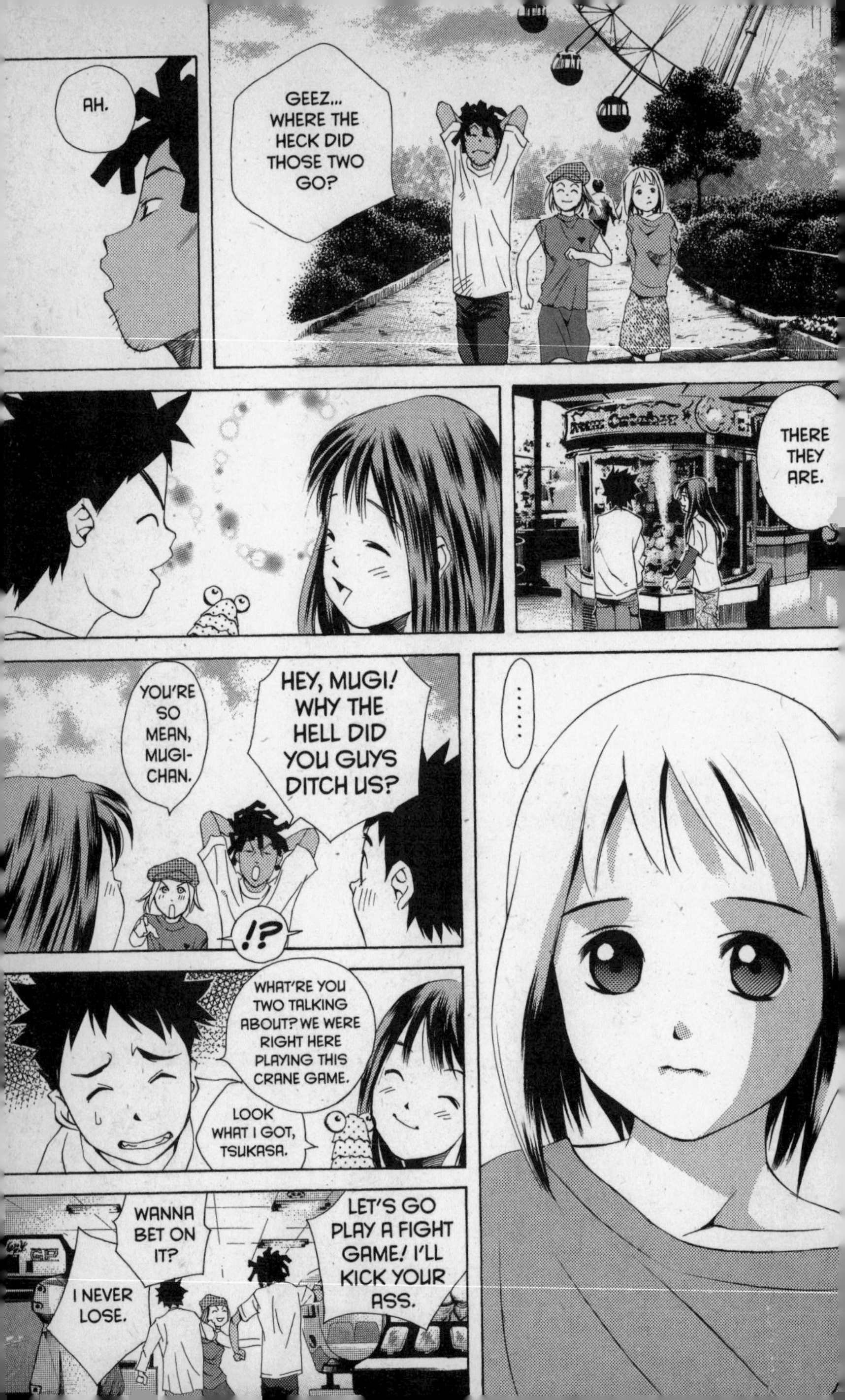
GEEZ... WHERE THE HECK DID THOSE TWO GO?
AH.
THERE THEY ARE.
......
HEY, MUGI! WHY THE HELL DID YOU GUYS DITCH US?
YOU'RE SO MEAN, MUGI-CHAN.
!?
WHAT'RE YOU TWO TALKING ABOUT? WE WERE RIGHT HERE PLAYING THIS CRANE GAME.
LOOK WHAT I GOT, TSUKASA.
LET'S GO PLAY A FIGHT GAME! I'LL KICK YOUR ASS.
WANNA BET ON IT?
I NEVER LOSE.

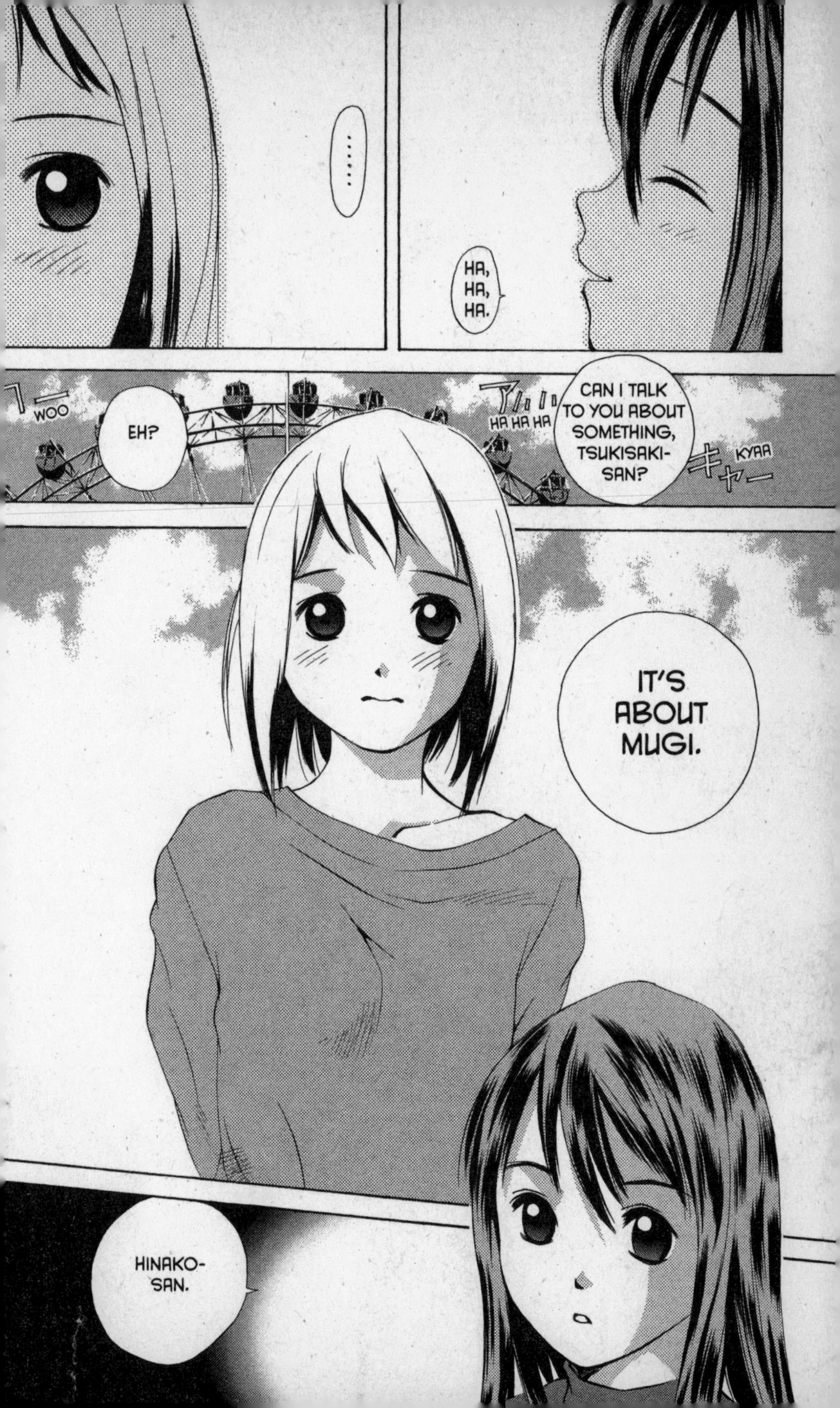

HA, HA, HA.
......
CAN I TALK TO YOU ABOUT SOMETHING, TSUKISAKI-SAN?
HA HA HA
キャー
KYAA
EH?
WOO
IT'S ABOUT MUGI.
HINAKO-SAN.

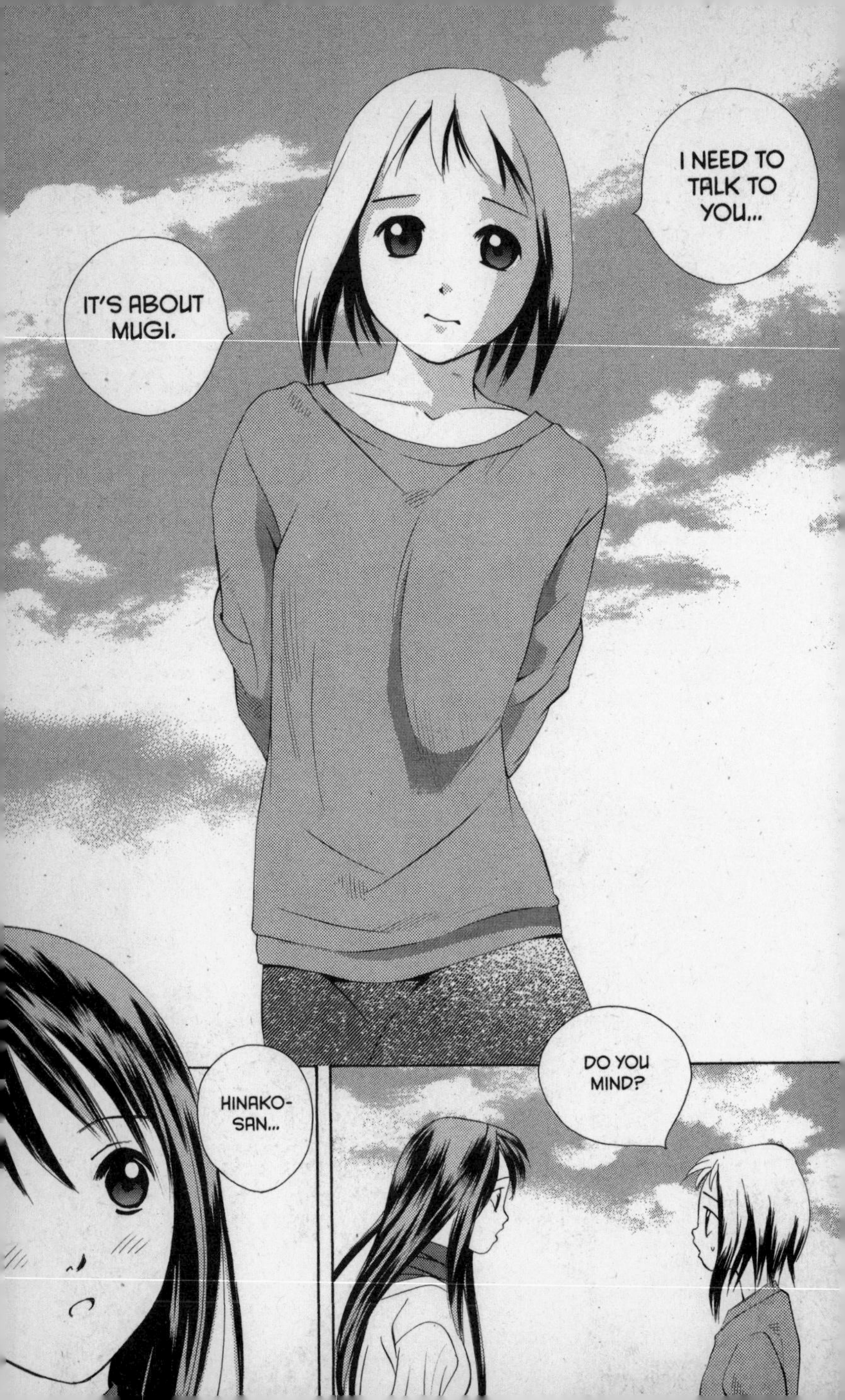
I NEED TO TALK TO YOU...
IT'S ABOUT MUGI.
DO YOU MIND?
HINAKO-SAN...

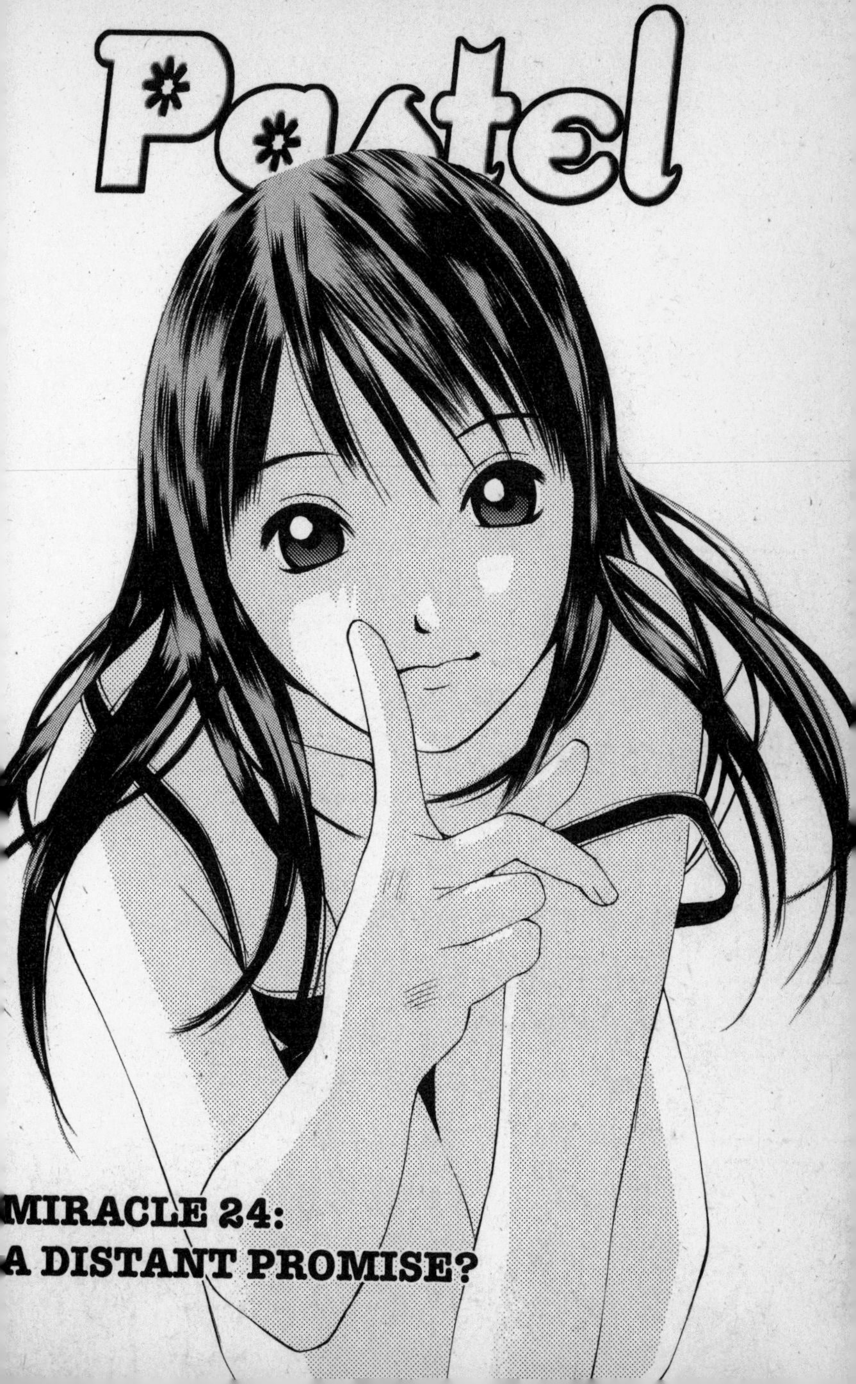
Pastel
MIRACLE 24:
A DISTANT PROMISE?

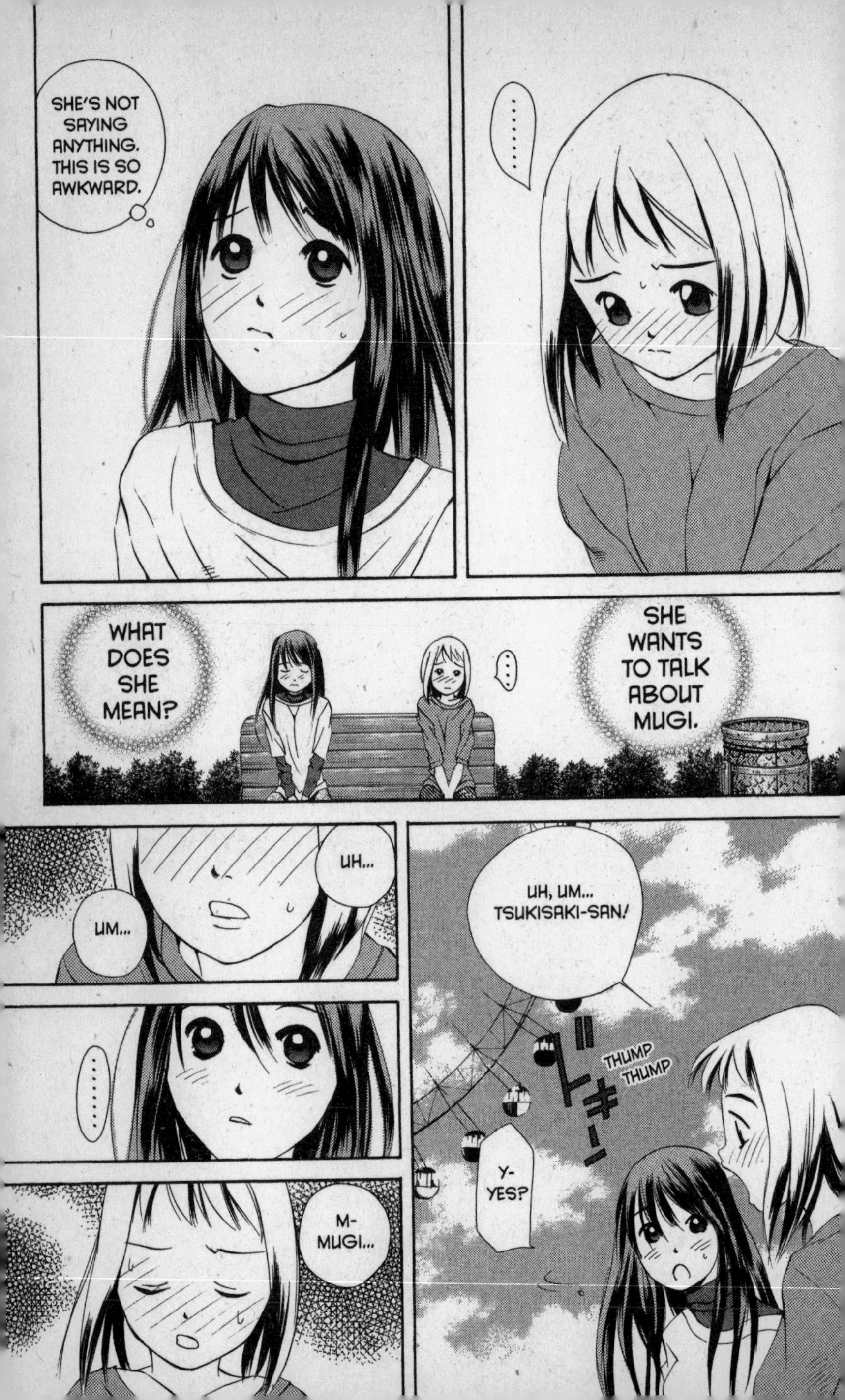
......
SHE'S NOT SAYING ANYTHING. THIS IS SO AWKWARD.
SHE WANTS TO TALK ABOUT MUGI.
...
WHAT DOES SHE MEAN?
UH, UM... TSUKISAKI-SAN!
THUMP THUMP
Y- YES?
UH...
UM...
......
M- MUGI...

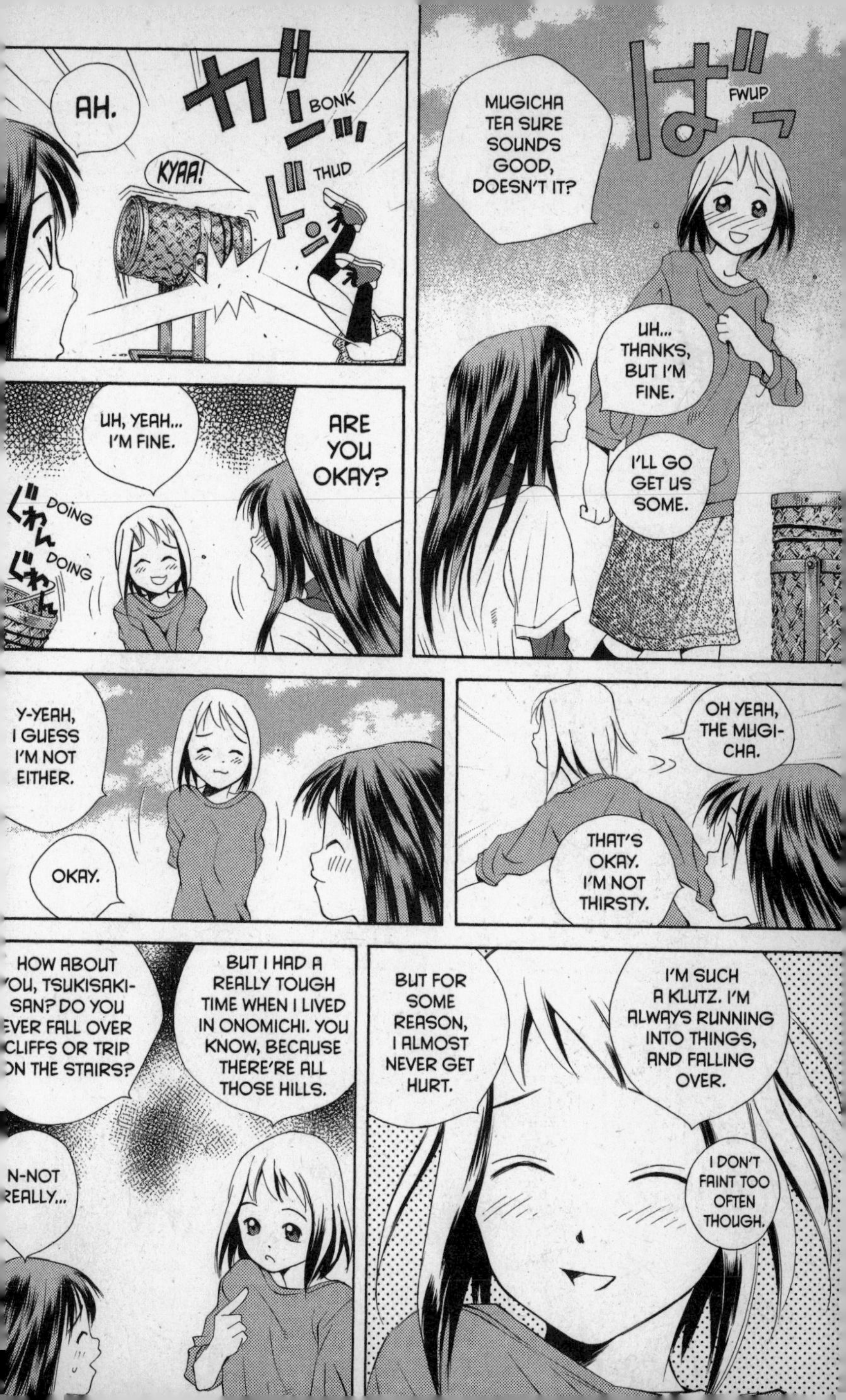
FWUP
MUGICHA TEA SURE SOUNDS GOOD, DOESN'T IT?
UH... THANKS, BUT I'M FINE.
I'LL GO GET US SOME.
BONK
AH.
KYAA!
THUD
ARE YOU OKAY?
UH, YEAH... I'M FINE.
DOING
DOING
OH YEAH, THE MUGI-CHA.
THAT'S OKAY. I'M NOT THIRSTY.
Y-YEAH, I GUESS I'M NOT EITHER.
OKAY.
I'M SUCH A KLUTZ. I'M ALWAYS RUNNING INTO THINGS, AND FALLING OVER.
BUT FOR SOME REASON, I ALMOST NEVER GET HURT.
I DON'T FAINT TOO OFTEN THOUGH.
BUT I HAD A REALLY TOUGH TIME WHEN I LIVED IN ONOMICHI. YOU KNOW, BECAUSE THERE'RE ALL THOSE HILLS.
HOW ABOUT YOU, TSUKISAKI-SAN? DO YOU EVER FALL OVER CLIFFS OR TRIP ON THE STAIRS?
N-NOT REALLY...

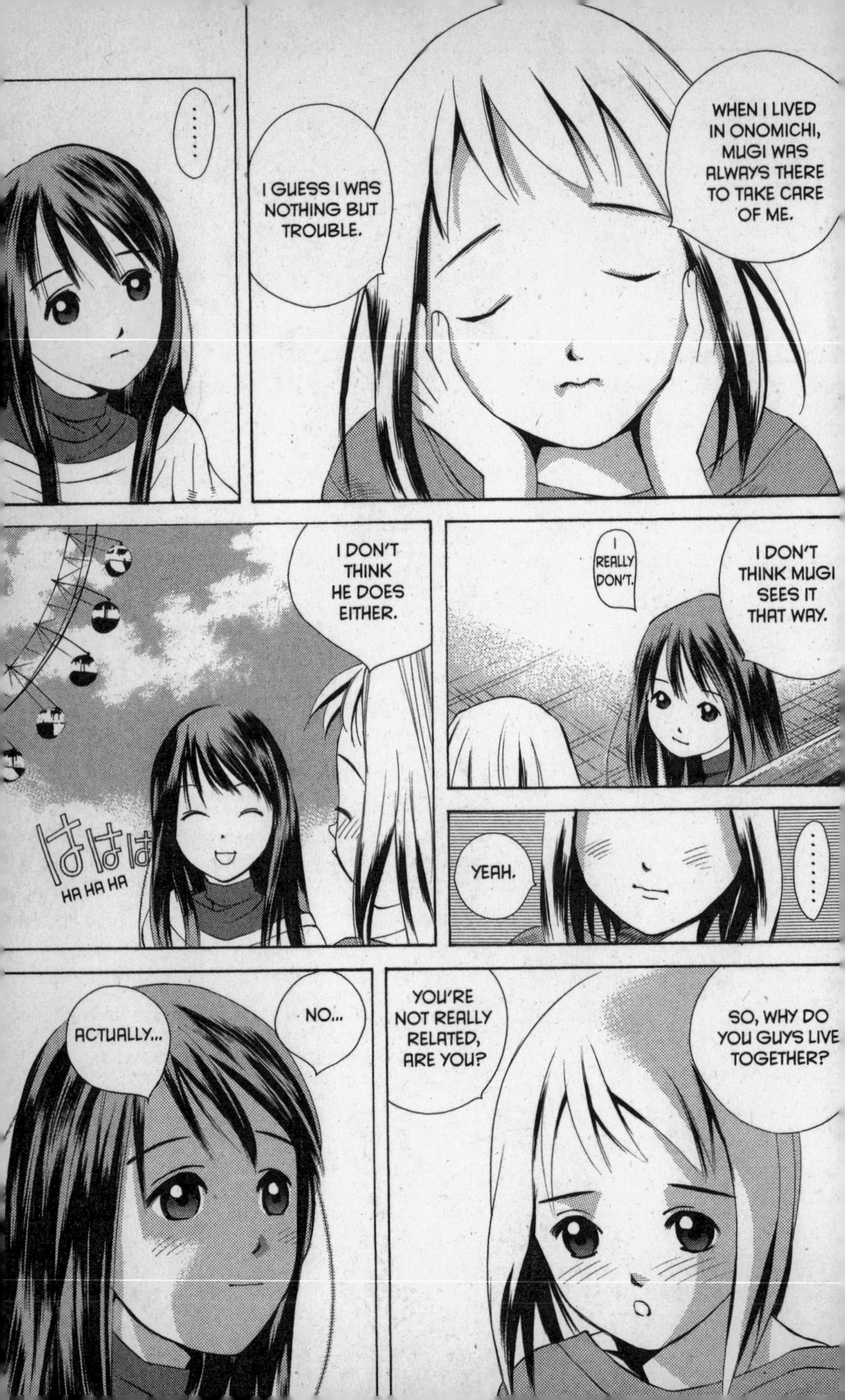
WHEN I LIVED IN ONOMICHI, MUGI WAS ALWAYS THERE TO TAKE CARE OF ME.
I GUESS I WAS NOTHING BUT TROUBLE.
......
I DON'T THINK MUGI SEES IT THAT WAY.
I REALLY DON'T.
....
YEAH.
I DON'T THINK HE DOES EITHER.
ははは
HA HA HA
SO, WHY DO YOU GUYS LIVE TOGETHER?
YOU'RE NOT REALLY RELATED, ARE YOU?
NO...
ACTUALLY...

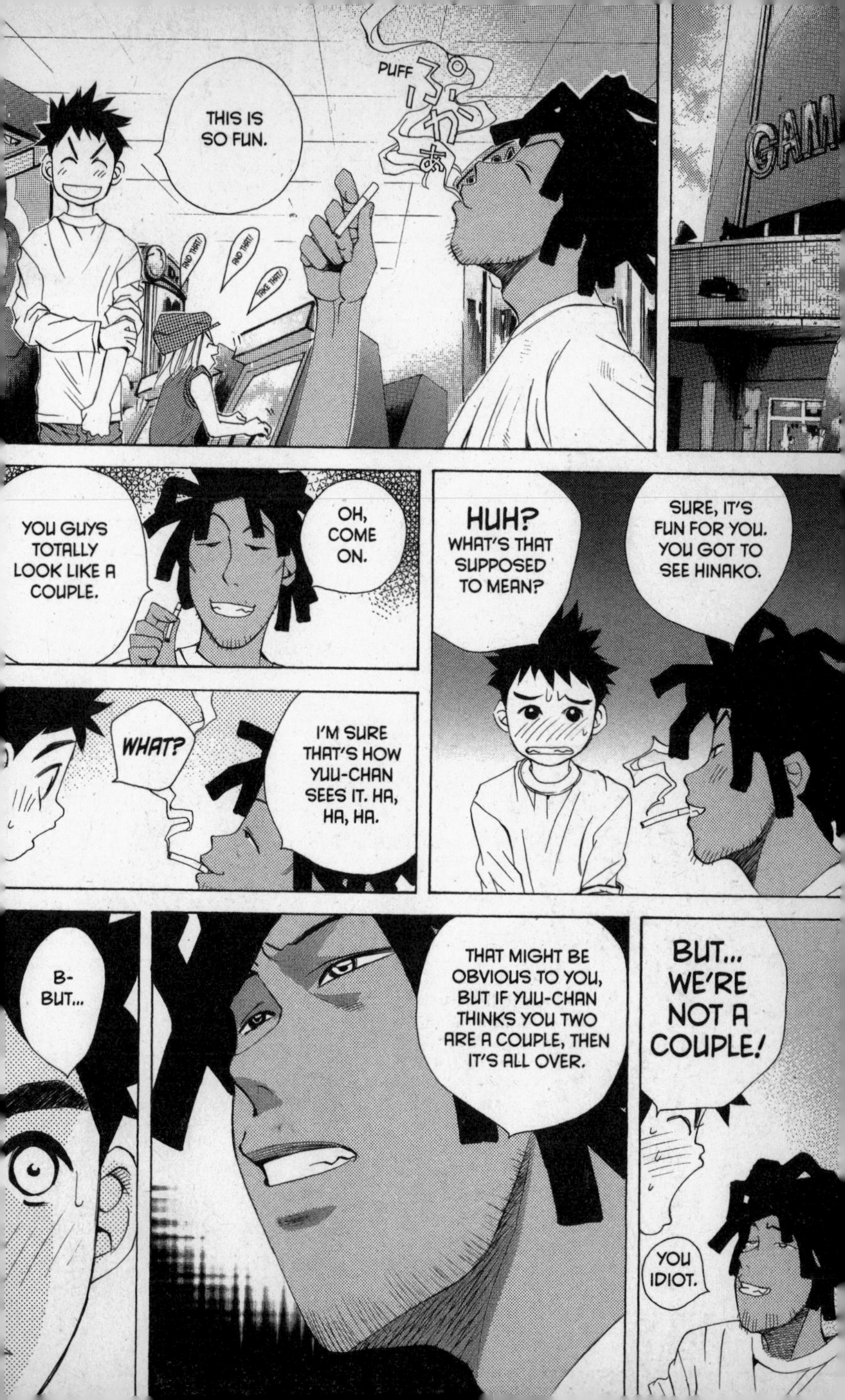
PUFF
THIS IS SO FUN.
AND THAT!
AND THAT!
TAKE THAT!
SURE, IT'S FUN FOR YOU. YOU GOT TO SEE HINAKO.
HUH? WHAT'S THAT SUPPOSED TO MEAN?
OH, COME ON.
YOU GUYS TOTALLY LOOK LIKE A COUPLE.
I'M SURE THAT'S HOW YUU-CHAN SEES IT. HA, HA, HA.
WHAT?
BUT... WE'RE NOT A COUPLE!
YOU IDIOT.
THAT MIGHT BE OBVIOUS TO YOU, BUT IF YUU-CHAN THINKS YOU TWO ARE A COUPLE, THEN IT'S ALL OVER.
B- BUT...

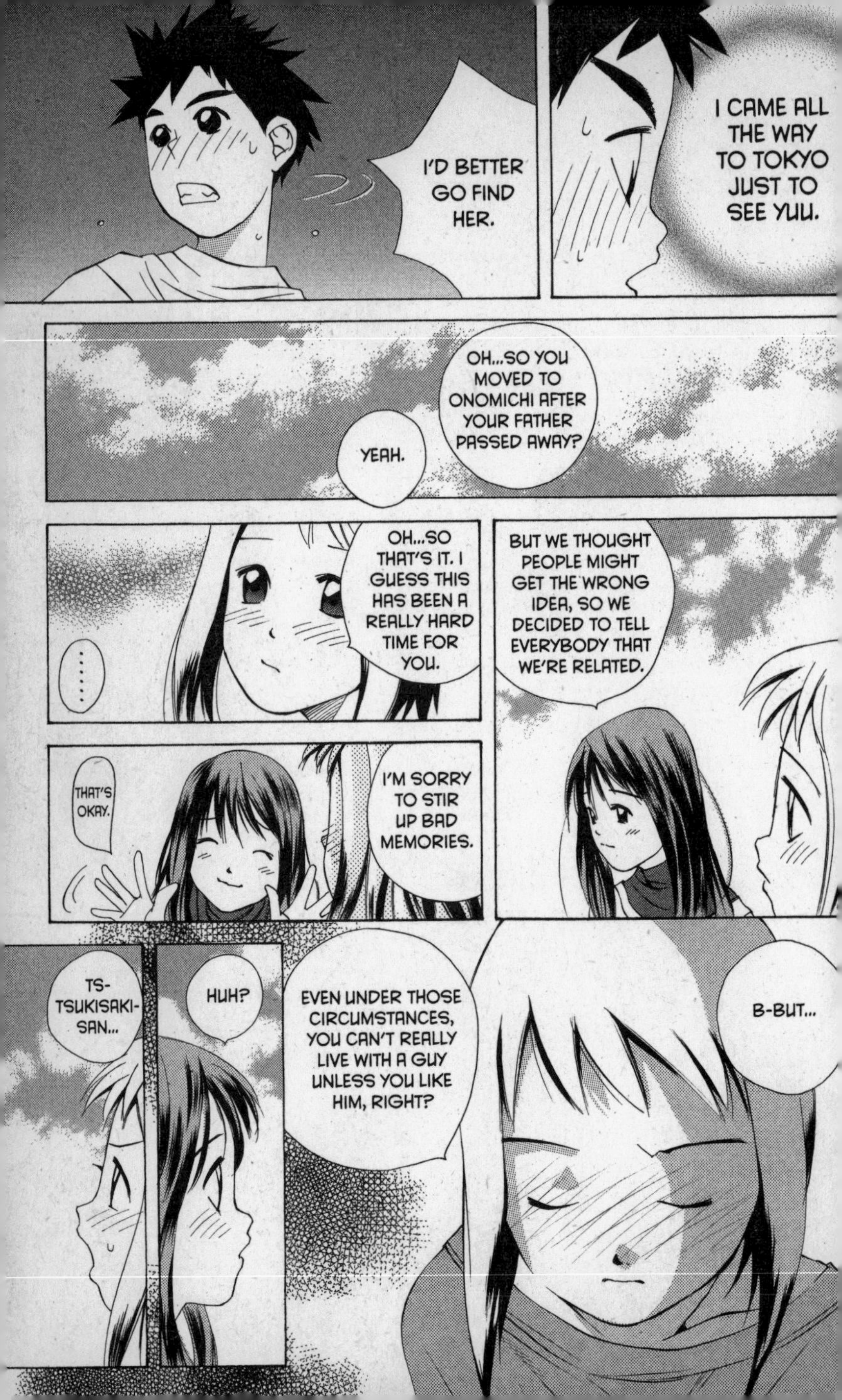
I CAME ALL THE WAY TO TOKYO JUST TO SEE YUU.
I'D BETTER GO FIND HER.
OH...SO YOU MOVED TO ONOMICHI AFTER YOUR FATHER PASSED AWAY?
YEAH.
BUT WE THOUGHT PEOPLE MIGHT GET THE WRONG IDEA, SO WE DECIDED TO TELL EVERYBODY THAT WE'RE RELATED.
OH...SO THAT'S IT. I GUESS THIS HAS BEEN A REALLY HARD TIME FOR YOU.
......
I'M SORRY TO STIR UP BAD MEMORIES.
THAT'S OKAY.
B-BUT...
EVEN UNDER THOSE CIRCUMSTANCES, YOU CAN'T REALLY LIVE WITH A GUY UNLESS YOU LIKE HIM, RIGHT?
HUH?
TS-TSUKISAKI-SAN...

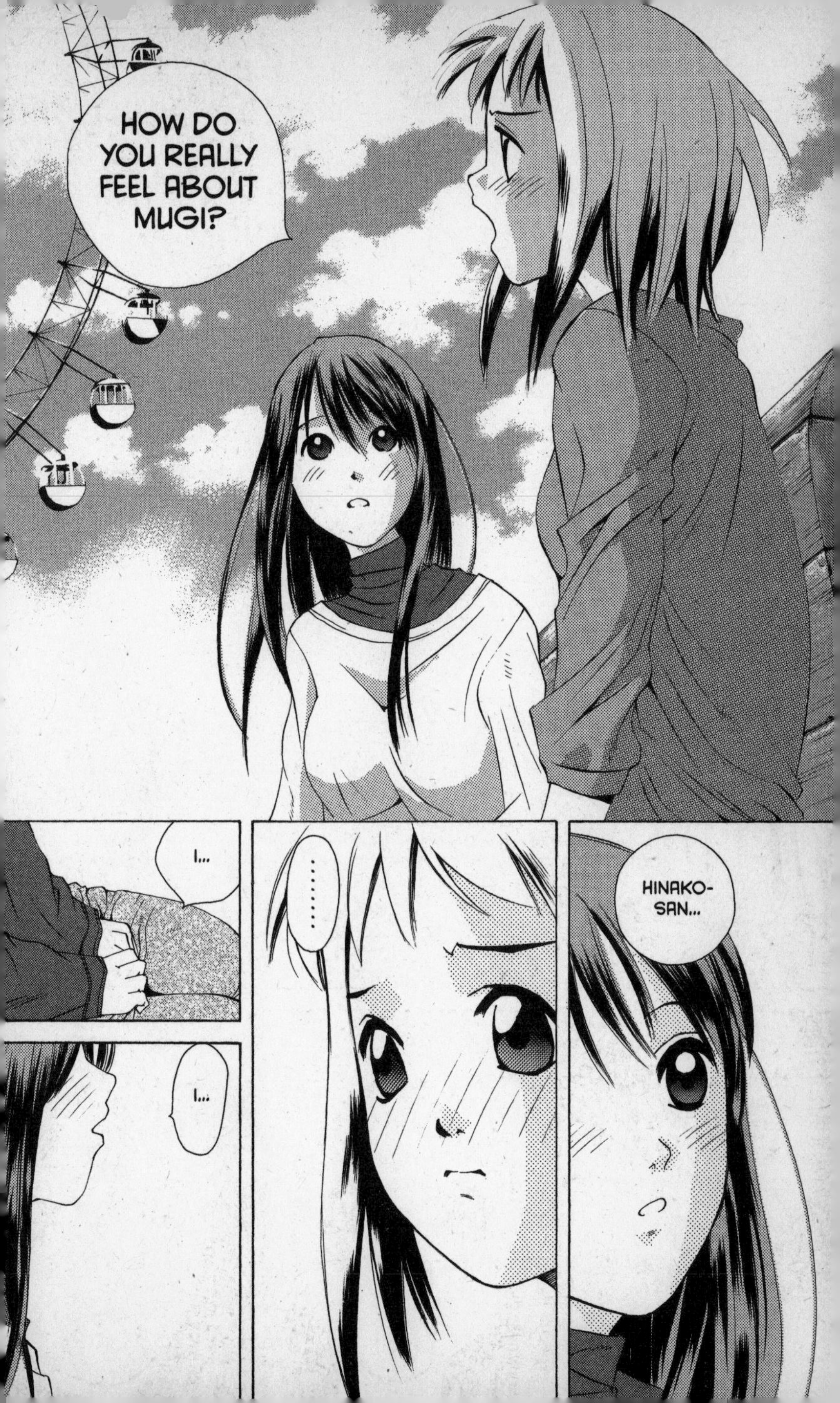
HOW DO YOU REALLY FEEL ABOUT MUGI?
HINAKO-SAN...
......
I...
I...

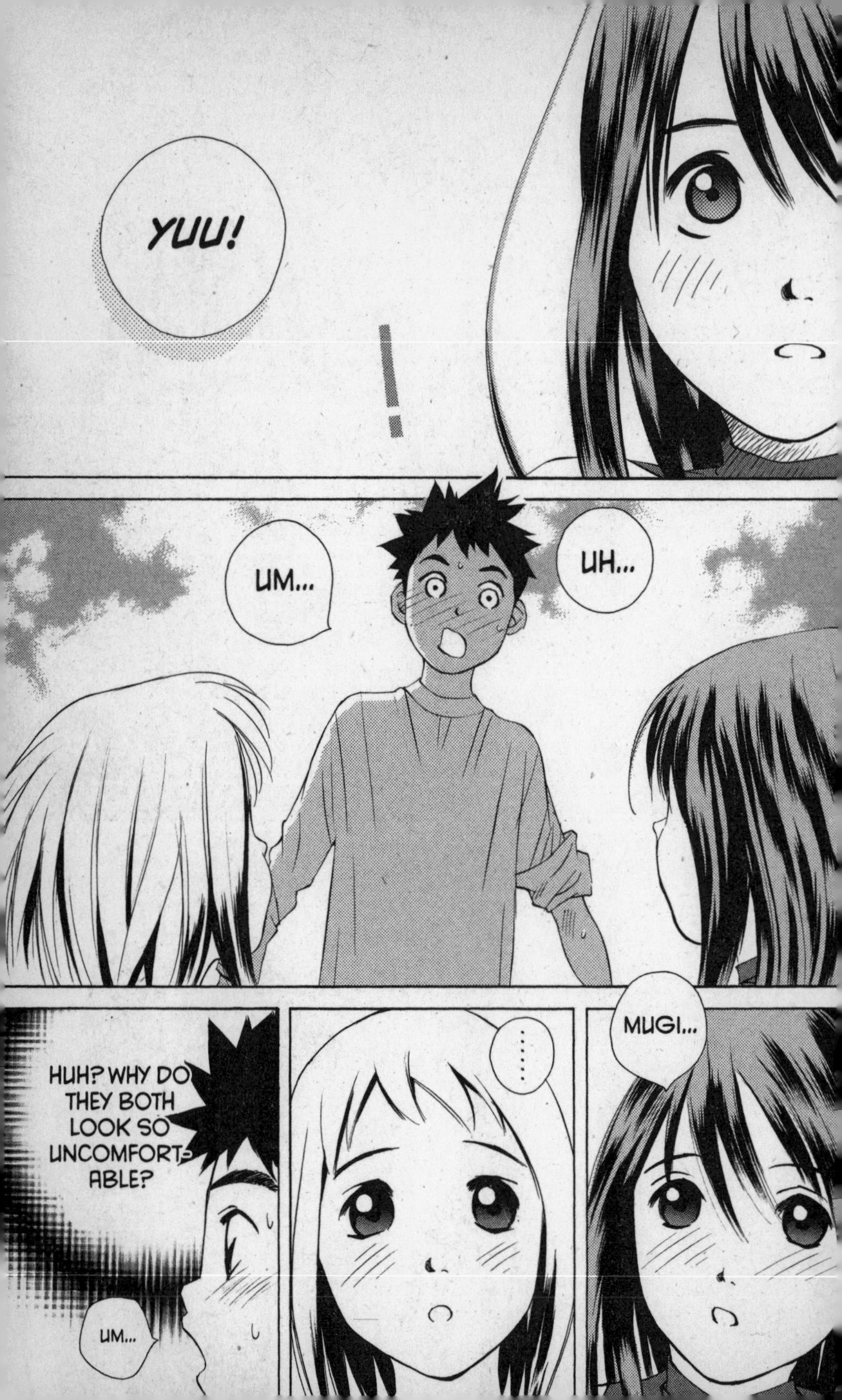
YUU!
!
UH...
UM...
MUGI...
......
HUH? WHY DO THEY BOTH LOOK SO UNCOMFORT-ABLE?
UM...

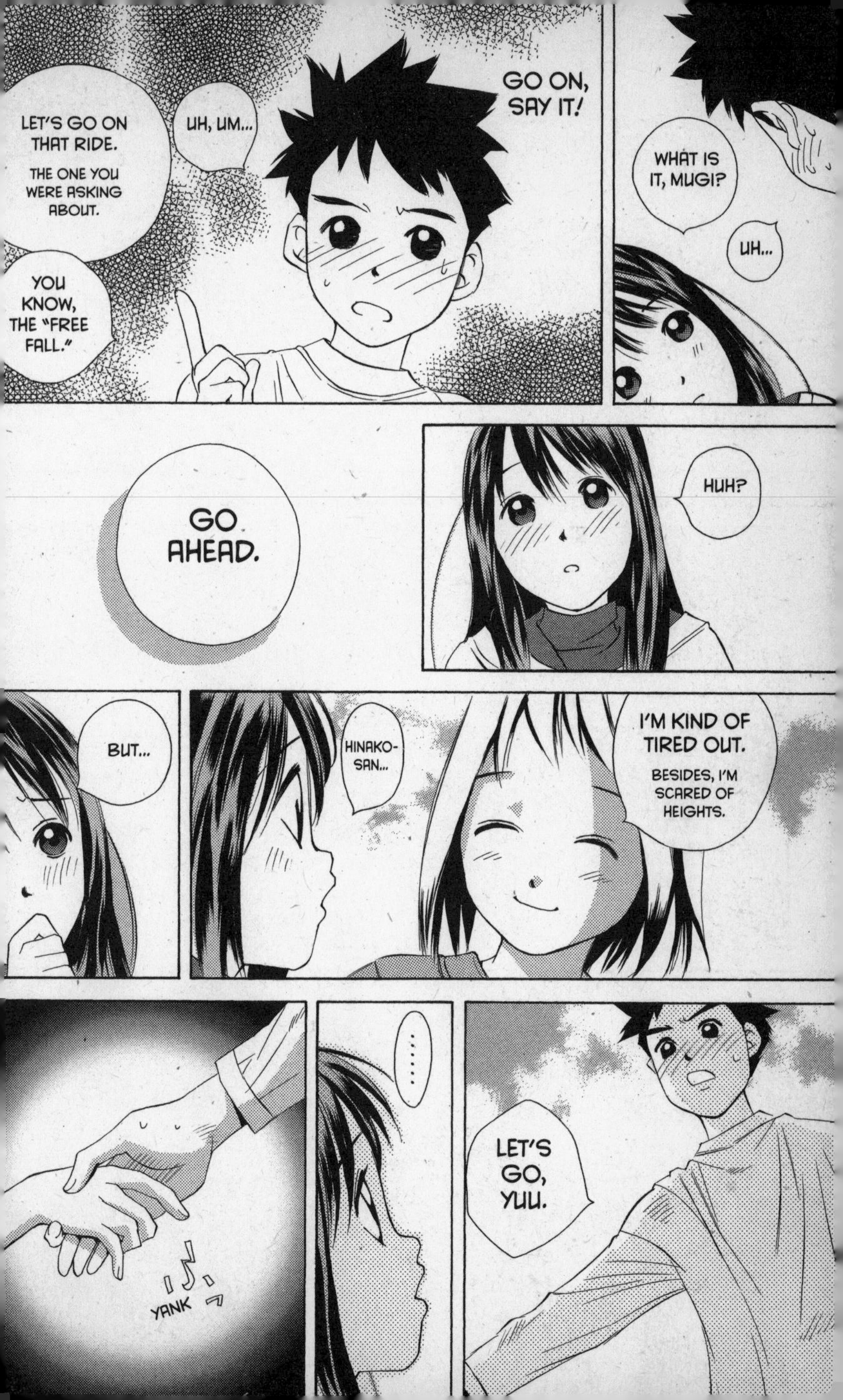
WHAT IS IT, MUGI?
UH...
GO ON, SAY IT!
UH, UM...
LET'S GO ON THAT RIDE.
THE ONE YOU WERE ASKING ABOUT.
YOU KNOW, THE "FREE FALL."
HUH?
GO AHEAD.
I'M KIND OF TIRED OUT.
BESIDES, I'M SCARED OF HEIGHTS.
HINAKO-SAN...
BUT...
LET'S GO, YUU.
......
YANK

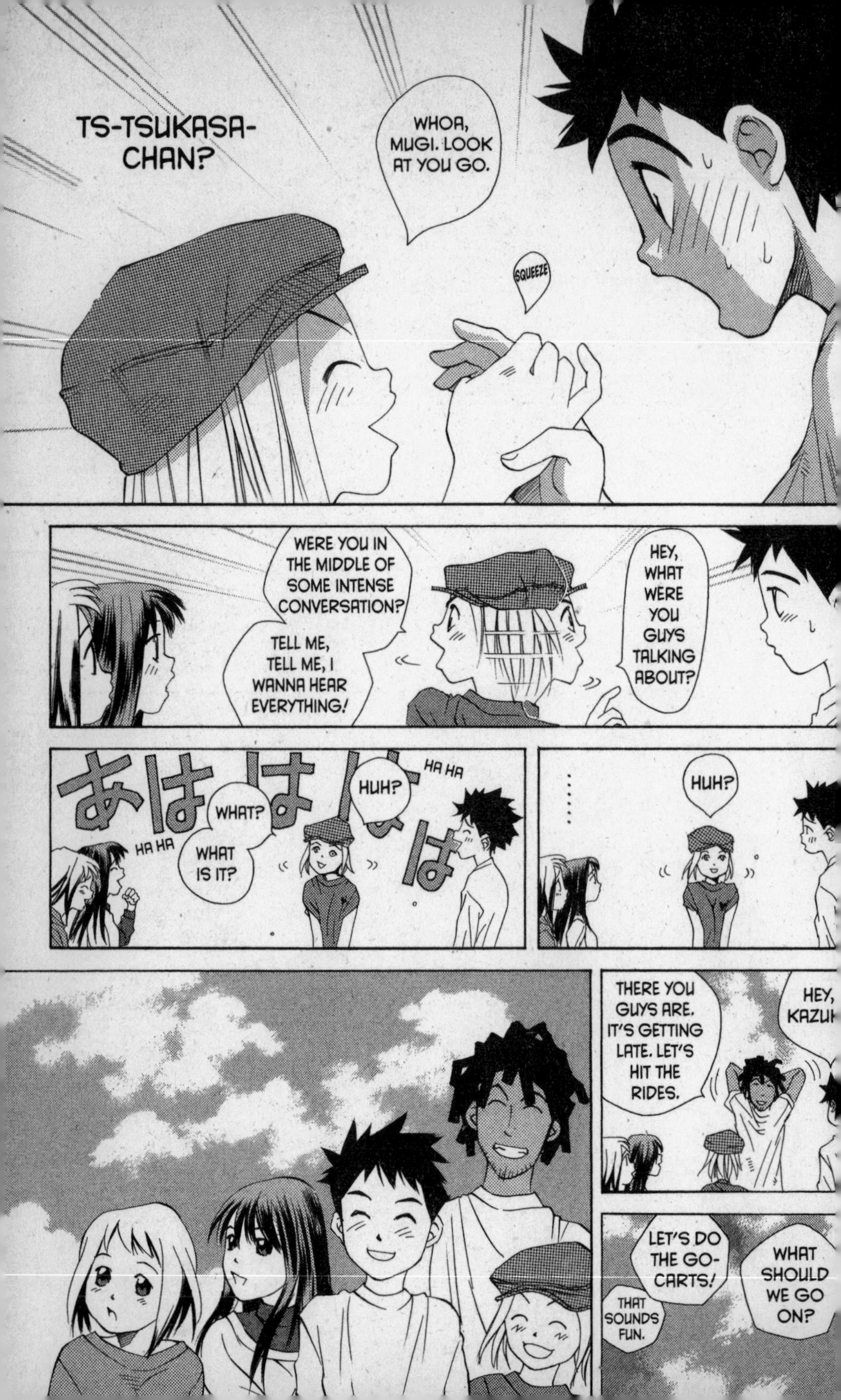
WHOA, MUGI. LOOK AT YOU GO.
TS-TSUKASA-CHAN?
SQUEEZE
HEY, WHAT WERE YOU GUYS TALKING ABOUT?
WERE YOU IN THE MIDDLE OF SOME INTENSE CONVERSATION?
TELL ME, TELL ME, I WANNA HEAR EVERYTHING!
HUH?
......
HA HA
HUH?
あははは
WHAT?
WHAT IS IT?
HA HA
HEY, KAZU
THERE YOU GUYS ARE. IT'S GETTING LATE. LET'S HIT THE RIDES.
WHAT SHOULD WE GO ON?
LET'S DO THE GO-CARTS!
THAT SOUNDS FUN.

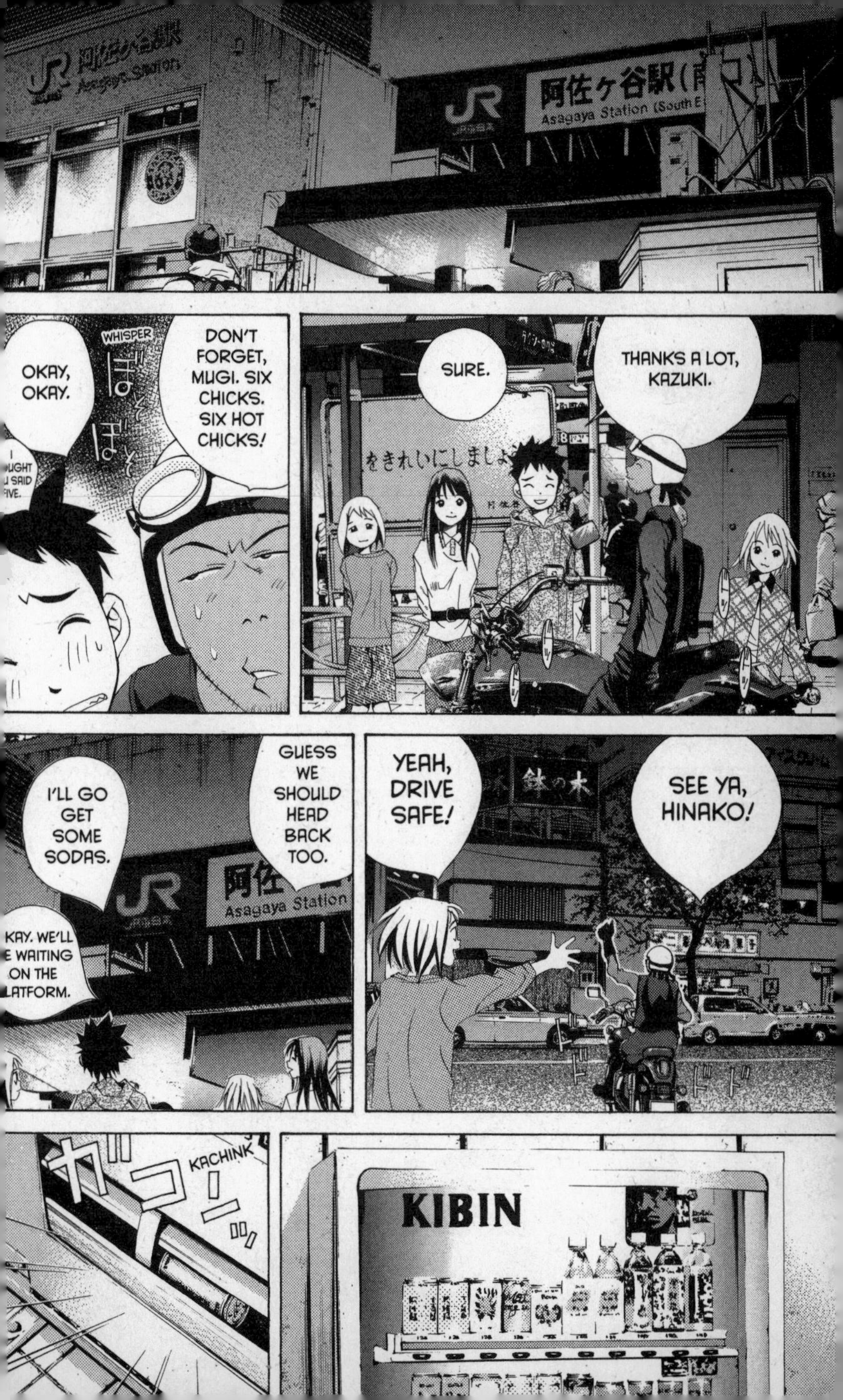
阿佐ヶ谷駅
Asagaya Station
THANKS A LOT, KAZUKI.
SURE.
DON'T FORGET, MUGI. SIX CHICKS. SIX HOT CHICKS!
WHISPER
OKAY, OKAY.
I UGHT U SAID FIVE.
SEE YA, HINAKO!
YEAH, DRIVE SAFE!
GUESS WE SHOULD HEAD BACK TOO.
I'LL GO GET SOME SODAS.
KAY. WE'LL E WAITING ON THE LATFORM.
Asagaya Station
KIBIN
KACHINK

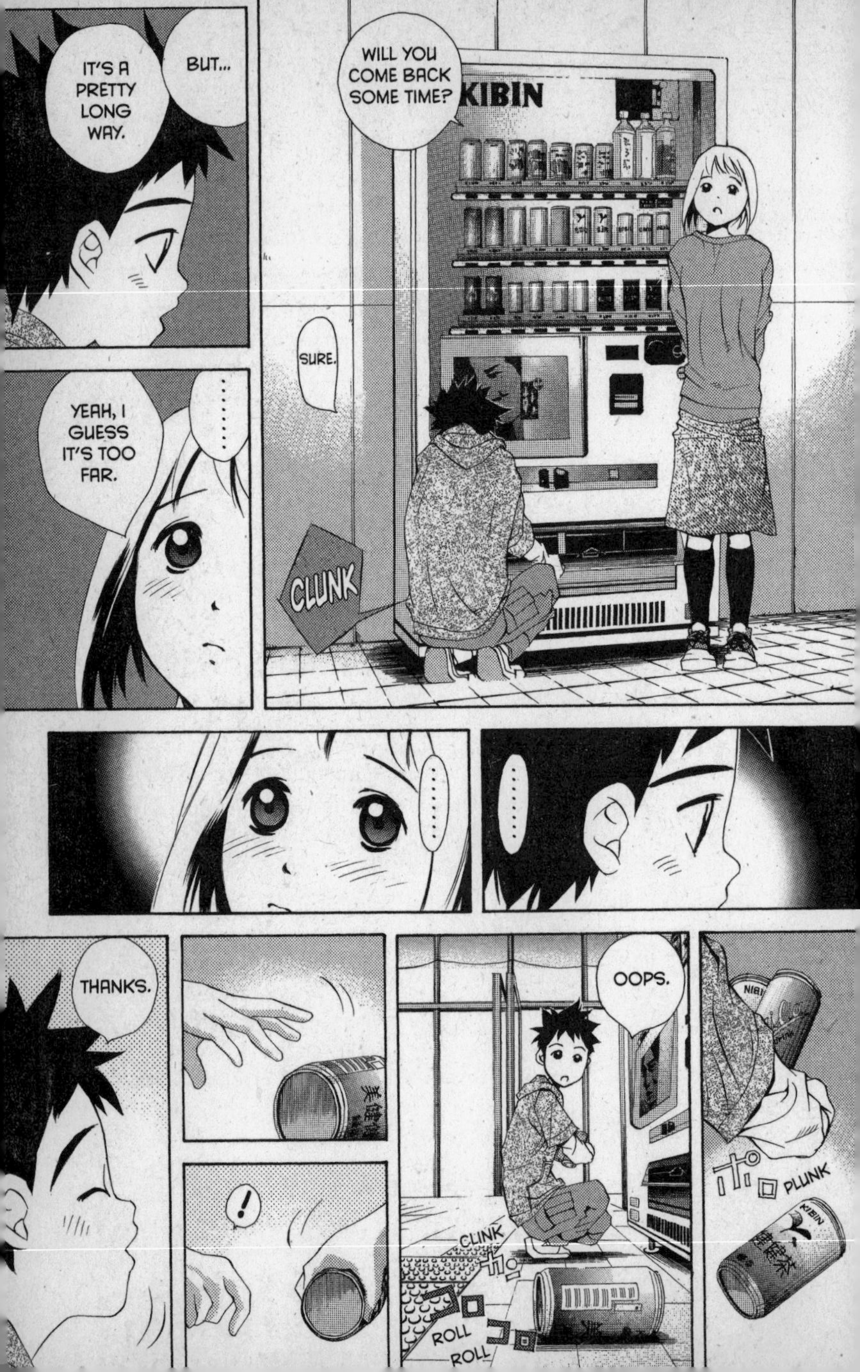
WILL YOU COME BACK SOME TIME?
SURE.
CLUNK
BUT...
IT'S A PRETTY LONG WAY.
......
YEAH, I GUESS IT'S TOO FAR.
......
......
ポロ
PLUNK
OOPS.
CLINK
コロ
ROLL
コロ
ROLL
!
THANKS.

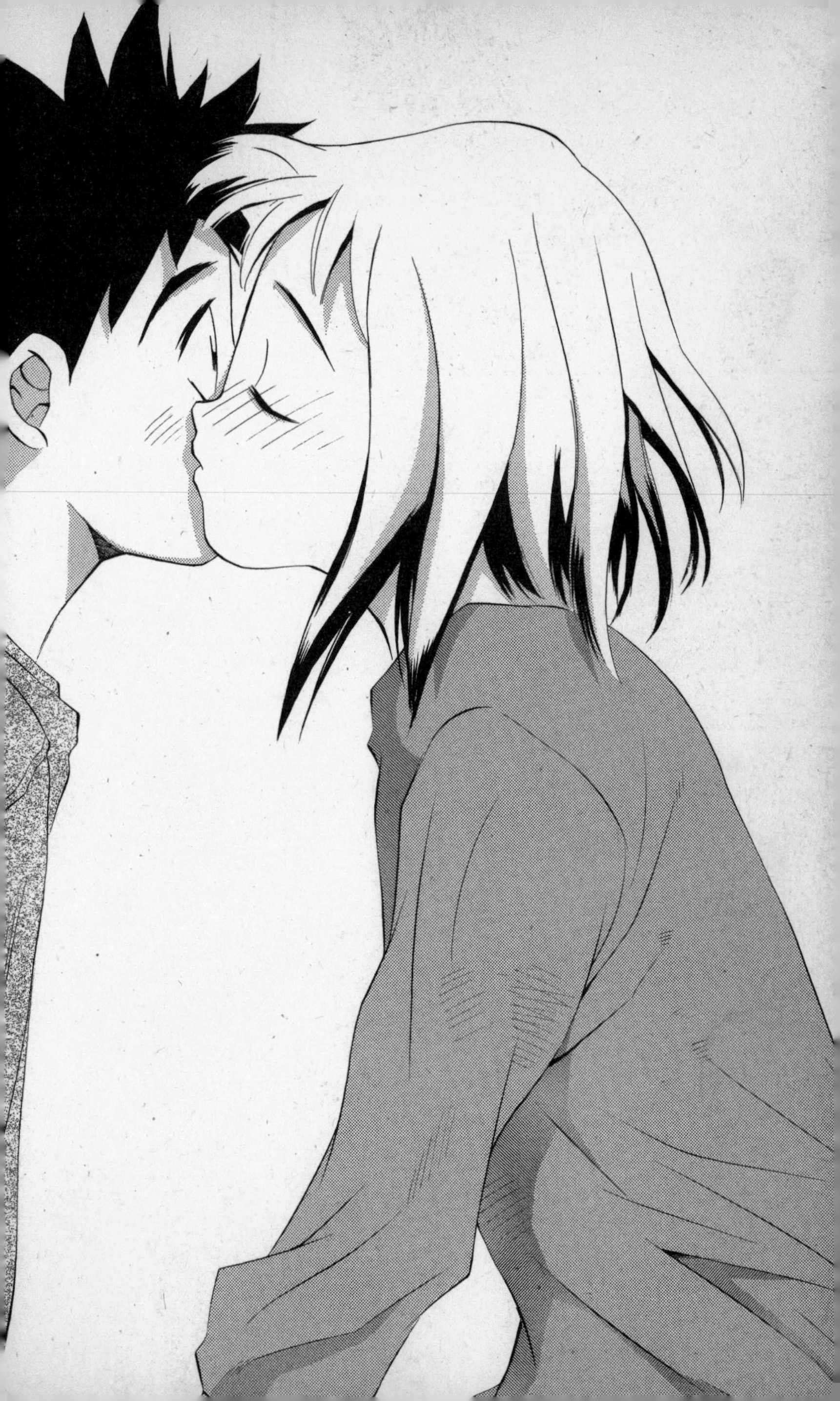

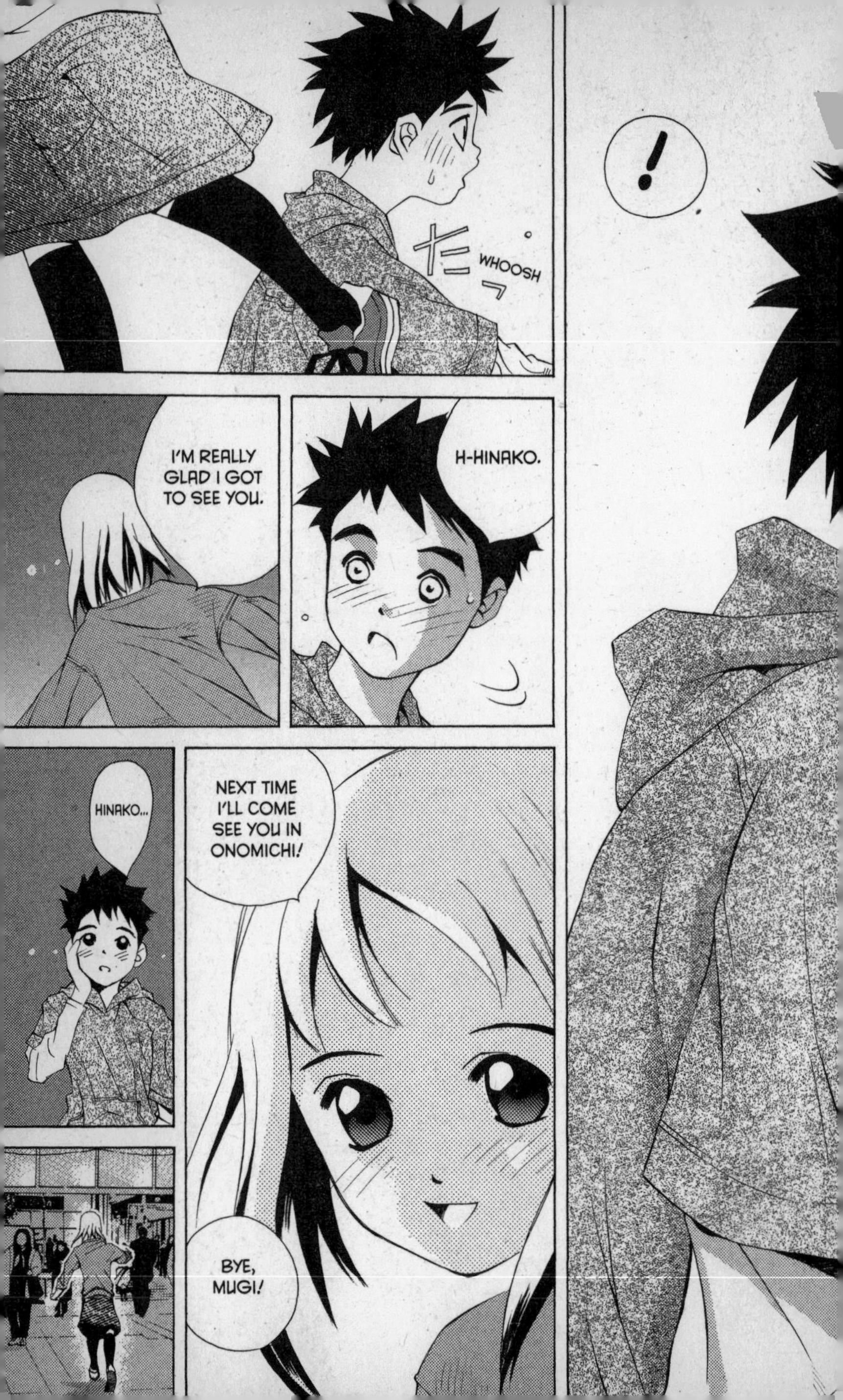
!
WHOOSH
H-HINAKO.
I'M REALLY GLAD I GOT TO SEE YOU.
NEXT TIME I'LL COME SEE YOU IN ONOMICHI!
BYE, MUGI!
HINAKO...

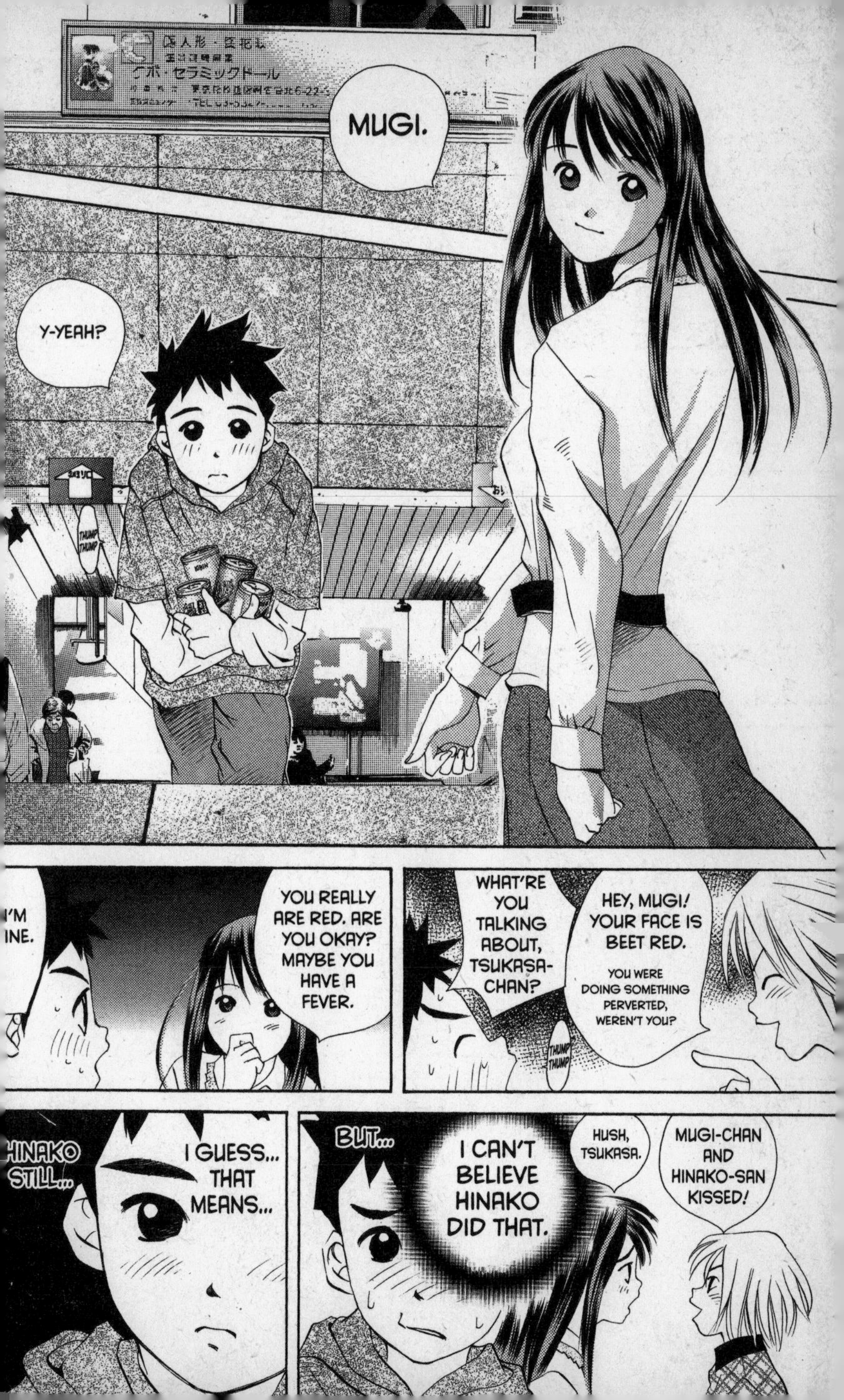
MUGI.
Y-YEAH?
THUMP THUMP
HEY, MUGI! YOUR FACE IS BEET RED.
YOU WERE DOING SOMETHING PERVERTED, WEREN'T YOU?
WHAT'RE YOU TALKING ABOUT, TSUKASA-CHAN?
THUMP THUMP
YOU REALLY ARE RED. ARE YOU OKAY? MAYBE YOU HAVE A FEVER.
'M INE.
MUGI-CHAN AND HINAKO-SAN KISSED!
HUSH, TSUKASA.
I CAN'T BELIEVE HINAKO DID THAT.
BUT...
I GUESS... THAT MEANS...
HINAKO STILL...

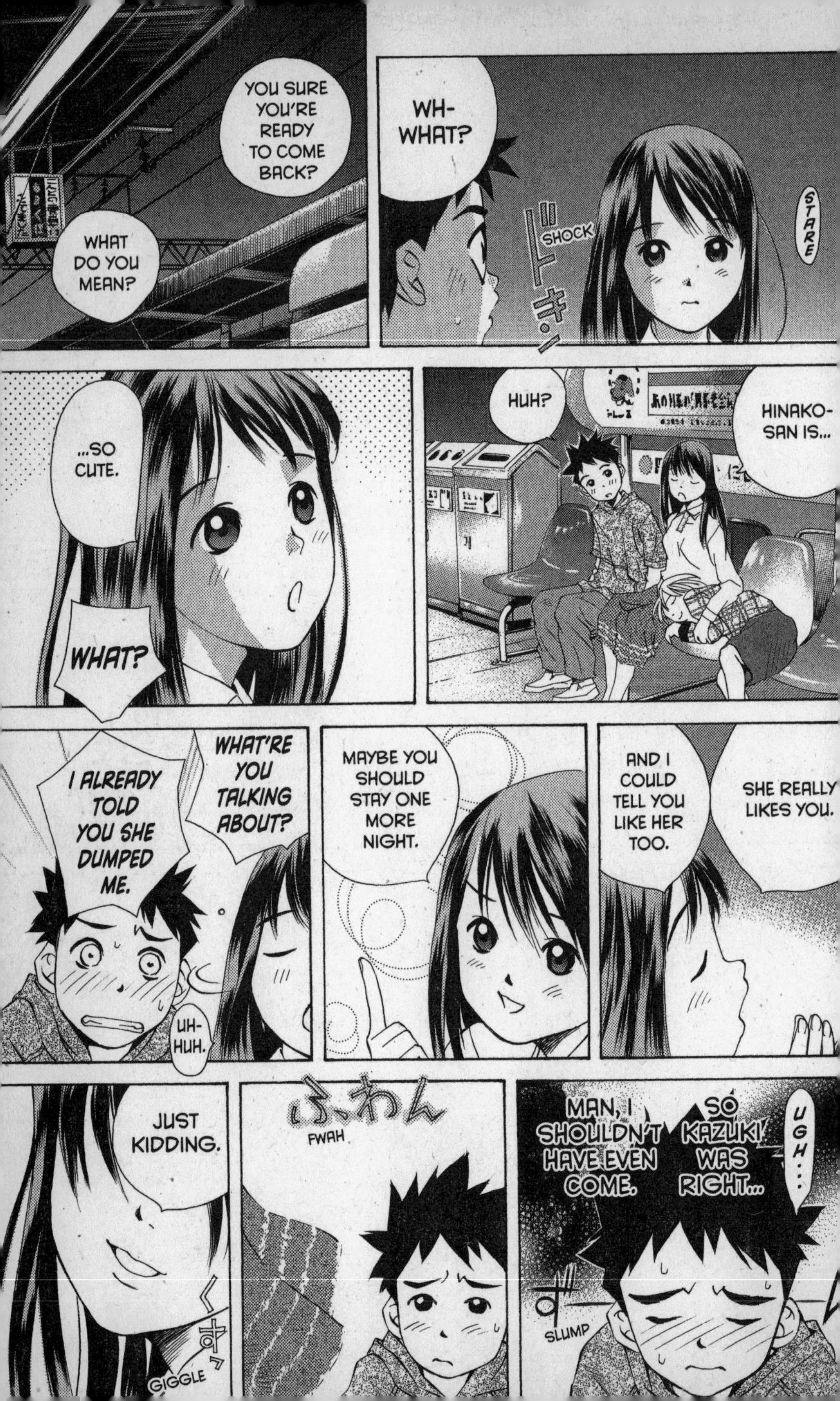
STARE
WH-WHAT?
SHOCK
YOU SURE YOU'RE READY TO COME BACK?
WHAT DO YOU MEAN?
HINAKO-SAN IS...
HUH?
...SO CUTE.
WHAT?
SHE REALLY LIKES YOU.
AND I COULD TELL YOU LIKE HER TOO.
MAYBE YOU SHOULD STAY ONE MORE NIGHT.
WHAT'RE YOU TALKING ABOUT?
I ALREADY TOLD YOU SHE DUMPED ME.
UH-HUH.
UGH...
SO KAZUKI WAS RIGHT...
MAN, I SHOULDN'T HAVE EVEN COME.
SLUMP
ふわん
FWAH
JUST KIDDING.
GIGGLE

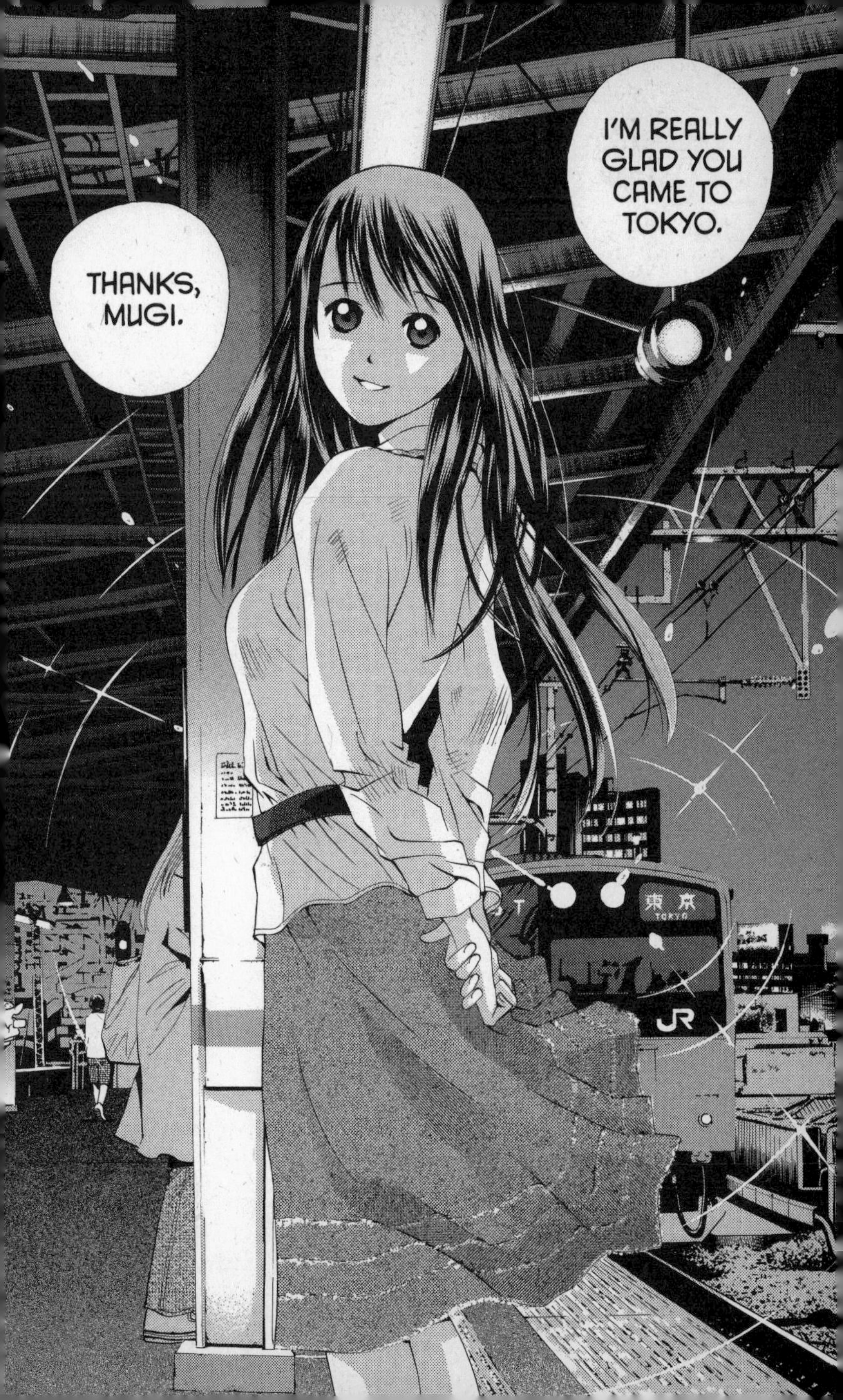
I'M REALLY GLAD YOU CAME TO TOKYO.
THANKS, MUGI.
JR

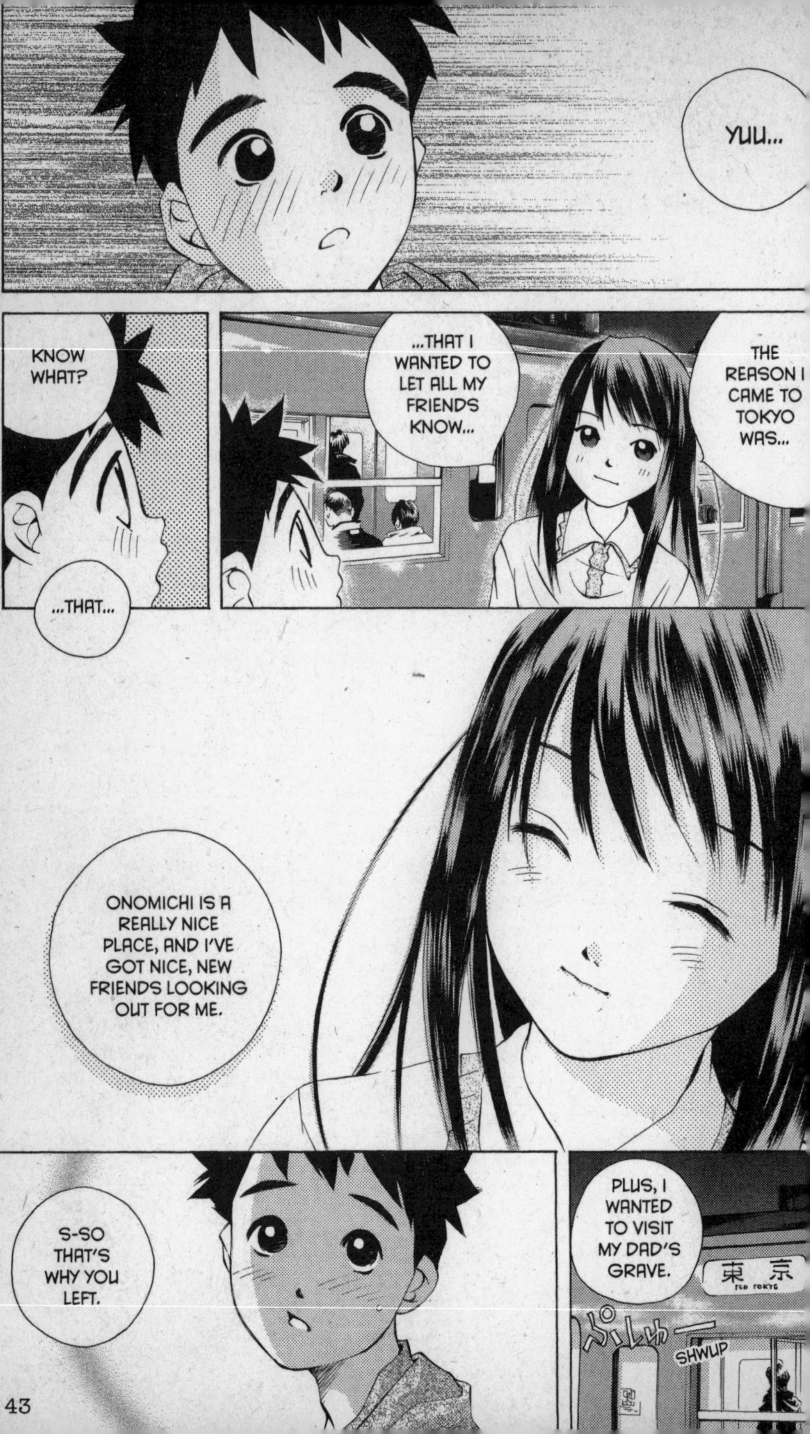
YUU...
THE REASON I CAME TO TOKYO WAS...
...THAT I WANTED TO LET ALL MY FRIENDS KNOW...
KNOW WHAT?
...THAT...
ONOMICHI IS A REALLY NICE PLACE, AND I'VE GOT NICE, NEW FRIENDS LOOKING OUT FOR ME.
PLUS, I WANTED TO VISIT MY DAD'S GRAVE.
東京
ぷしゅー
SHWUP
S-SO THAT'S WHY YOU LEFT.

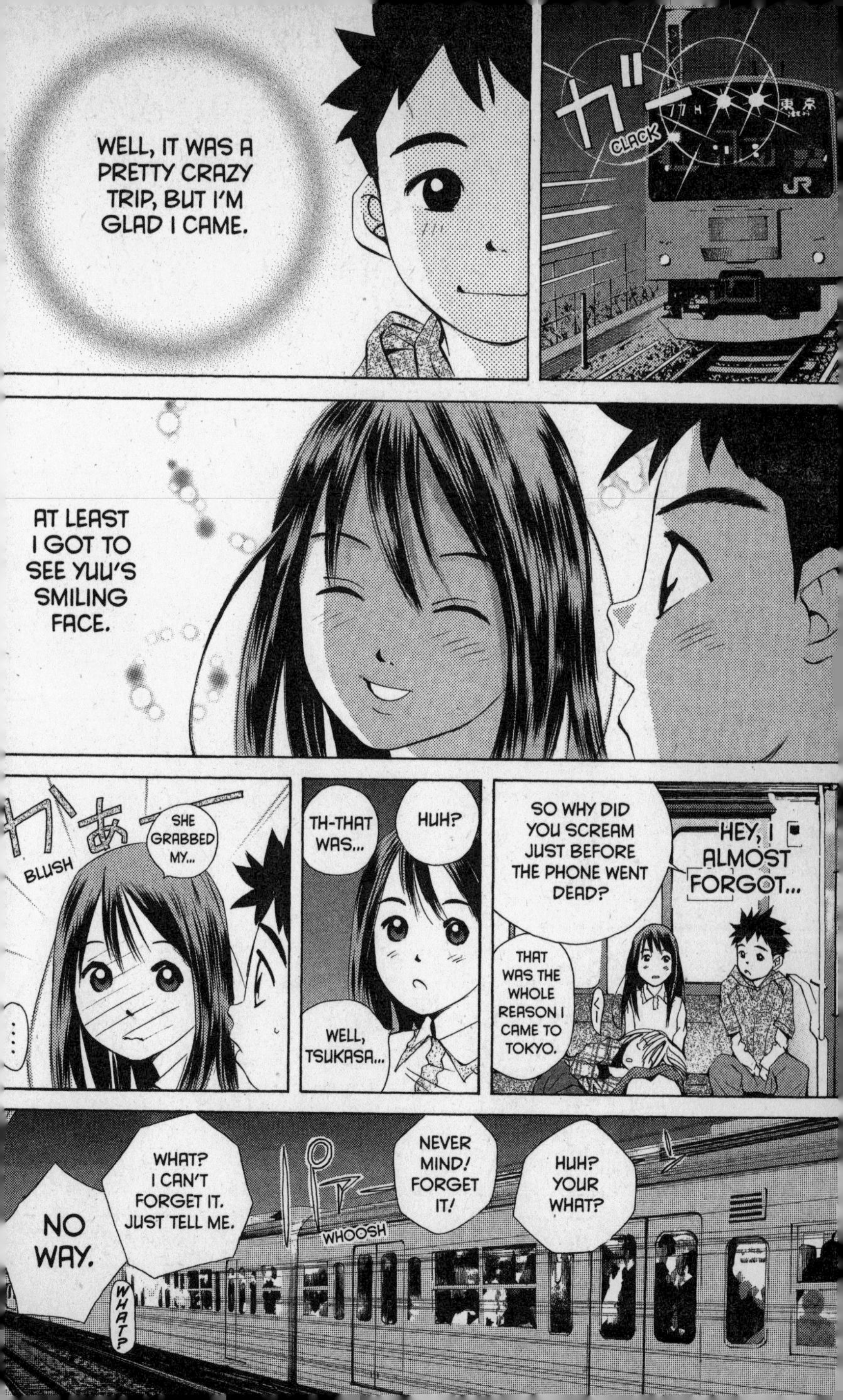
CLACK
東京
JR
WELL, IT WAS A PRETTY CRAZY TRIP, BUT I'M GLAD I CAME.
AT LEAST I GOT TO SEE YUU'S SMILING FACE.
HEY, I ALMOST FORGOT...
SO WHY DID YOU SCREAM JUST BEFORE THE PHONE WENT DEAD?
THAT WAS THE WHOLE REASON I CAME TO TOKYO.
HUH?
TH-THAT WAS...
WELL, TSUKASA...
SHE GRABBED MY...
BLUSH
......
HUH? YOUR WHAT?
NEVER MIND! FORGET IT!
WHOOSH
WHAT? I CAN'T FORGET IT. JUST TELL ME.
NO WAY.
WHAT?

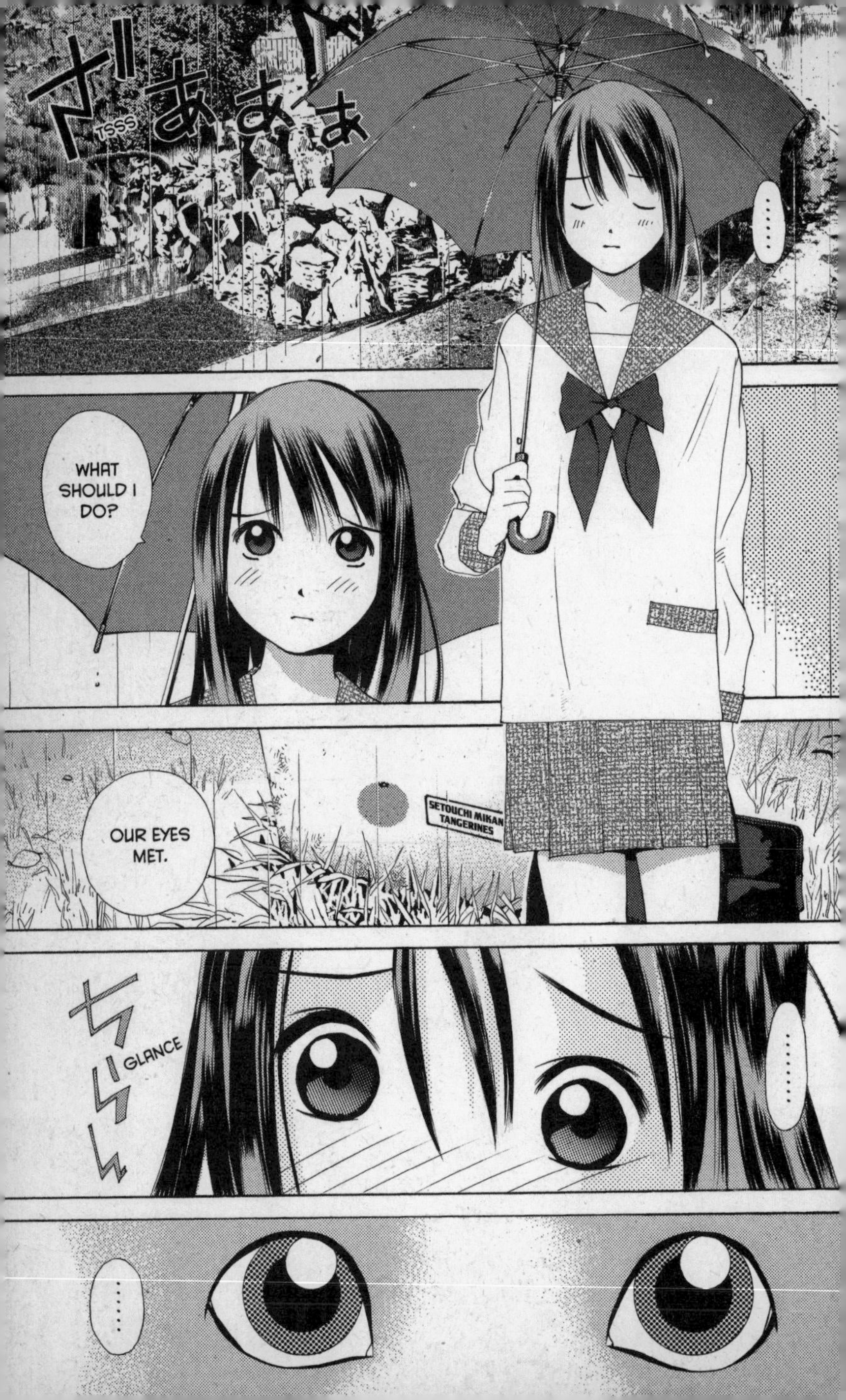
……
TSSS
WHAT SHOULD I DO?
SETOUCHI MIKAN TANGERINES
OUR EYES MET.
……
GLANCE
……

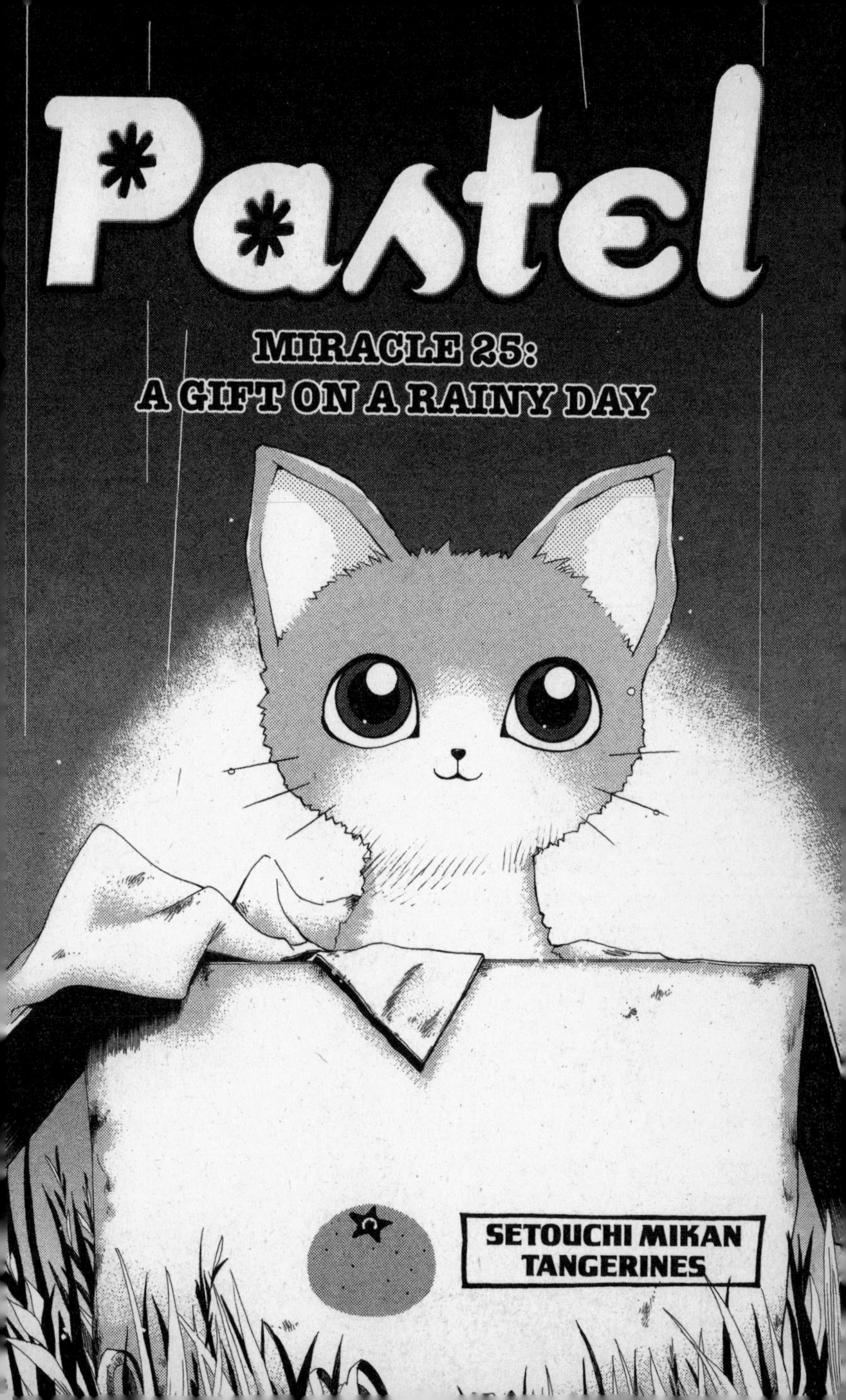
Pastel
MIRACLE 25:
A GIFT ON A RAINY DAY
SETOUCHI MIKAN
TANGERINES

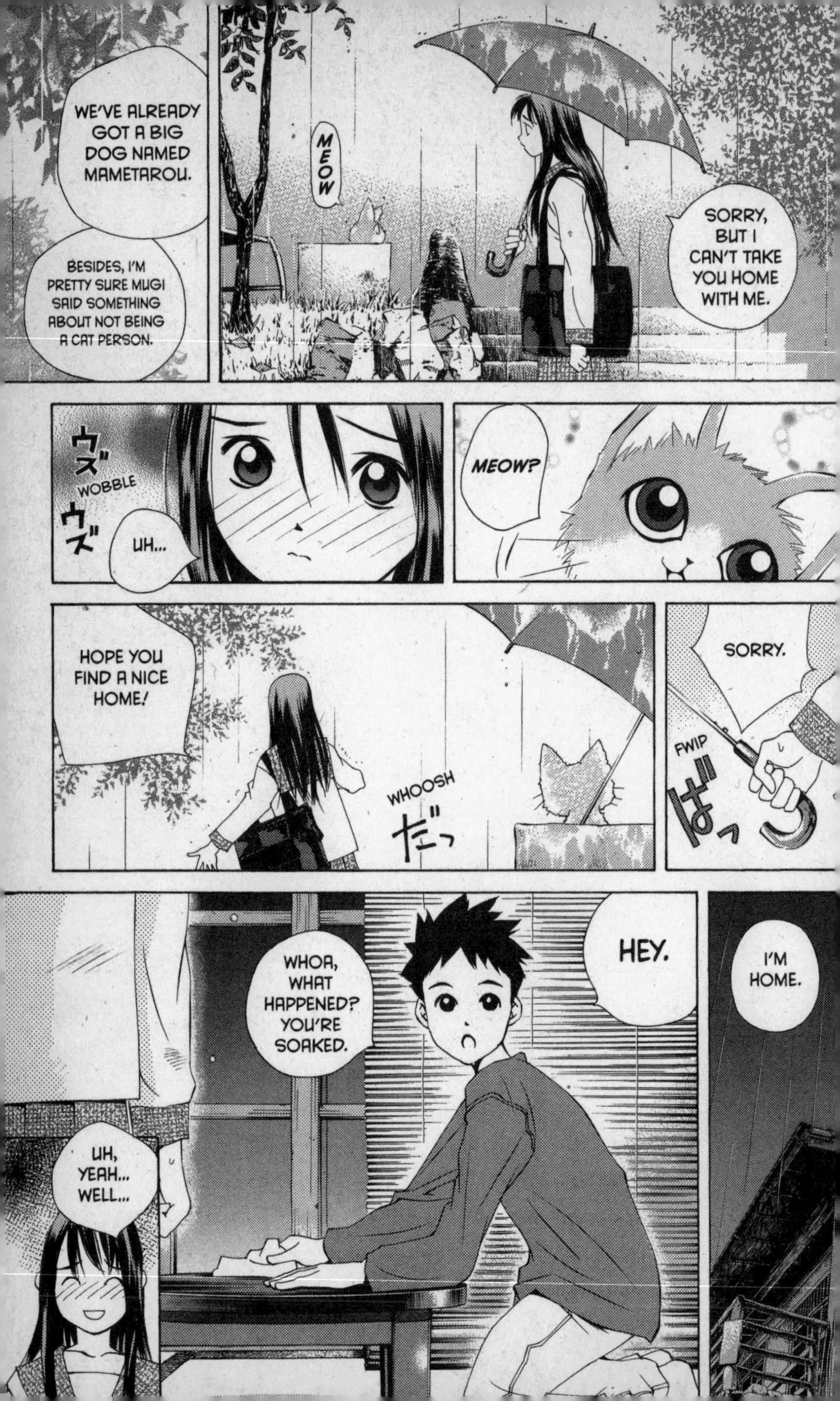
MEOW
SORRY, BUT I CAN'T TAKE YOU HOME WITH ME.
WE'VE ALREADY GOT A BIG DOG NAMED MAMETAROU.
BESIDES, I'M PRETTY SURE MUGI SAID SOMETHING ABOUT NOT BEING A CAT PERSON.
MEOW?
ウズウズ
WOBBLE
UH...
SORRY.
FWIP
ぱっ
WHOOSH
だっ
HOPE YOU FIND A NICE HOME!
I'M HOME.
HEY.
WHOA, WHAT HAPPENED? YOU'RE SOAKED.
UH, YEAH... WELL...

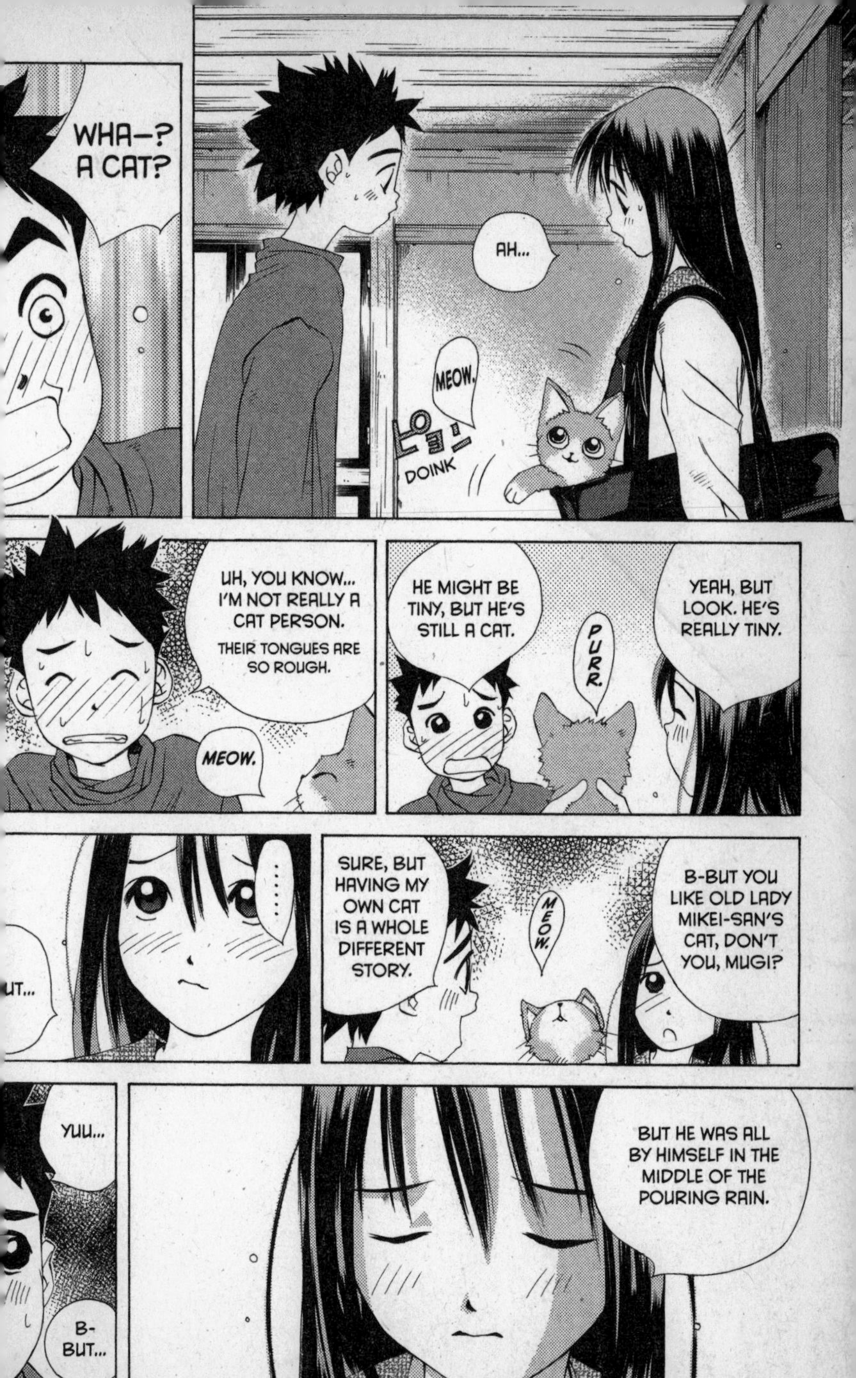

AH...
MEOW.
ピョン
DOINK
WHA—? A CAT?
YEAH, BUT LOOK. HE'S REALLY TINY.
PURR.
HE MIGHT BE TINY, BUT HE'S STILL A CAT.
UH, YOU KNOW... I'M NOT REALLY A CAT PERSON.
THEIR TONGUES ARE SO ROUGH.
MEOW.
B-BUT YOU LIKE OLD LADY MIKEI-SAN'S CAT, DON'T YOU, MUGI?
MEOW.
SURE, BUT HAVING MY OWN CAT IS A WHOLE DIFFERENT STORY.
......
UT...
BUT HE WAS ALL BY HIMSELF IN THE MIDDLE OF THE POURING RAIN.
YUU...
B- BUT...

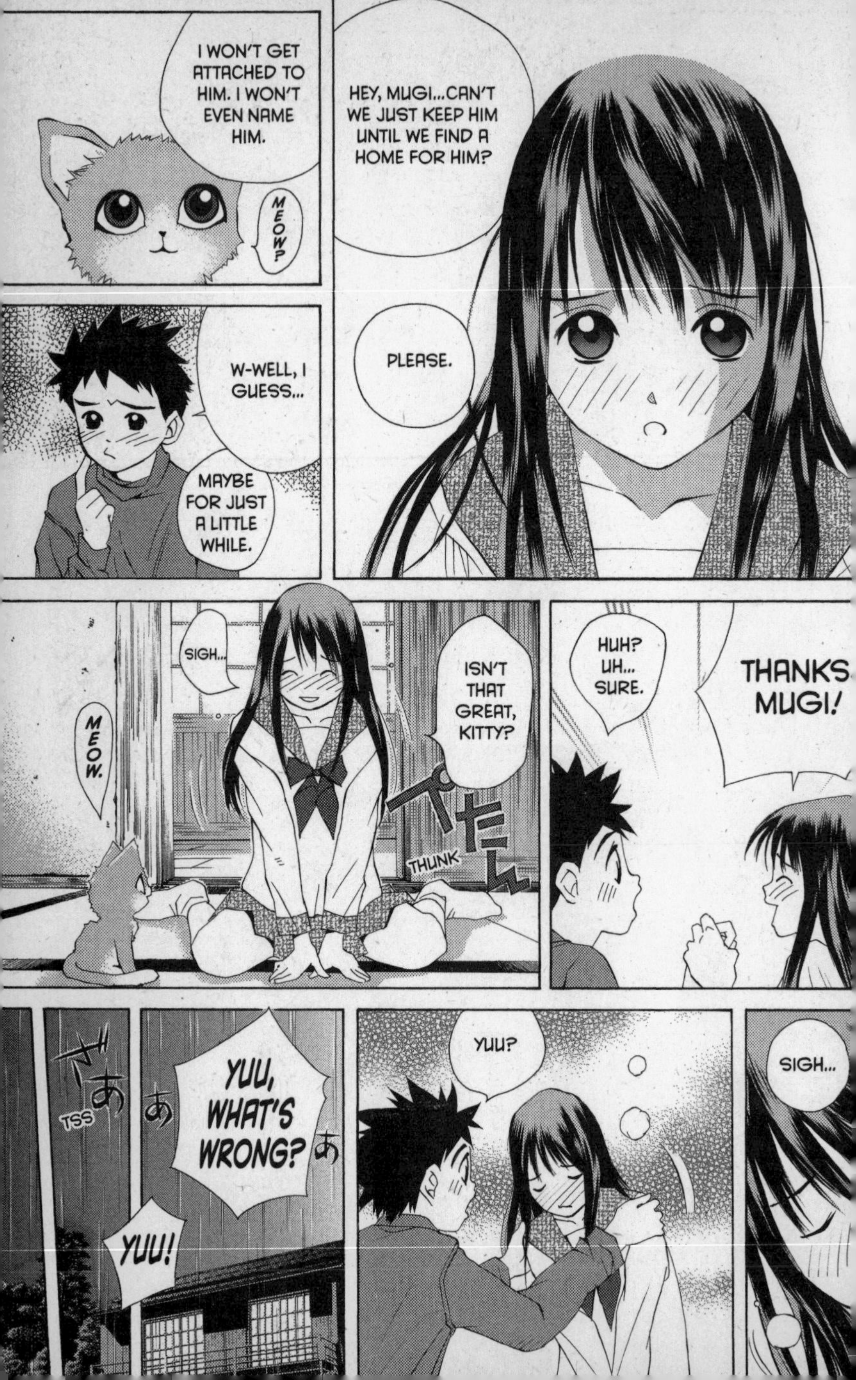
HEY, MUGI...CAN'T WE JUST KEEP HIM UNTIL WE FIND A HOME FOR HIM?
PLEASE.
I WON'T GET ATTACHED TO HIM. I WON'T EVEN NAME HIM.
MEOW?
W-WELL, I GUESS...
MAYBE FOR JUST A LITTLE WHILE.
THANKS MUGI!
HUH? UH... SURE.
ISN'T THAT GREAT, KITTY?
SIGH...
MEOW.
THUNK
SIGH...
YUU?
YUU, WHAT'S WRONG?
TSS
YUU!

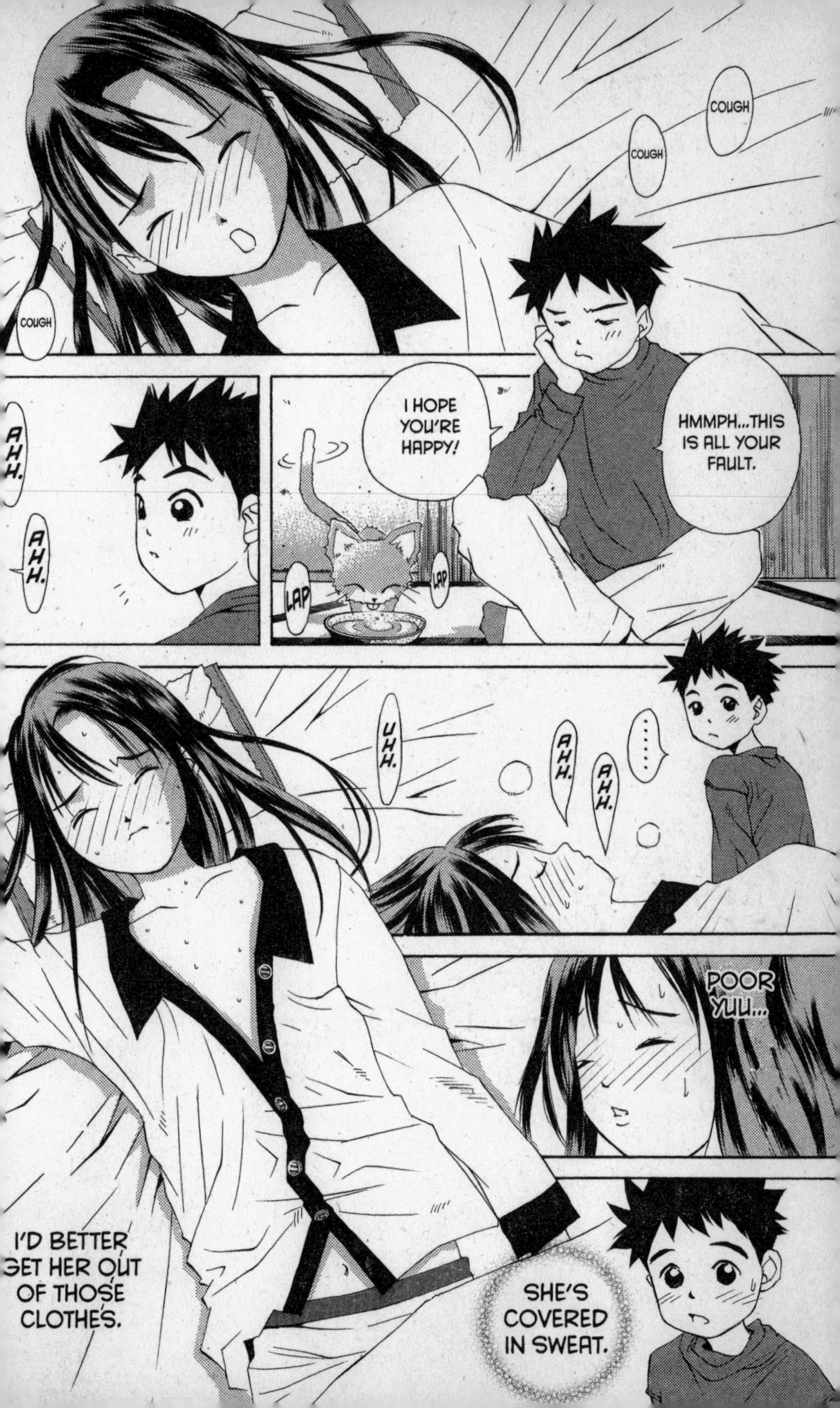
COUGH
COUGH
COUGH
HMMPH...THIS IS ALL YOUR FAULT.
I HOPE YOU'RE HAPPY!
LAP
LAP
AHH.
AHH.
......
AHH.
AHH.
UHH.
POOR YUU...
SHE'S COVERED IN SWEAT.
I'D BETTER GET HER OUT OF THOSE CLOTHES.

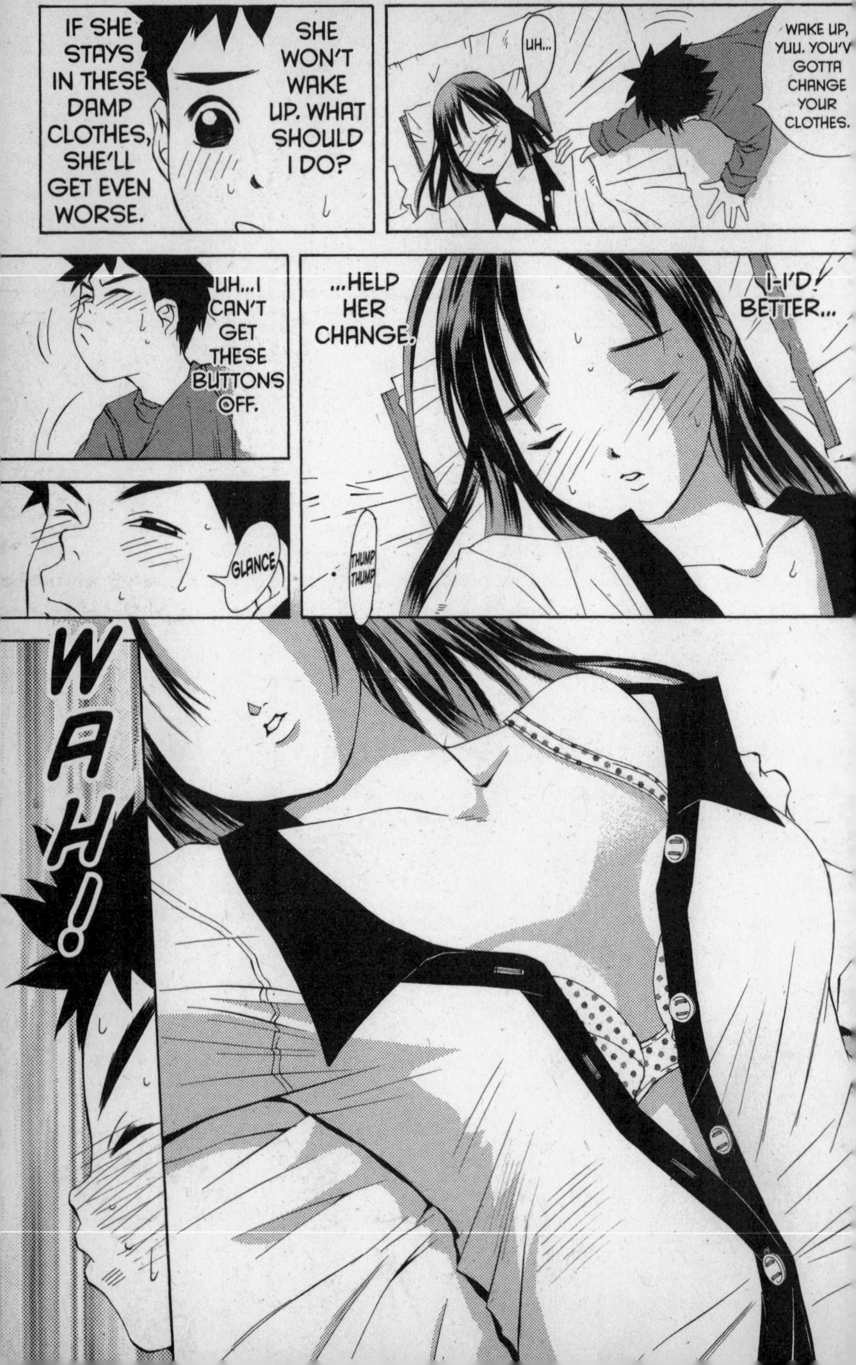
WAKE UP, YUU. YOU'V GOTTA CHANGE YOUR CLOTHES.
UH...
SHE WON'T WAKE UP. WHAT SHOULD I DO?
IF SHE STAYS IN THESE DAMP CLOTHES, SHE'LL GET EVEN WORSE.
I-I'D BETTER...
...HELP HER CHANGE.
THUMP THUMP
UH...I CAN'T GET THESE BUTTONS OFF.
GLANCE
WAH!

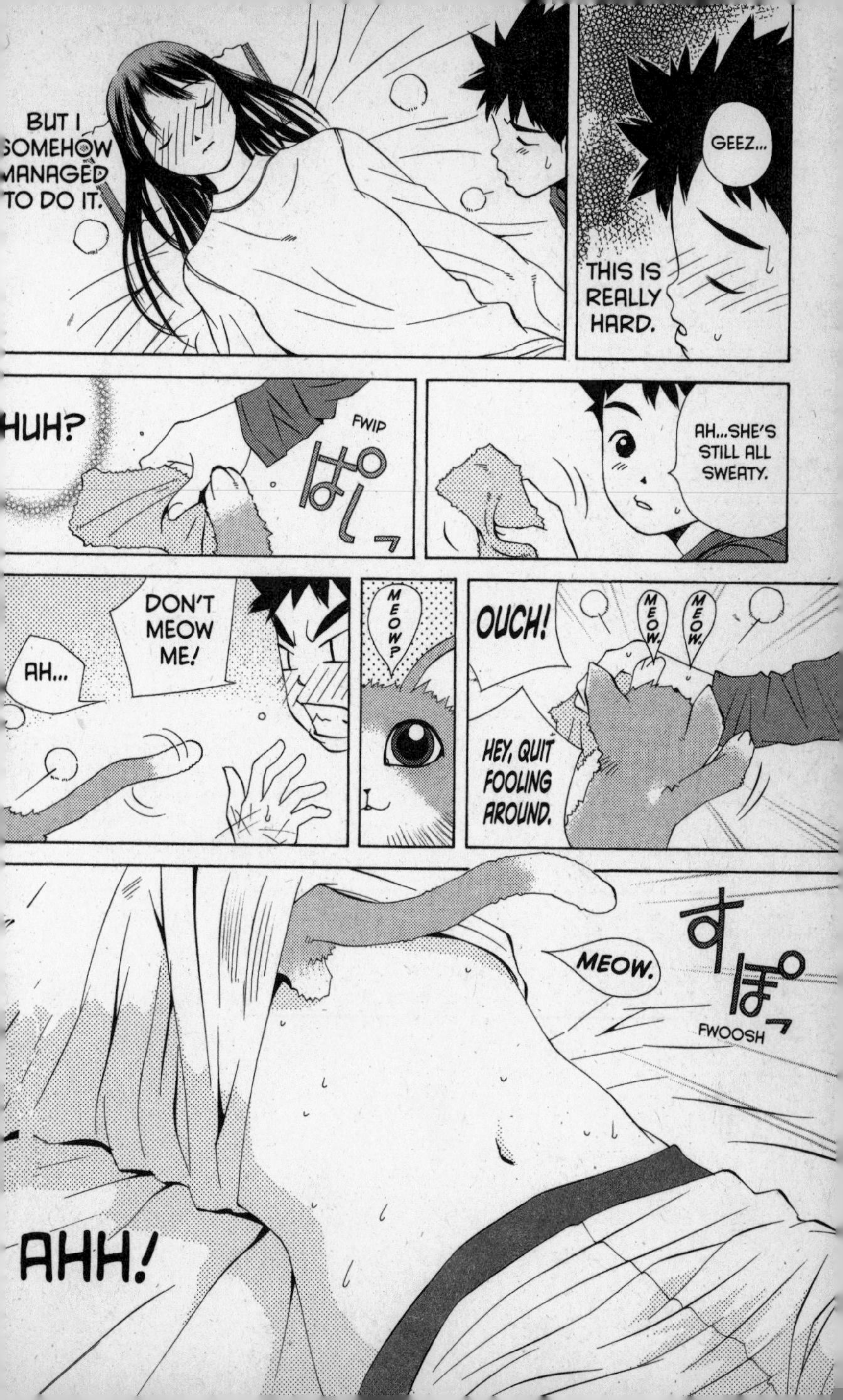
GEEZ...
THIS IS REALLY HARD.
BUT I SOMEHOW MANAGED TO DO IT.
AH...SHE'S STILL ALL SWEATY.
ぱしっ
FWIP
HUH?
MEOW.
MEOW.
OUCH!
HEY, QUIT FOOLING AROUND.
MEOW?
DON'T MEOW ME!
AH...
すぽっ
FWOOSH
MEOW.
AHH!

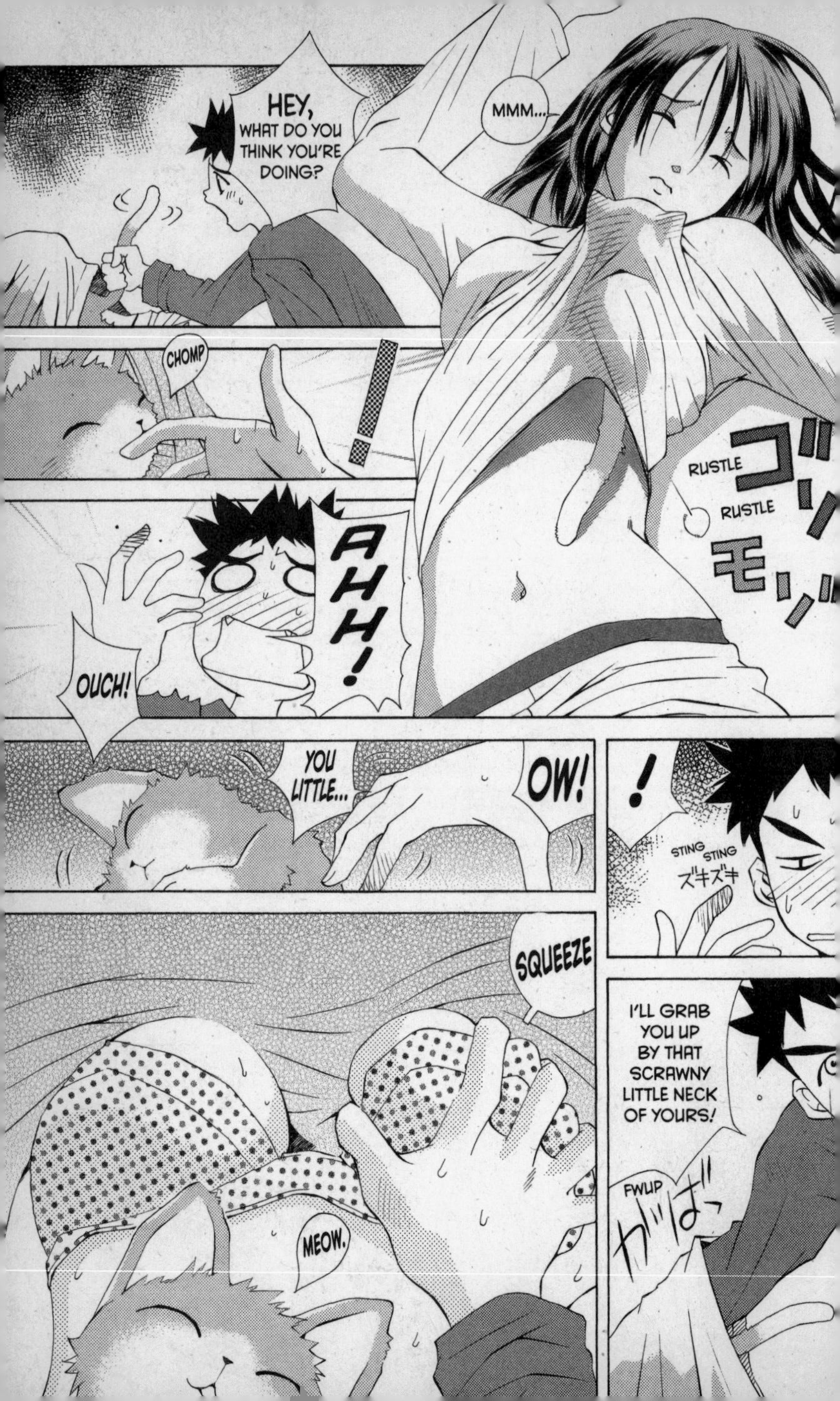
MMM...
RUSTLE
RUSTLE
ゴソ
モソッ
HEY, WHAT DO YOU THINK YOU'RE DOING?
CHOMP
!
AHHH!
OUCH!
!
STING STING
ズキズキ
OW!
YOU LITTLE...
I'LL GRAB YOU UP BY THAT SCRAWNY LITTLE NECK OF YOURS!
FWUP
がばっ
SQUEEZE
MEOW.

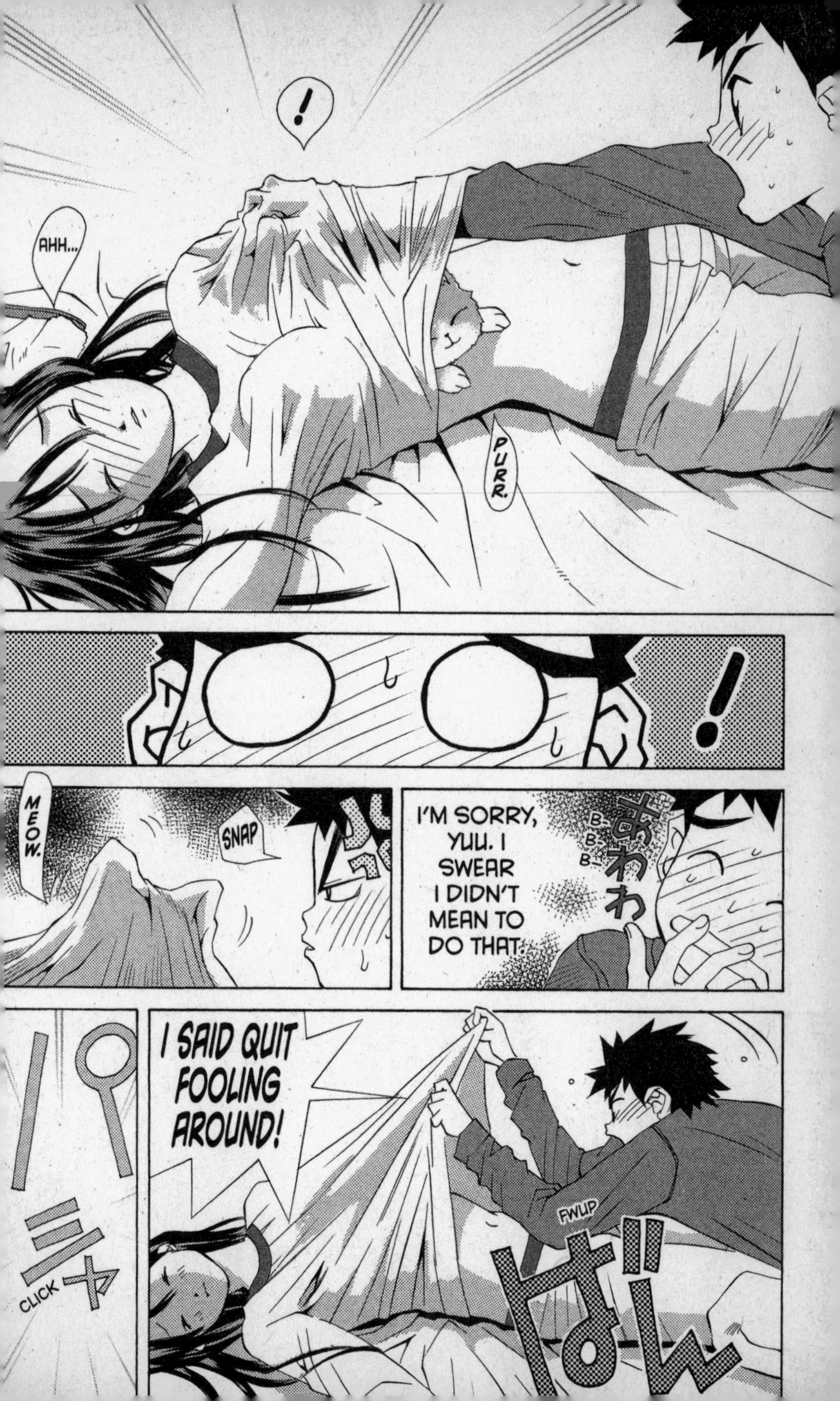

!
AHH...
PURR.
!
あわわ
B-B-B-
I'M SORRY, YUU. I SWEAR I DIDN'T MEAN TO DO THAT.
SNAP
MEOW.
I SAID QUIT FOOLING AROUND!
FWUP
ばん
ミャ
CLICK

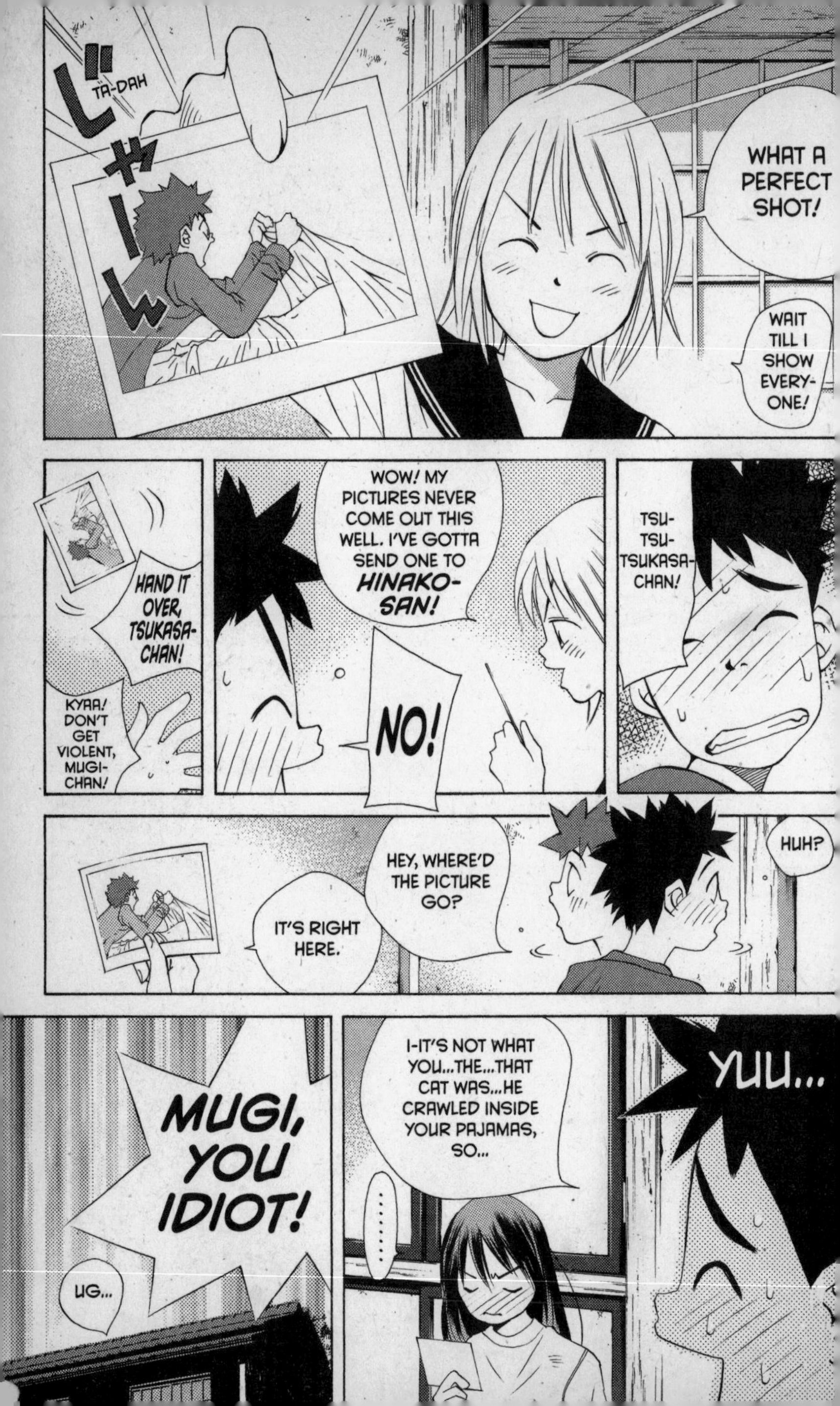
WHAT A PERFECT SHOT!
WAIT TILL I SHOW EVERY-ONE!
TA-DAH
TSU-TSU-TSUKASA-CHAN!
WOW! MY PICTURES NEVER COME OUT THIS WELL. I'VE GOTTA SEND ONE TO HINAKO-SAN!
NO!
HAND IT OVER, TSUKASA-CHAN!
KYAA! DON'T GET VIOLENT, MUGI-CHAN!
HUH?
HEY, WHERE'D THE PICTURE GO?
IT'S RIGHT HERE.
YUU...
I-IT'S NOT WHAT YOU...THE...THAT CAT WAS...HE CRAWLED INSIDE YOUR PAJAMAS, SO...
......
MUGI, YOU IDIOT!
UG...

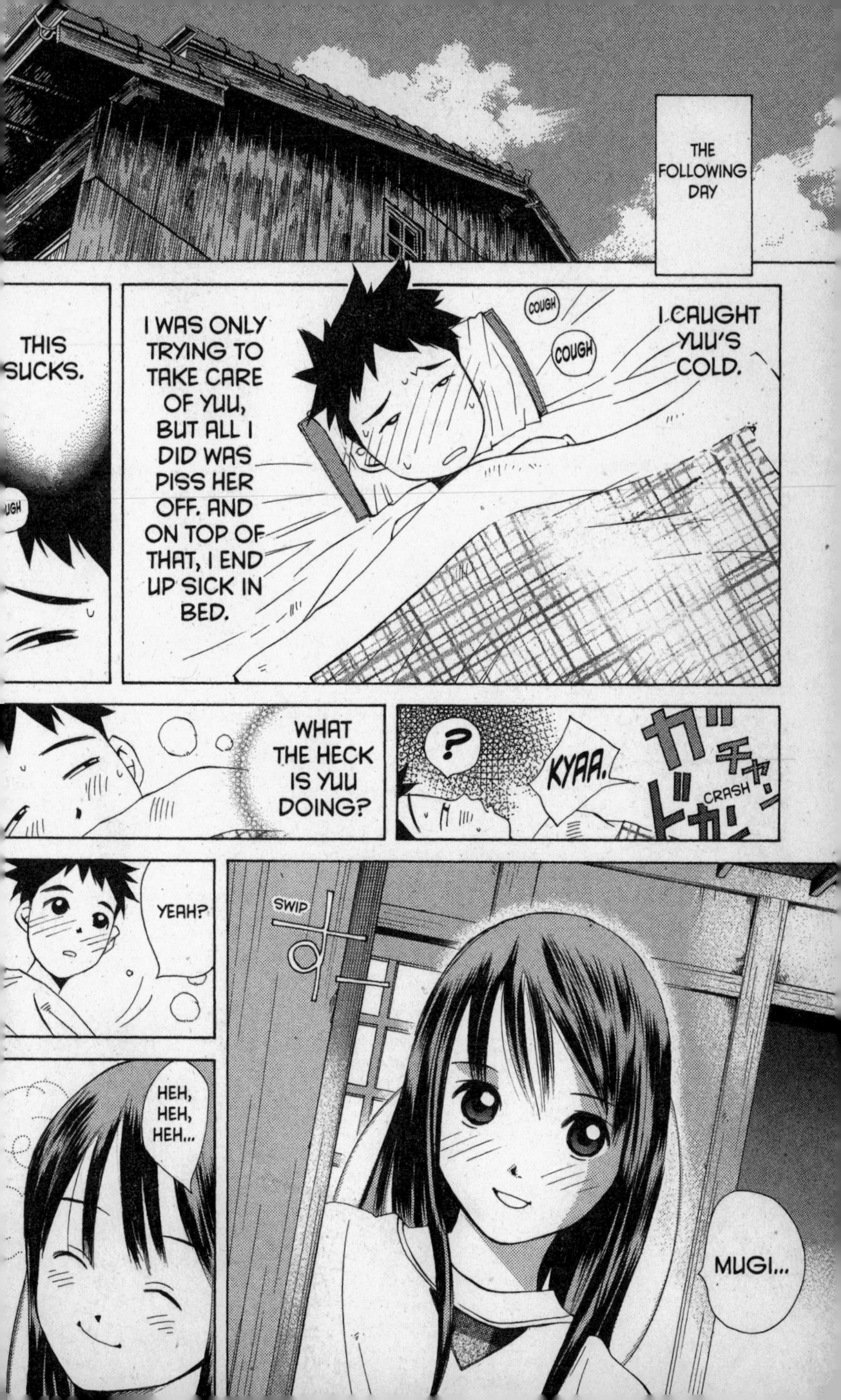
THE FOLLOWING DAY
COUGH
COUGH
I CAUGHT YUU'S COLD.
I WAS ONLY TRYING TO TAKE CARE OF YUU, BUT ALL I DID WAS PISS HER OFF. AND ON TOP OF THAT, I END UP SICK IN BED.
THIS SUCKS.
?
KYAA.
CRASH
WHAT THE HECK IS YUU DOING?
SWIP
MUGI...
YEAH?
HEH, HEH, HEH...

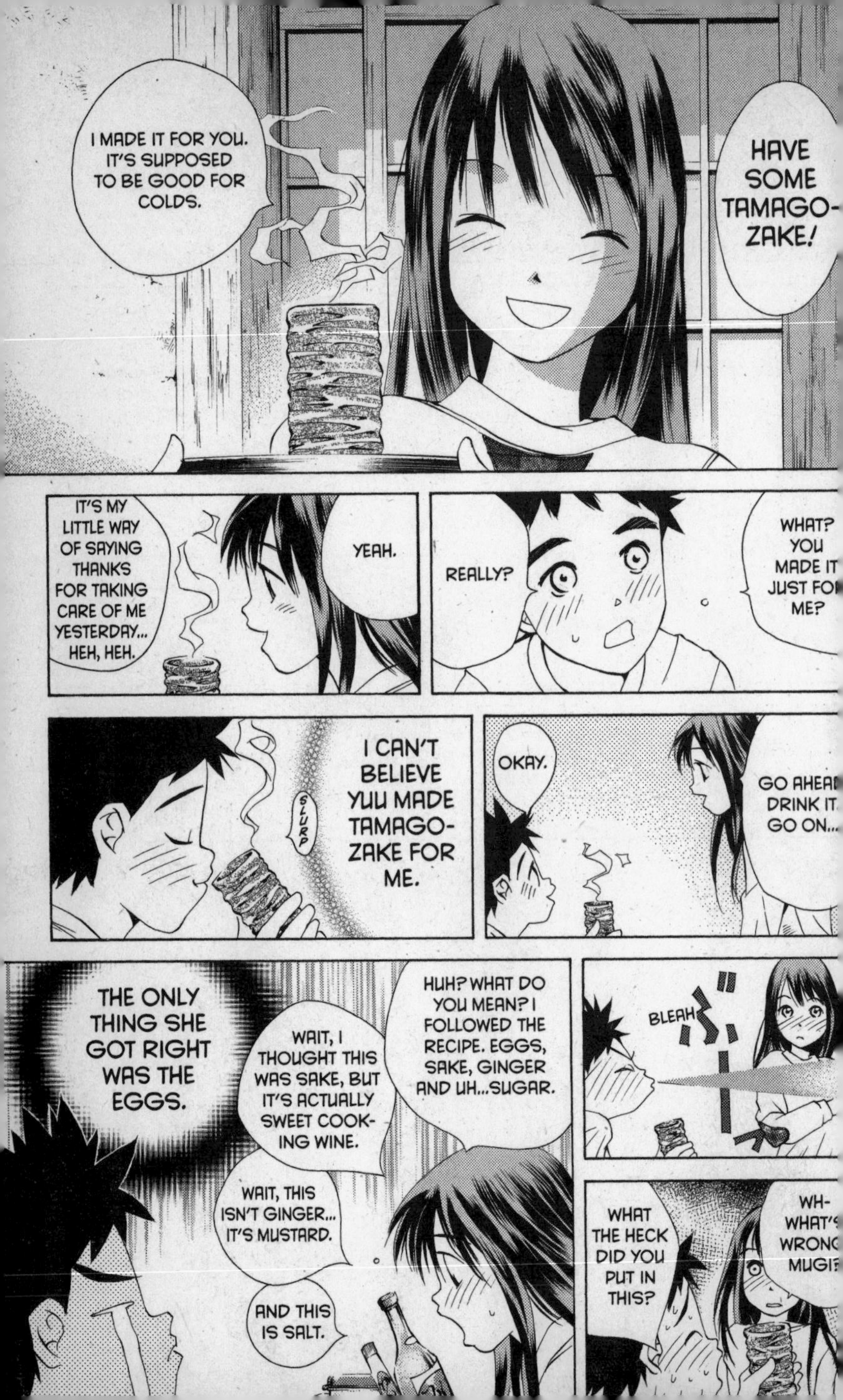
HAVE SOME TAMAGO-ZAKE!
I MADE IT FOR YOU. IT'S SUPPOSED TO BE GOOD FOR COLDS.
WHAT? YOU MADE IT JUST FO ME?
REALLY?
YEAH.
IT'S MY LITTLE WAY OF SAYING THANKS FOR TAKING CARE OF ME YESTERDAY... HEH, HEH.
GO AHEA DRINK IT. GO ON...
OKAY.
SLURP
I CAN'T BELIEVE YUU MADE TAMAGO-ZAKE FOR ME.
BLEAH
WH- WHAT'S WRONG MUGI?
WHAT THE HECK DID YOU PUT IN THIS?
HUH? WHAT DO YOU MEAN? I FOLLOWED THE RECIPE. EGGS, SAKE, GINGER AND UH...SUGAR.
WAIT, I THOUGHT THIS WAS SAKE, BUT IT'S ACTUALLY SWEET COOK-ING WINE.
WAIT, THIS ISN'T GINGER... IT'S MUSTARD.
AND THIS IS SALT.
THE ONLY THING SHE GOT RIGHT WAS THE EGGS.

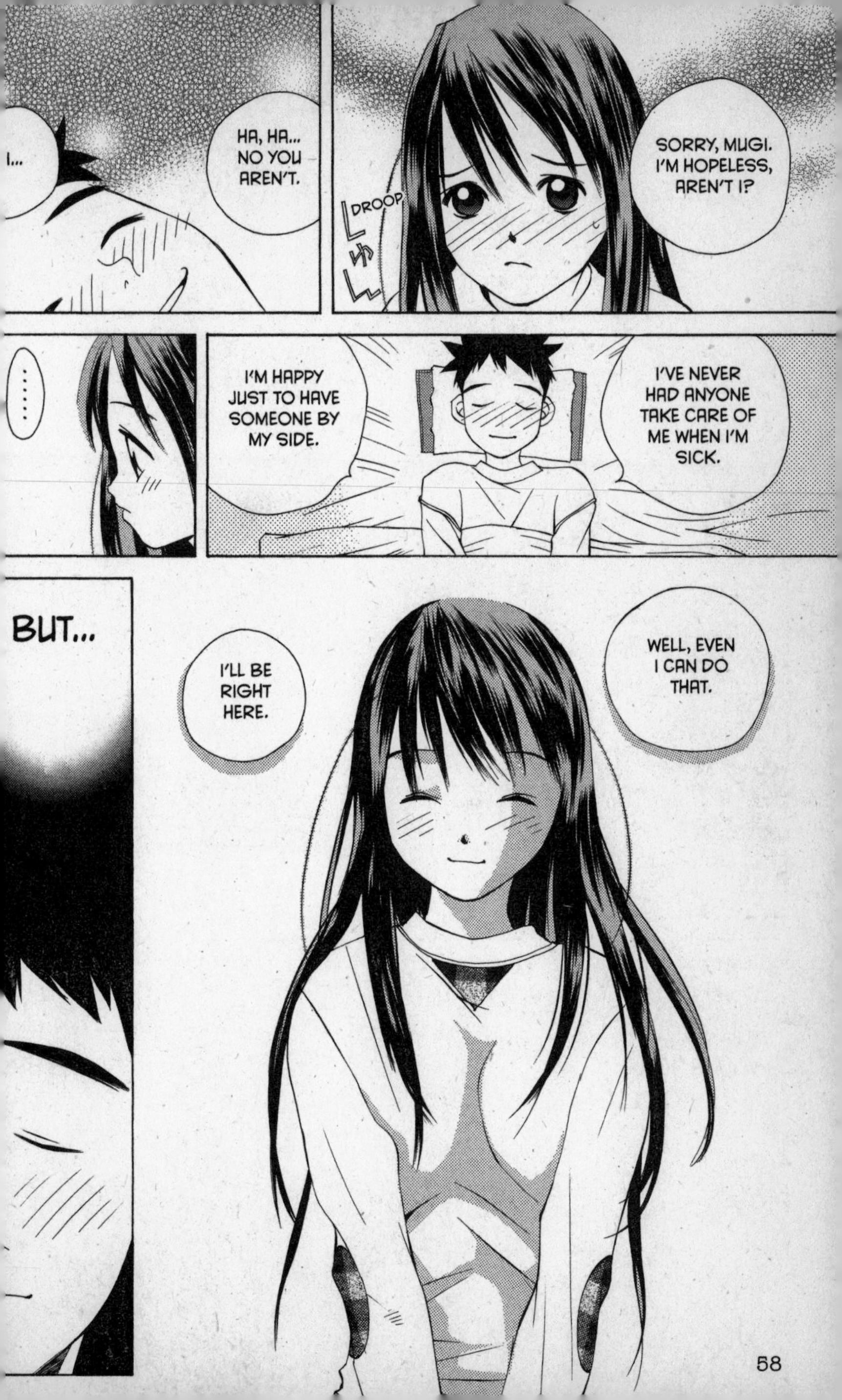
SORRY, MUGI. I'M HOPELESS, AREN'T I?
DROOP
しゅん
HA, HA... NO YOU AREN'T.
I...
I'VE NEVER HAD ANYONE TAKE CARE OF ME WHEN I'M SICK.
I'M HAPPY JUST TO HAVE SOMEONE BY MY SIDE.
......
WELL, EVEN I CAN DO THAT.
I'LL BE RIGHT HERE.
BUT...

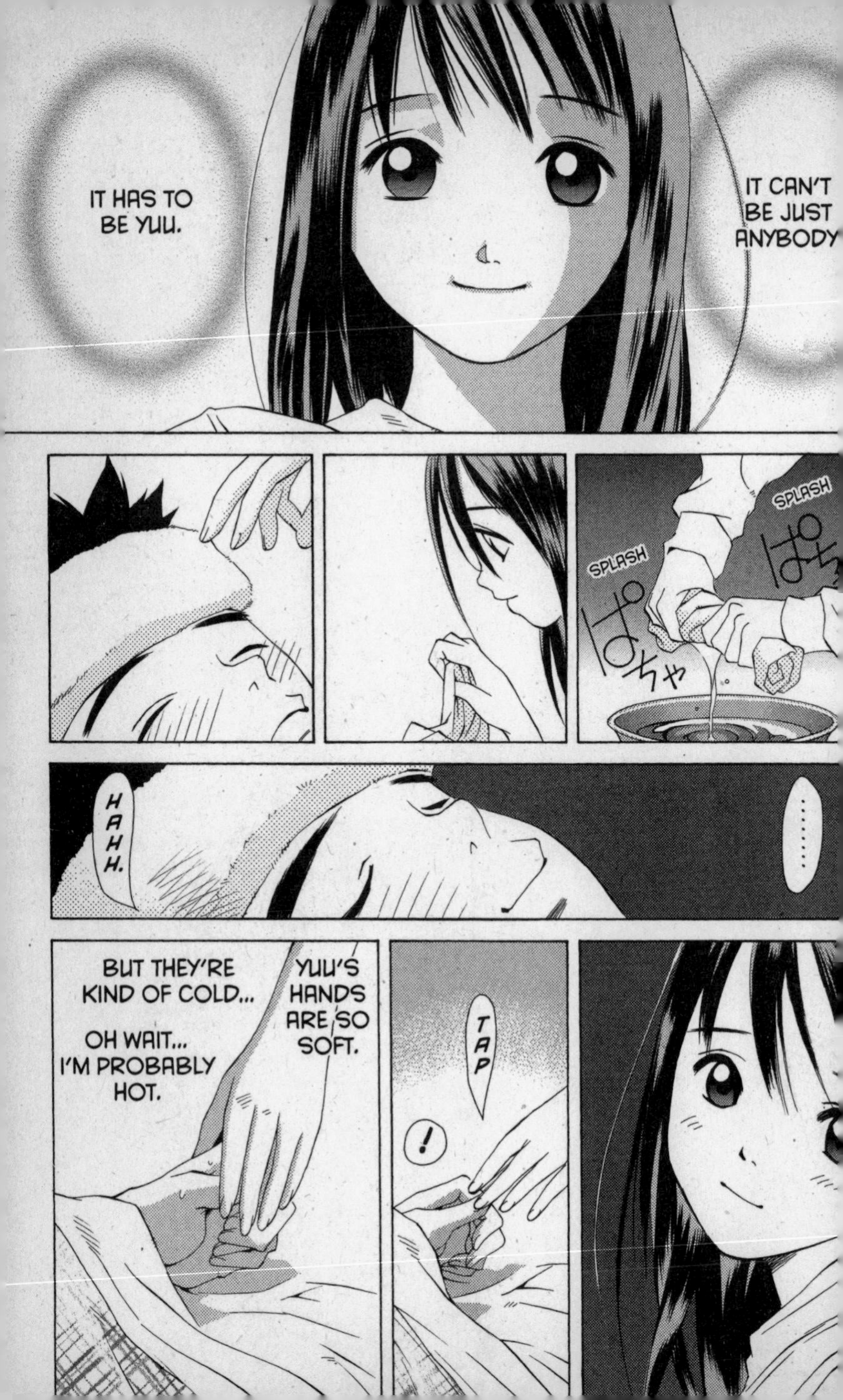
IT CAN'T BE JUST ANYBODY
IT HAS TO BE YUU.
SPLASH
SPLASH
ぱちゃ
......
HAHH.
TAP
!
YUU'S HANDS ARE SO SOFT.
BUT THEY'RE KIND OF COLD...
OH WAIT... I'M PROBABLY HOT.

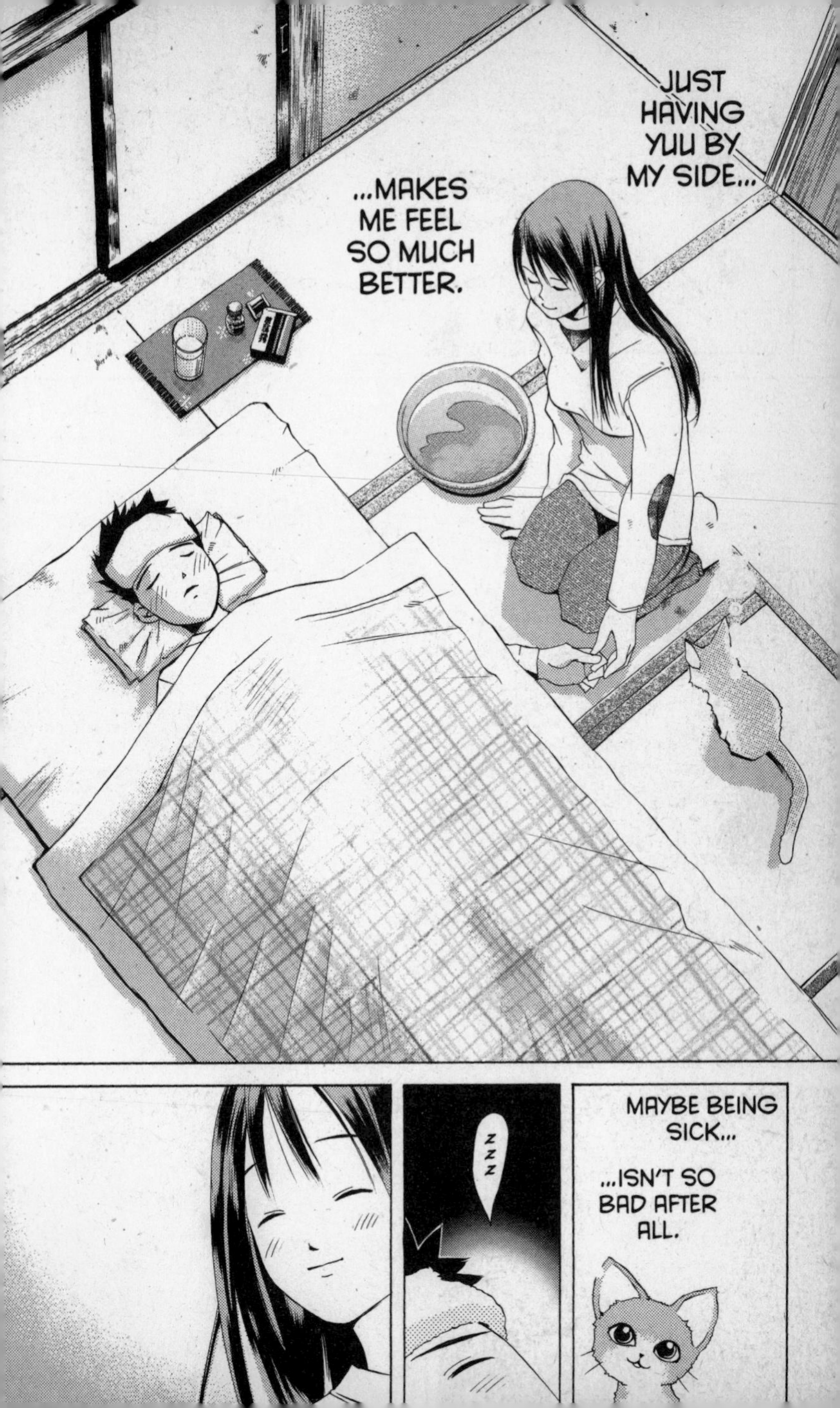
JUST HAVING YUU BY MY SIDE...
...MAKES ME FEEL SO MUCH BETTER.
MAYBE BEING SICK...
...ISN'T SO BAD AFTER ALL.
Z Z Z

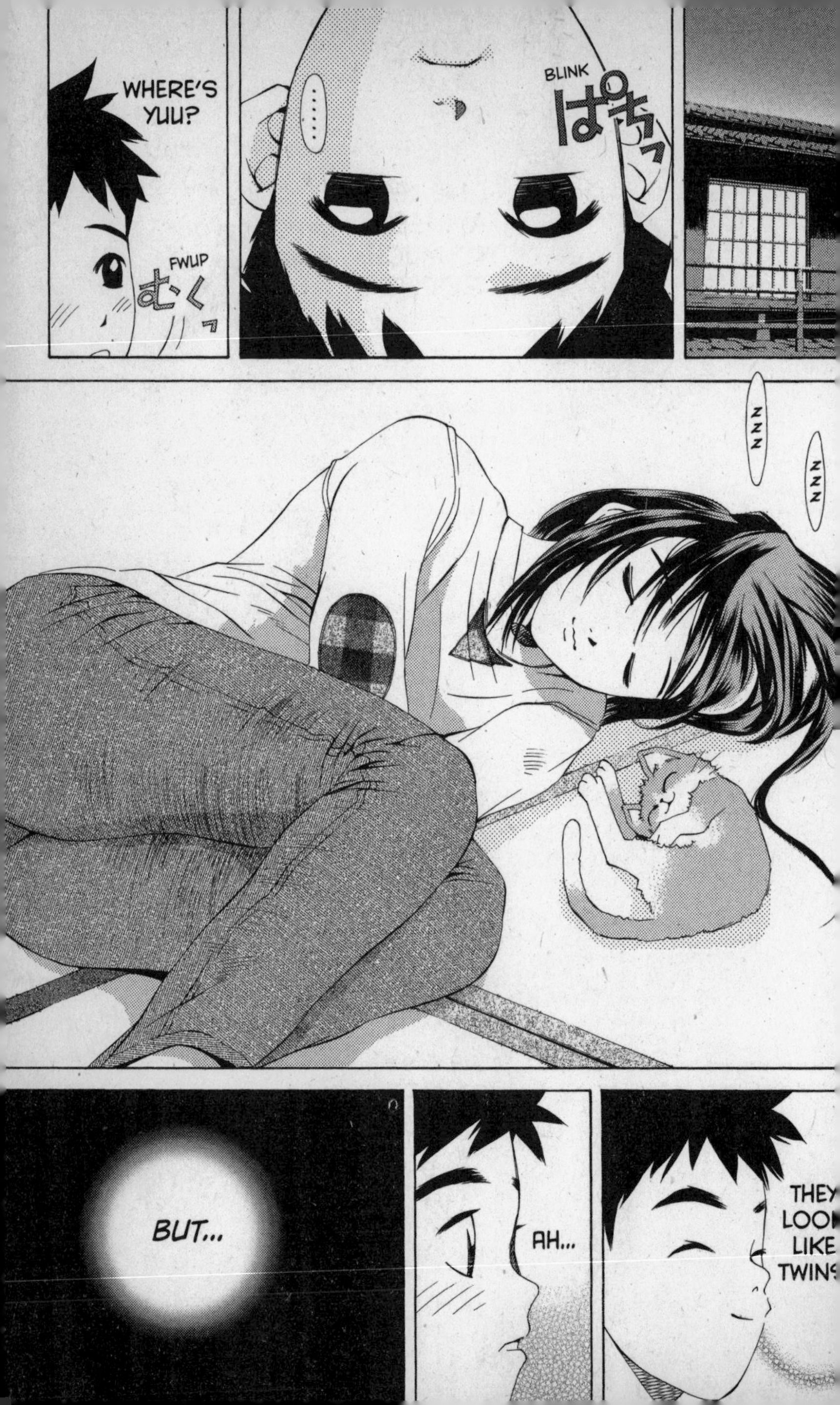
......
BLINK
ぱちっ
WHERE'S YUU?
FWUP
むくっ
ZZZ
ZZZ
THEY LOO LIKE TWIN
AH...
BUT...

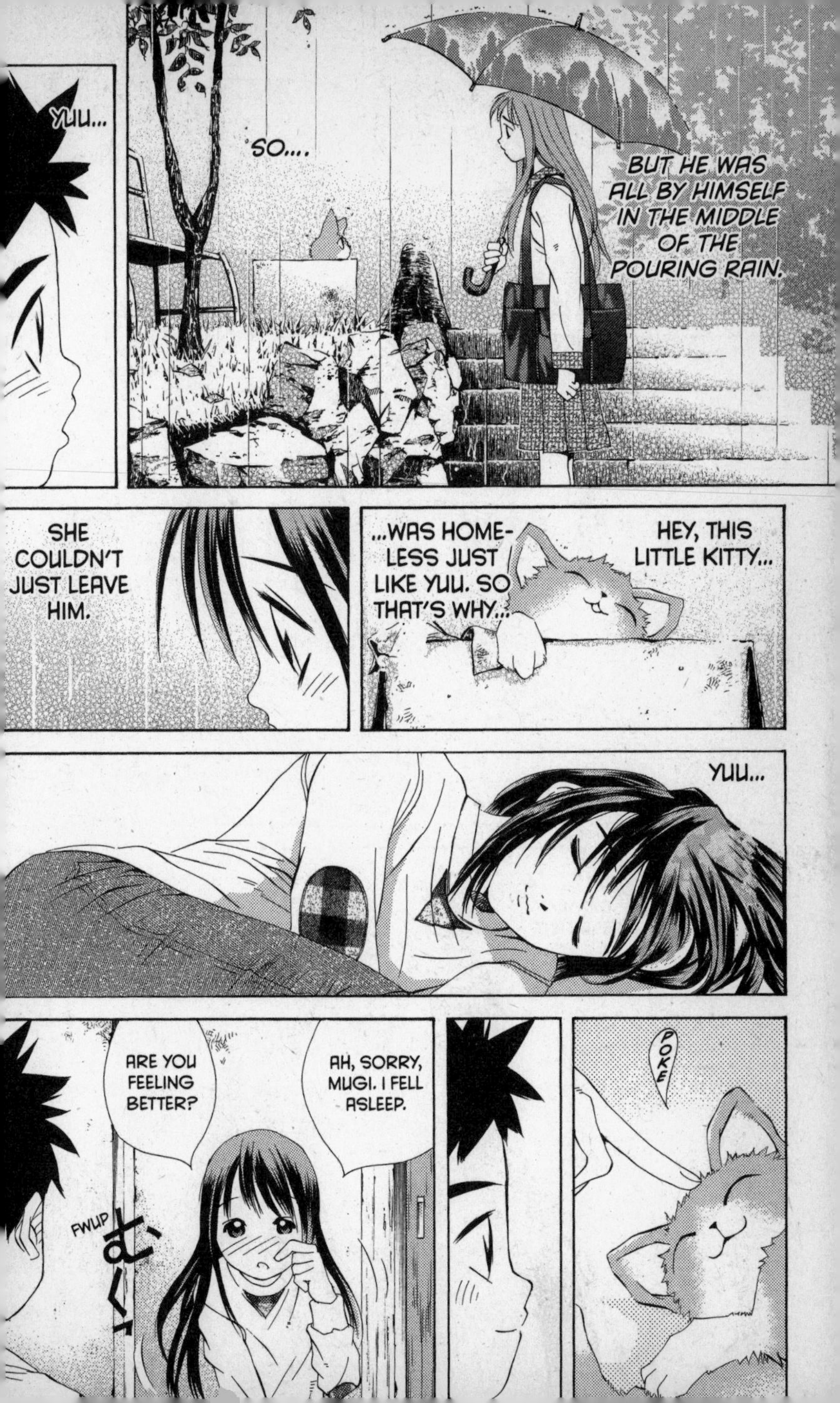
BUT HE WAS ALL BY HIMSELF IN THE MIDDLE OF THE POURING RAIN.
SO....
YUU...
HEY, THIS LITTLE KITTY...
...WAS HOME-LESS JUST LIKE YUU. SO THAT'S WHY...
SHE COULDN'T JUST LEAVE HIM.
YUU...
POKE
AH, SORRY, MUGI. I FELL ASLEEP.
ARE YOU FEELING BETTER?
FWUP

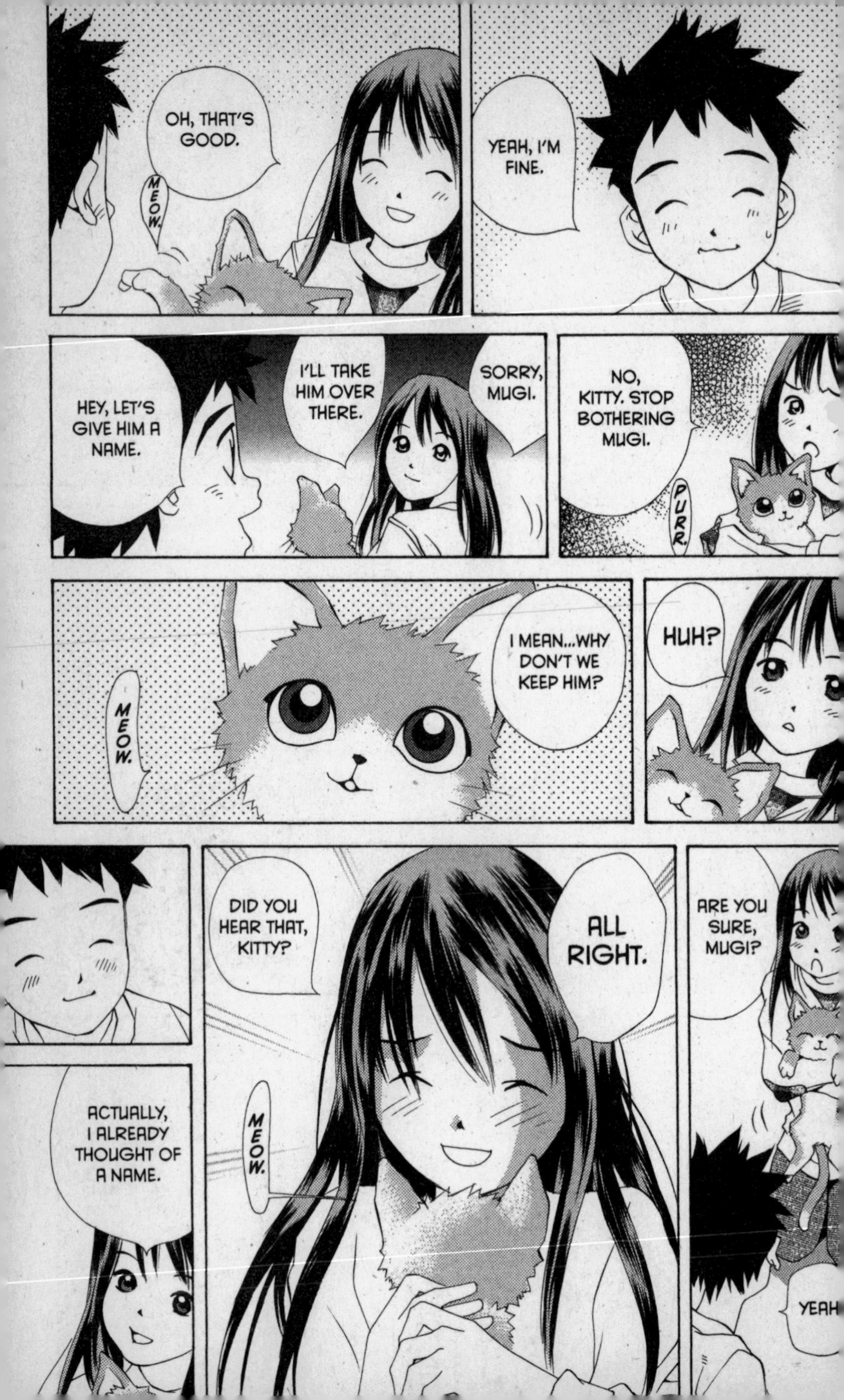
YEAH, I'M FINE.
OH, THAT'S GOOD.
MEOW.
NO, KITTY. STOP BOTHERING MUGI.
PURR.
SORRY, MUGI.
I'LL TAKE HIM OVER THERE.
HEY, LET'S GIVE HIM A NAME.
HUH?
I MEAN...WHY DON'T WE KEEP HIM?
MEOW.
ARE YOU SURE, MUGI?
YEAH
ALL RIGHT.
DID YOU HEAR THAT, KITTY?
MEOW.
ACTUALLY, I ALREADY THOUGHT OF A NAME.

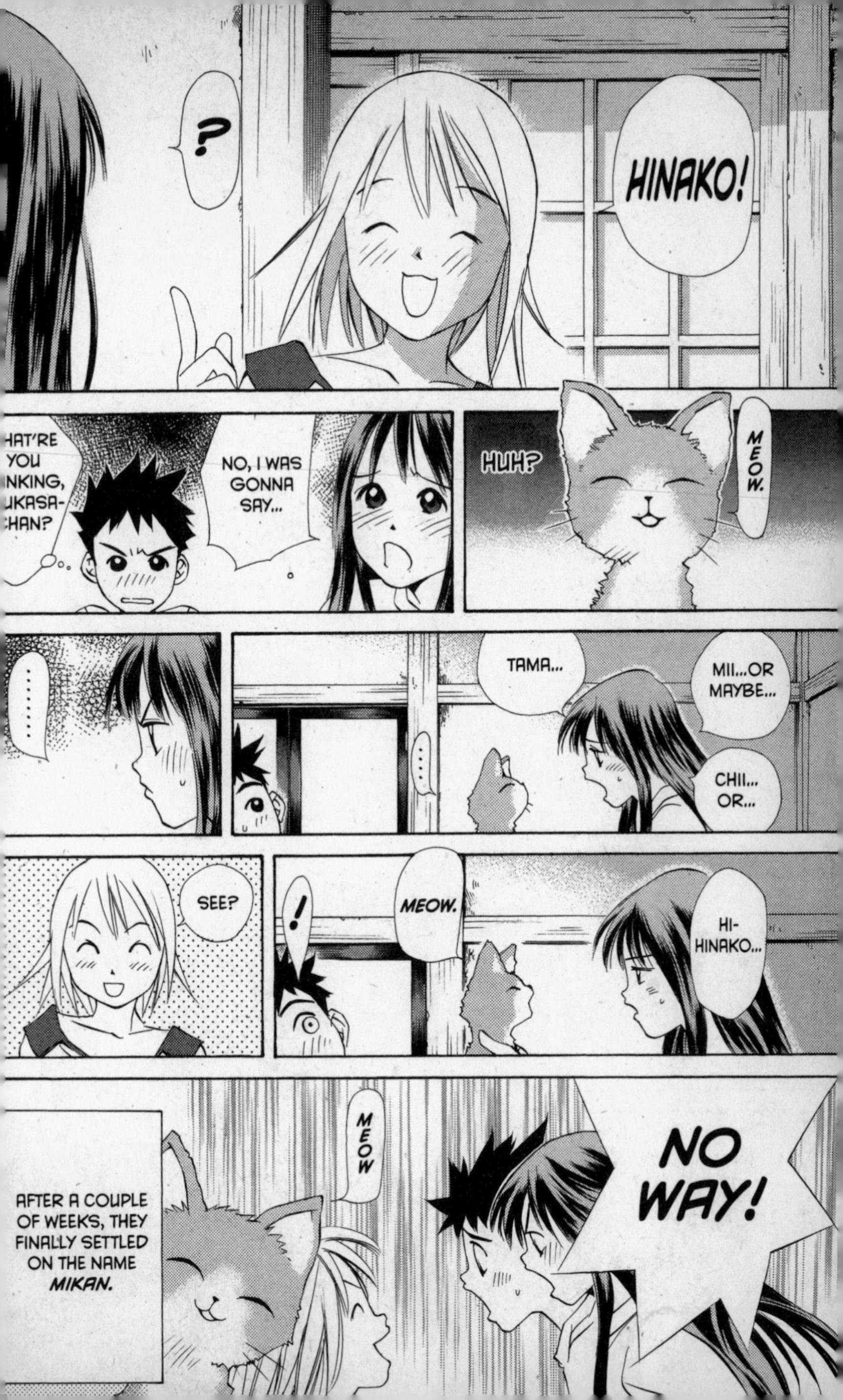
HINAKO!
?
MEOW.
HUH?
NO, I WAS GONNA SAY...
HAT'RE YOU NKING, UKASA-CHAN?
MII...OR MAYBE...
TAMA...
CHII... OR...
...
......
HI-HINAKO...
MEOW.
!
SEE?
NO WAY!
MEOW
AFTER A COUPLE OF WEEKS, THEY FINALLY SETTLED ON THE NAME *MIKAN*.

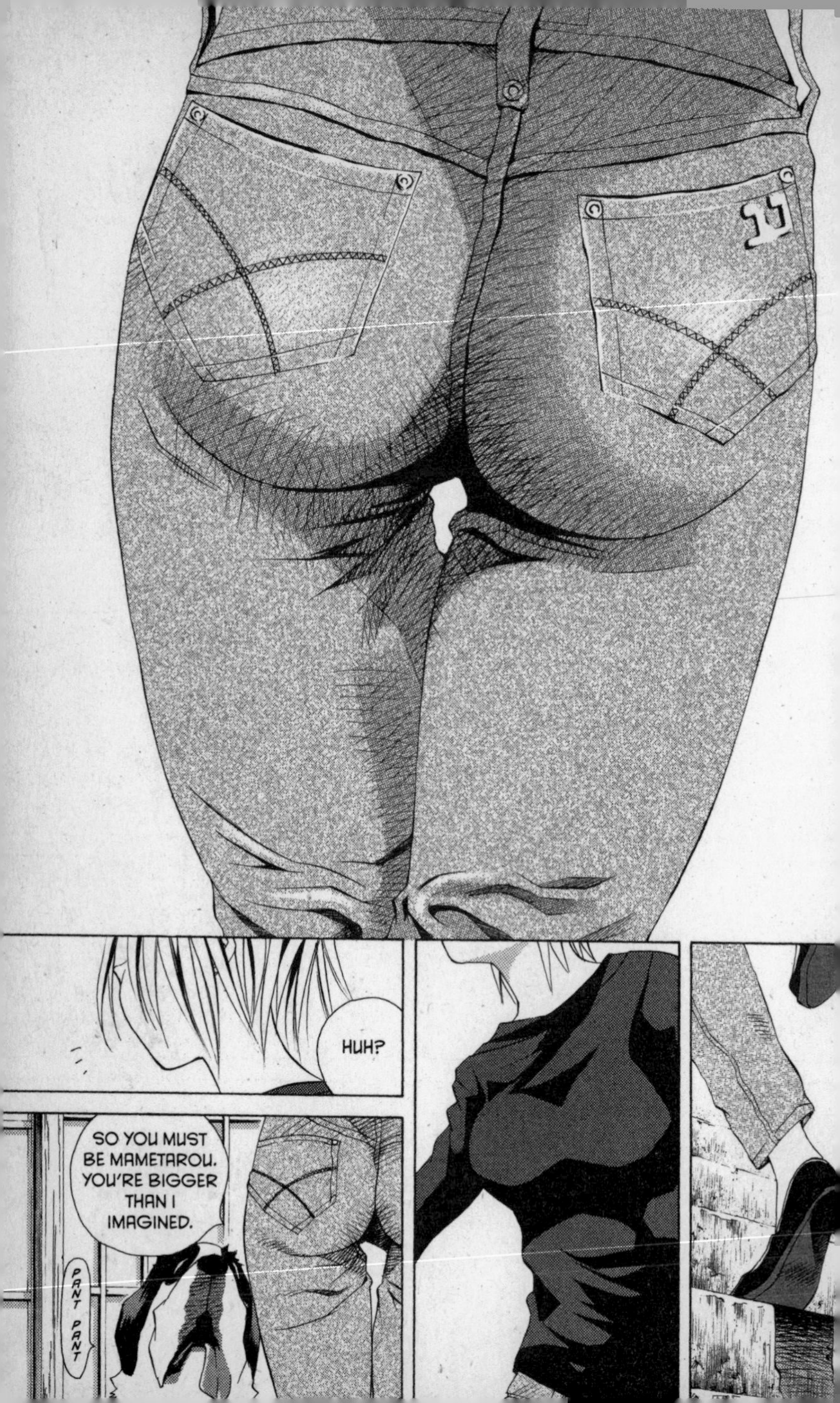
HUH?
SO YOU MUST BE MAMETAROU. YOU'RE BIGGER THAN I IMAGINED.
PANT PANT

Pastel

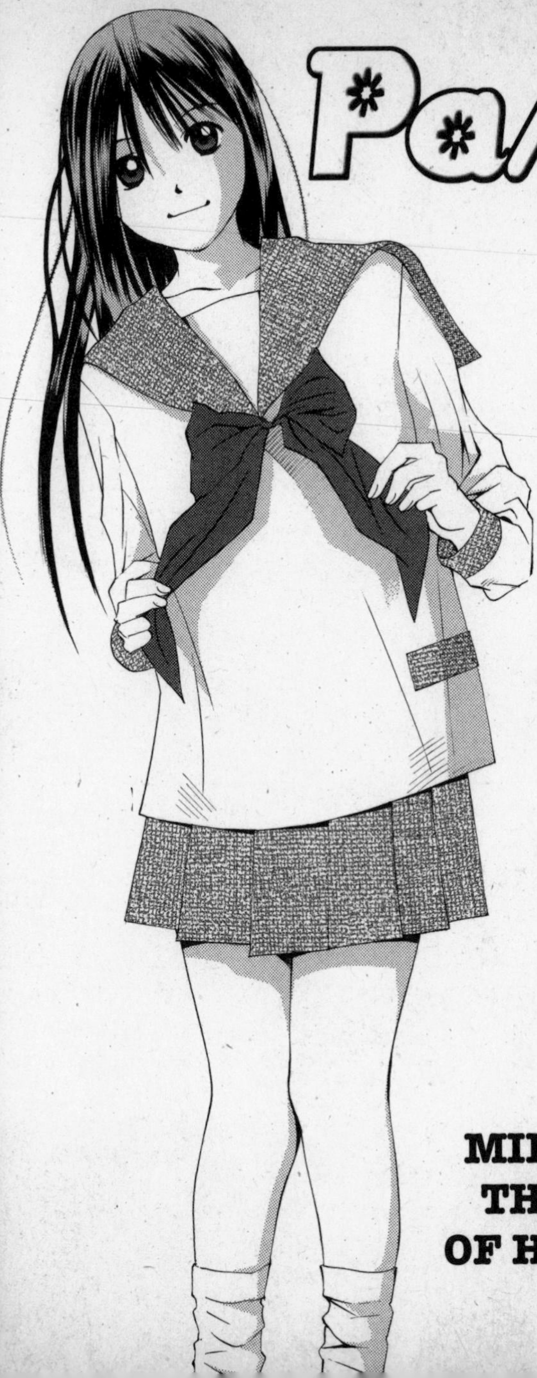

MIRACLE 26: THE SHAPE OF HAPPINESS

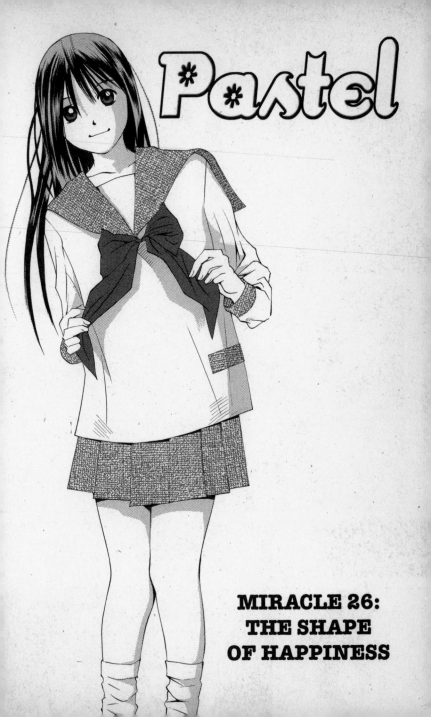

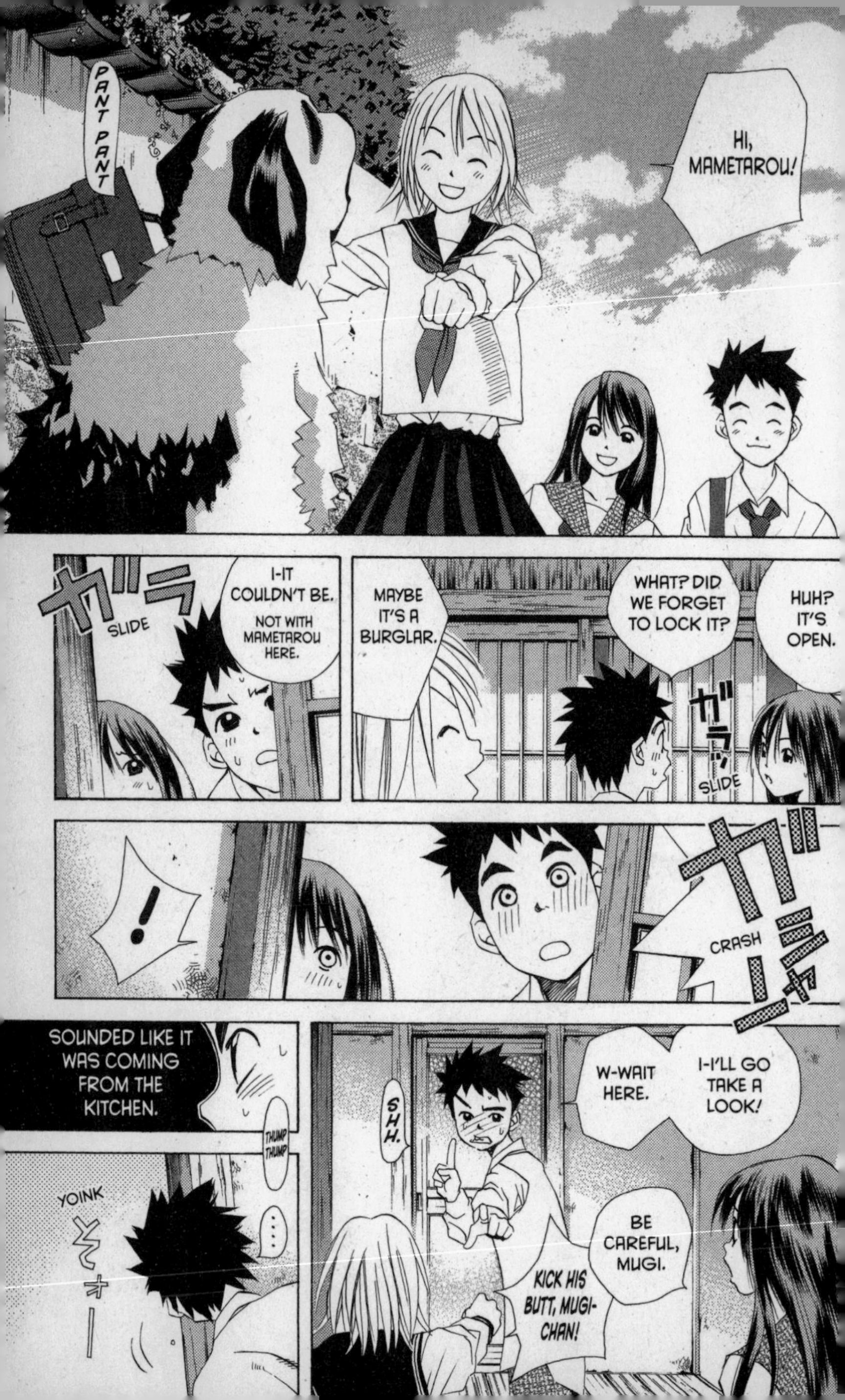
HI, MAMETAROU!
PANT PANT
HUH? IT'S OPEN.
WHAT? DID WE FORGET TO LOCK IT?
SLIDE
MAYBE IT'S A BURGLAR.
I-IT COULDN'T BE.
NOT WITH MAMETAROU HERE.
SLIDE
CRASH
!
I-I'LL GO TAKE A LOOK!
W-WAIT HERE.
SHH.
BE CAREFUL, MUGI.
KICK HIS BUTT, MUGI-CHAN!
SOUNDED LIKE IT WAS COMING FROM THE KITCHEN.
THUMP THUMP
....
YOINK

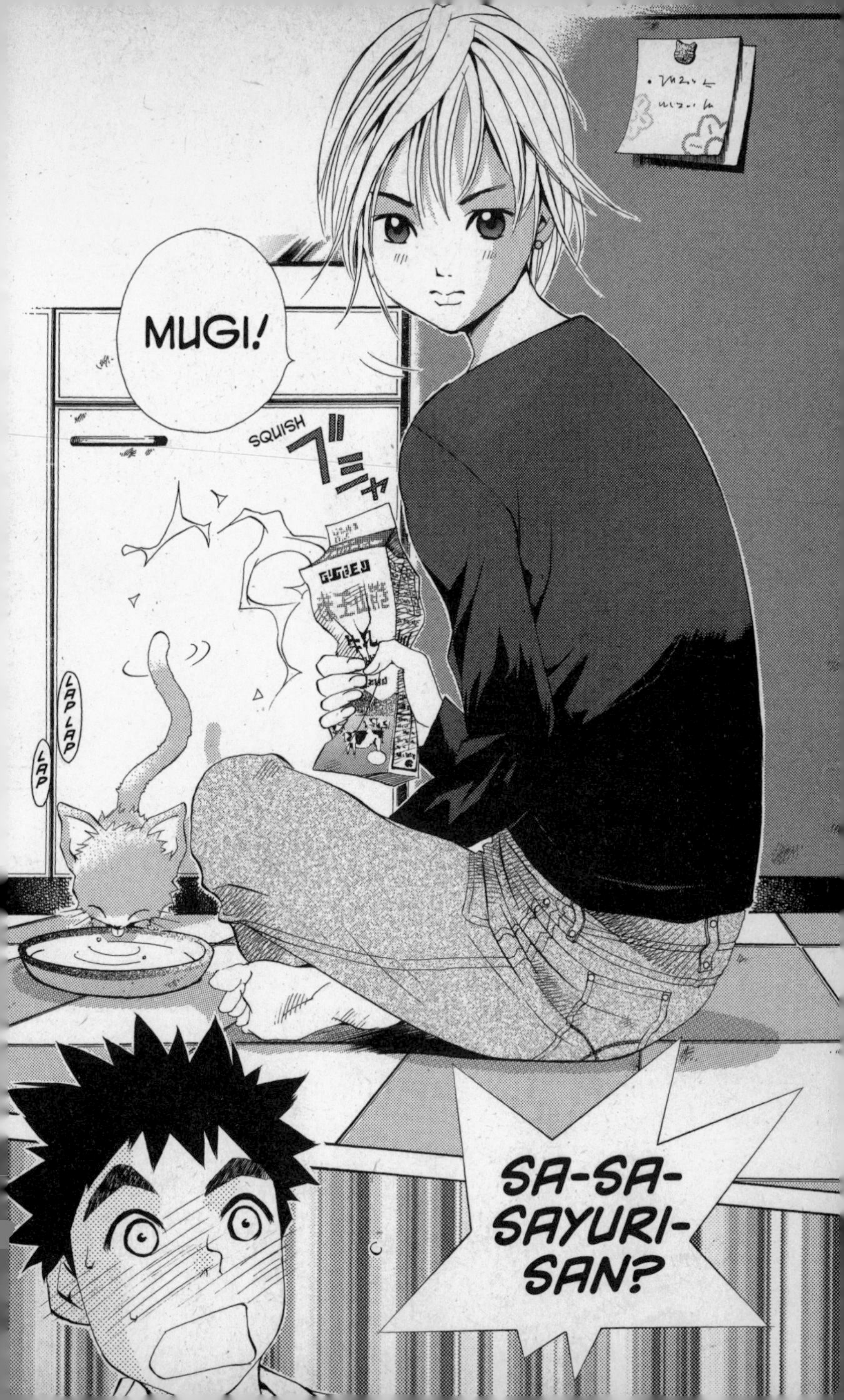
MUGI!
SQUISH
LAP LAP
LAP
SA-SA-SAYURI-SAN?

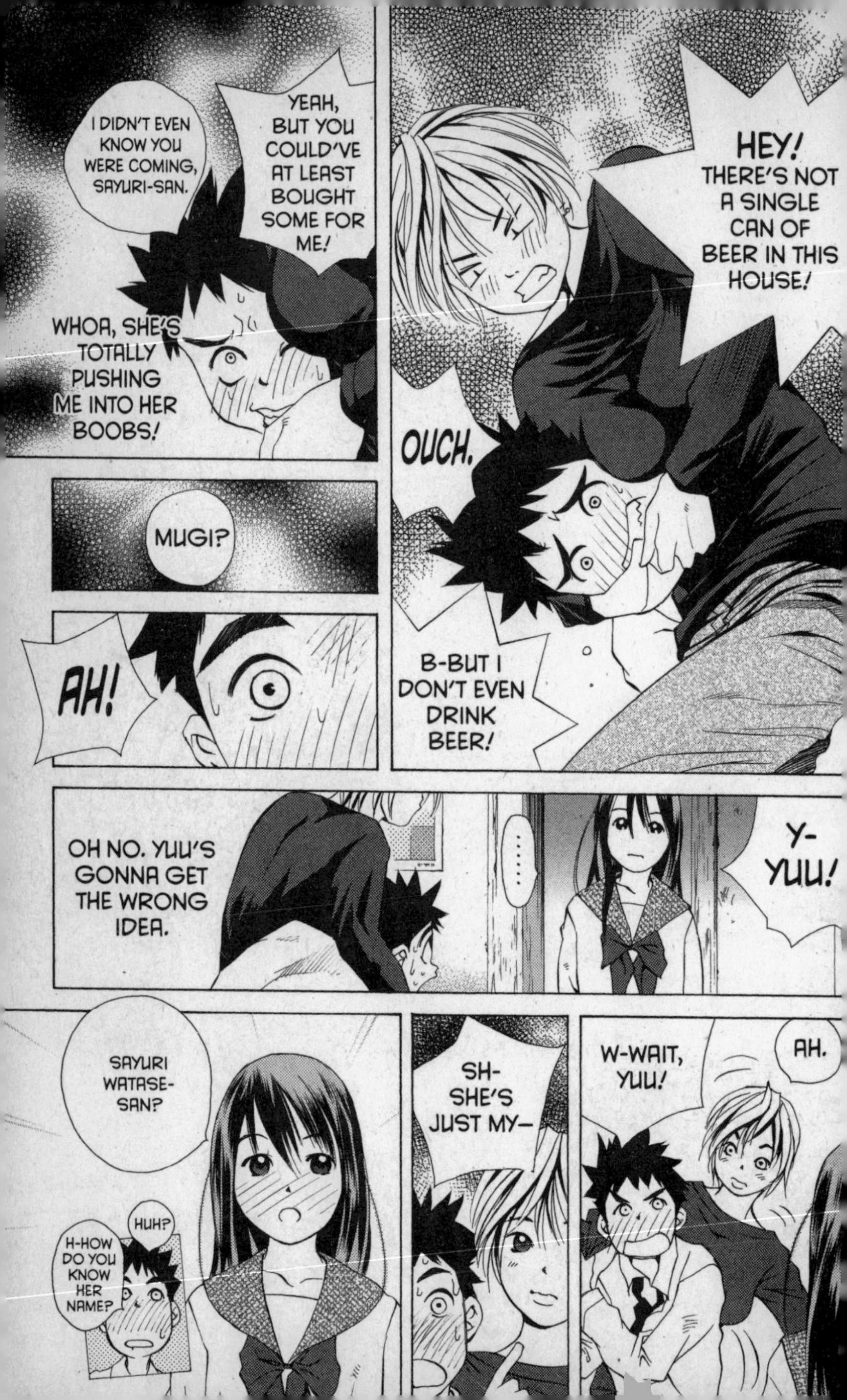
HEY! THERE'S NOT A SINGLE CAN OF BEER IN THIS HOUSE!
OUCH.
B-BUT I DON'T EVEN DRINK BEER!
YEAH, BUT YOU COULD'VE AT LEAST BOUGHT SOME FOR ME!
I DIDN'T EVEN KNOW YOU WERE COMING, SAYURI-SAN.
WHOA, SHE'S TOTALLY PUSHING ME INTO HER BOOBS!
MUGI?
AH!
Y-YUU!
......
OH NO. YUU'S GONNA GET THE WRONG IDEA.
AH.
W-WAIT, YUU!
SH-SHE'S JUST MY—
SAYURI WATASE-SAN?
HUH?
H-HOW DO YOU KNOW HER NAME?

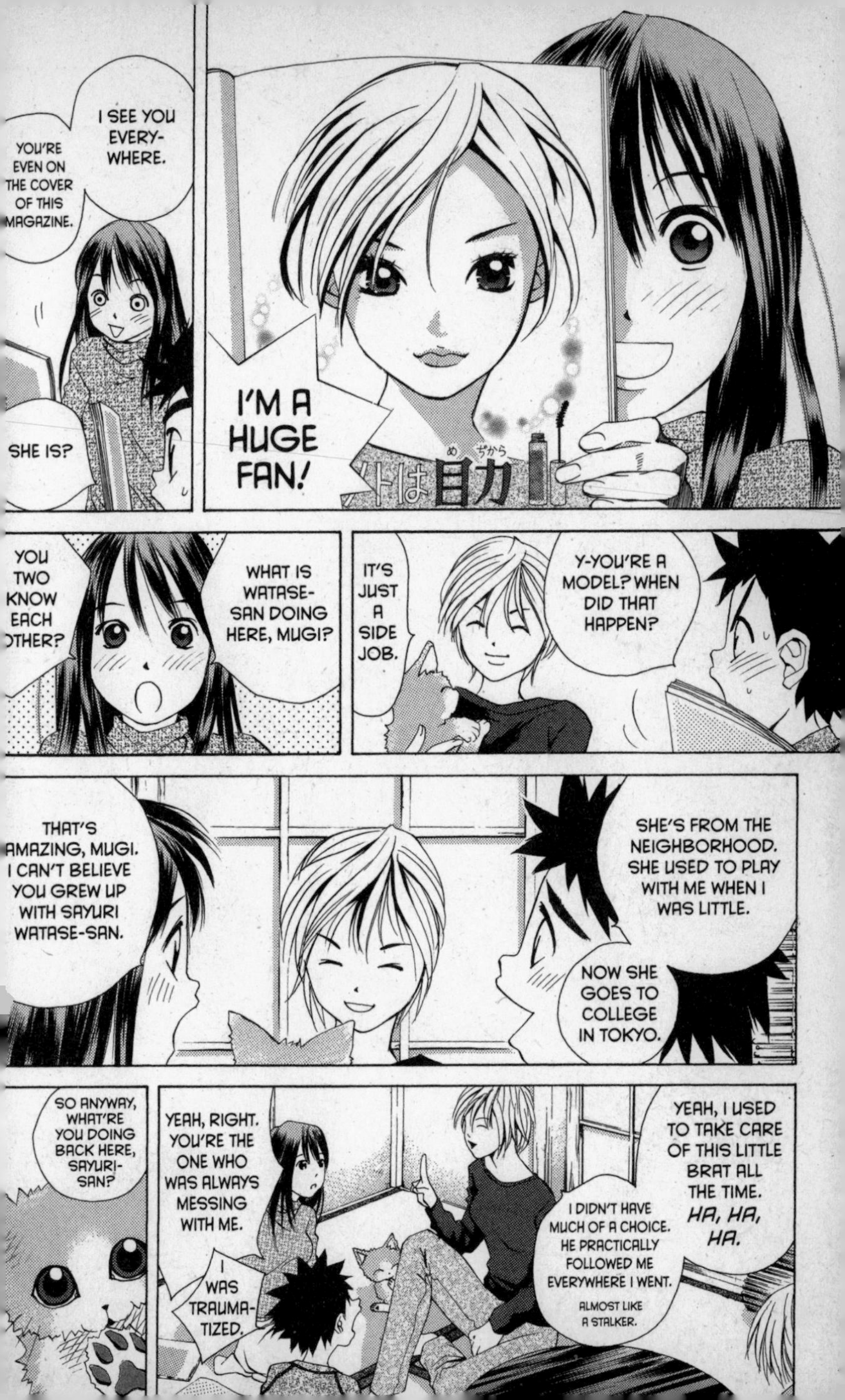
I'M A HUGE FAN!
トは目力
I SEE YOU EVERYWHERE.
YOU'RE EVEN ON THE COVER OF THIS MAGAZINE.
SHE IS?
Y-YOU'RE A MODEL? WHEN DID THAT HAPPEN?
IT'S JUST A SIDE JOB.
WHAT IS WATASE-SAN DOING HERE, MUGI?
YOU TWO KNOW EACH OTHER?
SHE'S FROM THE NEIGHBORHOOD. SHE USED TO PLAY WITH ME WHEN I WAS LITTLE.
NOW SHE GOES TO COLLEGE IN TOKYO.
THAT'S AMAZING, MUGI. I CAN'T BELIEVE YOU GREW UP WITH SAYURI WATASE-SAN.
YEAH, I USED TO TAKE CARE OF THIS LITTLE BRAT ALL THE TIME. HA, HA, HA.
YEAH, RIGHT. YOU'RE THE ONE WHO WAS ALWAYS MESSING WITH ME.
I DIDN'T HAVE MUCH OF A CHOICE. HE PRACTICALLY FOLLOWED ME EVERYWHERE I WENT.
ALMOST LIKE A STALKER.
I WAS TRAUMATIZED.
SO ANYWAY, WHAT'RE YOU DOING BACK HERE, SAYURI-SAN?

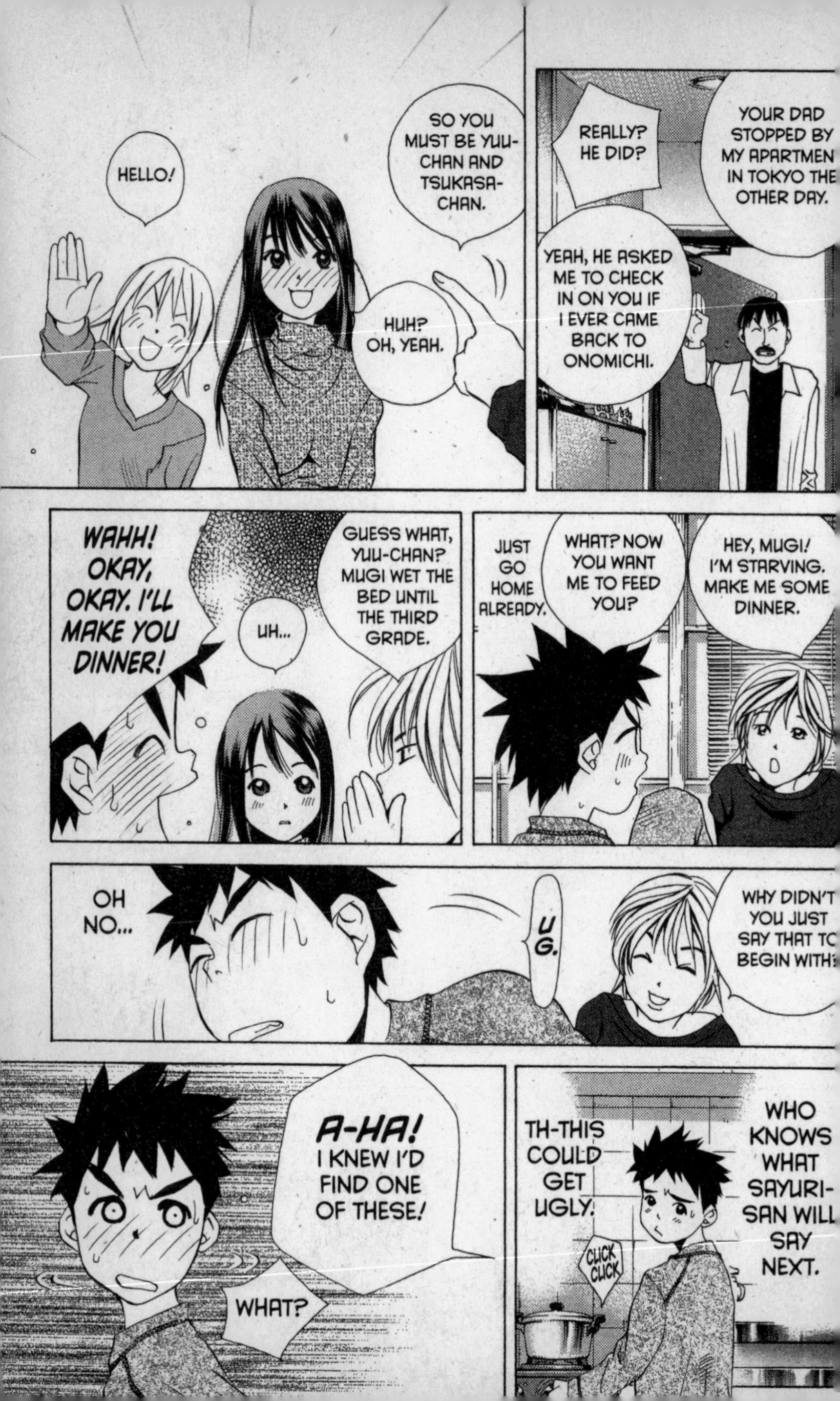
YOUR DAD STOPPED BY MY APARTMEN IN TOKYO THE OTHER DAY.
REALLY? HE DID?
YEAH, HE ASKED ME TO CHECK IN ON YOU IF I EVER CAME BACK TO ONOMICHI.
SO YOU MUST BE YUU-CHAN AND TSUKASA-CHAN.
HUH? OH, YEAH.
HELLO!
HEY, MUGI! I'M STARVING. MAKE ME SOME DINNER.
WHAT? NOW YOU WANT ME TO FEED YOU?
JUST GO HOME ALREADY.
GUESS WHAT, YUU-CHAN? MUGI WET THE BED UNTIL THE THIRD GRADE.
UH...
WAHH! OKAY, OKAY. I'LL MAKE YOU DINNER!
WHY DIDN'T YOU JUST SAY THAT T BEGIN WITH
UG.
OH NO...
WHO KNOWS WHAT SAYURI-SAN WILL SAY NEXT.
TH-THIS COULD GET UGLY.
CLICK CLICK
A-HA! I KNEW I'D FIND ONE OF THESE!
WHAT?

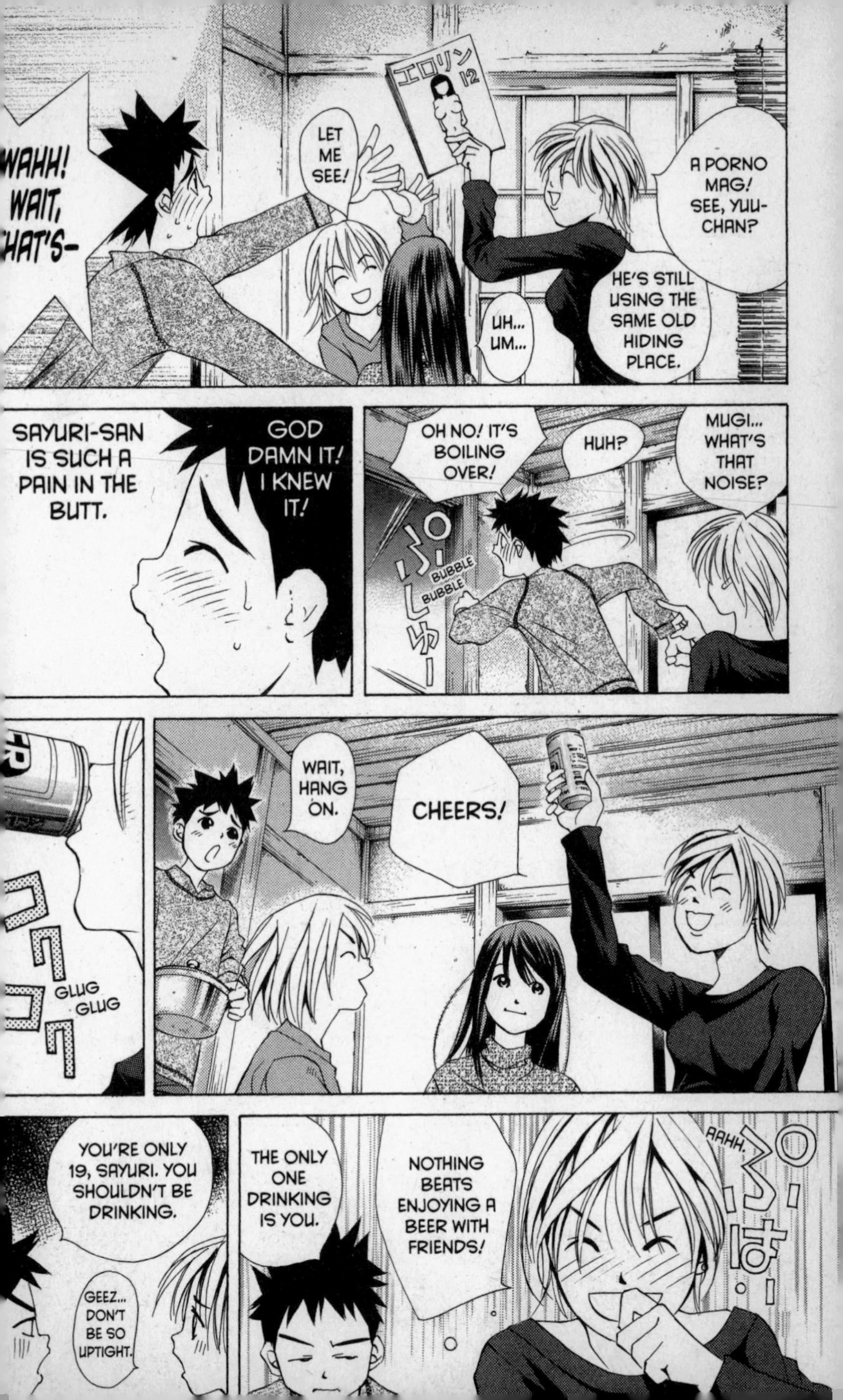
エロリン
12
A PORNO MAG! SEE, YUU-CHAN?
HE'S STILL USING THE SAME OLD HIDING PLACE.
LET ME SEE!
UH... UM...
WAHH! WAIT, HAT'S-
MUGI... WHAT'S THAT NOISE?
HUH?
OH NO! IT'S BOILING OVER!
ぷしゅー
BUBBLE BUBBLE
GOD DAMN IT! I KNEW IT!
SAYURI-SAN IS SUCH A PAIN IN THE BUTT.
CHEERS!
WAIT, HANG ON.
ゴクゴク
GLUG GLUG
ぷはー
AAHH.
NOTHING BEATS ENJOYING A BEER WITH FRIENDS!
THE ONLY ONE DRINKING IS YOU.
YOU'RE ONLY 19, SAYURI. YOU SHOULDN'T BE DRINKING.
GEEZ... DON'T BE SO UPTIGHT.

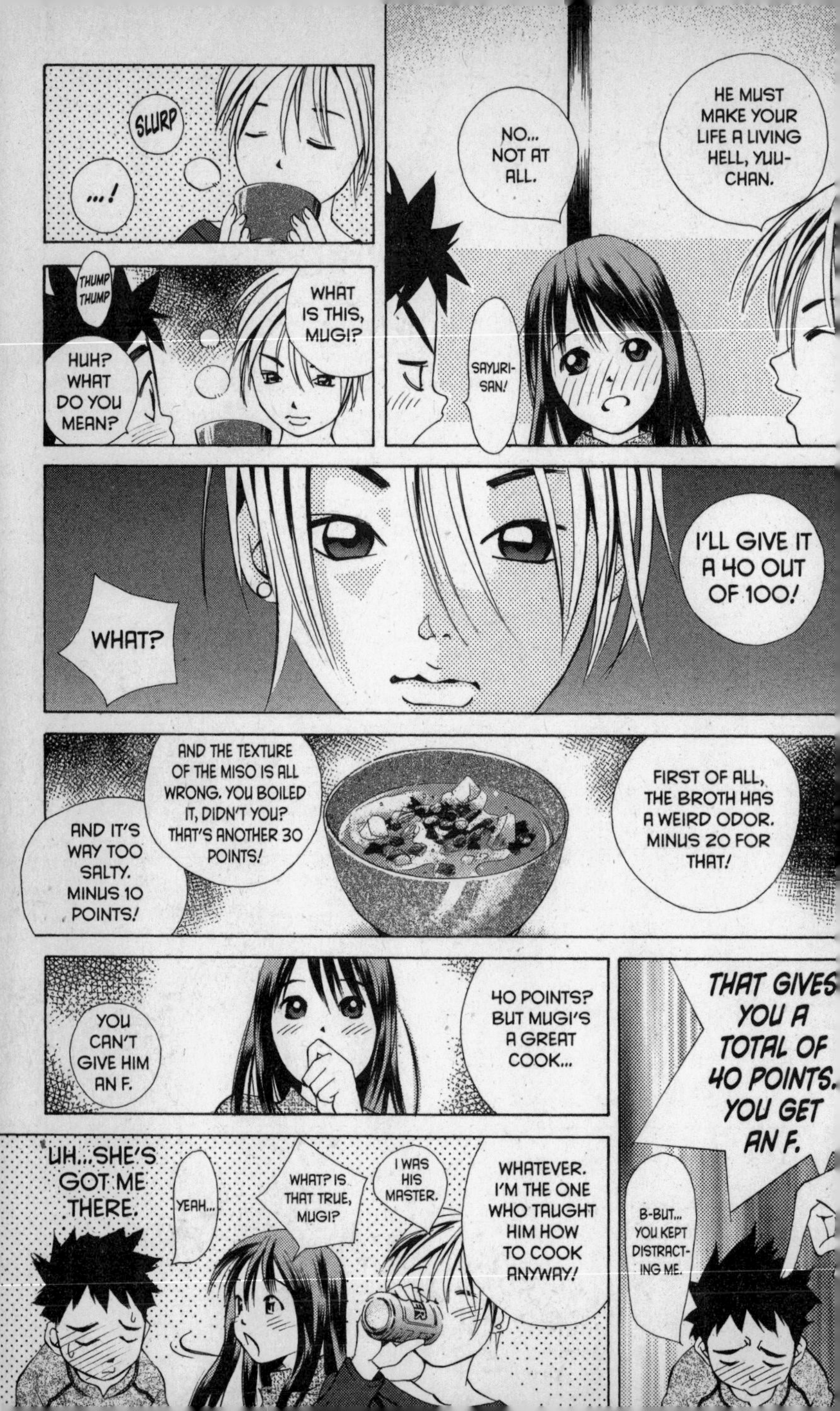
HE MUST MAKE YOUR LIFE A LIVING HELL, YUU-CHAN.
NO... NOT AT ALL.
SAYURI-SAN!
SLURP
...!
WHAT IS THIS, MUGI?
THUMP THUMP
HUH? WHAT DO YOU MEAN?
I'LL GIVE IT A 40 OUT OF 100!
WHAT?
FIRST OF ALL, THE BROTH HAS A WEIRD ODOR. MINUS 20 FOR THAT!
AND THE TEXTURE OF THE MISO IS ALL WRONG. YOU BOILED IT, DIDN'T YOU? THAT'S ANOTHER 30 POINTS!
AND IT'S WAY TOO SALTY. MINUS 10 POINTS!
THAT GIVES YOU A TOTAL OF 40 POINTS. YOU GET AN F.
B-BUT... YOU KEPT DISTRACTING ME.
40 POINTS? BUT MUGI'S A GREAT COOK...
YOU CAN'T GIVE HIM AN F.
WHATEVER. I'M THE ONE WHO TAUGHT HIM HOW TO COOK ANYWAY!
I WAS HIS MASTER.
WHAT? IS THAT TRUE, MUGI?
YEAH...
UH...SHE'S GOT ME THERE.

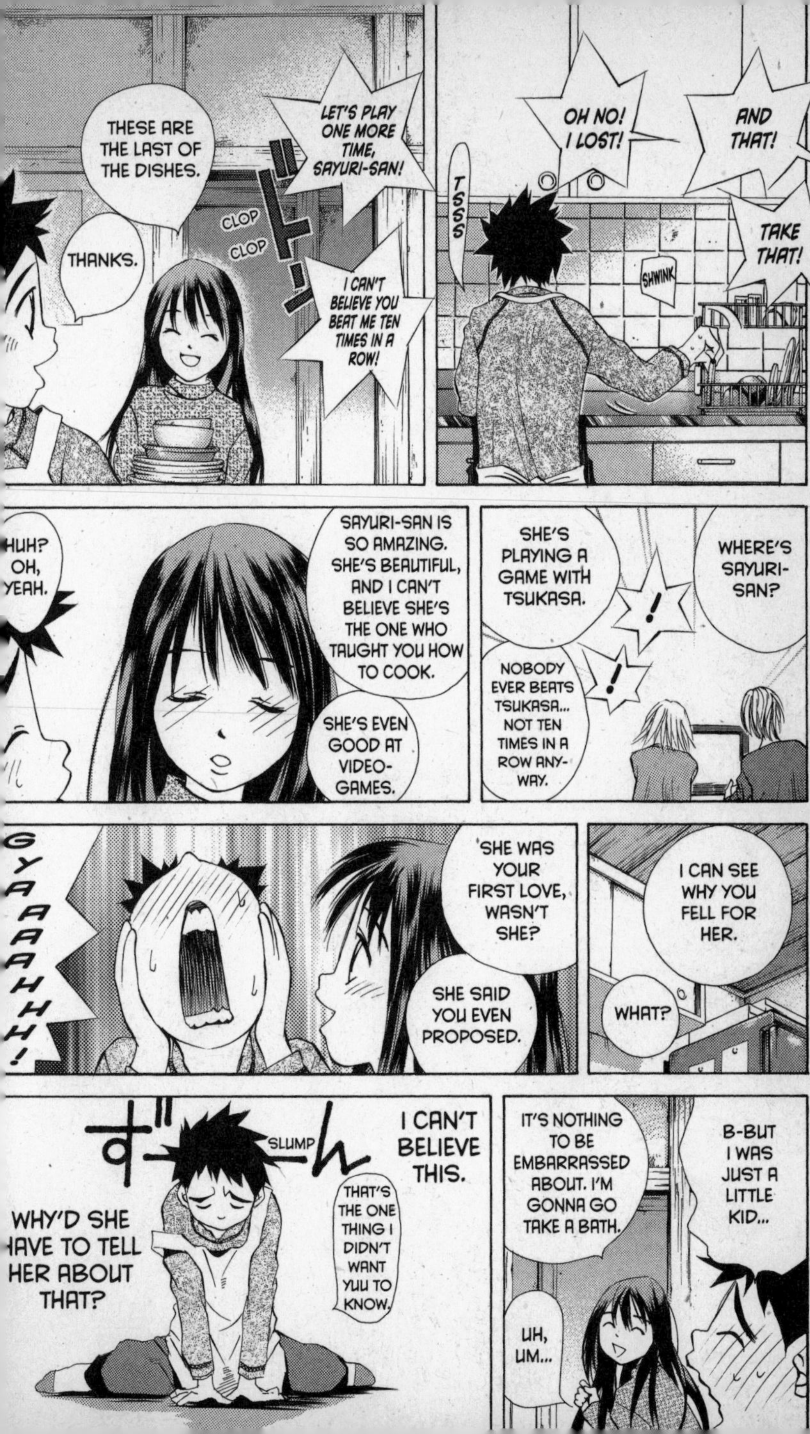
AND THAT!
TAKE THAT!
OH NO! I LOST!
SHWINK
TSSS
LET'S PLAY ONE MORE TIME, SAYURI-SAN!
I CAN'T BELIEVE YOU BEAT ME TEN TIMES IN A ROW!
THESE ARE THE LAST OF THE DISHES.
CLOP CLOP
THANKS.
WHERE'S SAYURI-SAN?
SHE'S PLAYING A GAME WITH TSUKASA.
!
!
NOBODY EVER BEATS TSUKASA... NOT TEN TIMES IN A ROW ANYWAY.
SAYURI-SAN IS SO AMAZING. SHE'S BEAUTIFUL, AND I CAN'T BELIEVE SHE'S THE ONE WHO TAUGHT YOU HOW TO COOK.
SHE'S EVEN GOOD AT VIDEO-GAMES.
HUH? OH, YEAH.
I CAN SEE WHY YOU FELL FOR HER.
WHAT?
SHE WAS YOUR FIRST LOVE, WASN'T SHE?
SHE SAID YOU EVEN PROPOSED.
GYAAAAHHH!
B-BUT I WAS JUST A LITTLE KID...
IT'S NOTHING TO BE EMBARRASSED ABOUT. I'M GONNA GO TAKE A BATH.
UH, UM...
I CAN'T BELIEVE THIS.
ずーん
SLUMP
THAT'S THE ONE THING I DIDN'T WANT YUU TO KNOW.
WHY'D SHE HAVE TO TELL HER ABOUT THAT?

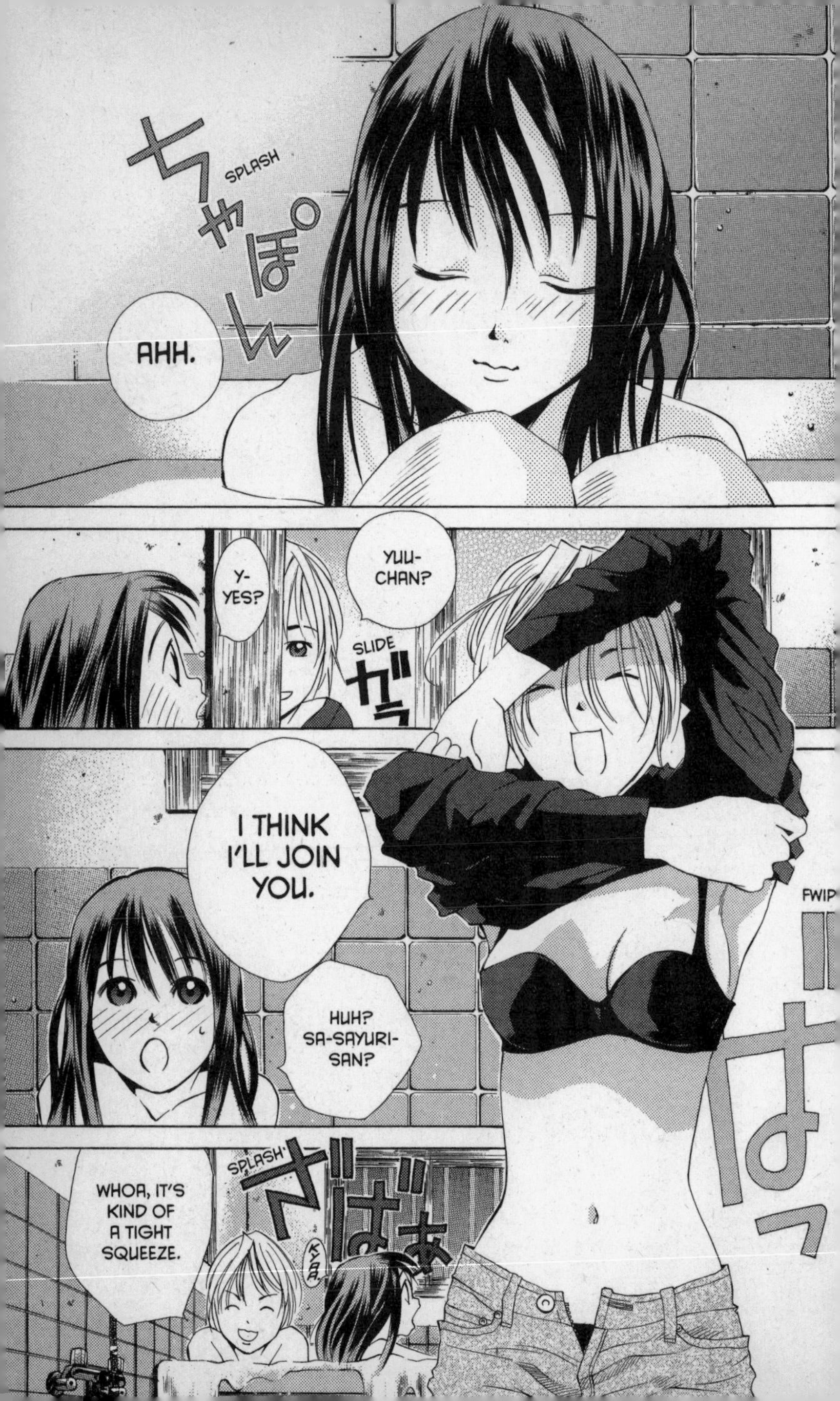

ちゃぽん
SPLASH
AHH.
YUU-CHAN?
Y-YES?
SLIDE
ガラ
I THINK I'LL JOIN YOU.
FWIP
ぱっ
HUH? SA-SAYURI-SAN?
SPLASH
ざばぁ
KYA
WHOA, IT'S KIND OF A TIGHT SQUEEZE.

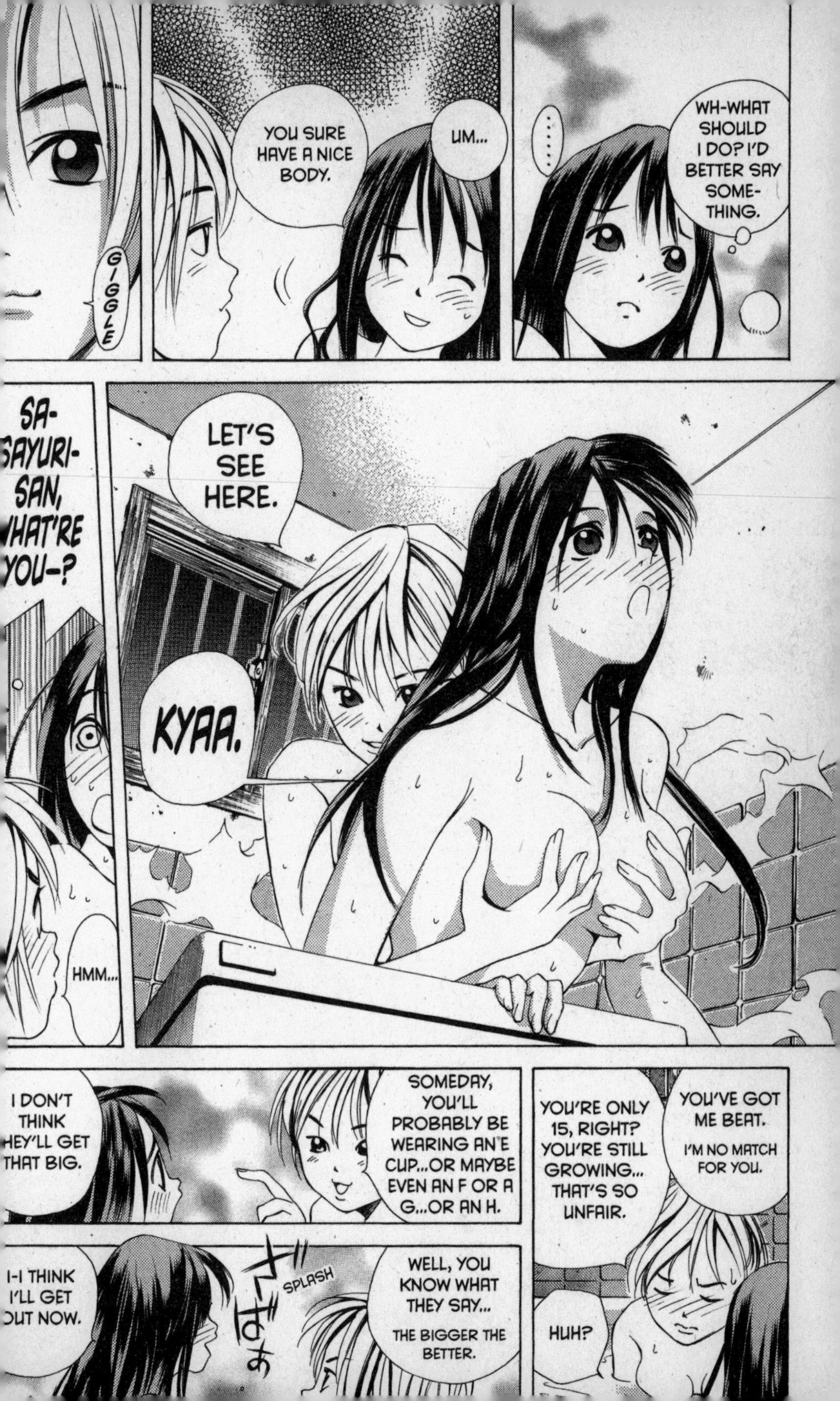
WH-WHAT SHOULD I DO? I'D BETTER SAY SOME-THING.
......
UM...
YOU SURE HAVE A NICE BODY.
GIGGLE
LET'S SEE HERE.
KYAA.
SA- AYURI- SAN, HAT'RE YOU-?
HMM...
YOU'VE GOT ME BEAT.
I'M NO MATCH FOR YOU.
YOU'RE ONLY 15, RIGHT? YOU'RE STILL GROWING... THAT'S SO UNFAIR.
HUH?
SOMEDAY, YOU'LL PROBABLY BE WEARING AN E CUP...OR MAYBE EVEN AN F OR A G...OR AN H.
I DON'T THINK HEY'LL GET THAT BIG.
WELL, YOU KNOW WHAT THEY SAY...
THE BIGGER THE BETTER.
SPLASH
I-I THINK I'LL GET OUT NOW.

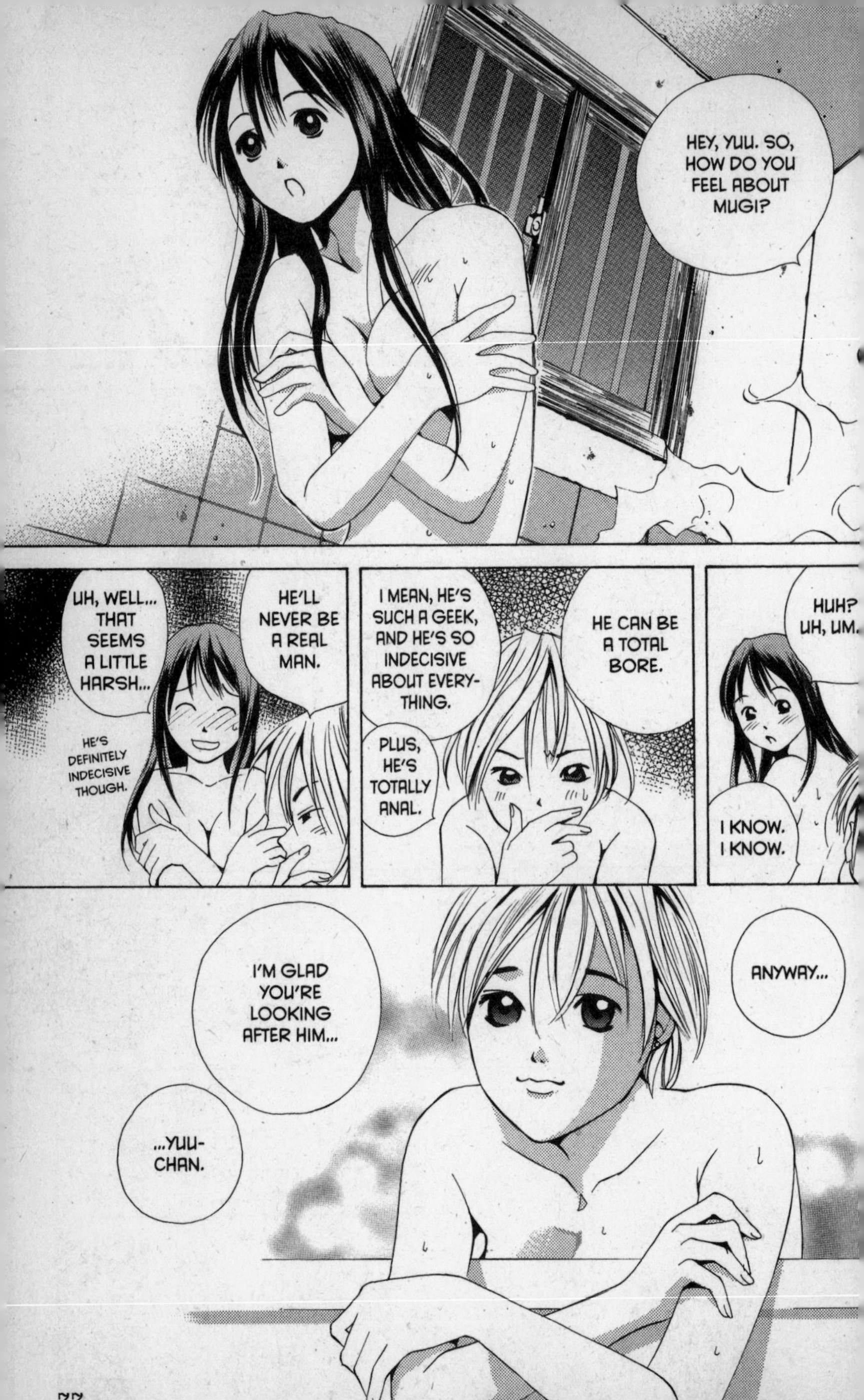
HEY, YUU. SO, HOW DO YOU FEEL ABOUT MUGI?
HUH? UH, UM.
I KNOW. I KNOW.
HE CAN BE A TOTAL BORE.
I MEAN, HE'S SUCH A GEEK, AND HE'S SO INDECISIVE ABOUT EVERY-THING.
PLUS, HE'S TOTALLY ANAL.
HE'LL NEVER BE A REAL MAN.
UH, WELL... THAT SEEMS A LITTLE HARSH...
HE'S DEFINITELY INDECISIVE THOUGH.
ANYWAY...
I'M GLAD YOU'RE LOOKING AFTER HIM...
...YUU-CHAN.

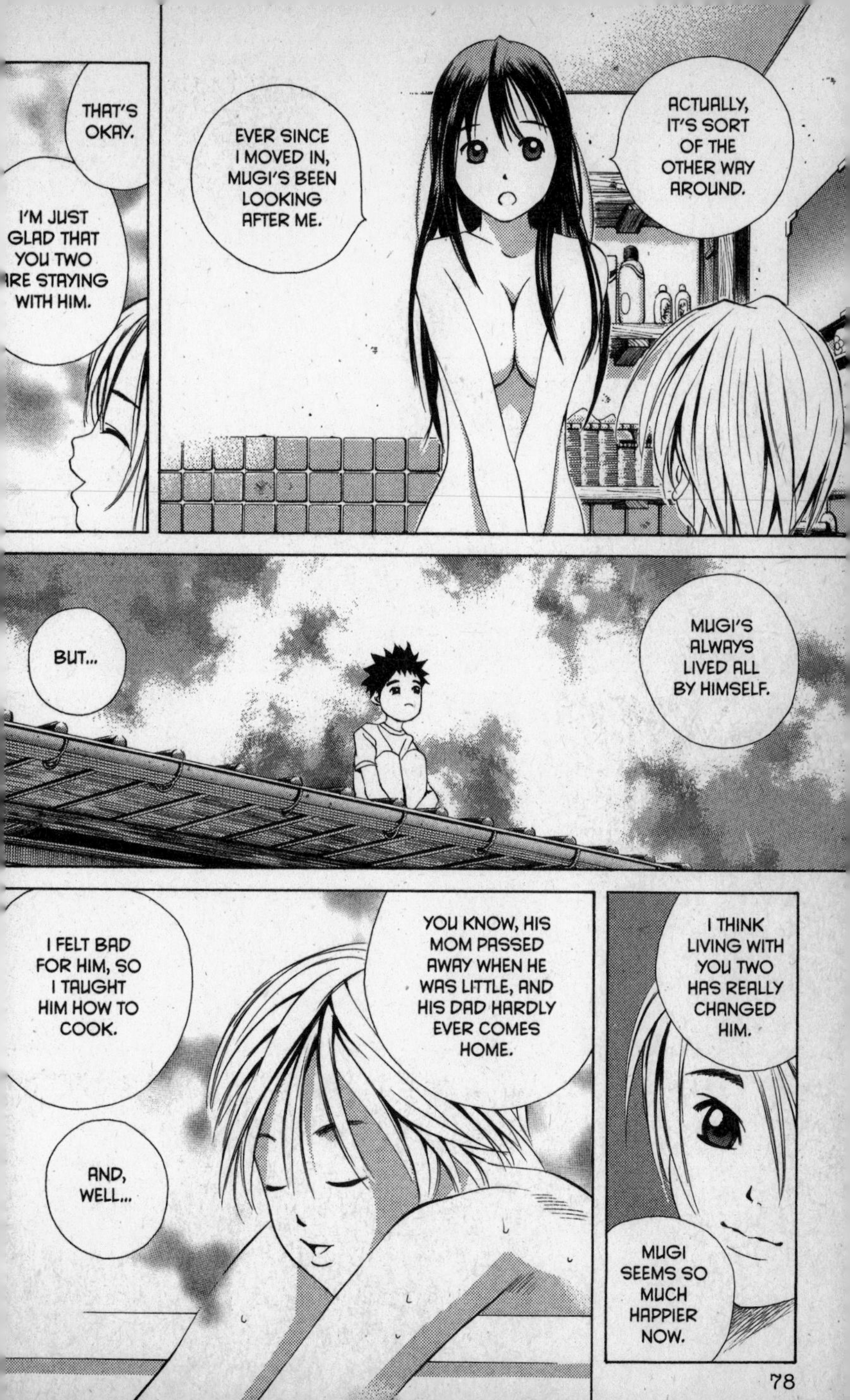
ACTUALLY, IT'S SORT OF THE OTHER WAY AROUND.
EVER SINCE I MOVED IN, MUGI'S BEEN LOOKING AFTER ME.
THAT'S OKAY.
I'M JUST GLAD THAT YOU TWO ARE STAYING WITH HIM.
MUGI'S ALWAYS LIVED ALL BY HIMSELF.
BUT...
I THINK LIVING WITH YOU TWO HAS REALLY CHANGED HIM.
MUGI SEEMS SO MUCH HAPPIER NOW.
YOU KNOW, HIS MOM PASSED AWAY WHEN HE WAS LITTLE, AND HIS DAD HARDLY EVER COMES HOME.
I FELT BAD FOR HIM, SO I TAUGHT HIM HOW TO COOK.
AND, WELL...

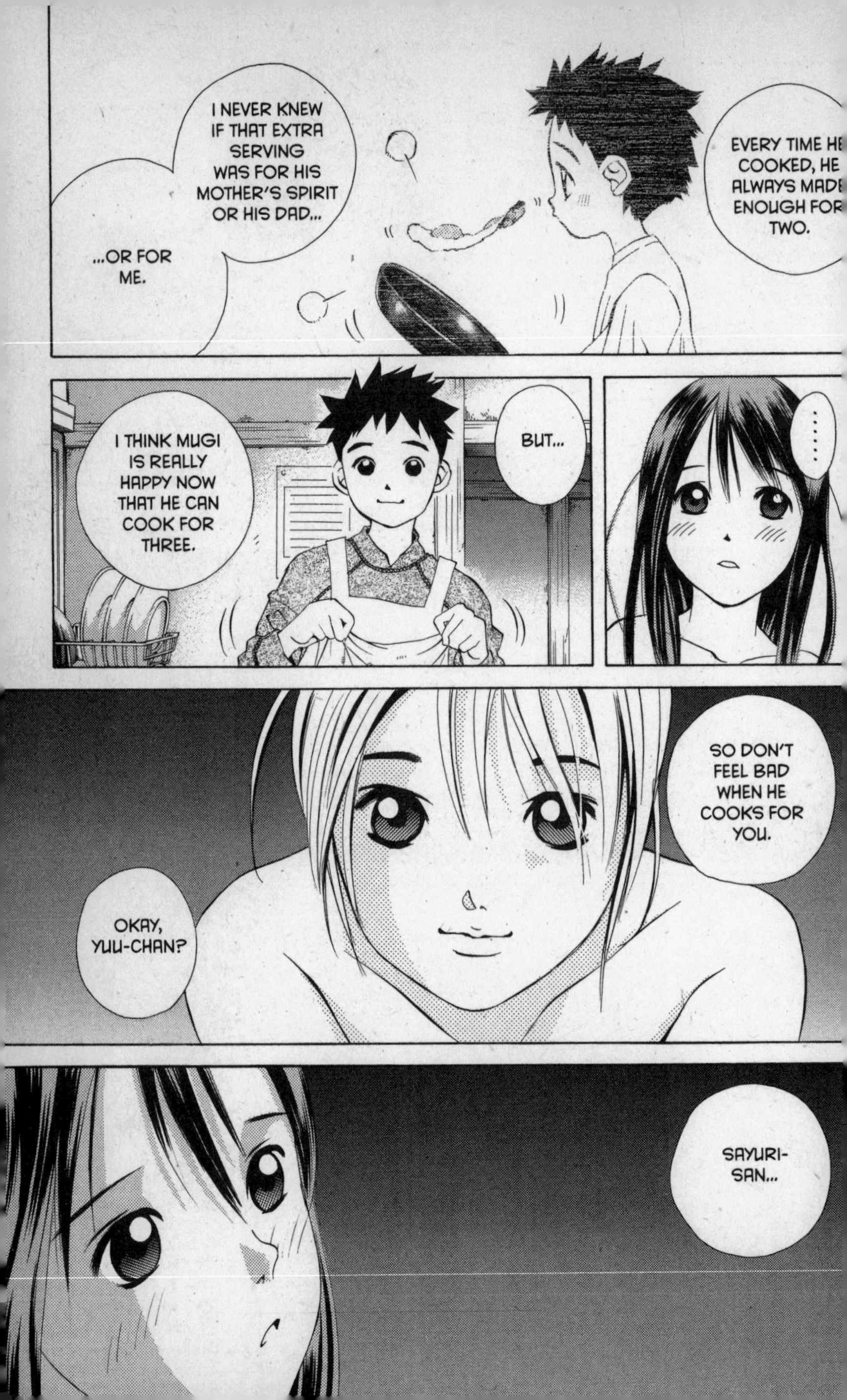
EVERY TIME HE COOKED, HE ALWAYS MADE ENOUGH FOR TWO.
I NEVER KNEW IF THAT EXTRA SERVING WAS FOR HIS MOTHER'S SPIRIT OR HIS DAD...
...OR FOR ME.
......
BUT...
I THINK MUGI IS REALLY HAPPY NOW THAT HE CAN COOK FOR THREE.
SO DON'T FEEL BAD WHEN HE COOKS FOR YOU.
OKAY, YUU-CHAN?
SAYURI-SAN...

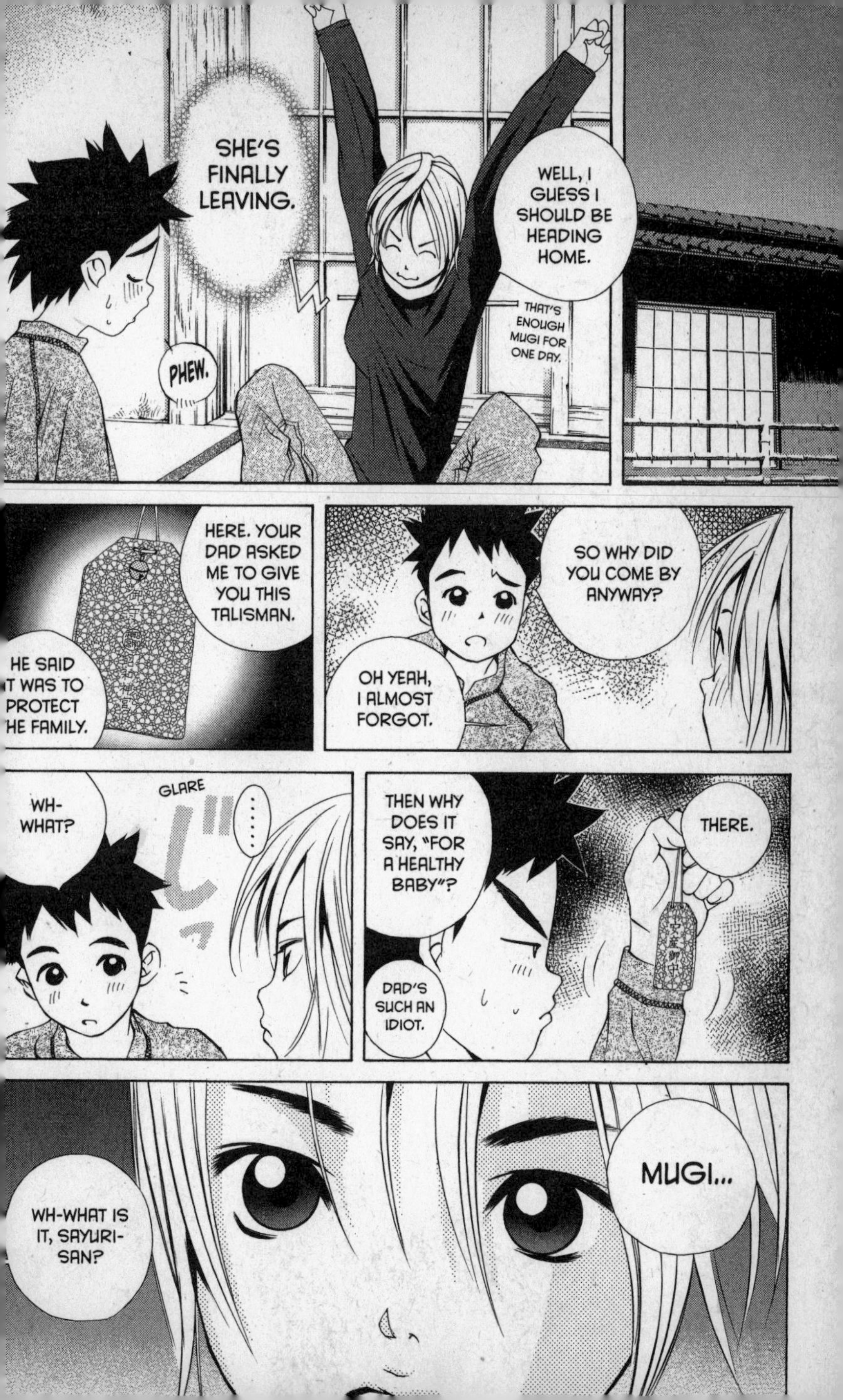

WELL, I GUESS I SHOULD BE HEADING HOME.
THAT'S ENOUGH MUGI FOR ONE DAY.
SHE'S FINALLY LEAVING.
PHEW.
SO WHY DID YOU COME BY ANYWAY?
OH YEAH, I ALMOST FORGOT.
HERE. YOUR DAD ASKED ME TO GIVE YOU THIS TALISMAN.
HE SAID T WAS TO PROTECT HE FAMILY.
THERE.
THEN WHY DOES IT SAY, "FOR A HEALTHY BABY"?
DAD'S SUCH AN IDIOT.
......
GLARE
WH- WHAT?
MUGI...
WH-WHAT IS IT, SAYURI-SAN?

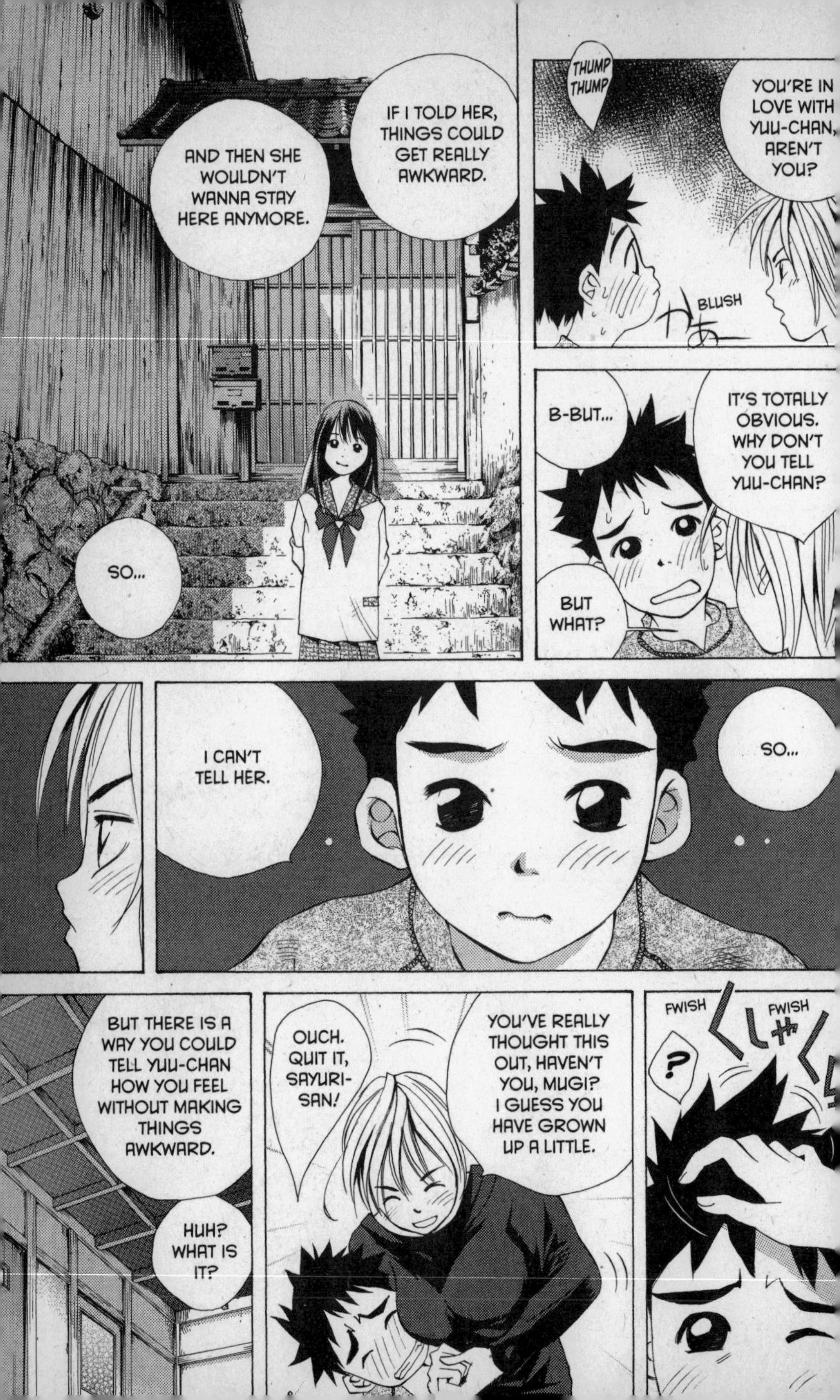
YOU'RE IN LOVE WITH YUU-CHAN, AREN'T YOU?
THUMP THUMP
BLUSH
IT'S TOTALLY OBVIOUS. WHY DON'T YOU TELL YUU-CHAN?
B-BUT...
BUT WHAT?
IF I TOLD HER, THINGS COULD GET REALLY AWKWARD.
AND THEN SHE WOULDN'T WANNA STAY HERE ANYMORE.
SO...
SO...
I CAN'T TELL HER.
FWISH
FWISH
?
YOU'VE REALLY THOUGHT THIS OUT, HAVEN'T YOU, MUGI? I GUESS YOU HAVE GROWN UP A LITTLE.
OUCH. QUIT IT, SAYURI-SAN!
BUT THERE IS A WAY YOU COULD TELL YUU-CHAN HOW YOU FEEL WITHOUT MAKING THINGS AWKWARD.
HUH? WHAT IS IT?

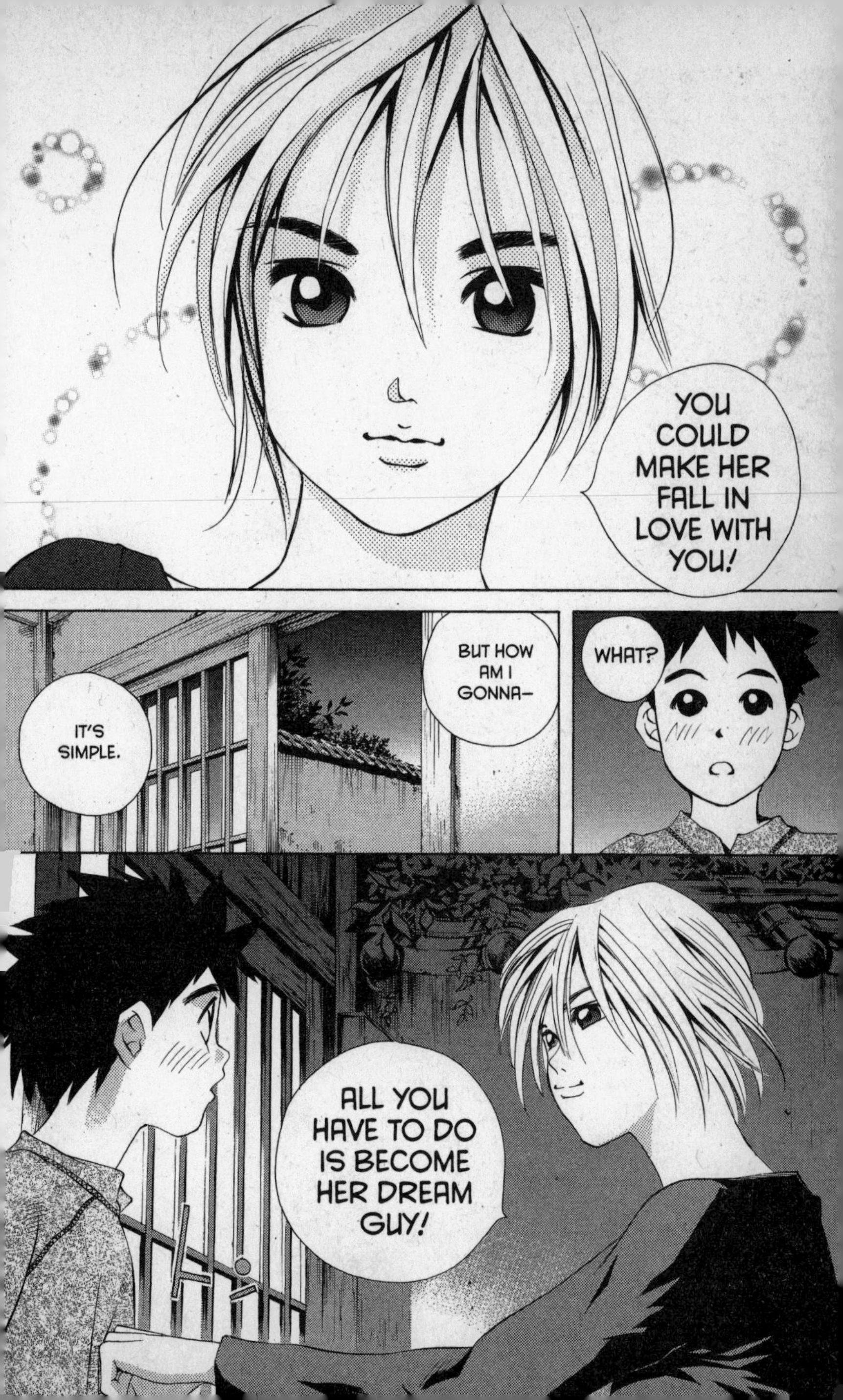
YOU COULD MAKE HER FALL IN LOVE WITH YOU!
WHAT?
BUT HOW AM I GONNA—
IT'S SIMPLE.
ALL YOU HAVE TO DO IS BECOME HER DREAM GUY!

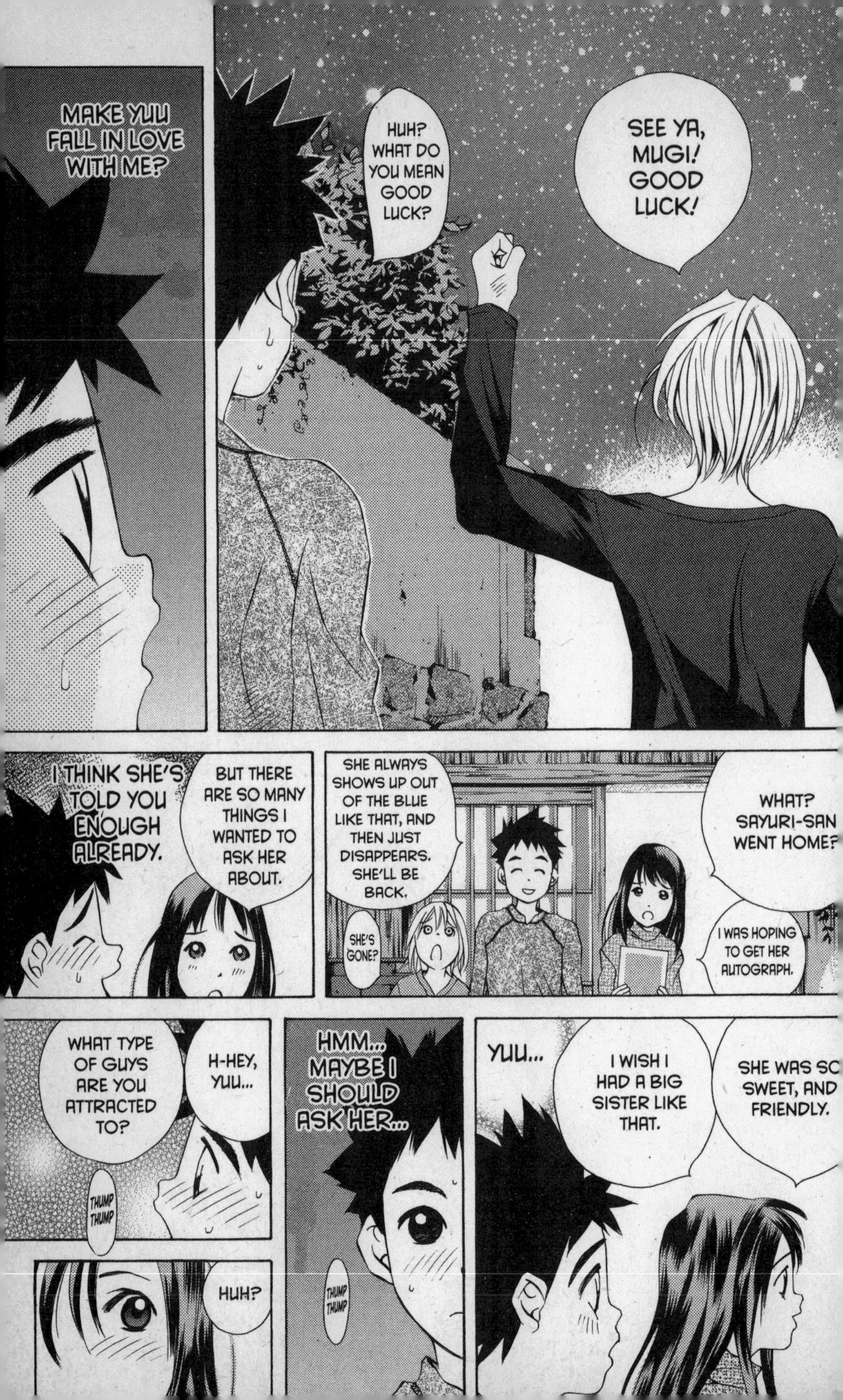
SEE YA, MUGI! GOOD LUCK!
HUH? WHAT DO YOU MEAN GOOD LUCK?
MAKE YUU FALL IN LOVE WITH ME?
WHAT? SAYURI-SAN WENT HOME?
SHE ALWAYS SHOWS UP OUT OF THE BLUE LIKE THAT, AND THEN JUST DISAPPEARS. SHE'LL BE BACK.
I WAS HOPING TO GET HER AUTOGRAPH.
SHE'S GONE?
BUT THERE ARE SO MANY THINGS I WANTED TO ASK HER ABOUT.
I THINK SHE'S TOLD YOU ENOUGH ALREADY.
SHE WAS SO SWEET, AND FRIENDLY.
I WISH I HAD A BIG SISTER LIKE THAT.
YUU...
HMM... MAYBE I SHOULD ASK HER...
THUMP THUMP
H-HEY, YUU...
WHAT TYPE OF GUYS ARE YOU ATTRACTED TO?
THUMP THUMP
HUH?

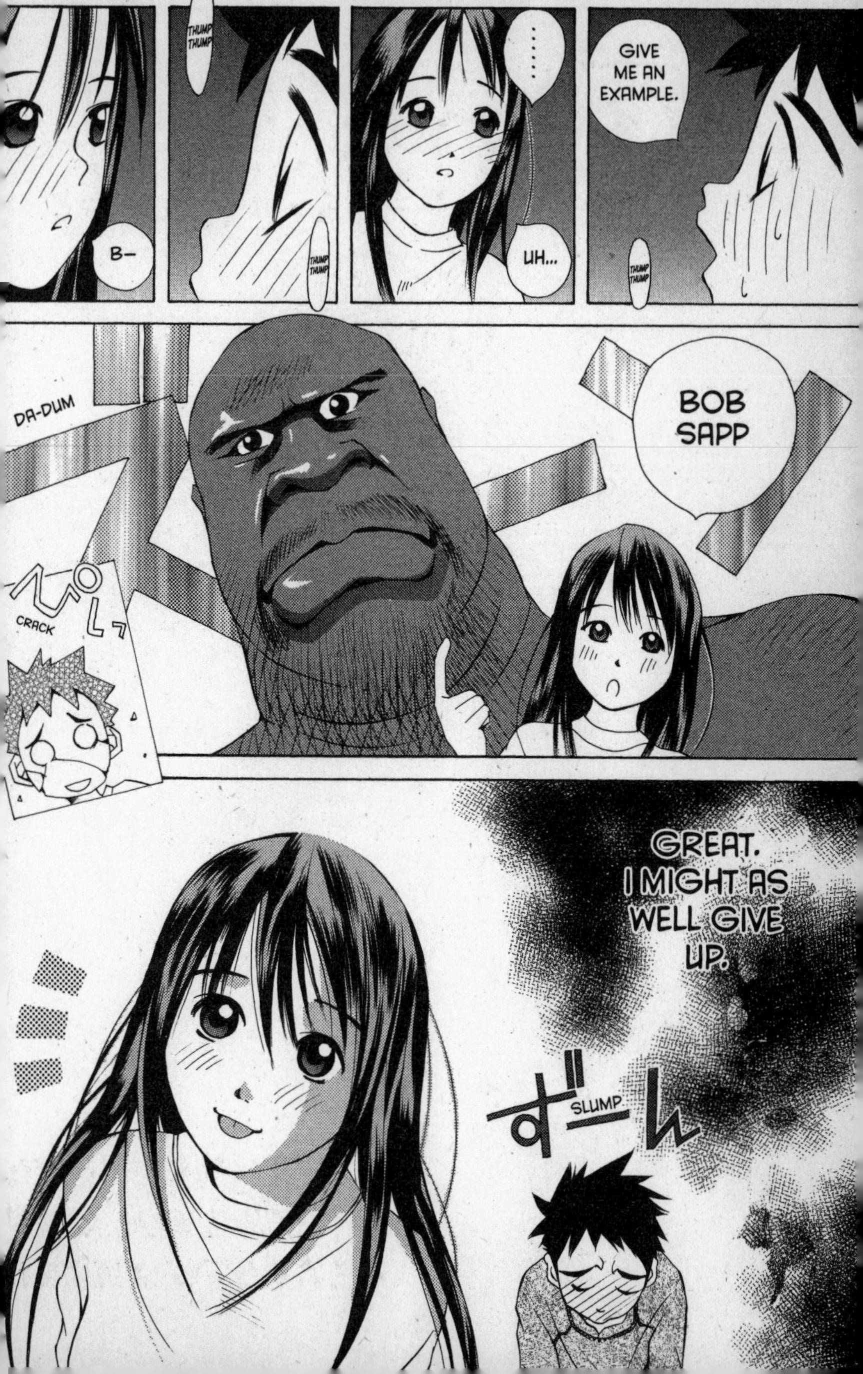
GIVE ME AN EXAMPLE.
THUMP THUMP
......
UH...
THUMP THUMP
THUMP THUMP
B–
BOB SAPP
DA-DUM
CRACK
GREAT. I MIGHT AS WELL GIVE UP.
ずーん
SLUMP

Pastel

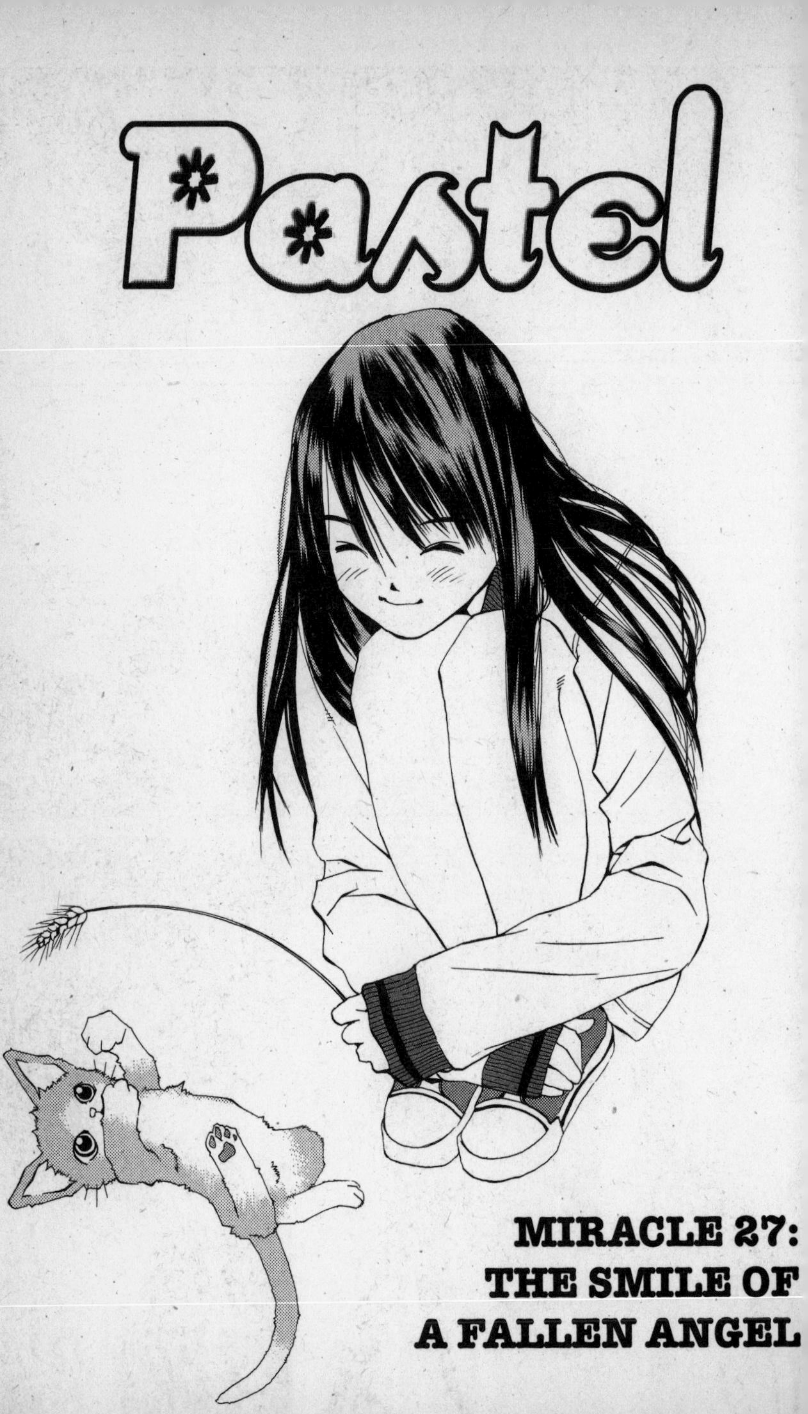

MIRACLE 27: THE SMILE OF A FALLEN ANGEL

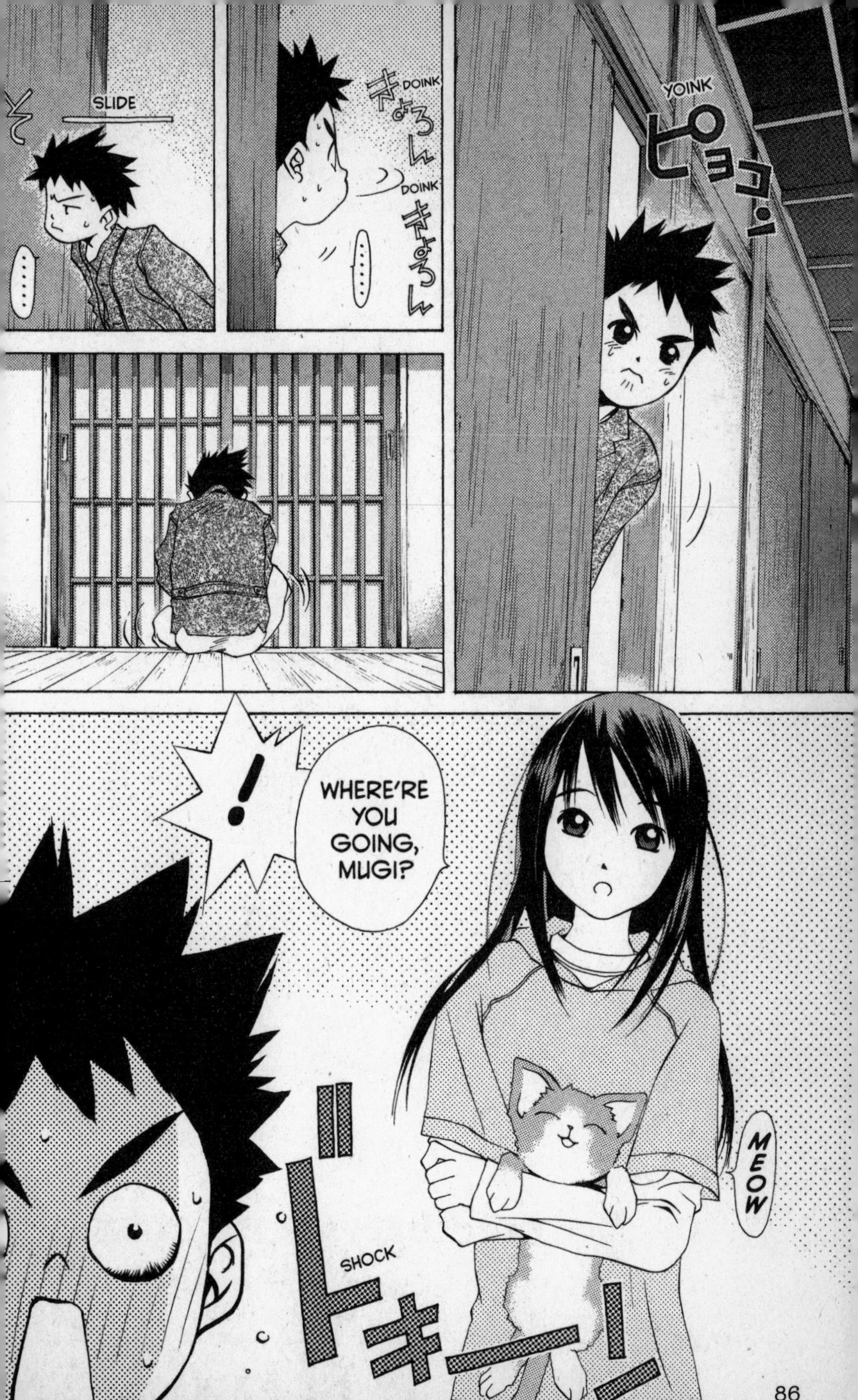

YOINK
ピョコ!
DOINK
きょろん
DOINK
きょろん
……
SLIDE
そ
……
!
WHERE'RE YOU GOING, MUGI?
MEOW
SHOCK
ドキー

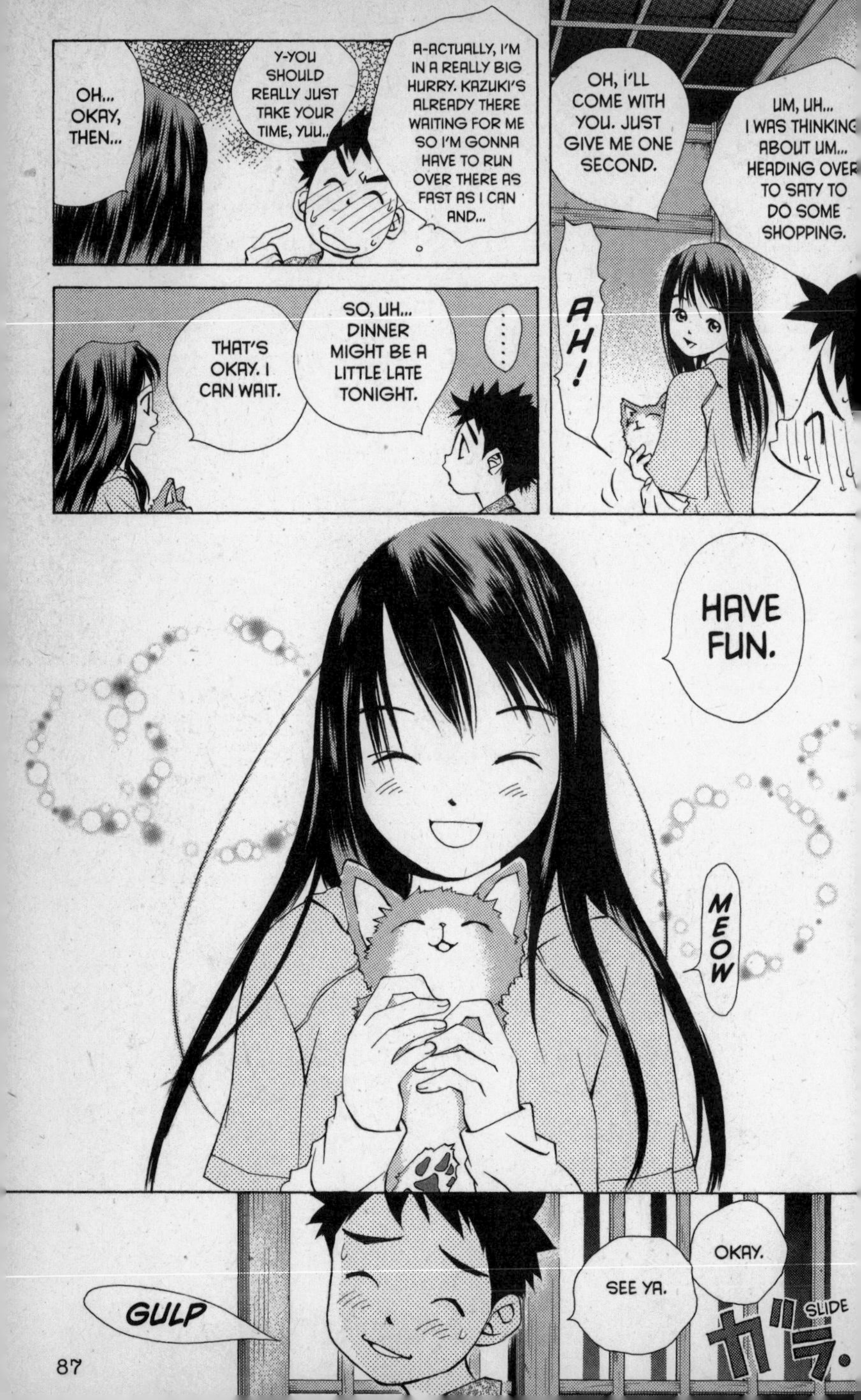
UM, UH... I WAS THINKING ABOUT UM... HEADING OVER TO SATY TO DO SOME SHOPPING.
OH, I'LL COME WITH YOU. JUST GIVE ME ONE SECOND.
AH!
A-ACTUALLY, I'M IN A REALLY BIG HURRY. KAZUKI'S ALREADY THERE WAITING FOR ME SO I'M GONNA HAVE TO RUN OVER THERE AS FAST AS I CAN AND...
Y-YOU SHOULD REALLY JUST TAKE YOUR TIME, YUU...
OH... OKAY, THEN...
......
SO, UH... DINNER MIGHT BE A LITTLE LATE TONIGHT.
THAT'S OKAY. I CAN WAIT.
HAVE FUN.
MEOW
SLIDE
OKAY.
SEE YA.
GULP

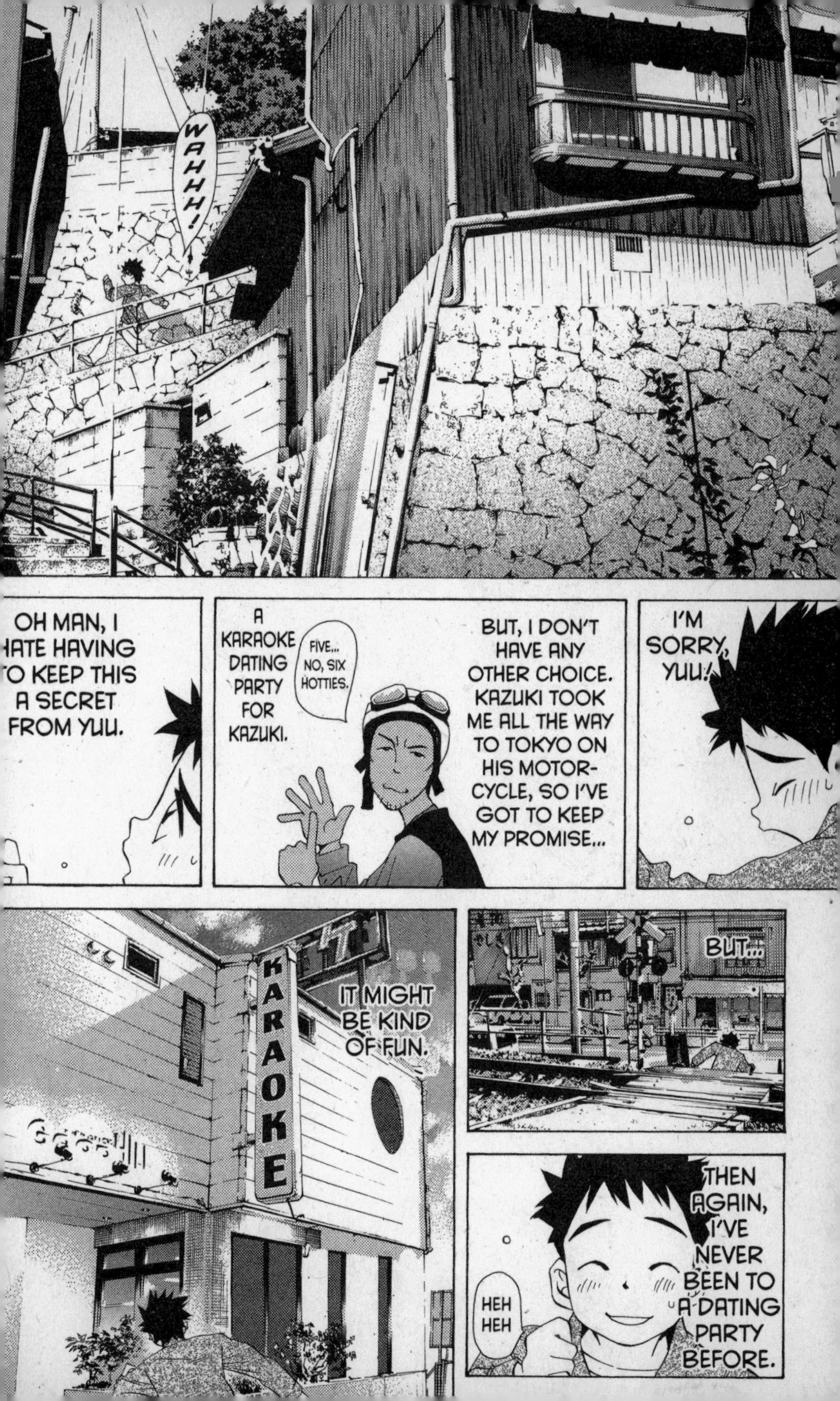
WAHHH!
I'M SORRY, YUU!
A KARAOKE DATING PARTY FOR KAZUKI.
FIVE... NO, SIX HOTTIES.
BUT, I DON'T HAVE ANY OTHER CHOICE. KAZUKI TOOK ME ALL THE WAY TO TOKYO ON HIS MOTOR-CYCLE, SO I'VE GOT TO KEEP MY PROMISE...
OH MAN, I HATE HAVING TO KEEP THIS A SECRET FROM YUU.
BUT...
THEN AGAIN, I'VE NEVER BEEN TO A DATING PARTY BEFORE.
HEH HEH
KARAOKE
IT MIGHT BE KIND OF FUN.

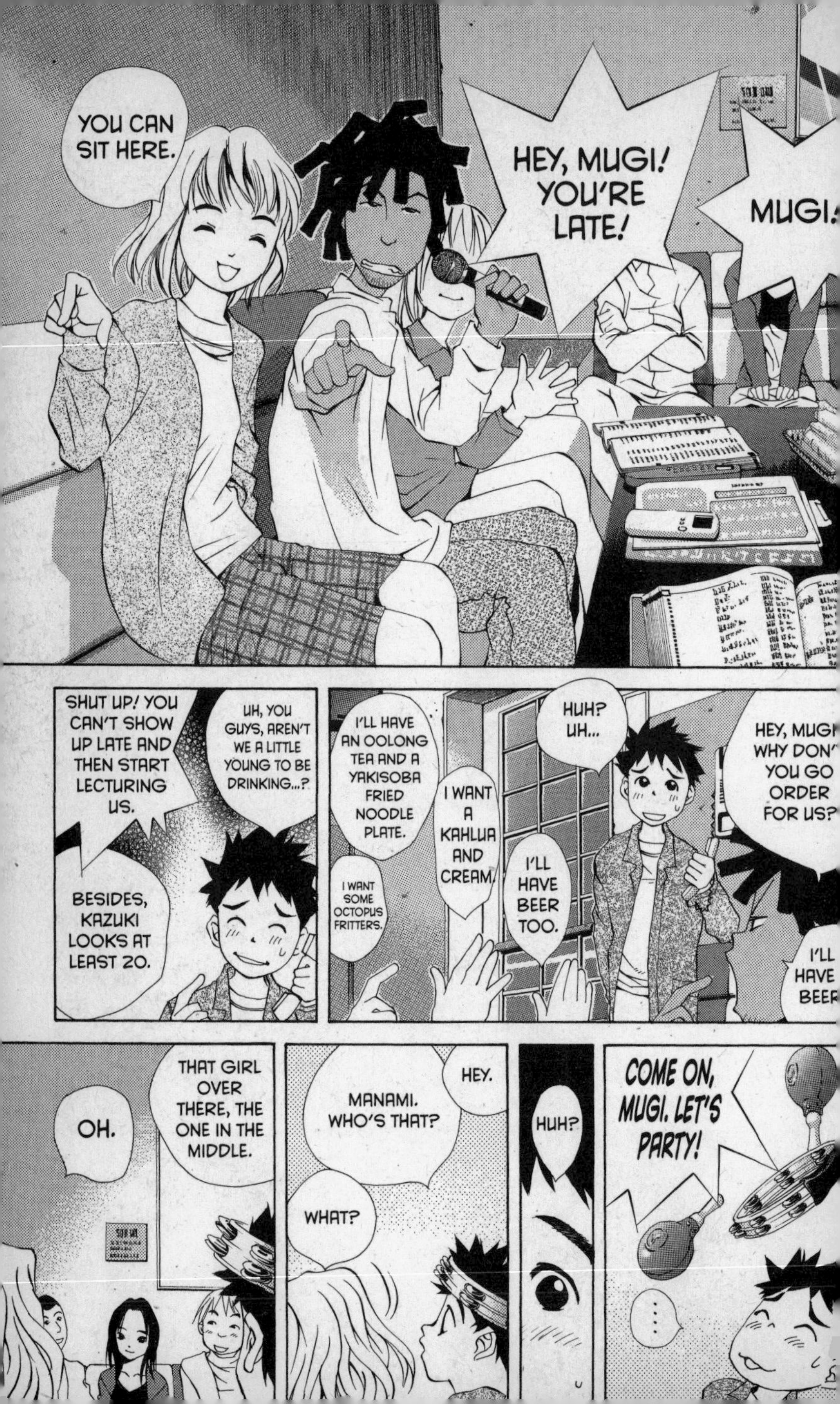
MUGI!
HEY, MUGI! YOU'RE LATE!
YOU CAN SIT HERE.
HEY, MUGI WHY DON' YOU GO ORDER FOR US?
HUH? UH...
I'LL HAVE AN OOLONG TEA AND A YAKISOBA FRIED NOODLE PLATE.
I WANT A KAHLUA AND CREAM.
I'LL HAVE BEER
I'LL HAVE BEER TOO.
I WANT SOME OCTOPUS FRITTERS.
UH, YOU GUYS, AREN'T WE A LITTLE YOUNG TO BE DRINKING...?
SHUT UP! YOU CAN'T SHOW UP LATE AND THEN START LECTURING US.
BESIDES, KAZUKI LOOKS AT LEAST 20.
COME ON, MUGI. LET'S PARTY!
....
HUH?
HEY.
MANAMI. WHO'S THAT?
WHAT?
THAT GIRL OVER THERE, THE ONE IN THE MIDDLE.
OH.

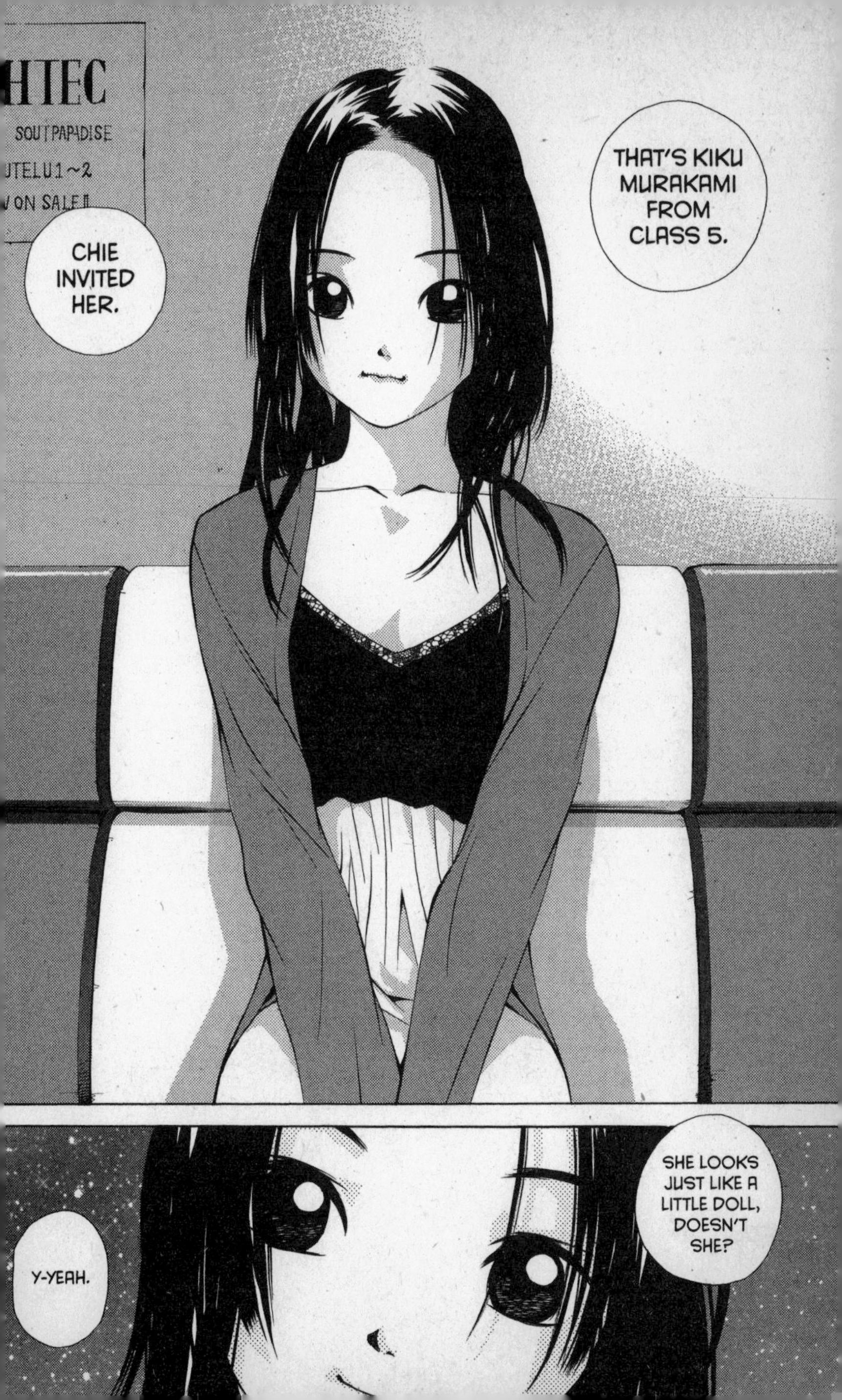
THAT'S KIKU MURAKAMI FROM CLASS 5.
CHIE INVITED HER.
SHE LOOKS JUST LIKE A LITTLE DOLL, DOESN'T SHE?
Y-YEAH.

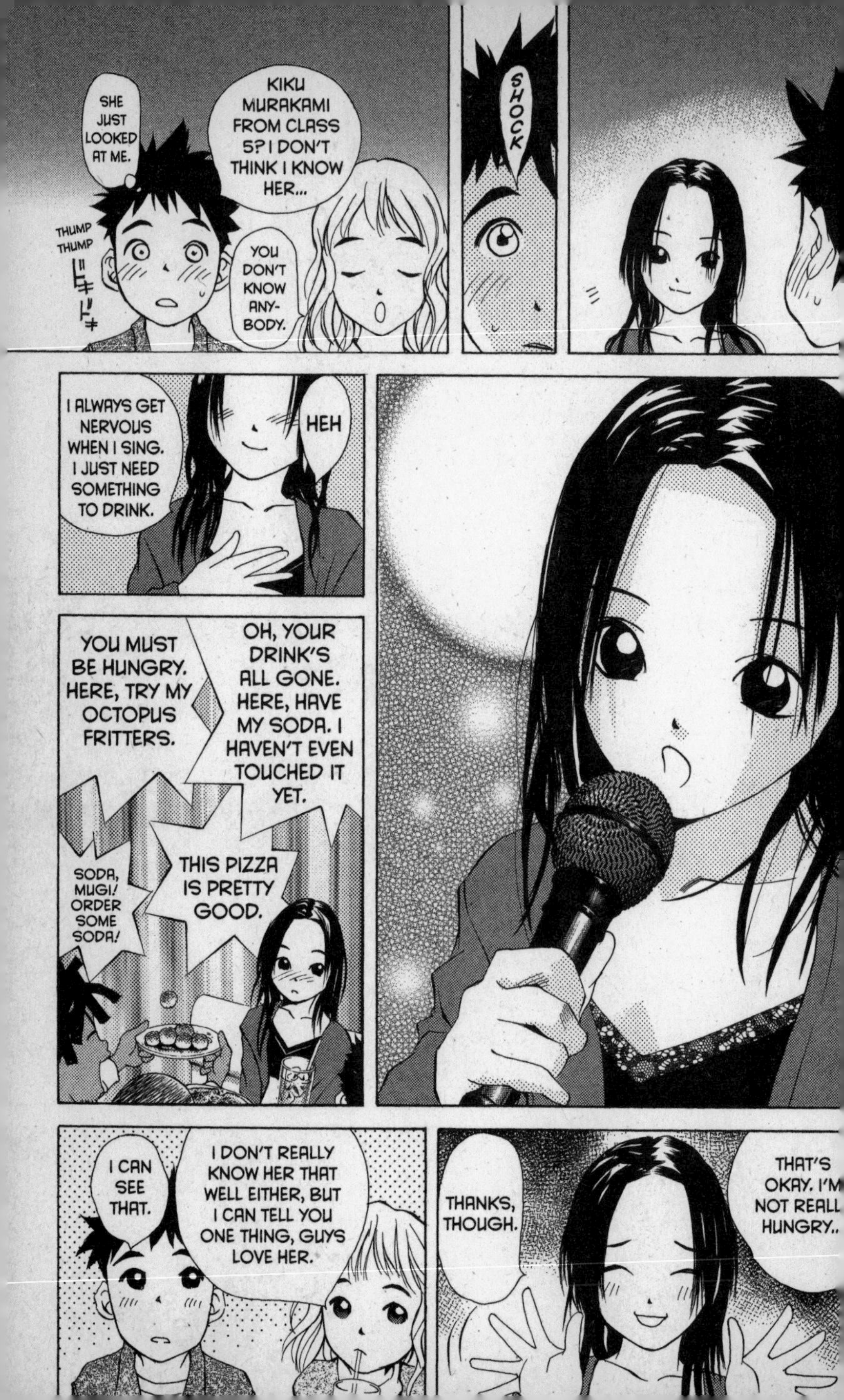
SHOCK
KIKU MURAKAMI FROM CLASS 5? I DON'T THINK I KNOW HER...
SHE JUST LOOKED AT ME.
YOU DON'T KNOW ANY-BODY.
THUMP THUMP
HEH
I ALWAYS GET NERVOUS WHEN I SING. I JUST NEED SOMETHING TO DRINK.
OH, YOUR DRINK'S ALL GONE. HERE, HAVE MY SODA. I HAVEN'T EVEN TOUCHED IT YET.
YOU MUST BE HUNGRY. HERE, TRY MY OCTOPUS FRITTERS.
THIS PIZZA IS PRETTY GOOD.
SODA, MUGI! ORDER SOME SODA!
THAT'S OKAY. I'M NOT REALL HUNGRY..
THANKS, THOUGH.
I DON'T REALLY KNOW HER THAT WELL EITHER, BUT I CAN TELL YOU ONE THING, GUYS LOVE HER.
I CAN SEE THAT.

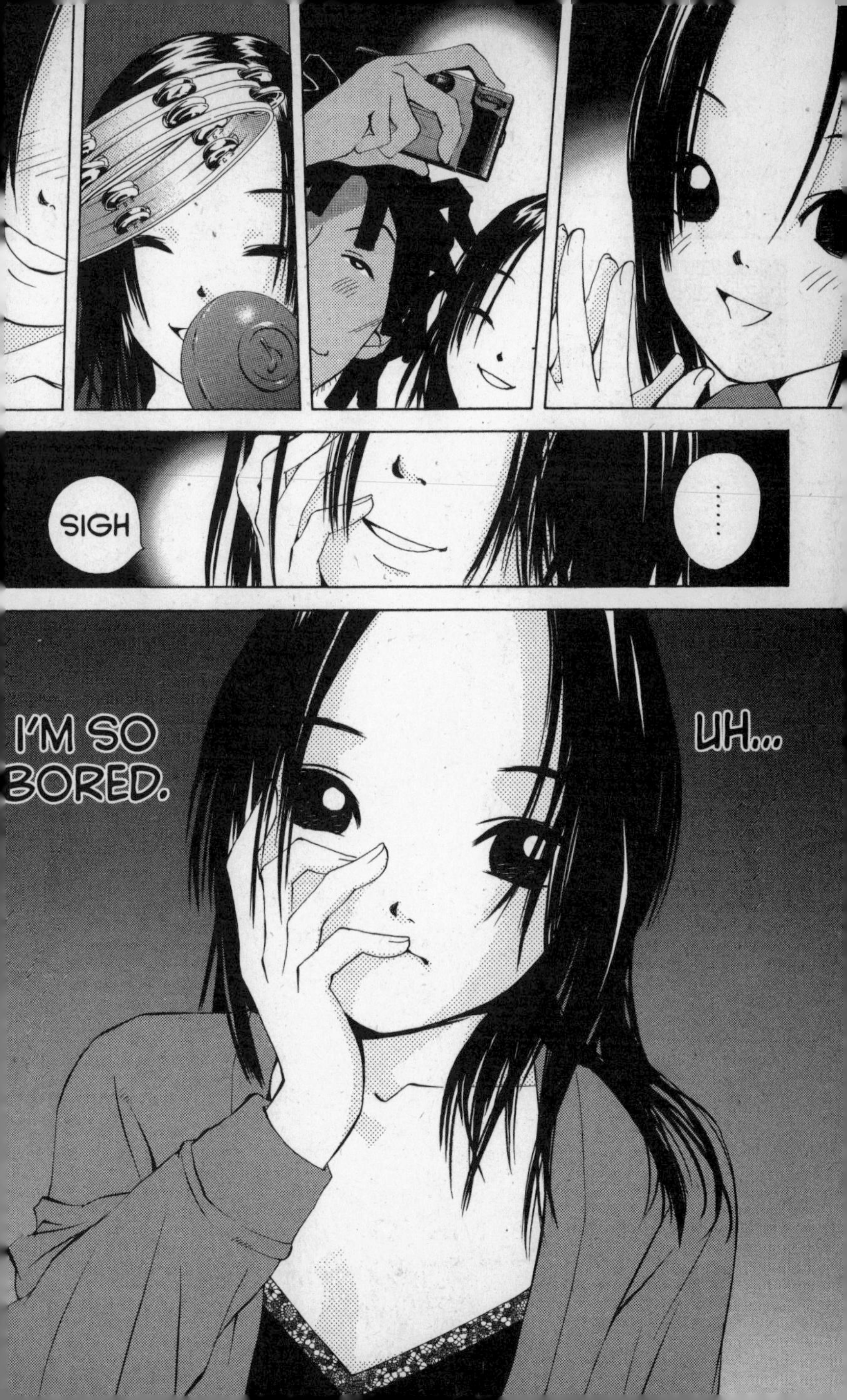
......
SIGH
UH...
I'M SO BORED.

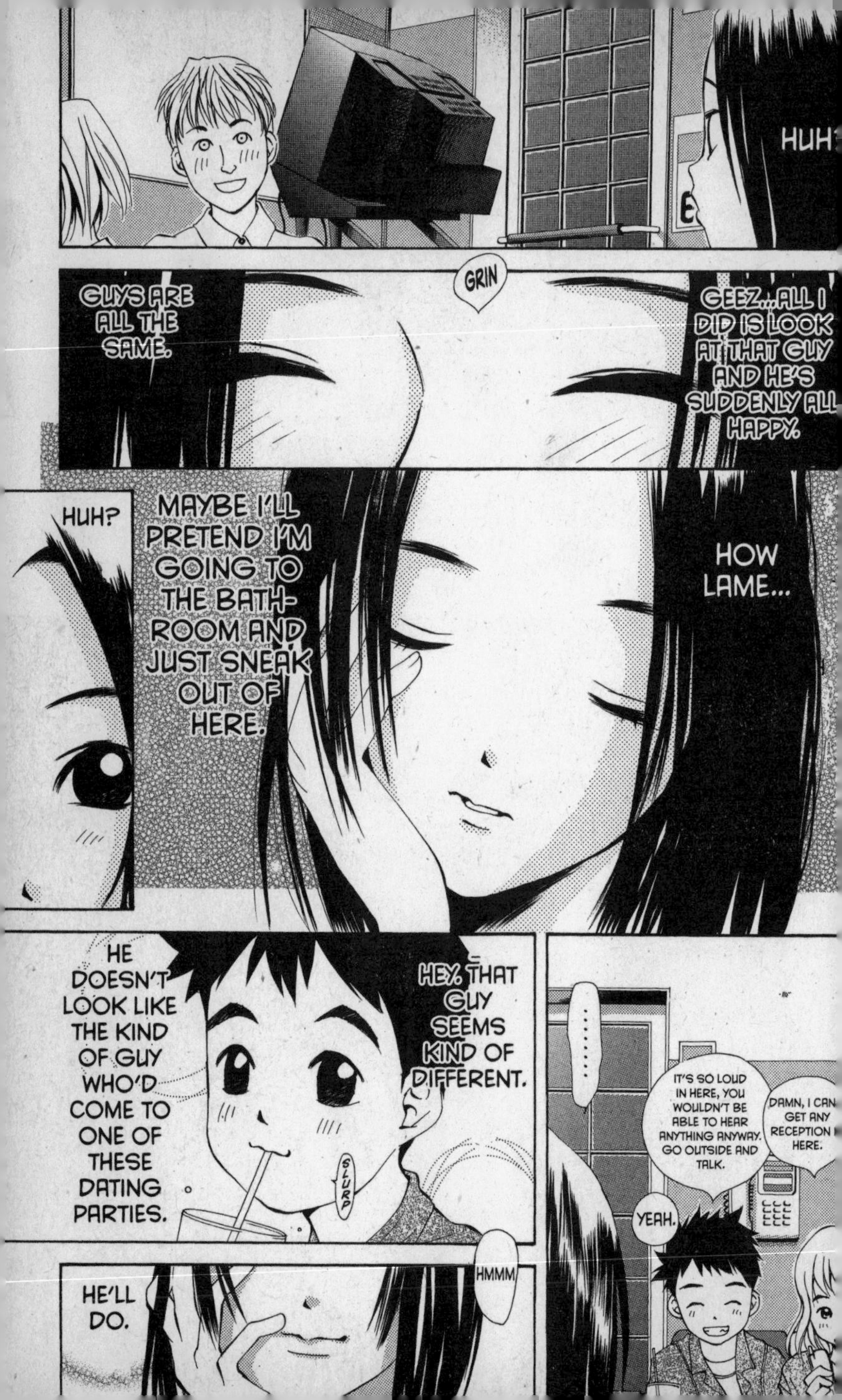
HUH
GEEZ...ALL I DID IS LOOK AT THAT GUY AND HE'S SUDDENLY ALL HAPPY.
GRIN
GUYS ARE ALL THE SAME.
HOW LAME...
MAYBE I'LL PRETEND I'M GOING TO THE BATH-ROOM AND JUST SNEAK OUT OF HERE.
HUH?
......
DAMN, I CAN GET ANY RECEPTION HERE.
IT'S SO LOUD IN HERE, YOU WOULDN'T BE ABLE TO HEAR ANYTHING ANYWAY. GO OUTSIDE AND TALK.
YEAH.
HEY. THAT GUY SEEMS KIND OF DIFFERENT.
HE DOESN'T LOOK LIKE THE KIND OF GUY WHO'D COME TO ONE OF THESE DATING PARTIES.
SLURP
HMMM
HE'LL DO.

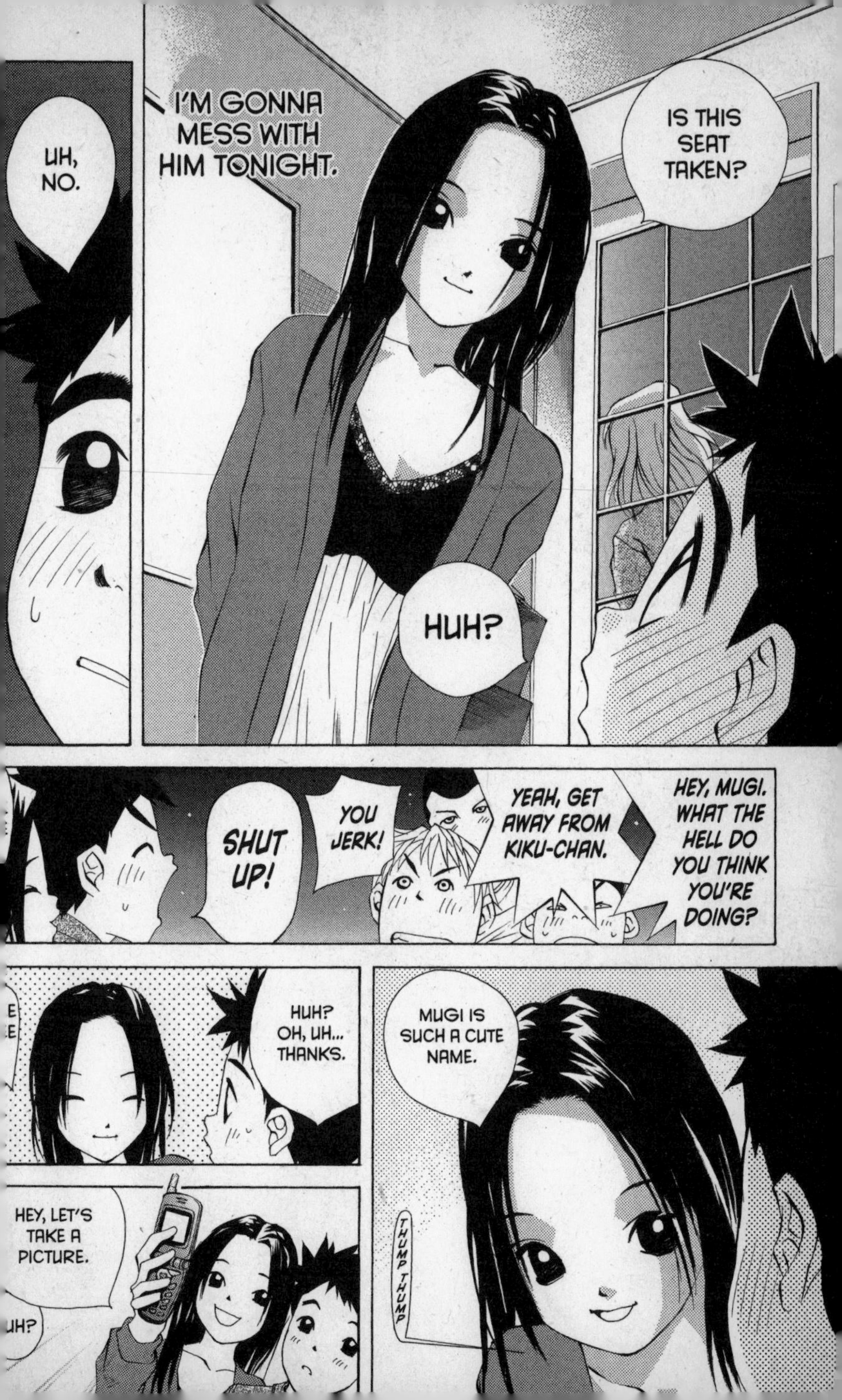
IS THIS SEAT TAKEN?
I'M GONNA MESS WITH HIM TONIGHT.
HUH?
UH, NO.
HEY, MUGI. WHAT THE HELL DO YOU THINK YOU'RE DOING?
YEAH, GET AWAY FROM KIKU-CHAN.
YOU JERK!
SHUT UP!
MUGI IS SUCH A CUTE NAME.
THUMP THUMP
HUH? OH, UH... THANKS.
HEY, LET'S TAKE A PICTURE.

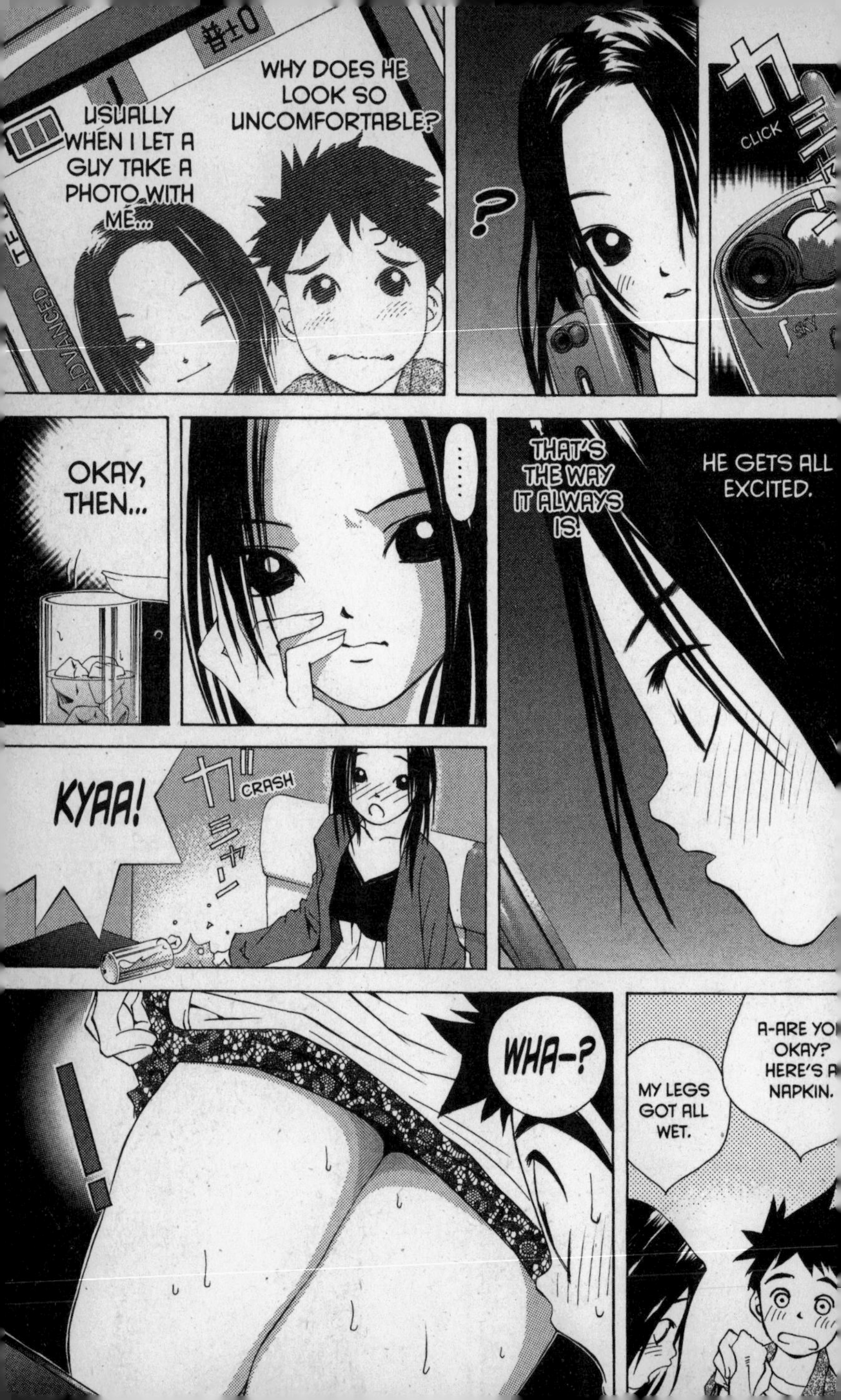
CLICK
?
WHY DOES HE LOOK SO UNCOMFORTABLE?
USUALLY WHEN I LET A GUY TAKE A PHOTO WITH ME...
ADVANCED
HE GETS ALL EXCITED.
THAT'S THE WAY IT ALWAYS IS.
......
OKAY, THEN...
CRASH
KYAA!
A-ARE YO OKAY? HERE'S A NAPKIN.
MY LEGS GOT ALL WET.
WHA-?
!

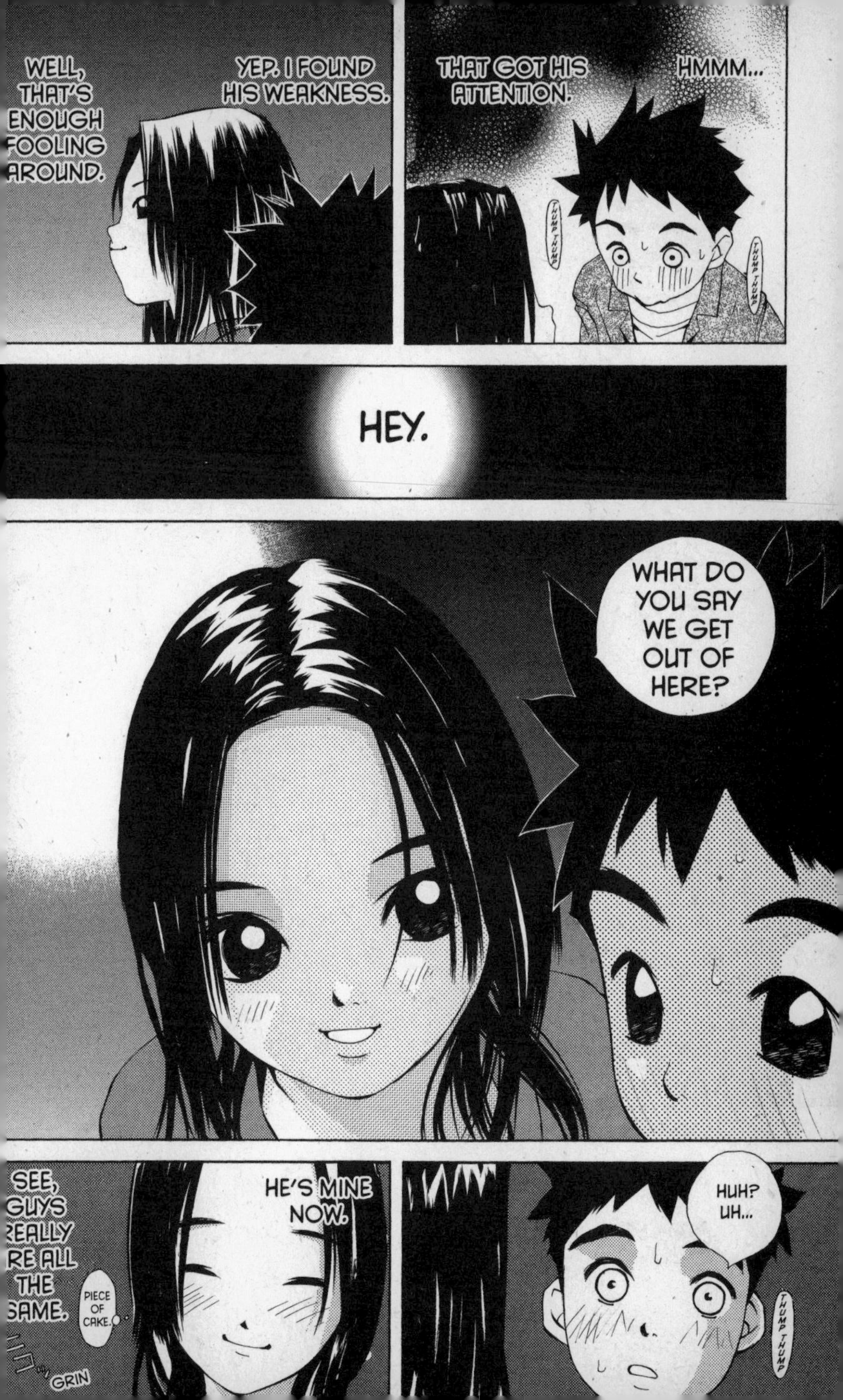
HMMM...
THAT GOT HIS ATTENTION.
THUMP THUMP
THUMP THUMP
YEP. I FOUND HIS WEAKNESS.
WELL, THAT'S ENOUGH FOOLING AROUND.
HEY.
WHAT DO YOU SAY WE GET OUT OF HERE?
HUH? UH...
THUMP THUMP
HE'S MINE NOW.
SEE, GUYS REALLY ARE ALL THE SAME.
PIECE OF CAKE.
GRIN

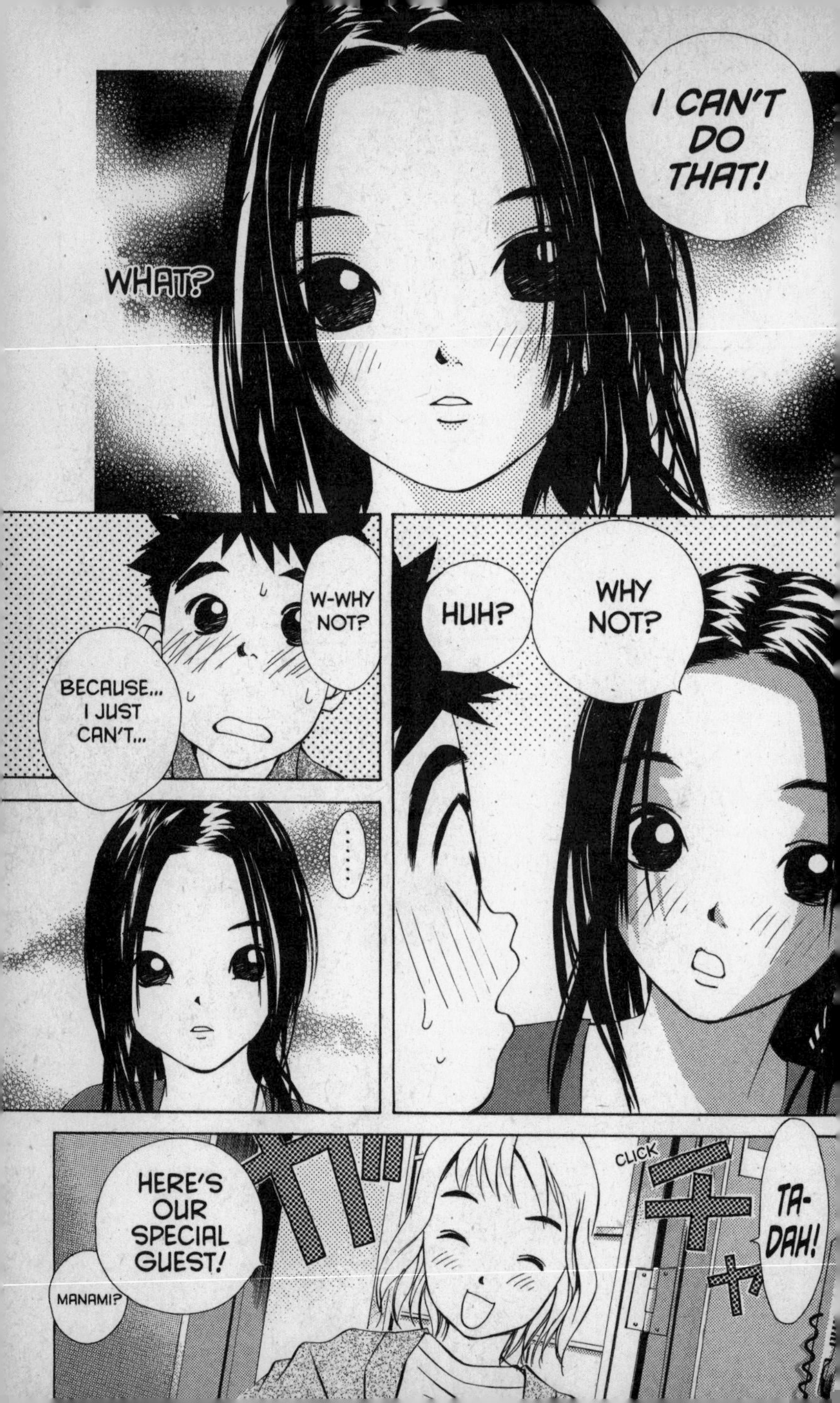
I CAN'T DO THAT!
WHAT?
WHY NOT?
HUH?
W-WHY NOT?
BECAUSE... I JUST CAN'T...
......
TA-DAH!
CLICK
HERE'S OUR SPECIAL GUEST!
MANAMI?

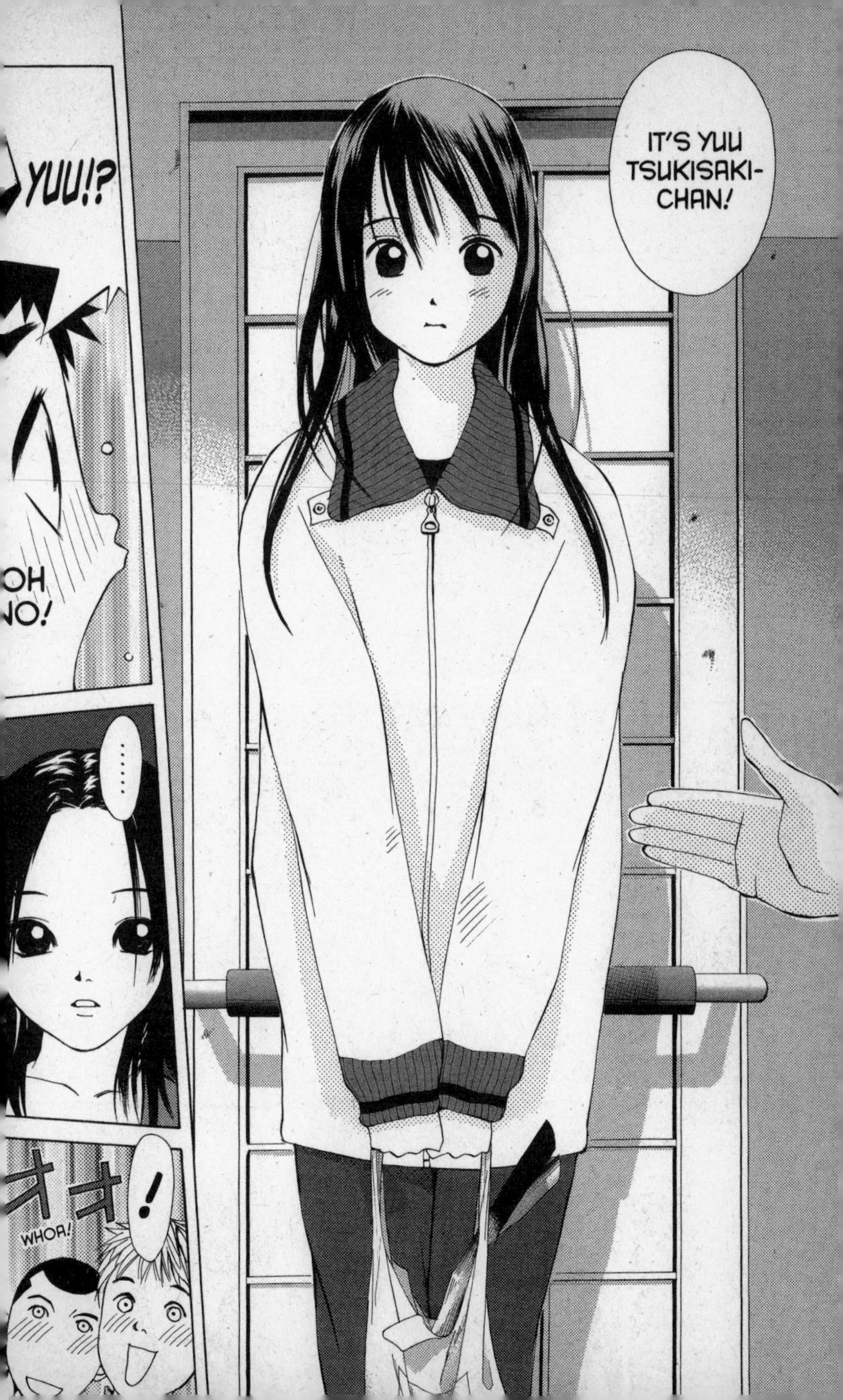

IT'S YUU TSUKISAKI-CHAN!
YUU!?
OH NO!
......
!
WHOA!

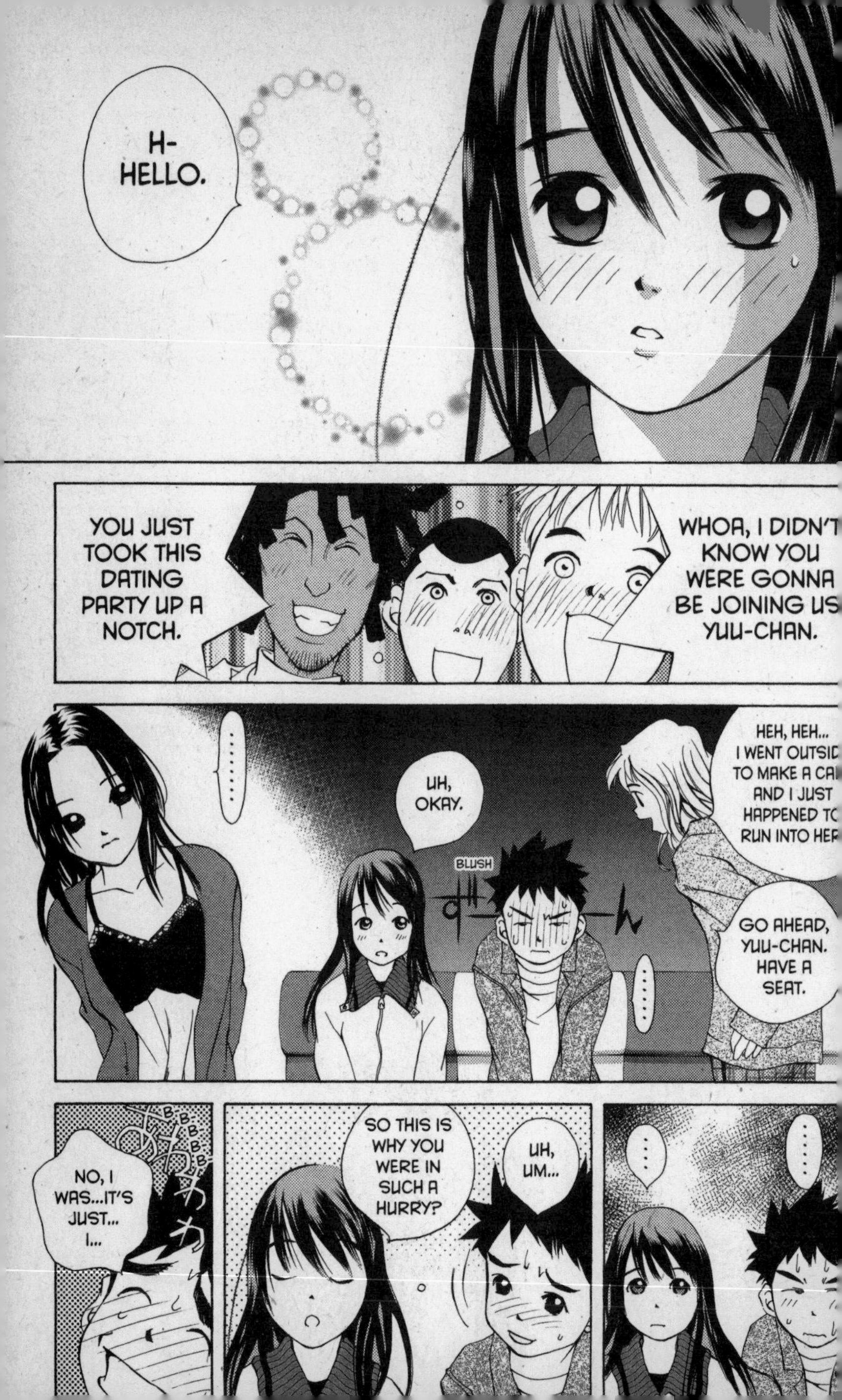
H-
HELLO.
WHOA, I DIDN'T KNOW YOU WERE GONNA BE JOINING US YUU-CHAN.
YOU JUST TOOK THIS DATING PARTY UP A NOTCH.
HEH, HEH... I WENT OUTSID TO MAKE A CA AND I JUST HAPPENED TO RUN INTO HER
GO AHEAD, YUU-CHAN. HAVE A SEAT.
......
BLUSH
UH, OKAY.
......
......
......
UH, UM...
SO THIS IS WHY YOU WERE IN SUCH A HURRY?
B-B-B-B
NO, I WAS...IT'S JUST... I...

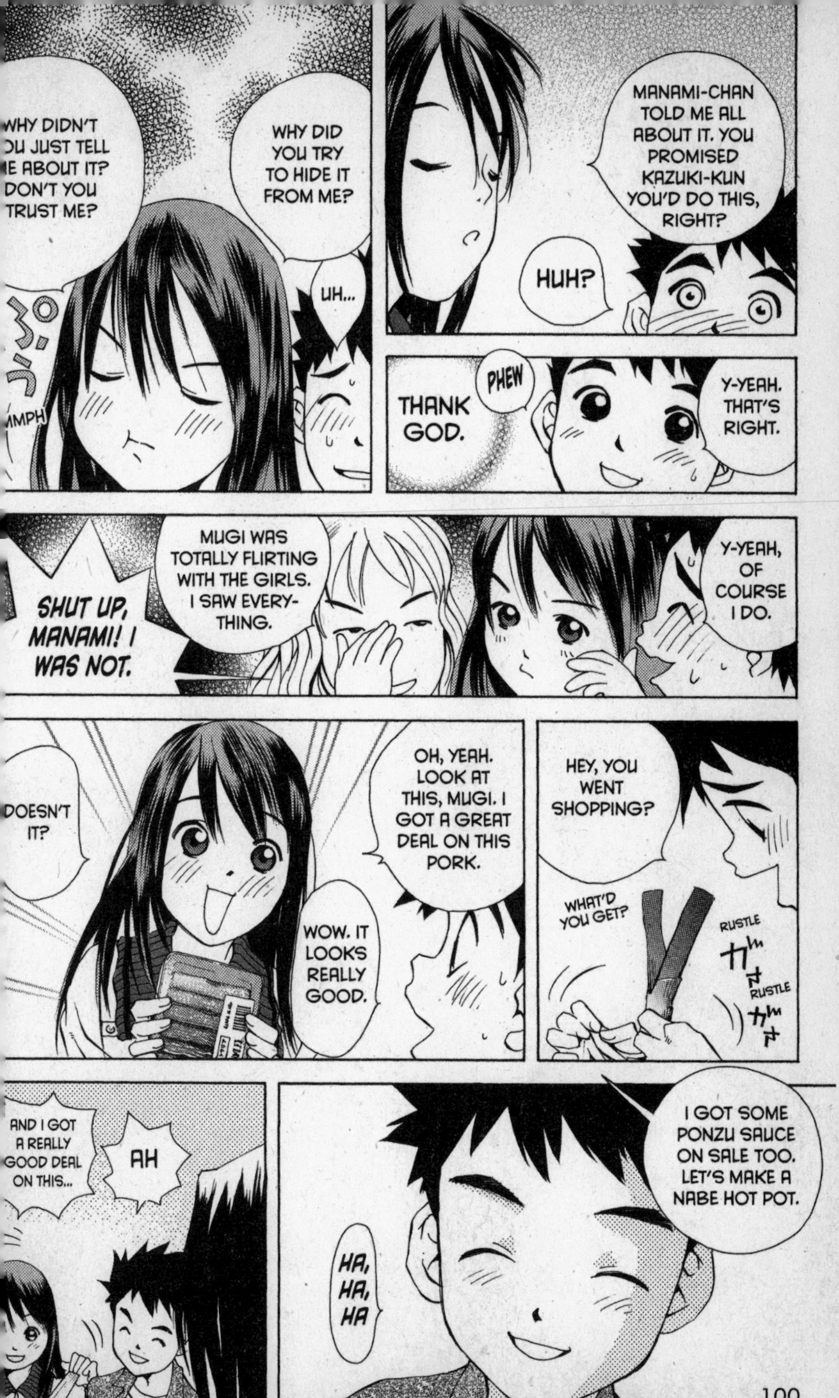
MANAMI-CHAN TOLD ME ALL ABOUT IT. YOU PROMISED KAZUKI-KUN YOU'D DO THIS, RIGHT?
HUH?
Y-YEAH. THAT'S RIGHT.
PHEW
THANK GOD.
WHY DID YOU TRY TO HIDE IT FROM ME?
WHY DIDN'T OU JUST TELL E ABOUT IT? DON'T YOU TRUST ME?
UH...
MPH
Y-YEAH, OF COURSE I DO.
MUGI WAS TOTALLY FLIRTING WITH THE GIRLS. I SAW EVERY-THING.
SHUT UP, MANAMI! I WAS NOT.
HEY, YOU WENT SHOPPING?
WHAT'D YOU GET?
RUSTLE
RUSTLE
OH, YEAH. LOOK AT THIS, MUGI. I GOT A GREAT DEAL ON THIS PORK.
WOW. IT LOOKS REALLY GOOD.
DOESN'T IT?
I GOT SOME PONZU SAUCE ON SALE TOO. LET'S MAKE A NABE HOT POT.
HA, HA, HA
AH
AND I GOT A REALLY GOOD DEAL ON THIS...

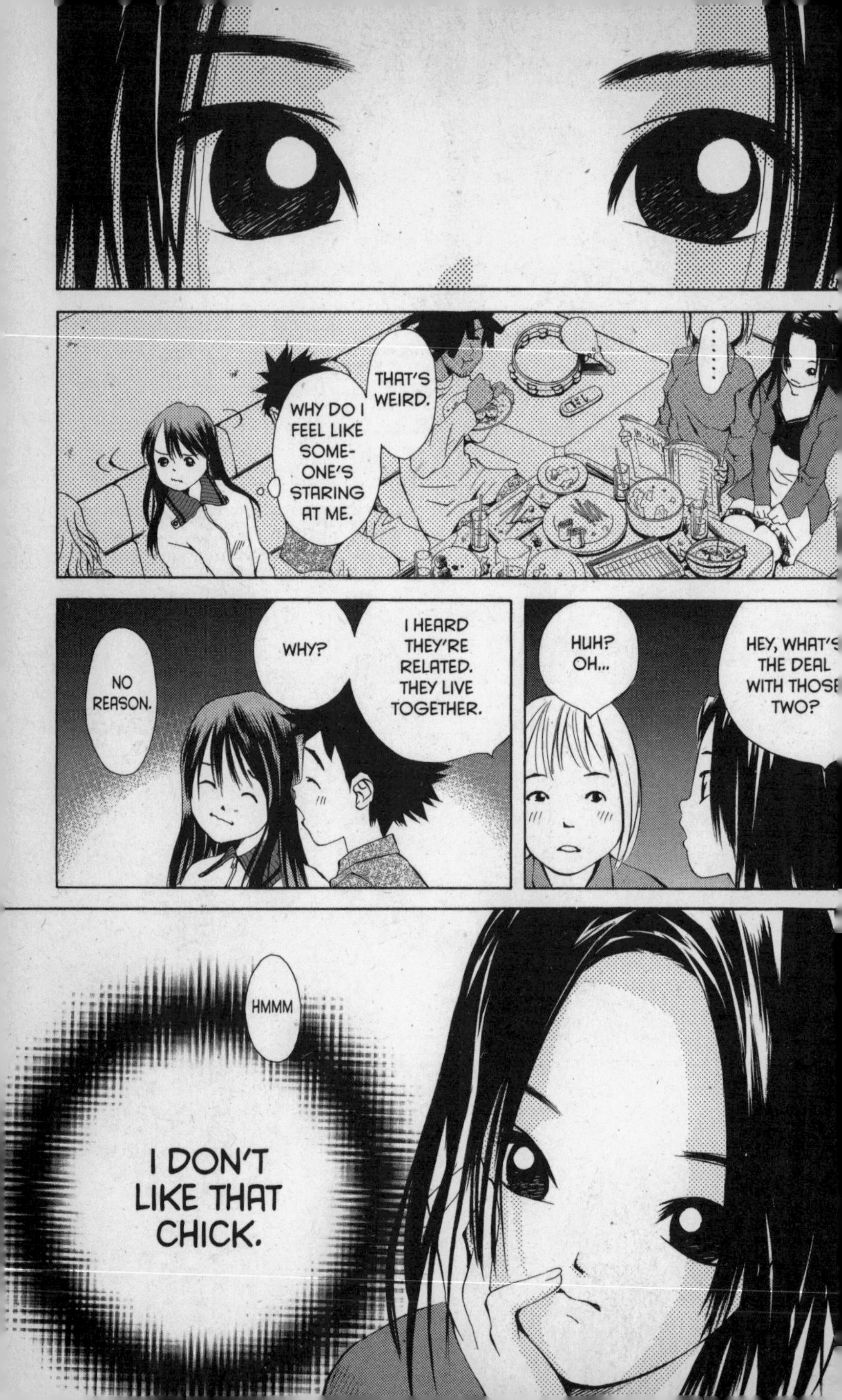
......
THAT'S WEIRD.
WHY DO I FEEL LIKE SOME-ONE'S STARING AT ME.
HEY, WHAT'S THE DEAL WITH THOSE TWO?
HUH? OH...
I HEARD THEY'RE RELATED. THEY LIVE TOGETHER.
WHY?
NO REASON.
HMMM
I DON'T LIKE THAT CHICK.

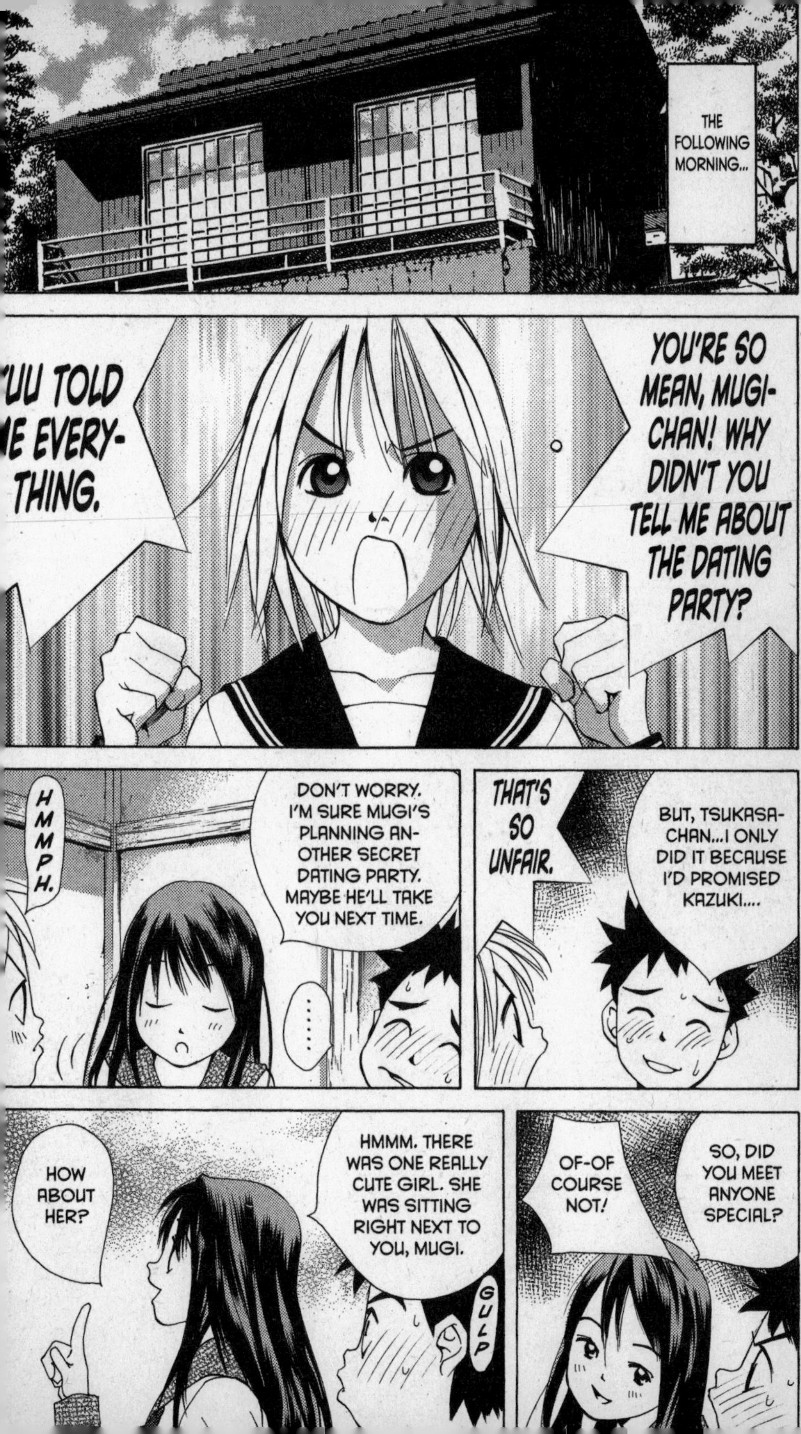
THE FOLLOWING MORNING...
YOU'RE SO MEAN, MUGI-CHAN! WHY DIDN'T YOU TELL ME ABOUT THE DATING PARTY?
UU TOLD E EVERY-THING.
BUT, TSUKASA-CHAN...I ONLY DID IT BECAUSE I'D PROMISED KAZUKI....
THAT'S SO UNFAIR.
DON'T WORRY. I'M SURE MUGI'S PLANNING AN-OTHER SECRET DATING PARTY. MAYBE HE'LL TAKE YOU NEXT TIME.
HMMPH.
......
SO, DID YOU MEET ANYONE SPECIAL?
OF-OF COURSE NOT!
HMMM. THERE WAS ONE REALLY CUTE GIRL. SHE WAS SITTING RIGHT NEXT TO YOU, MUGI.
HOW ABOUT HER?
GULP

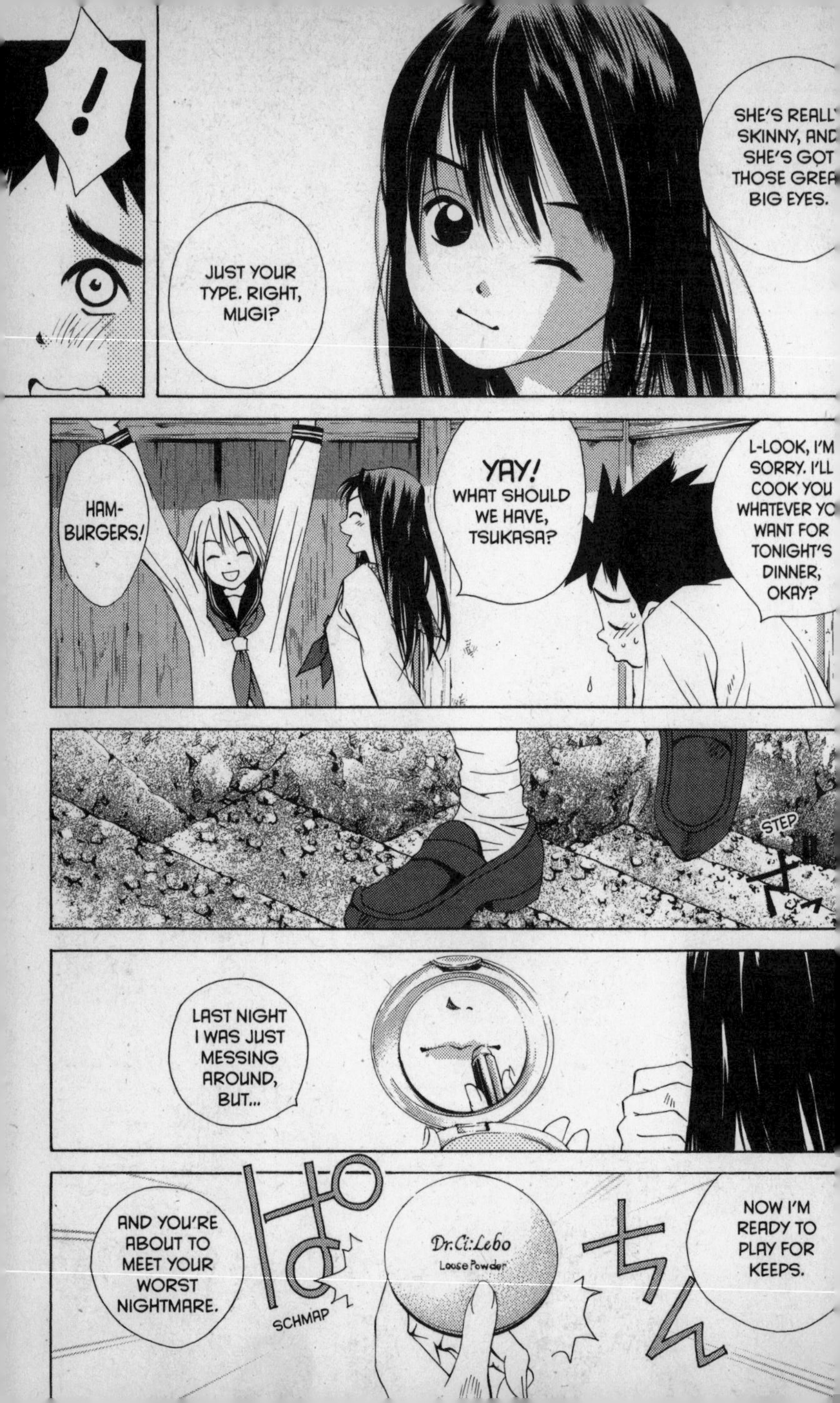
SHE'S REALL SKINNY, AND SHE'S GOT THOSE GREA BIG EYES.
JUST YOUR TYPE. RIGHT, MUGI?
!
L-LOOK, I'M SORRY. I'LL COOK YOU WHATEVER YO WANT FOR TONIGHT'S DINNER, OKAY?
YAY! WHAT SHOULD WE HAVE, TSUKASA?
HAM-BURGERS!
STEP
LAST NIGHT I WAS JUST MESSING AROUND, BUT...
NOW I'M READY TO PLAY FOR KEEPS.
ぱちん
Dr.Ci:Lebo
Loose Powder
SCHMAP
AND YOU'RE ABOUT TO MEET YOUR WORST NIGHTMARE.

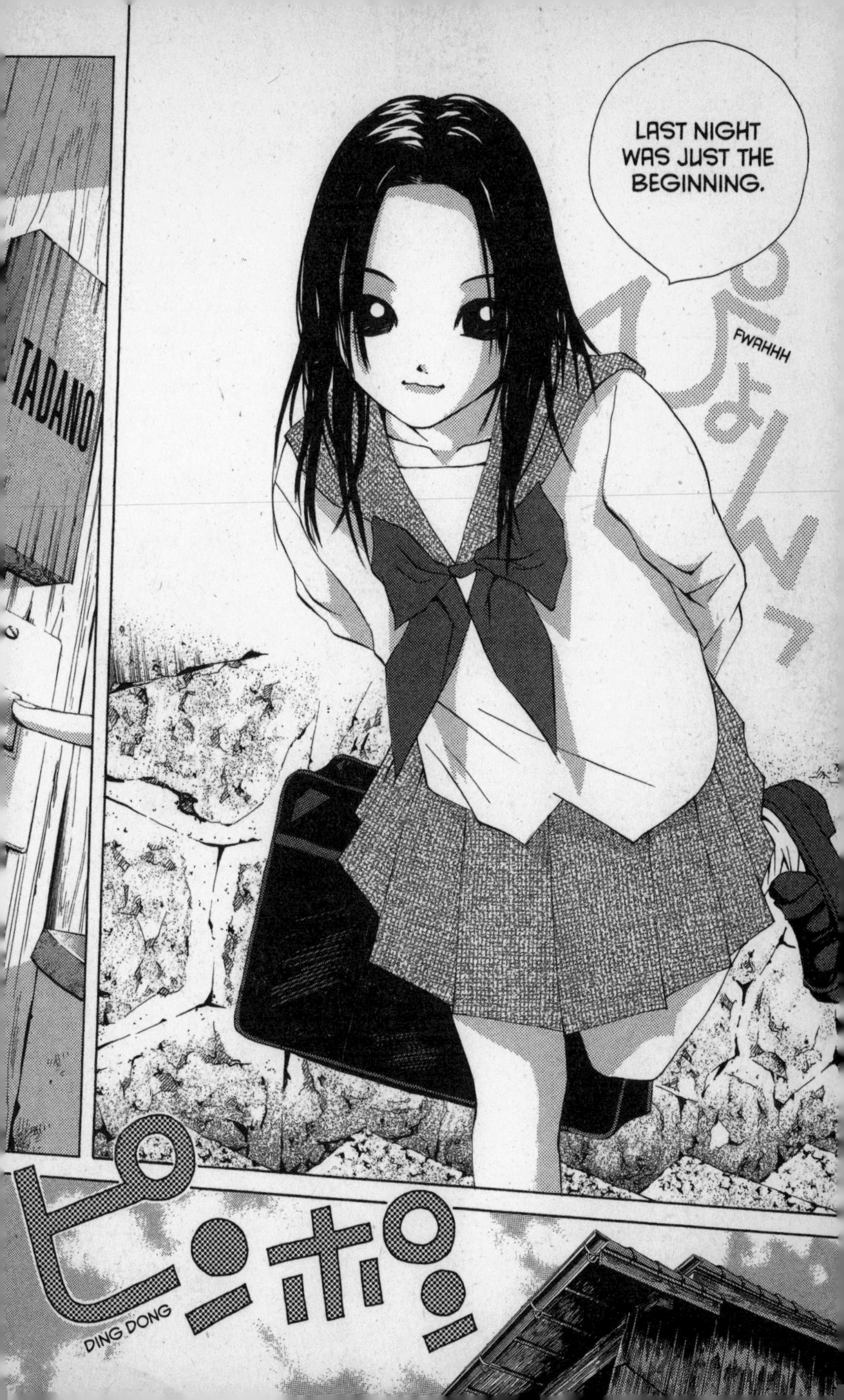

LAST NIGHT WAS JUST THE BEGINNING.
FWAHHH
TADANO
DING DONG

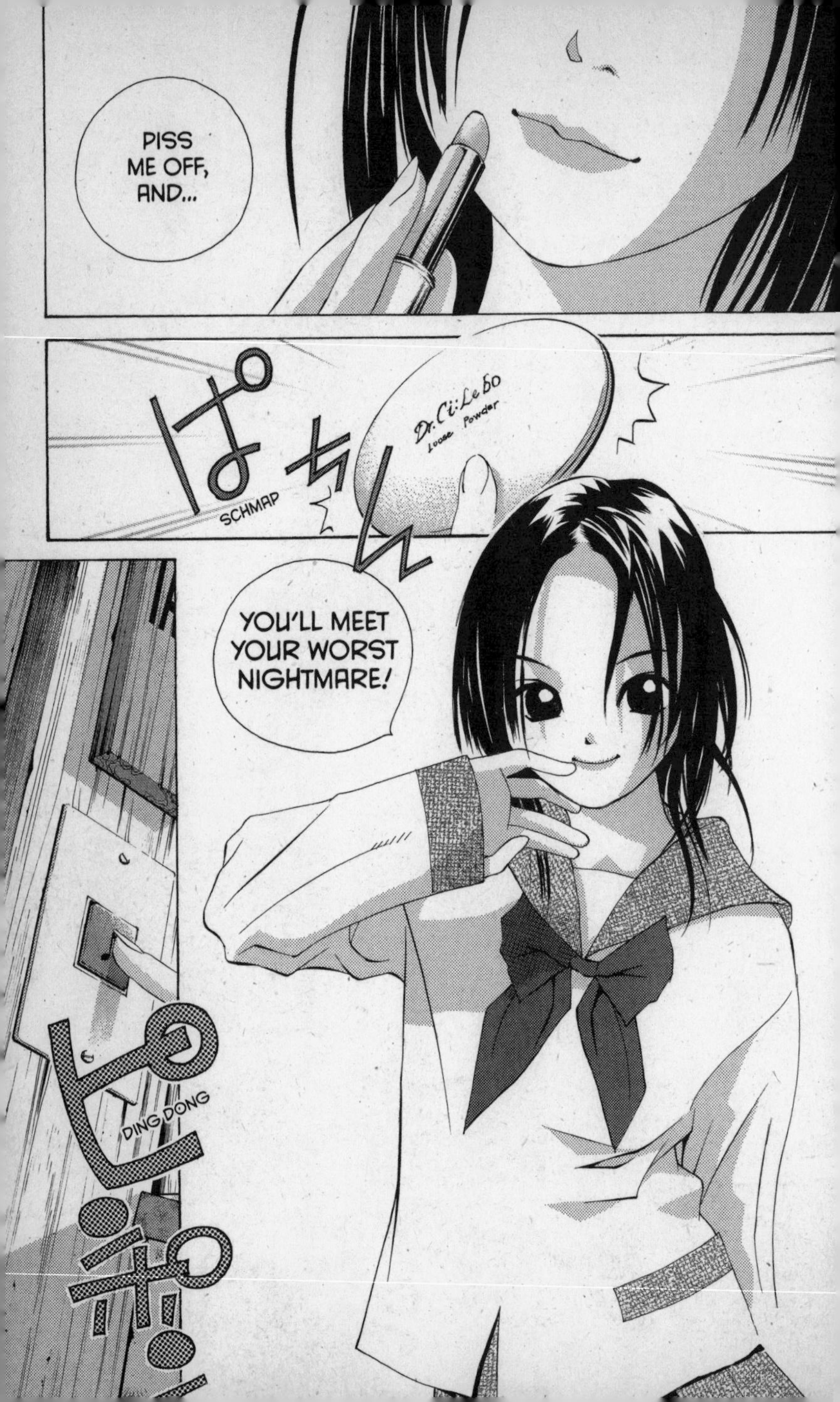

PISS ME OFF, AND...
ぱちん
SCHMAP
Dr. Ci:Labo
Loose Powder
YOU'LL MEET YOUR WORST NIGHTMARE!
DING DONG

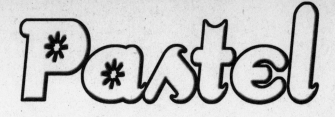

Pastel

MIRACLE 28: AN INVISIBLE TRAP

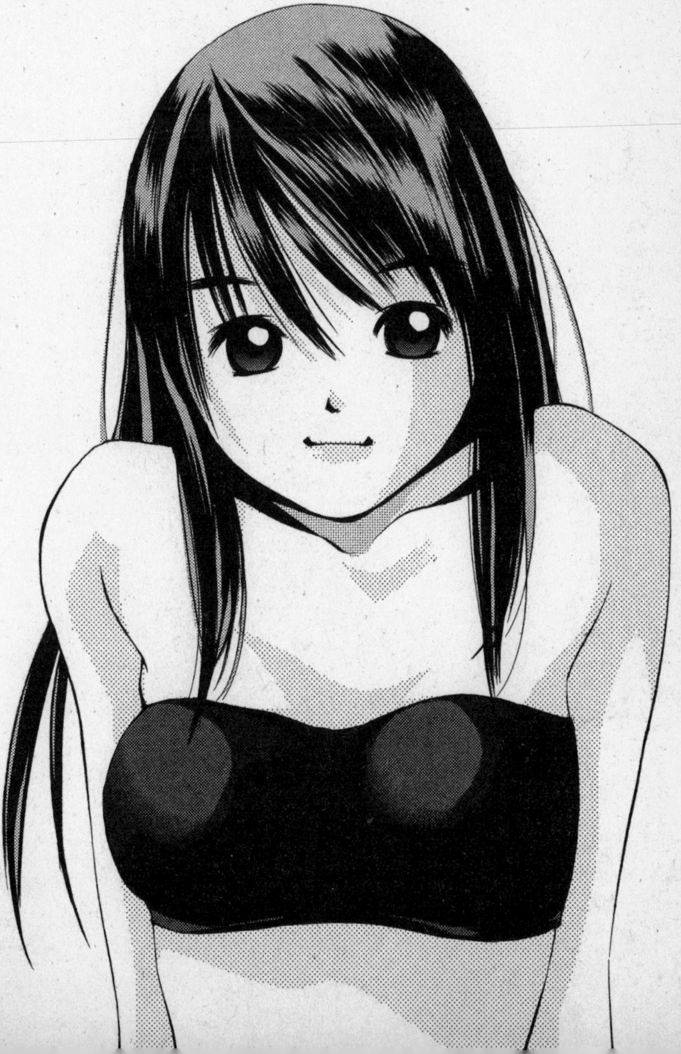

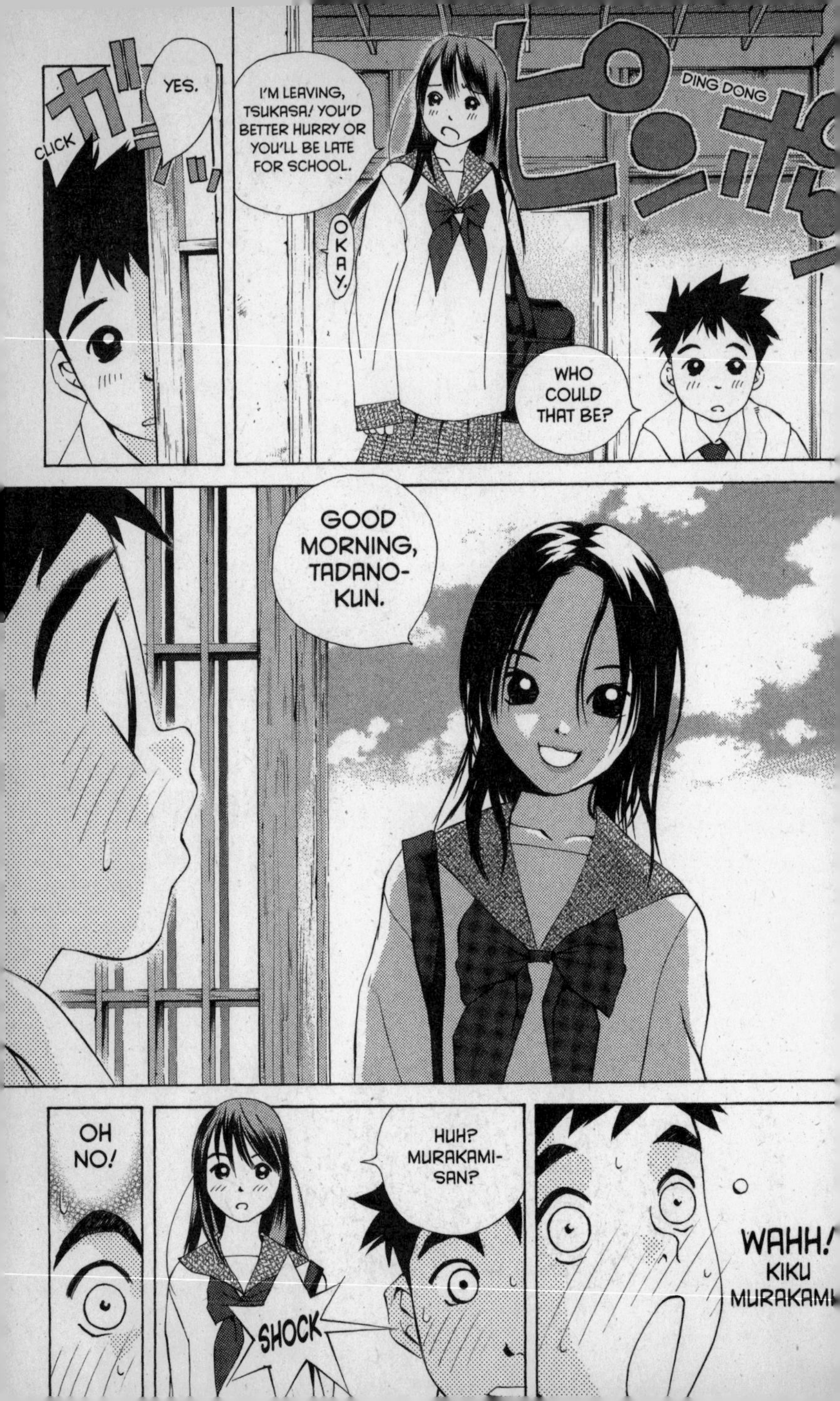
DING DONG
I'M LEAVING, TSUKASA! YOU'D BETTER HURRY OR YOU'LL BE LATE FOR SCHOOL.
OKAY.
WHO COULD THAT BE?
YES.
CLICK
GOOD MORNING, TADANO-KUN.
WAHH! KIKU MURAKAMI
HUH? MURAKAMI-SAN?
SHOCK
OH NO!

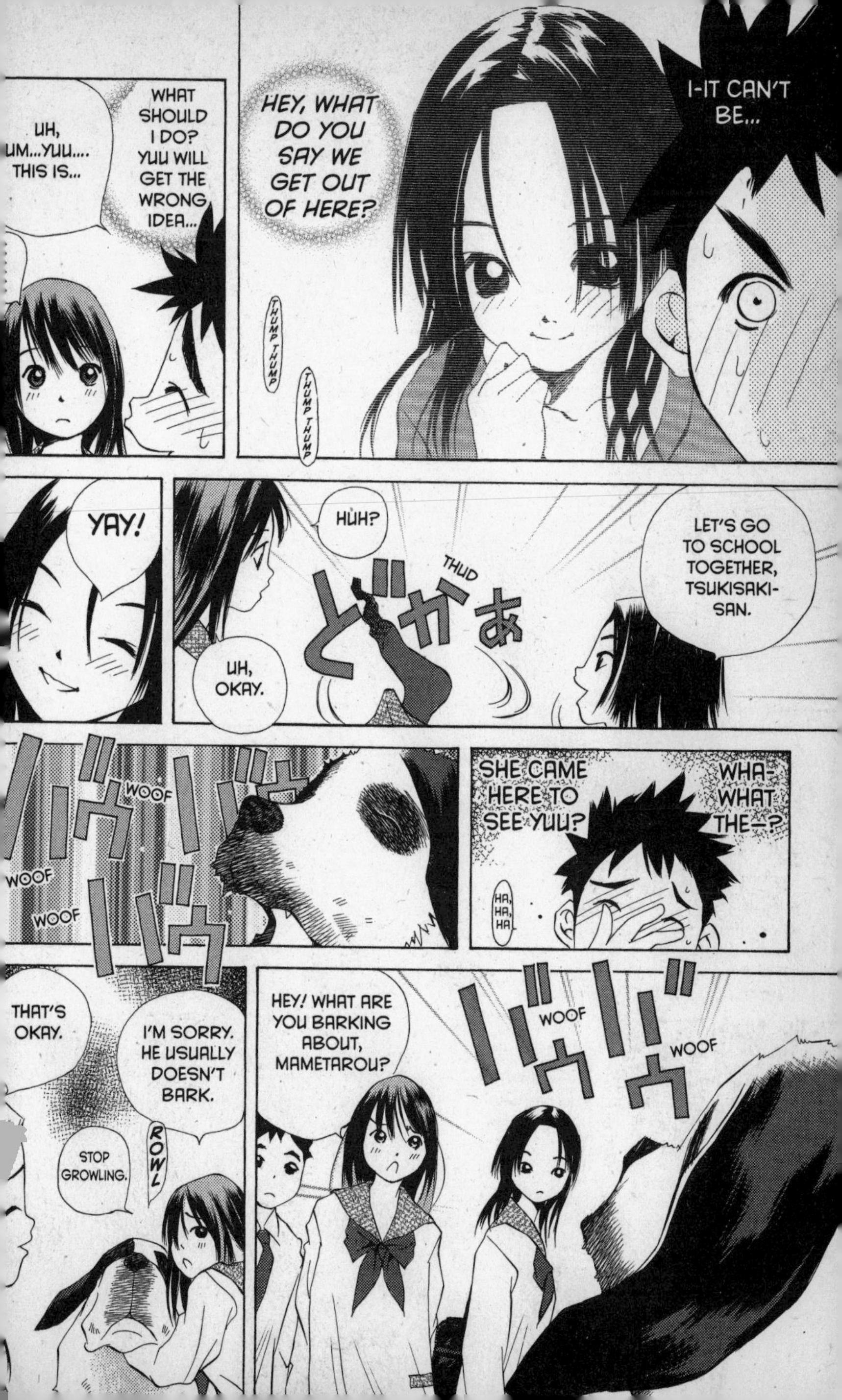
I-IT CAN'T BE...
HEY, WHAT DO YOU SAY WE GET OUT OF HERE?
THUMP THUMP
THUMP THUMP
WHAT SHOULD I DO? YUU WILL GET THE WRONG IDEA...
UH, UM...YUU.... THIS IS...
LET'S GO TO SCHOOL TOGETHER, TSUKISAKI-SAN.
THUD
HUH?
UH, OKAY.
YAY!
WHA- WHAT THE—?
SHE CAME HERE TO SEE YUU?
HA, HA, HA
WOOF
WOOF
WOOF
HEY! WHAT ARE YOU BARKING ABOUT, MAMETAROU?
WOOF
WOOF
I'M SORRY. HE USUALLY DOESN'T BARK.
THAT'S OKAY.
ROWL
STOP GROWLING.

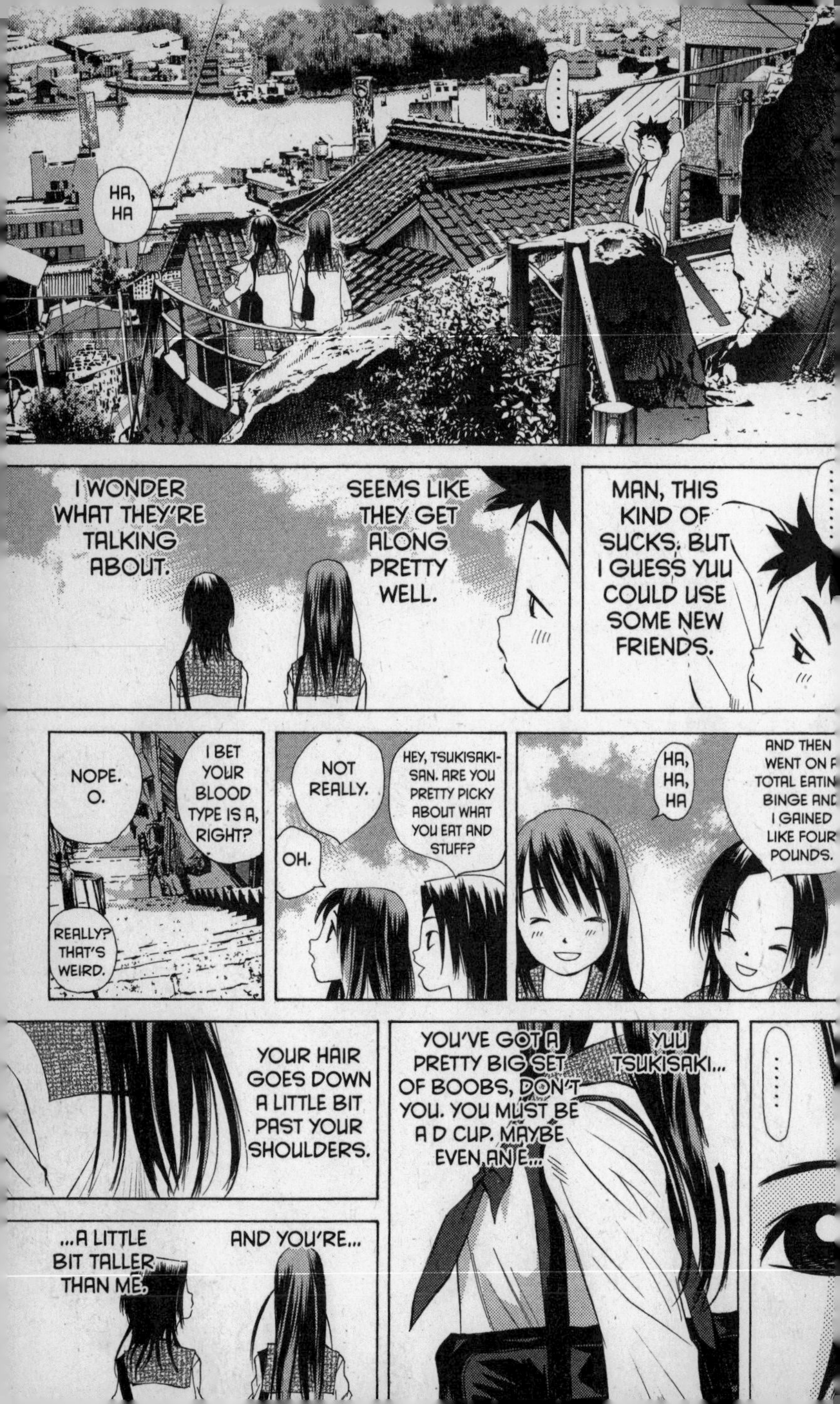

......
HA, HA
MAN, THIS KIND OF SUCKS. BUT I GUESS YUU COULD USE SOME NEW FRIENDS.
SEEMS LIKE THEY GET ALONG PRETTY WELL.
I WONDER WHAT THEY'RE TALKING ABOUT.
AND THEN WENT ON A TOTAL EATIN BINGE AND I GAINED LIKE FOUR POUNDS.
HA, HA, HA
HEY, TSUKISAKI-SAN. ARE YOU PRETTY PICKY ABOUT WHAT YOU EAT AND STUFF?
NOT REALLY.
OH.
I BET YOUR BLOOD TYPE IS A, RIGHT?
NOPE. O.
REALLY? THAT'S WEIRD.
......
YUU TSUKISAKI...
YOU'VE GOT A PRETTY BIG SET OF BOOBS, DON'T YOU. YOU MUST BE A D CUP. MAYBE EVEN AN E...
YOUR HAIR GOES DOWN A LITTLE BIT PAST YOUR SHOULDERS.
AND YOU'RE...
...A LITTLE BIT TALLER THAN ME.

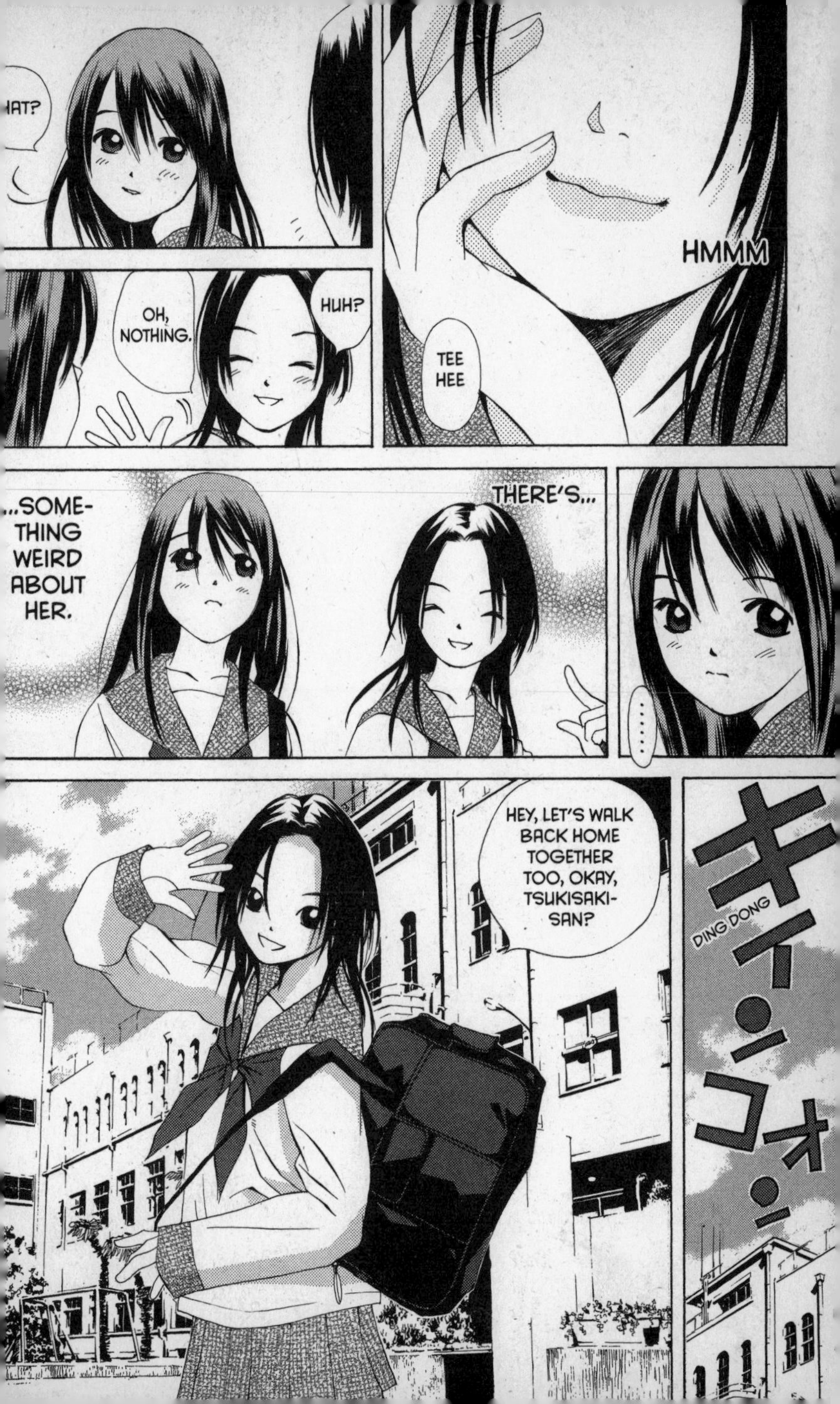

HMMM
TEE HEE
HAT?
HUH?
OH, NOTHING.
......
THERE'S...
...SOME-THING WEIRD ABOUT HER.
DING DONG
HEY, LET'S WALK BACK HOME TOGETHER TOO, OKAY, TSUKISAKI-SAN?

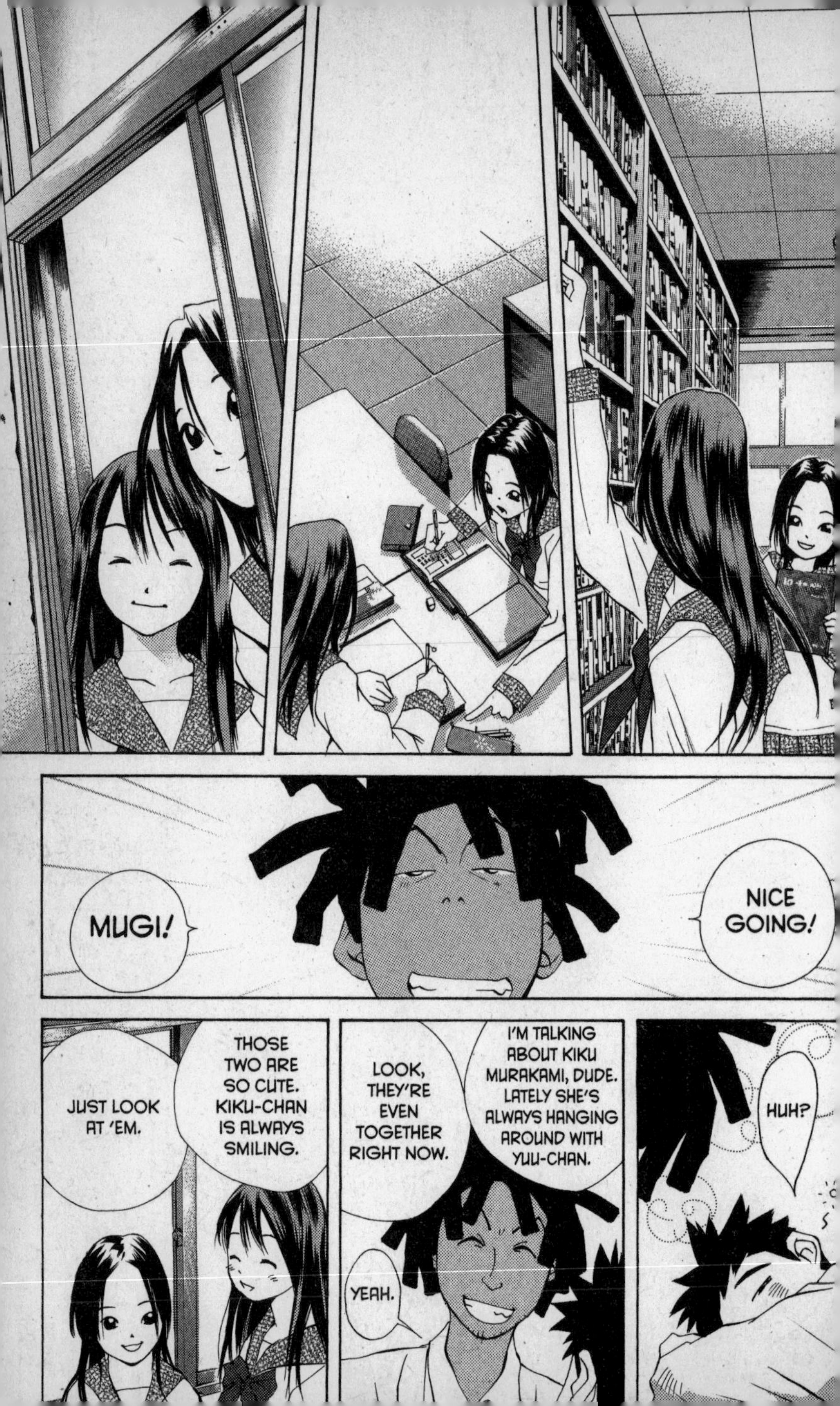
NICE GOING!
MUGI!
HUH?
I'M TALKING ABOUT KIKU MURAKAMI, DUDE. LATELY SHE'S ALWAYS HANGING AROUND WITH YUU-CHAN.
LOOK, THEY'RE EVEN TOGETHER RIGHT NOW.
YEAH.
THOSE TWO ARE SO CUTE. KIKU-CHAN IS ALWAYS SMILING.
JUST LOOK AT 'EM.

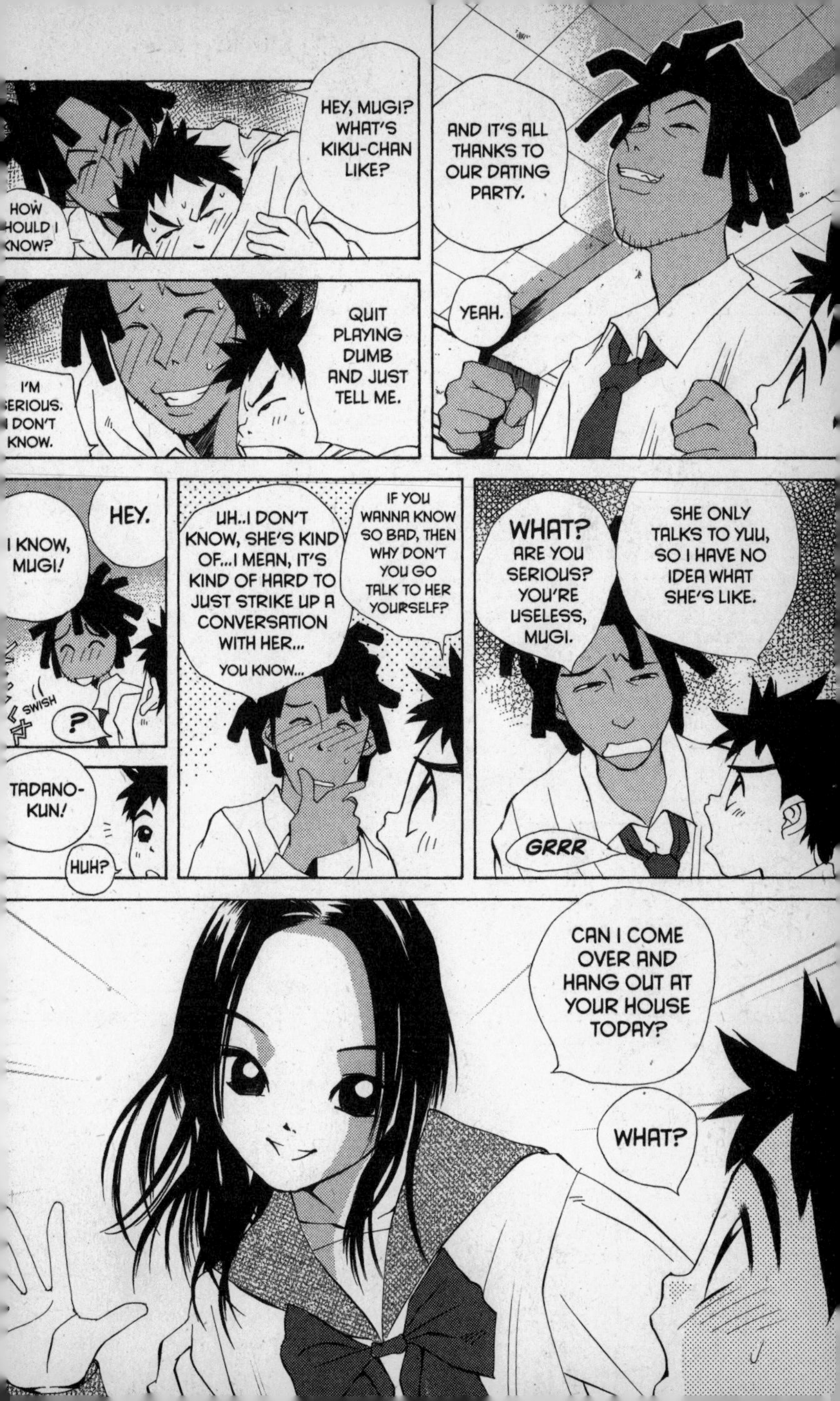
AND IT'S ALL THANKS TO OUR DATING PARTY.
YEAH.
HEY, MUGI? WHAT'S KIKU-CHAN LIKE?
HOW HOULD I KNOW?
QUIT PLAYING DUMB AND JUST TELL ME.
I'M ERIOUS. DON'T KNOW.
SHE ONLY TALKS TO YUU, SO I HAVE NO IDEA WHAT SHE'S LIKE.
WHAT? ARE YOU SERIOUS? YOU'RE USELESS, MUGI.
GRRR
IF YOU WANNA KNOW SO BAD, THEN WHY DON'T YOU GO TALK TO HER YOURSELF?
UH..I DON'T KNOW, SHE'S KIND OF...I MEAN, IT'S KIND OF HARD TO JUST STRIKE UP A CONVERSATION WITH HER...
YOU KNOW...
HEY.
I KNOW, MUGI!
SWISH
?
TADANO-KUN!
HUH?
CAN I COME OVER AND HANG OUT AT YOUR HOUSE TODAY?
WHAT?

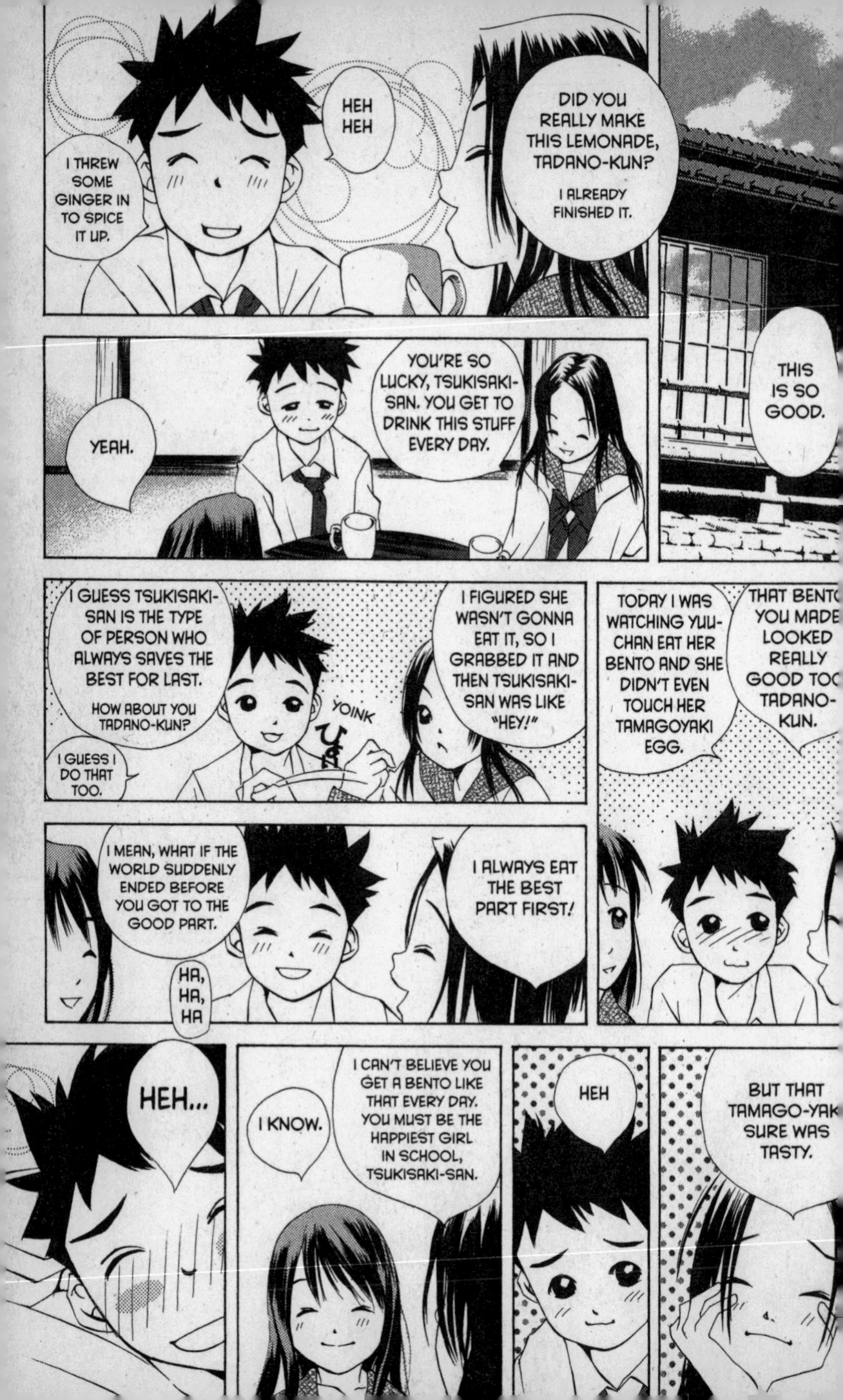
THIS IS SO GOOD.
DID YOU REALLY MAKE THIS LEMONADE, TADANO-KUN?
I ALREADY FINISHED IT.
HEH HEH
I THREW SOME GINGER IN TO SPICE IT UP.
YOU'RE SO LUCKY, TSUKISAKI-SAN. YOU GET TO DRINK THIS STUFF EVERY DAY.
YEAH.
THAT BENTO YOU MADE LOOKED REALLY GOOD TOO TADANO-KUN.
TODAY I WAS WATCHING YUU-CHAN EAT HER BENTO AND SHE DIDN'T EVEN TOUCH HER TAMAGOYAKI EGG.
I FIGURED SHE WASN'T GONNA EAT IT, SO I GRABBED IT AND THEN TSUKISAKI-SAN WAS LIKE "HEY!"
YOINK
I GUESS TSUKISAKI-SAN IS THE TYPE OF PERSON WHO ALWAYS SAVES THE BEST FOR LAST.
HOW ABOUT YOU TADANO-KUN?
I GUESS I DO THAT TOO.
I ALWAYS EAT THE BEST PART FIRST!
I MEAN, WHAT IF THE WORLD SUDDENLY ENDED BEFORE YOU GOT TO THE GOOD PART.
HA, HA, HA
BUT THAT TAMAGO-YAK SURE WAS TASTY.
HEH
I CAN'T BELIEVE YOU GET A BENTO LIKE THAT EVERY DAY. YOU MUST BE THE HAPPIEST GIRL IN SCHOOL, TSUKISAKI-SAN.
I KNOW.
HEH...

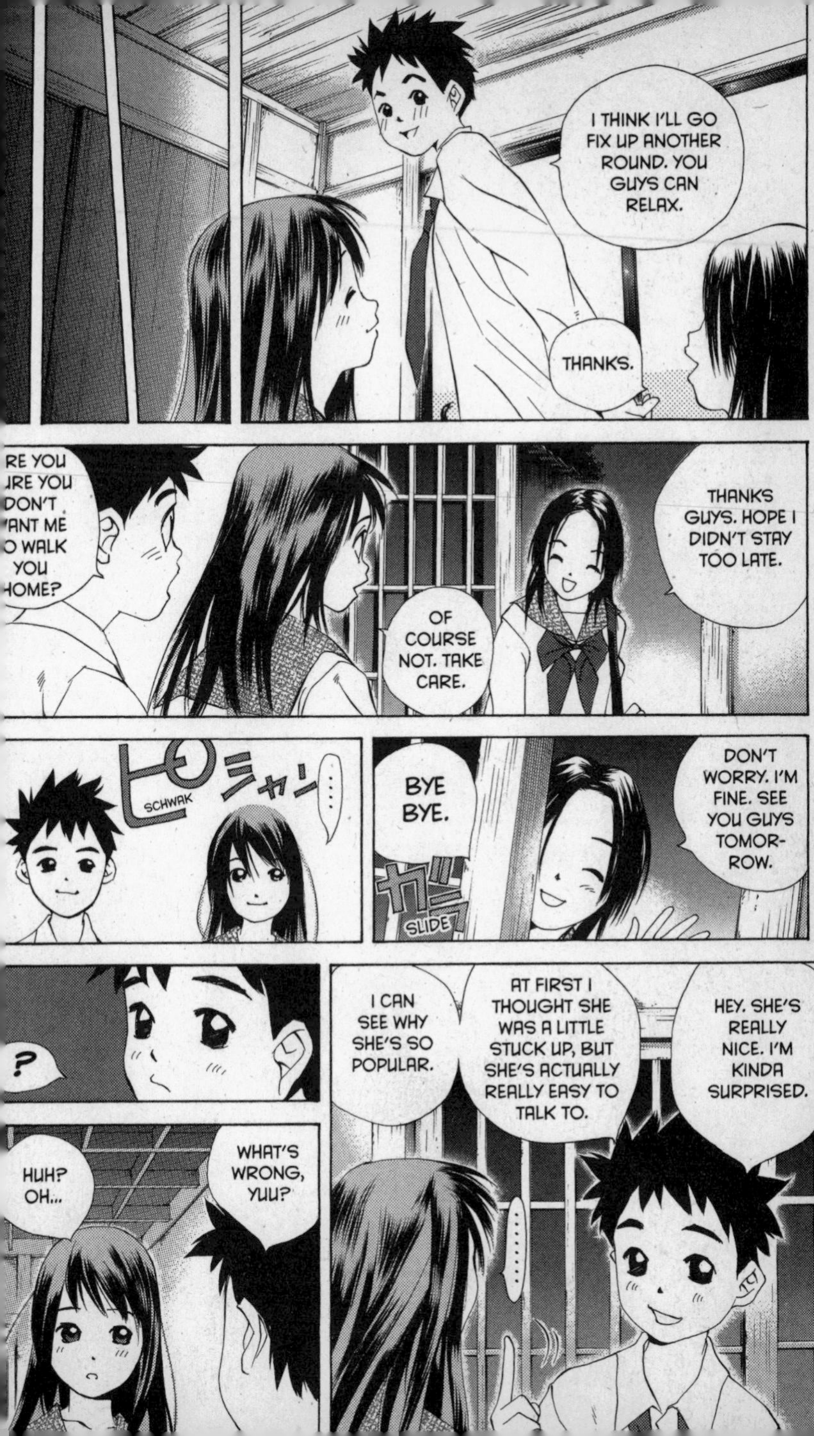
I THINK I'LL GO FIX UP ANOTHER ROUND. YOU GUYS CAN RELAX.
THANKS.
THANKS GUYS. HOPE I DIDN'T STAY TOO LATE.
OF COURSE NOT. TAKE CARE.
RE YOU URE YOU DON'T ANT ME O WALK YOU HOME?
DON'T WORRY. I'M FINE. SEE YOU GUYS TOMOR-ROW.
BYE BYE.
SLIDE
ピシャン
SCHWAK
.....
HEY. SHE'S REALLY NICE. I'M KINDA SURPRISED.
AT FIRST I THOUGHT SHE WAS A LITTLE STUCK UP, BUT SHE'S ACTUALLY REALLY EASY TO TALK TO.
I CAN SEE WHY SHE'S SO POPULAR.
.....
?
WHAT'S WRONG, YUU?
HUH? OH...

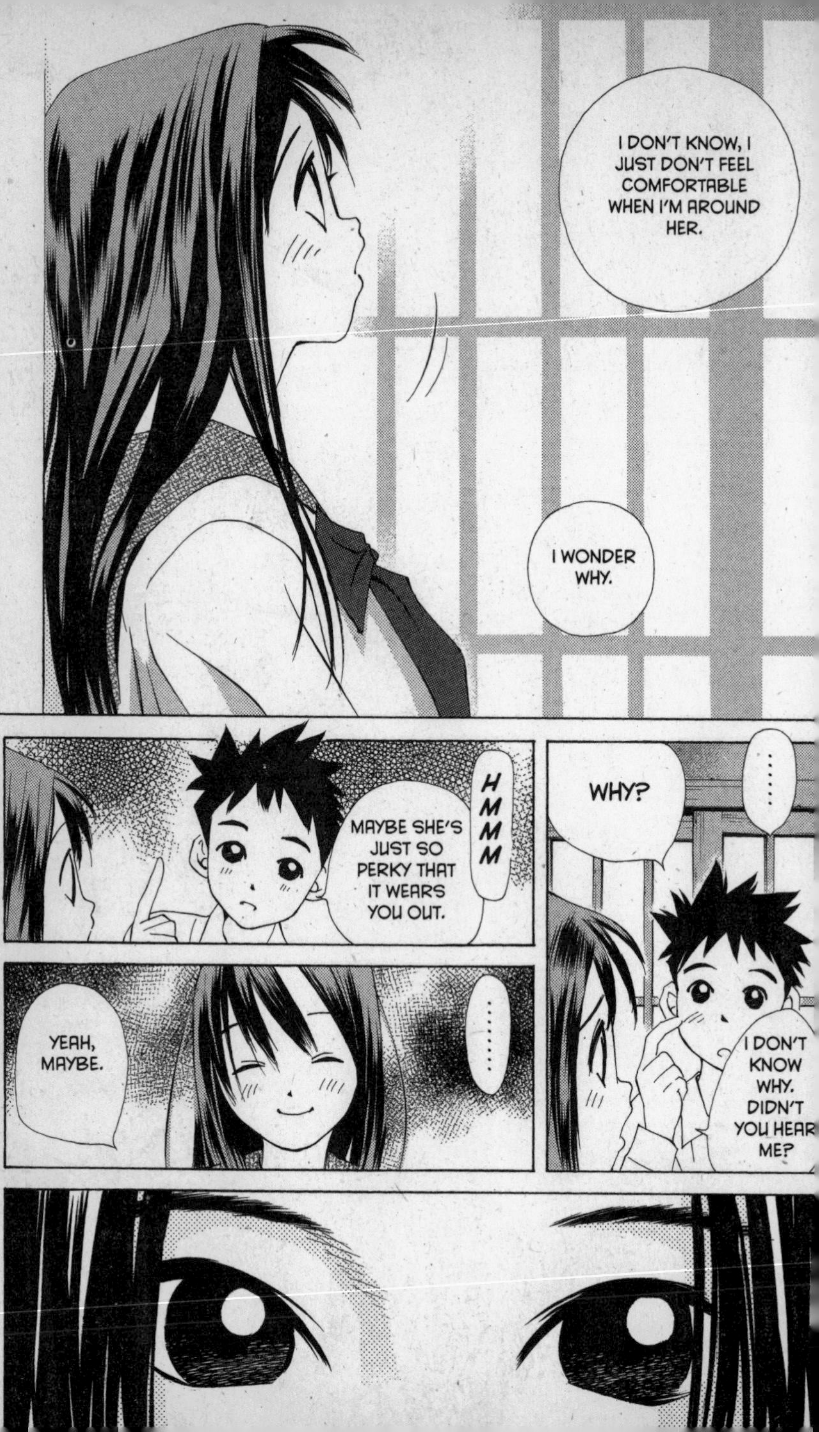

I DON'T KNOW, I JUST DON'T FEEL COMFORTABLE WHEN I'M AROUND HER.
I WONDER WHY.
......
WHY?
I DON'T KNOW WHY. DIDN'T YOU HEAR ME?
HMMM
MAYBE SHE'S JUST SO PERKY THAT IT WEARS YOU OUT.
......
YEAH, MAYBE.

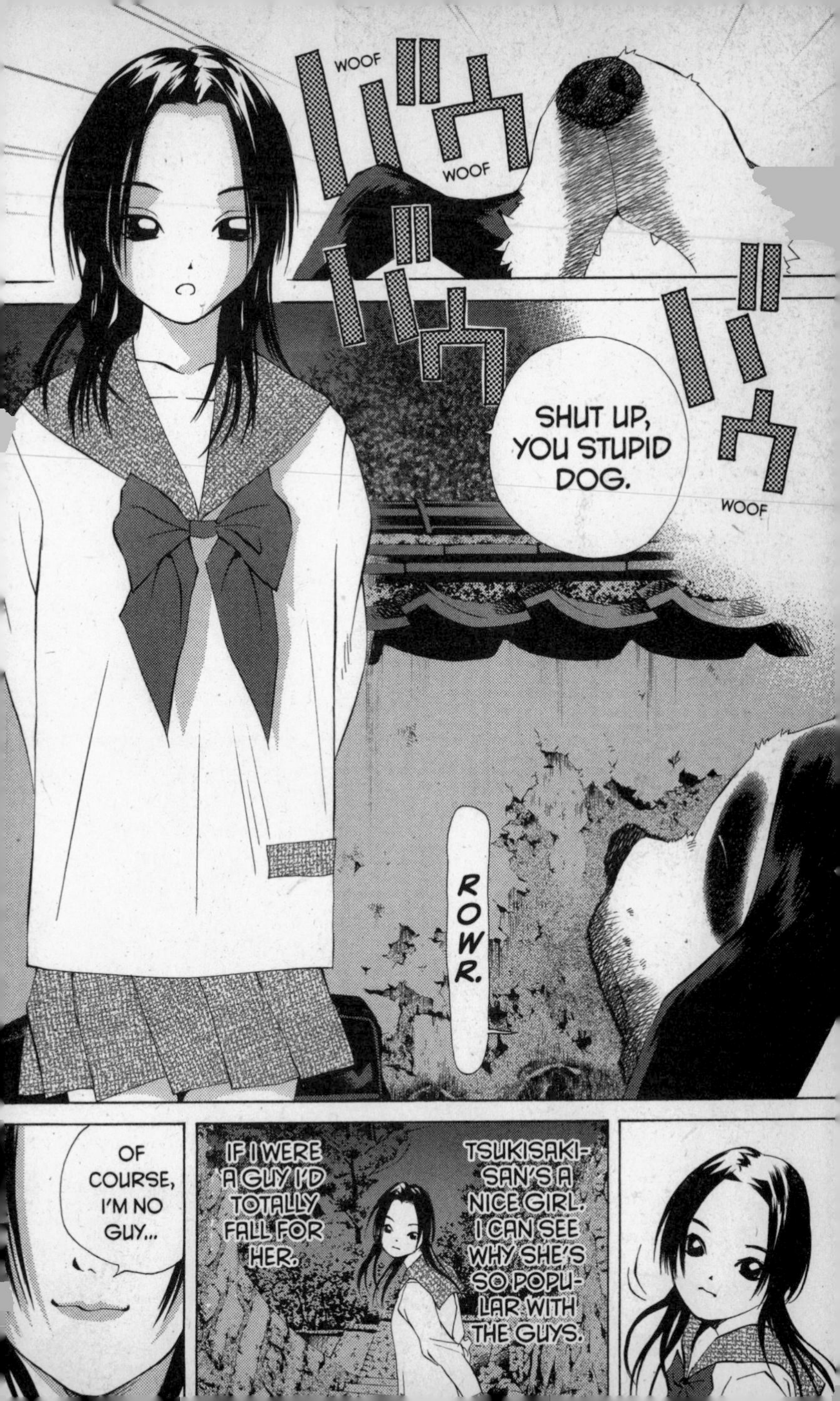
WOOF
WOOF
SHUT UP, YOU STUPID DOG.
WOOF
ROWR.
TSUKISAKI-SAN'S A NICE GIRL. I CAN SEE WHY SHE'S SO POPULAR WITH THE GUYS.
IF I WERE A GUY I'D TOTALLY FALL FOR HER.
OF COURSE, I'M NO GUY...

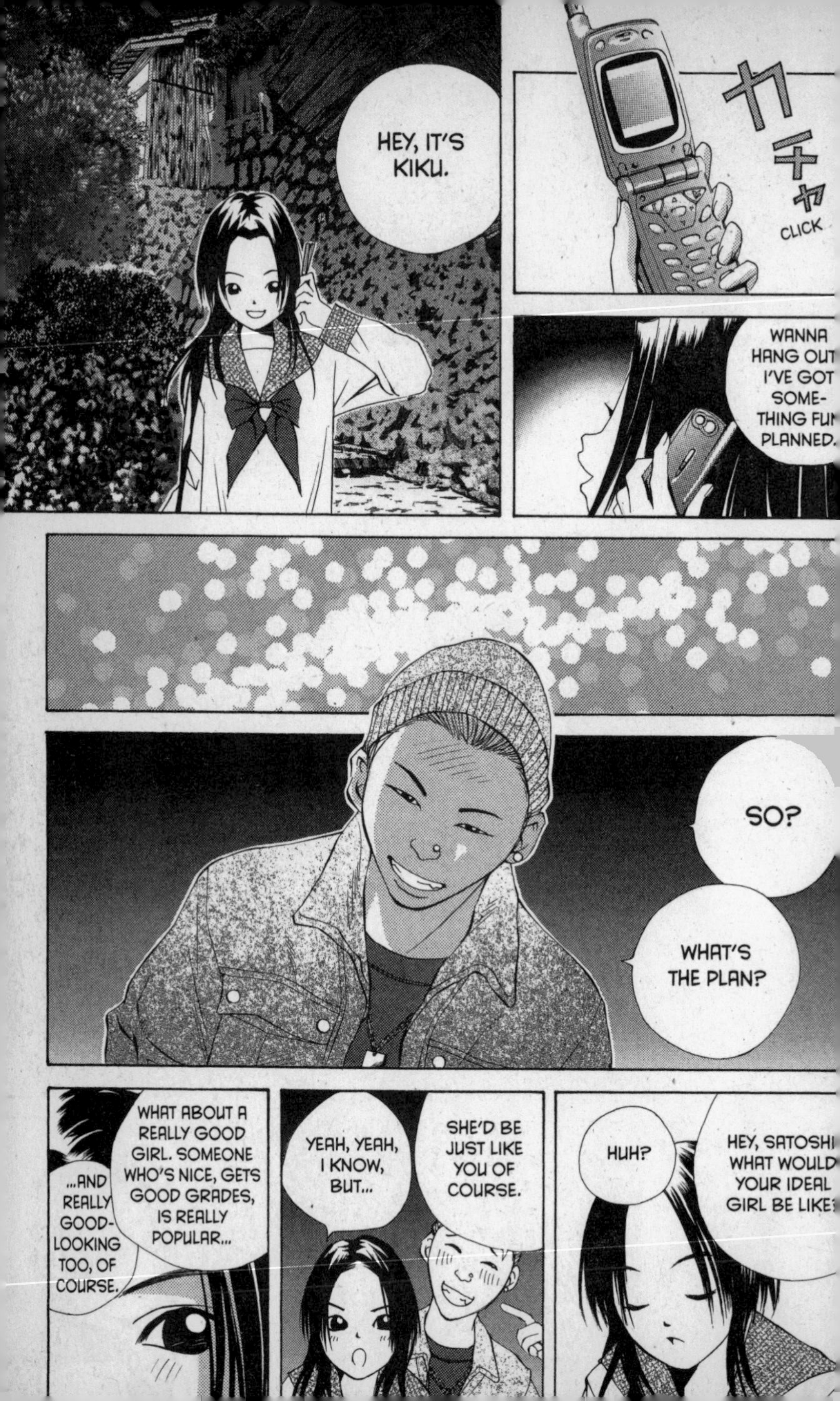
カチャ
CLICK
WANNA HANG OUT I'VE GOT SOME-THING FU PLANNED.
HEY, IT'S KIKU.
SO?
WHAT'S THE PLAN?
HEY, SATOSHI WHAT WOULD YOUR IDEAL GIRL BE LIKE
HUH?
SHE'D BE JUST LIKE YOU OF COURSE.
YEAH, YEAH, I KNOW, BUT...
WHAT ABOUT A REALLY GOOD GIRL. SOMEONE WHO'S NICE, GETS GOOD GRADES, IS REALLY POPULAR...
...AND REALLY GOOD-LOOKING TOO, OF COURSE.

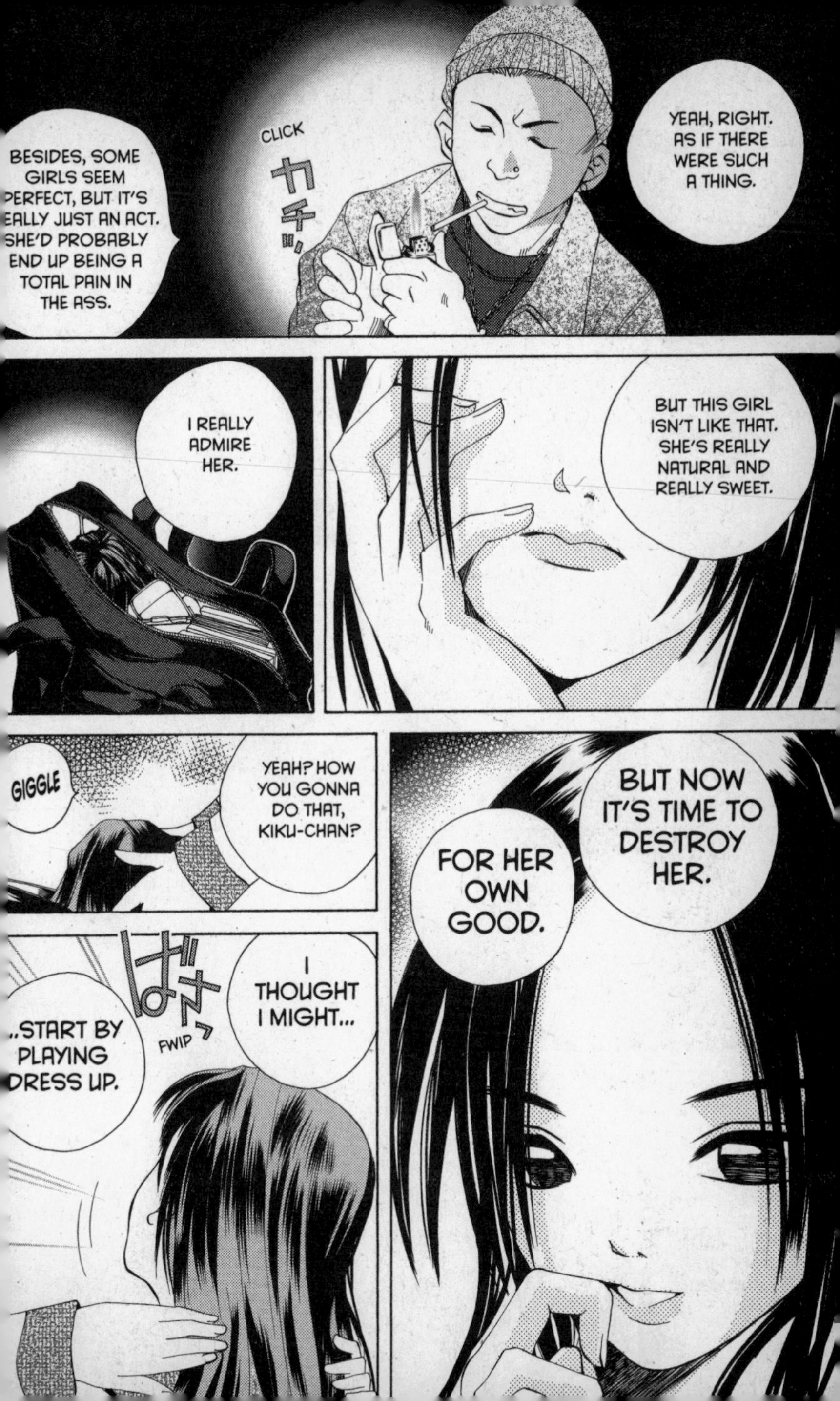
YEAH, RIGHT. AS IF THERE WERE SUCH A THING.
CLICK
カチッ
BESIDES, SOME GIRLS SEEM PERFECT, BUT IT'S EALLY JUST AN ACT. SHE'D PROBABLY END UP BEING A TOTAL PAIN IN THE ASS.
BUT THIS GIRL ISN'T LIKE THAT. SHE'S REALLY NATURAL AND REALLY SWEET.
I REALLY ADMIRE HER.
BUT NOW IT'S TIME TO DESTROY HER.
FOR HER OWN GOOD.
YEAH? HOW YOU GONNA DO THAT, KIKU-CHAN?
GIGGLE
I THOUGHT I MIGHT...
ばさっ
FWIP
..START BY PLAYING DRESS UP.

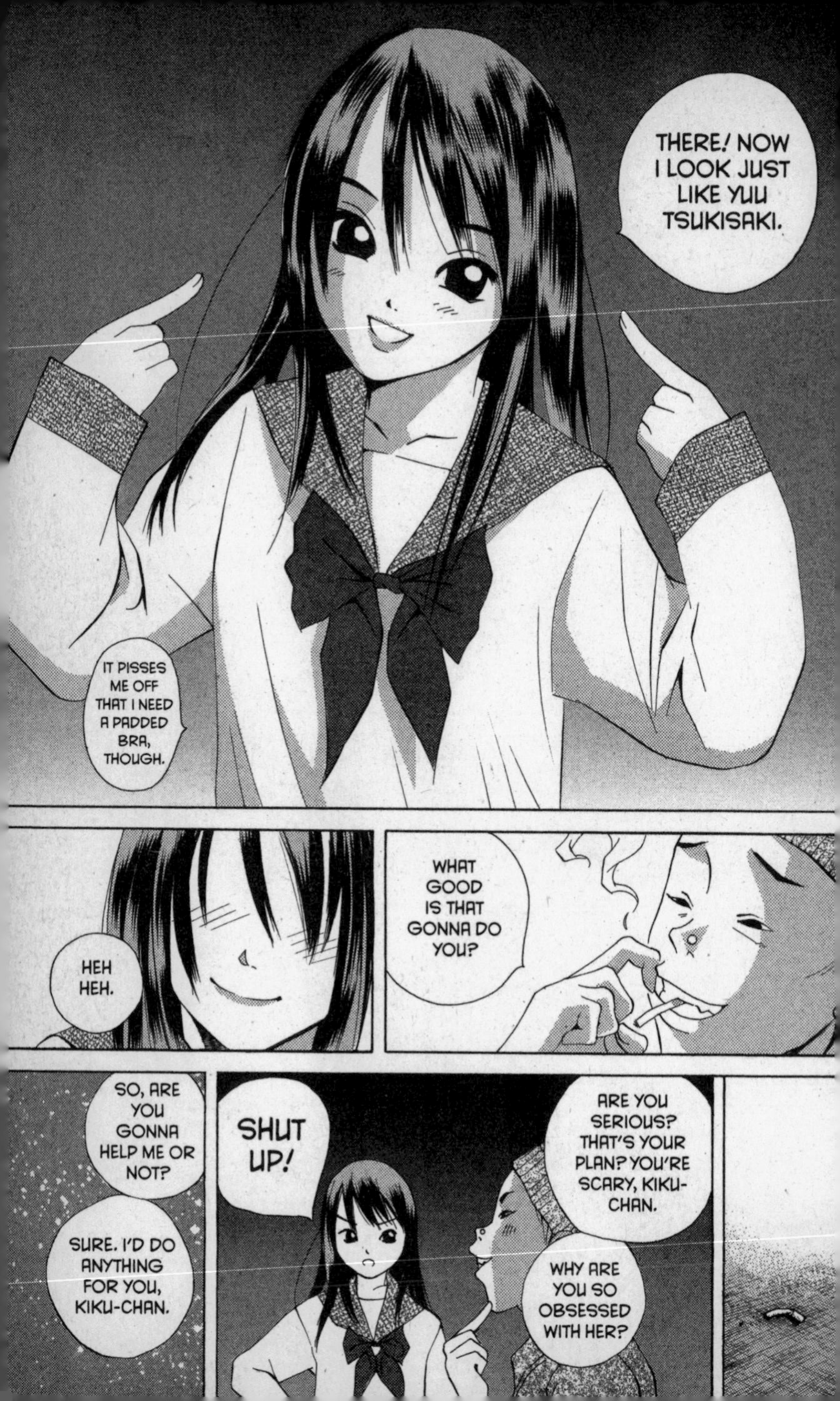
THERE! NOW I LOOK JUST LIKE YUU TSUKISAKI.
IT PISSES ME OFF THAT I NEED A PADDED BRA, THOUGH.
WHAT GOOD IS THAT GONNA DO YOU?
HEH HEH.
ARE YOU SERIOUS? THAT'S YOUR PLAN? YOU'RE SCARY, KIKU-CHAN.
WHY ARE YOU SO OBSESSED WITH HER?
SHUT UP!
SO, ARE YOU GONNA HELP ME OR NOT?
SURE. I'D DO ANYTHING FOR YOU, KIKU-CHAN.

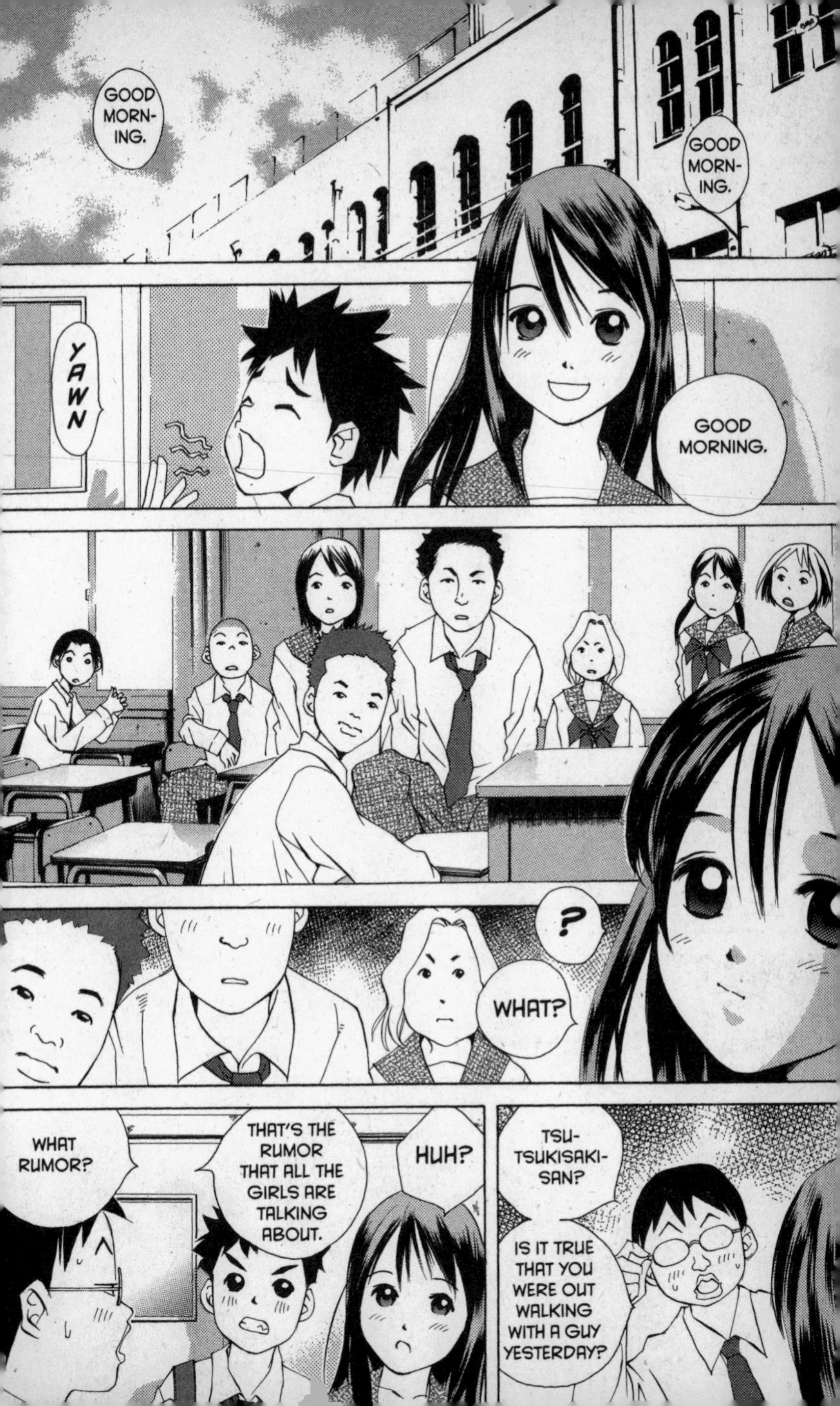
GOOD MORN-ING.
GOOD MORN-ING.
GOOD MORNING.
YAWN
?
WHAT?
TSU-TSUKISAKI-SAN?
IS IT TRUE THAT YOU WERE OUT WALKING WITH A GUY YESTERDAY?
HUH?
THAT'S THE RUMOR THAT ALL THE GIRLS ARE TALKING ABOUT.
WHAT RUMOR?

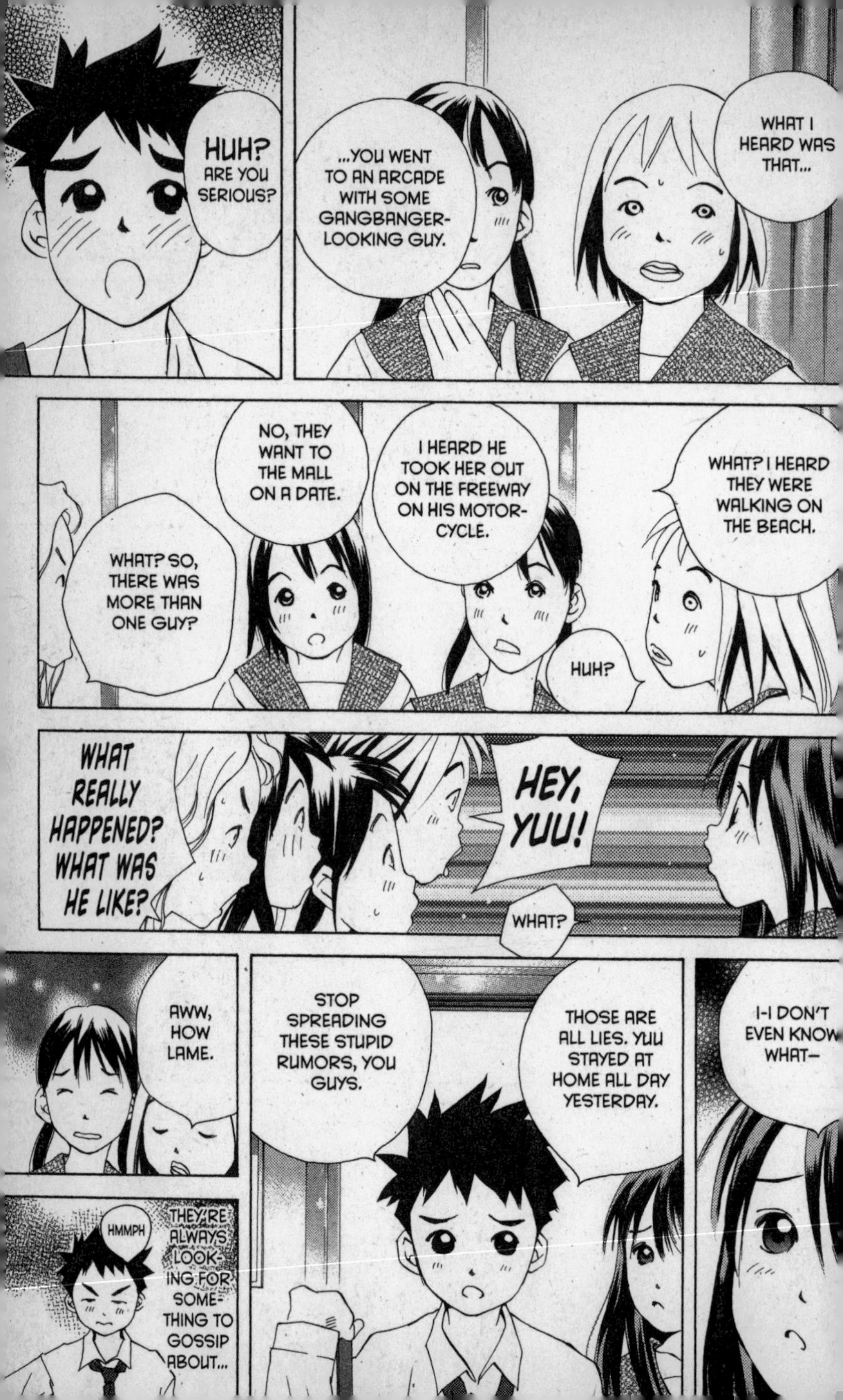
WHAT I HEARD WAS THAT...
...YOU WENT TO AN ARCADE WITH SOME GANGBANGER-LOOKING GUY.
HUH? ARE YOU SERIOUS?
WHAT? I HEARD THEY WERE WALKING ON THE BEACH.
I HEARD HE TOOK HER OUT ON THE FREEWAY ON HIS MOTOR-CYCLE.
NO, THEY WANT TO THE MALL ON A DATE.
HUH?
WHAT? SO, THERE WAS MORE THAN ONE GUY?
HEY, YUU!
WHAT?
WHAT REALLY HAPPENED? WHAT WAS HE LIKE?
I-I DON'T EVEN KNOW WHAT—
STOP SPREADING THESE STUPID RUMORS, YOU GUYS.
THOSE ARE ALL LIES. YUU STAYED AT HOME ALL DAY YESTERDAY.
AWW, HOW LAME.
HMMPH
THEY'RE ALWAYS LOOK-ING FOR SOME-THING TO GOSSIP ABOUT...

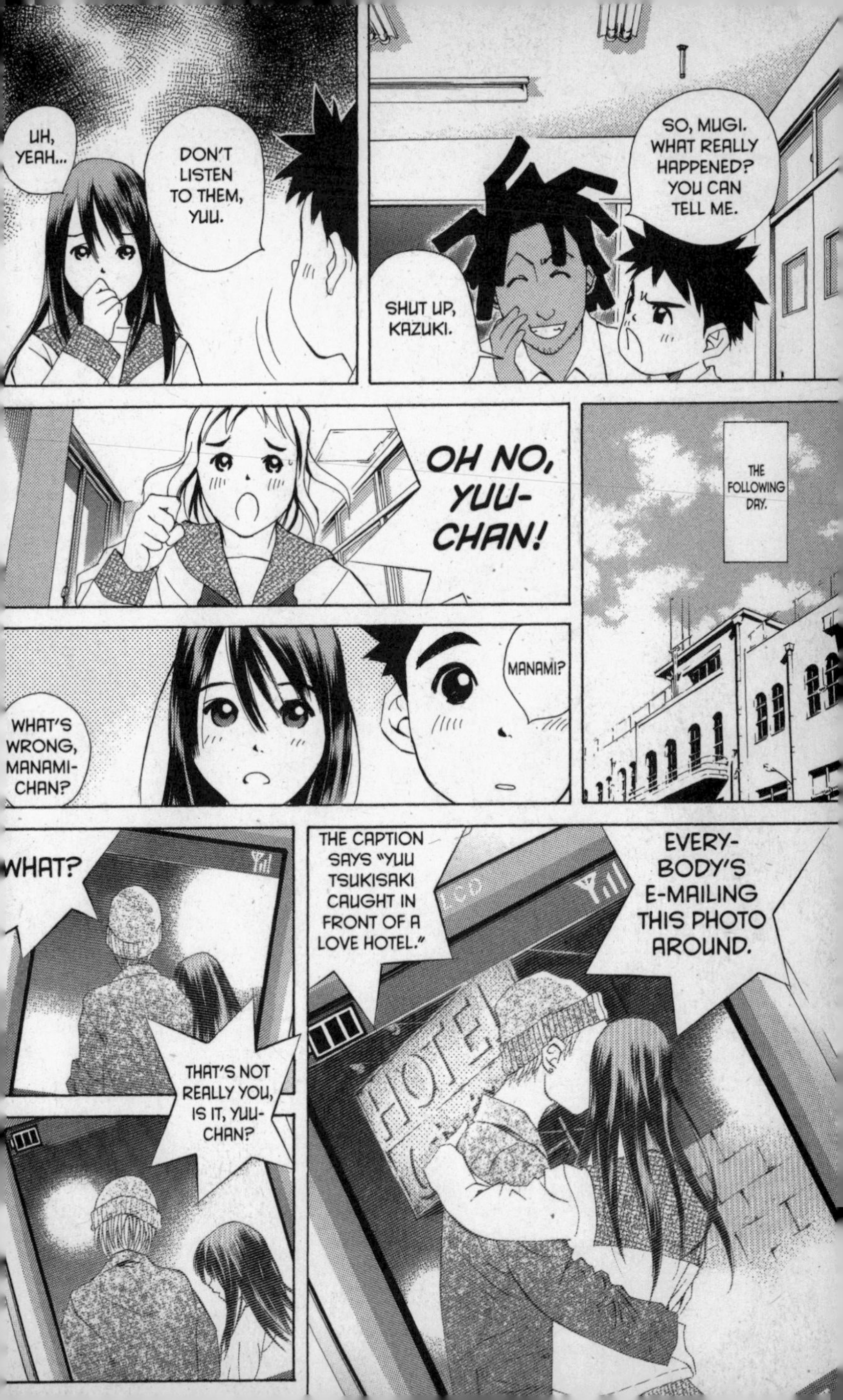
SO, MUGI. WHAT REALLY HAPPENED? YOU CAN TELL ME.
SHUT UP, KAZUKI.
DON'T LISTEN TO THEM, YUU.
UH, YEAH...
THE FOLLOWING DAY.
OH NO, YUU-CHAN!
MANAMI?
WHAT'S WRONG, MANAMI-CHAN?
EVERY-BODY'S E-MAILING THIS PHOTO AROUND.
THE CAPTION SAYS "YUU TSUKISAKI CAUGHT IN FRONT OF A LOVE HOTEL."
WHAT?
THAT'S NOT REALLY YOU, IS IT, YUU-CHAN?

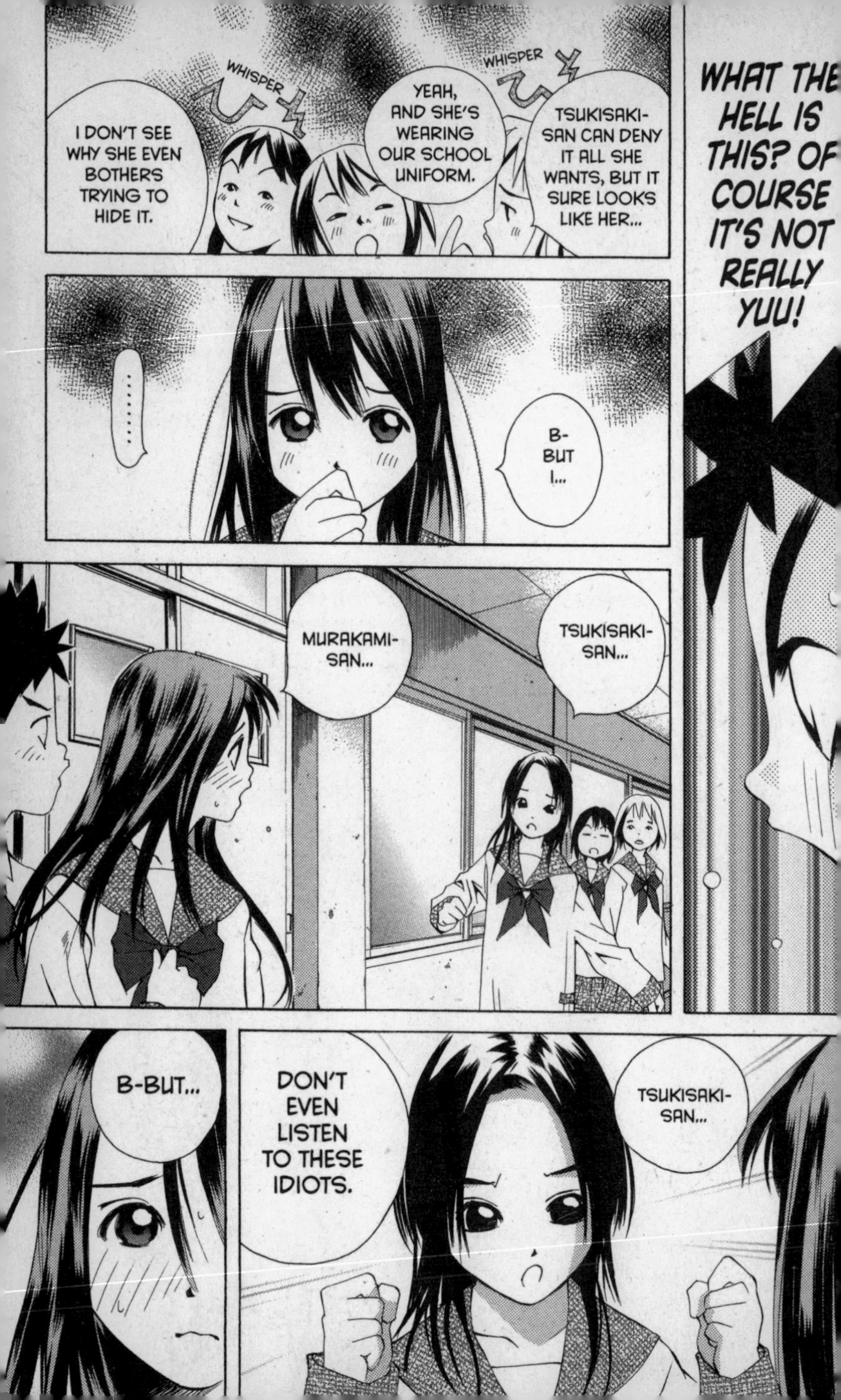
WHAT THE HELL IS THIS? OF COURSE IT'S NOT REALLY YUU!
WHISPER
TSUKISAKI-SAN CAN DENY IT ALL SHE WANTS, BUT IT SURE LOOKS LIKE HER...
YEAH, AND SHE'S WEARING OUR SCHOOL UNIFORM.
WHISPER
I DON'T SEE WHY SHE EVEN BOTHERS TRYING TO HIDE IT.
B-BUT I...
....
TSUKISAKI-SAN...
MURAKAMI-SAN...
TSUKISAKI-SAN...
DON'T EVEN LISTEN TO THESE IDIOTS.
B-BUT...

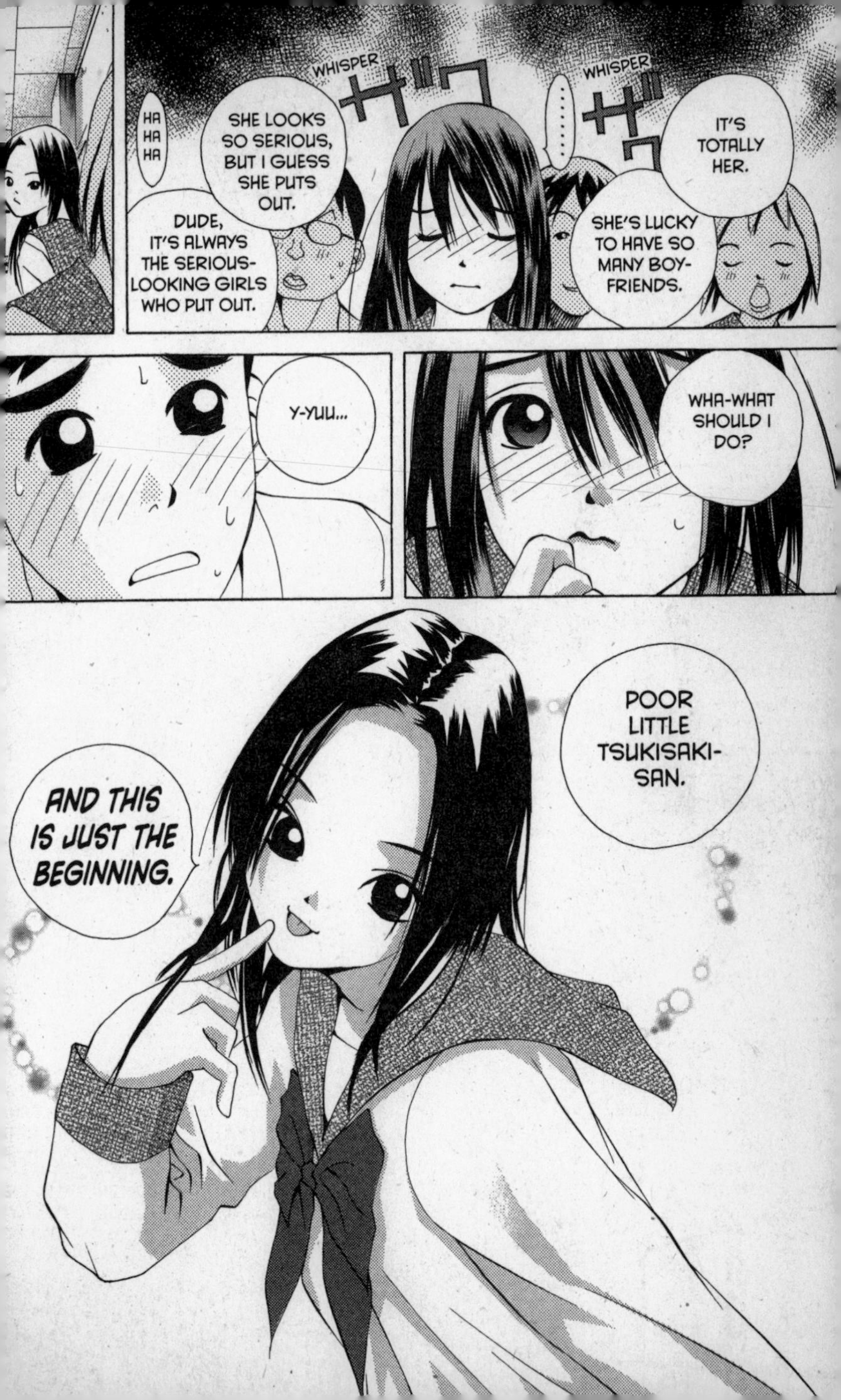
WHISPER
IT'S TOTALLY HER.
......
SHE'S LUCKY TO HAVE SO MANY BOY-FRIENDS.
WHISPER
SHE LOOKS SO SERIOUS, BUT I GUESS SHE PUTS OUT.
HA HA HA
DUDE, IT'S ALWAYS THE SERIOUS-LOOKING GIRLS WHO PUT OUT.
WHA-WHAT SHOULD I DO?
Y-YUU...
POOR LITTLE TSUKISAKI-SAN.
AND THIS IS JUST THE BEGINNING.

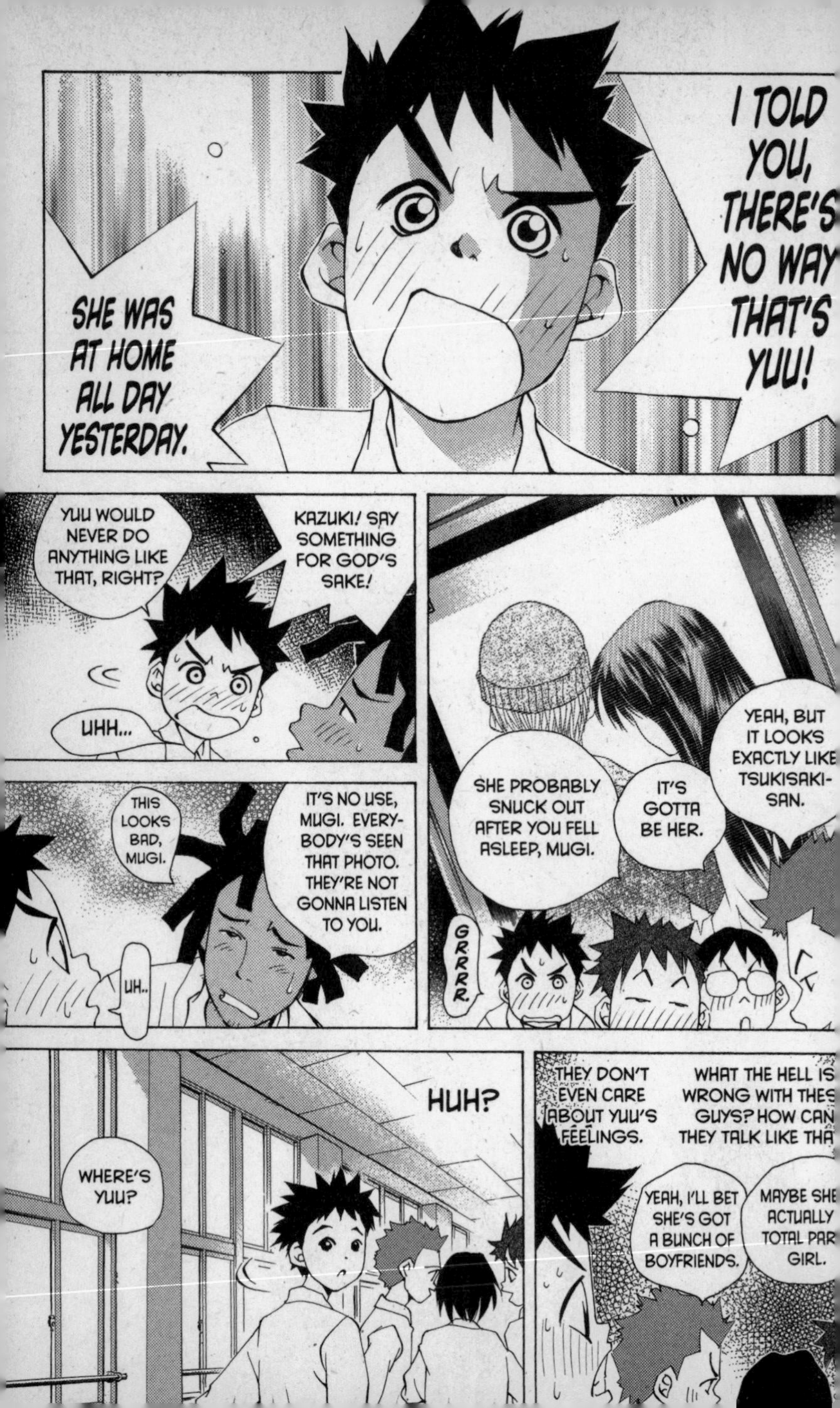
I TOLD YOU, THERE'S NO WAY THAT'S YUU!
SHE WAS AT HOME ALL DAY YESTERDAY.
YEAH, BUT IT LOOKS EXACTLY LIKE TSUKISAKI-SAN.
IT'S GOTTA BE HER.
SHE PROBABLY SNUCK OUT AFTER YOU FELL ASLEEP, MUGI.
GRRRR.
KAZUKI! SAY SOMETHING FOR GOD'S SAKE!
YUU WOULD NEVER DO ANYTHING LIKE THAT, RIGHT?
UHH...
IT'S NO USE, MUGI. EVERYBODY'S SEEN THAT PHOTO. THEY'RE NOT GONNA LISTEN TO YOU.
THIS LOOKS BAD, MUGI.
UH..
WHAT THE HELL IS WRONG WITH THES GUYS? HOW CAN THEY TALK LIKE THA
THEY DON'T EVEN CARE ABOUT YUU'S FEELINGS.
MAYBE SHE ACTUALLY TOTAL PAR GIRL.
YEAH, I'LL BET SHE'S GOT A BUNCH OF BOYFRIENDS.
HUH?
WHERE'S YUU?

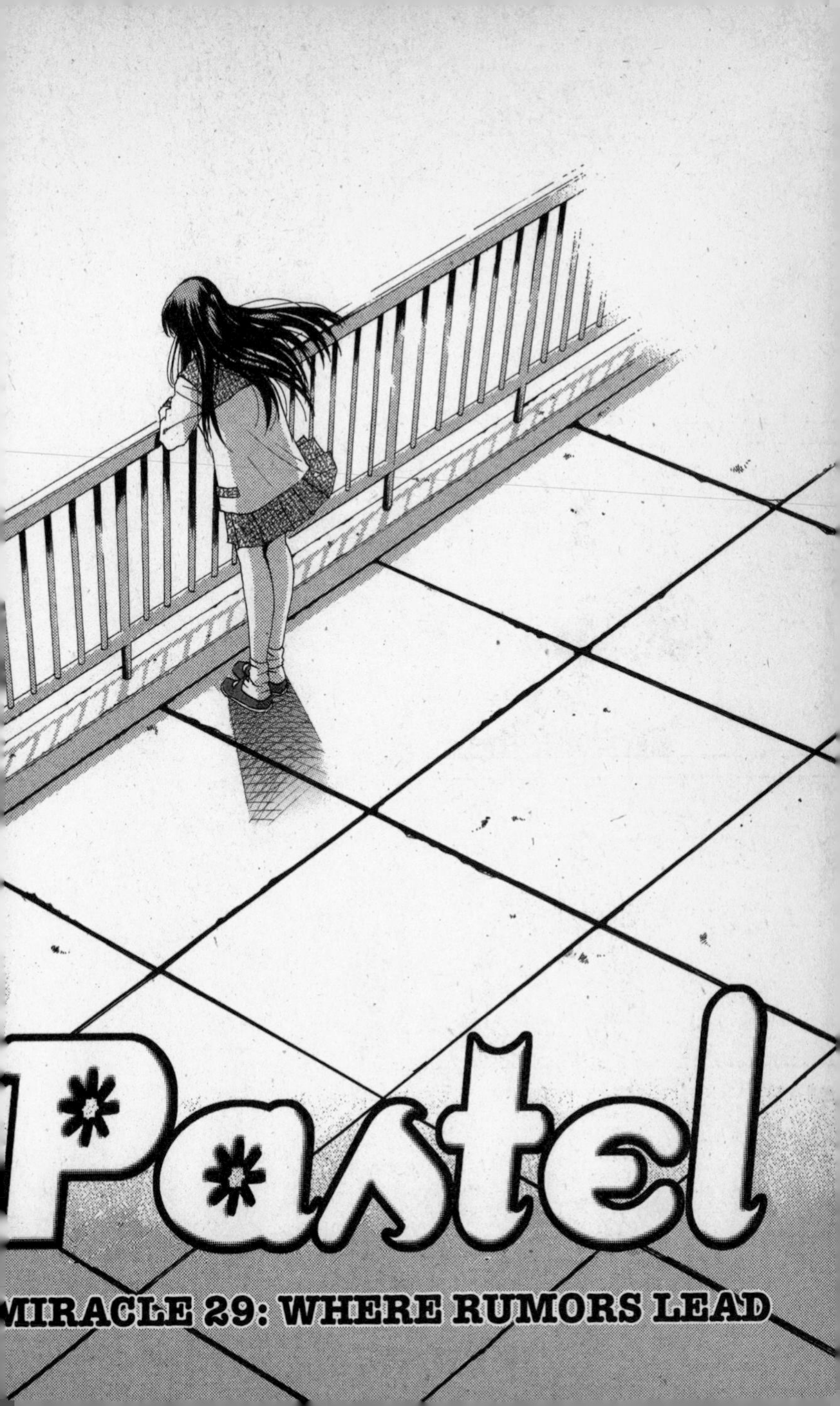

Pastel
MIRACLE 29: WHERE RUMORS LEAD

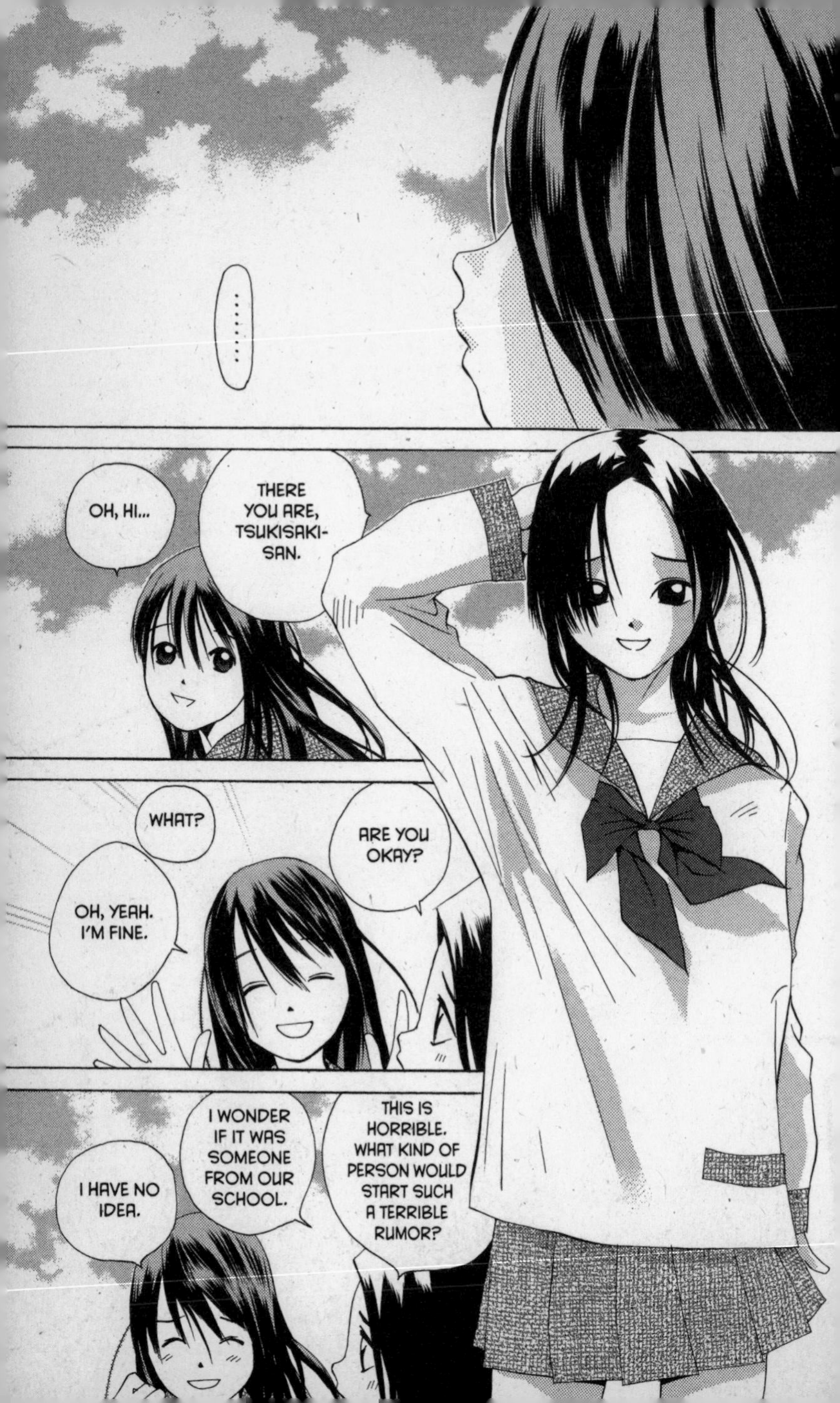
......
THERE YOU ARE, TSUKISAKI-SAN.
OH, HI...
ARE YOU OKAY?
WHAT?
OH, YEAH. I'M FINE.
THIS IS HORRIBLE. WHAT KIND OF PERSON WOULD START SUCH A TERRIBLE RUMOR?
I WONDER IF IT WAS SOMEONE FROM OUR SCHOOL.
I HAVE NO IDEA.

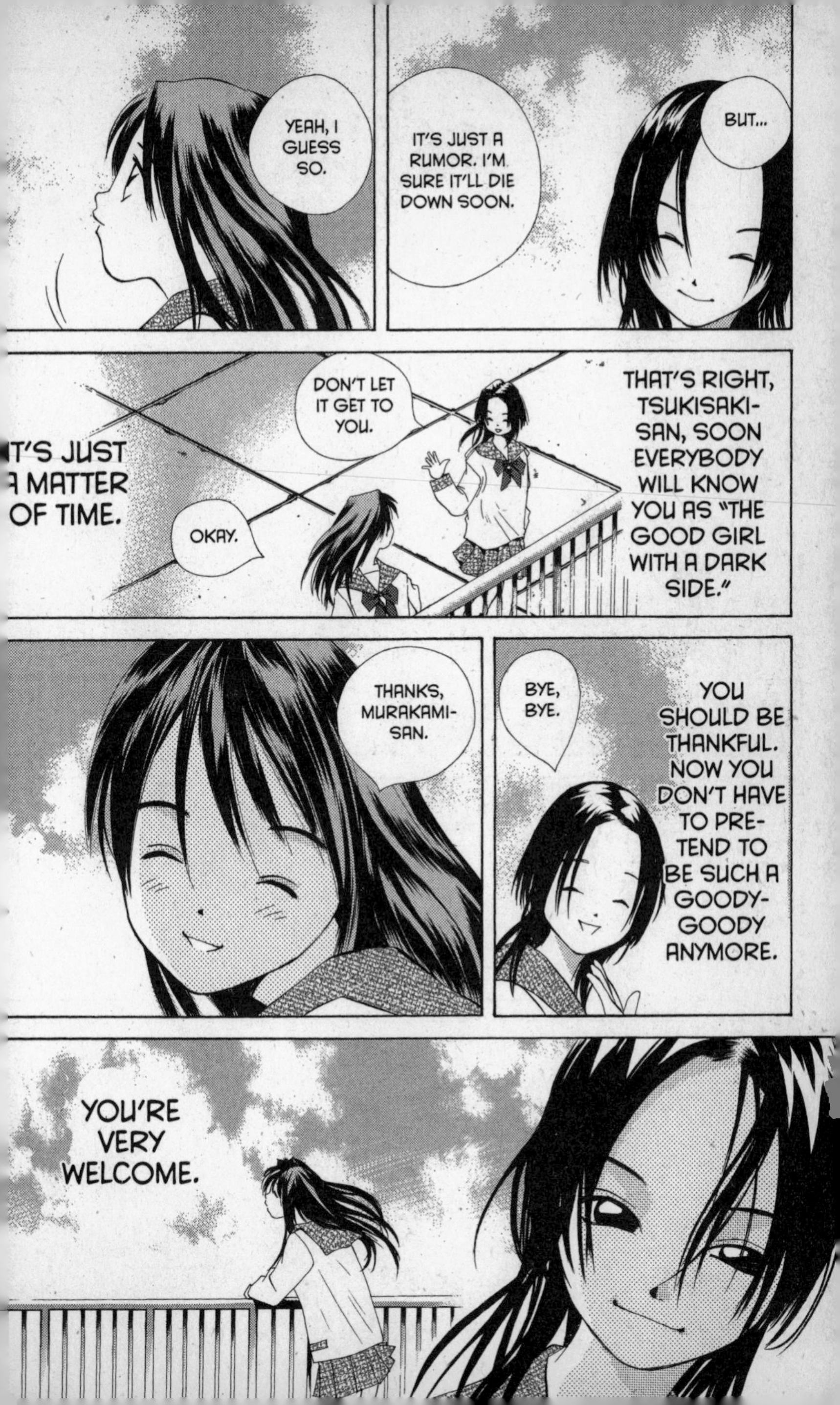
BUT...
IT'S JUST A RUMOR. I'M SURE IT'LL DIE DOWN SOON.
YEAH, I GUESS SO.
THAT'S RIGHT, TSUKISAKI-SAN, SOON EVERYBODY WILL KNOW YOU AS "THE GOOD GIRL WITH A DARK SIDE."
DON'T LET IT GET TO YOU.
OKAY.
IT'S JUST A MATTER OF TIME.
YOU SHOULD BE THANKFUL. NOW YOU DON'T HAVE TO PRE-TEND TO BE SUCH A GOODY-GOODY ANYMORE.
BYE, BYE.
THANKS, MURAKAMI-SAN.
YOU'RE VERY WELCOME.

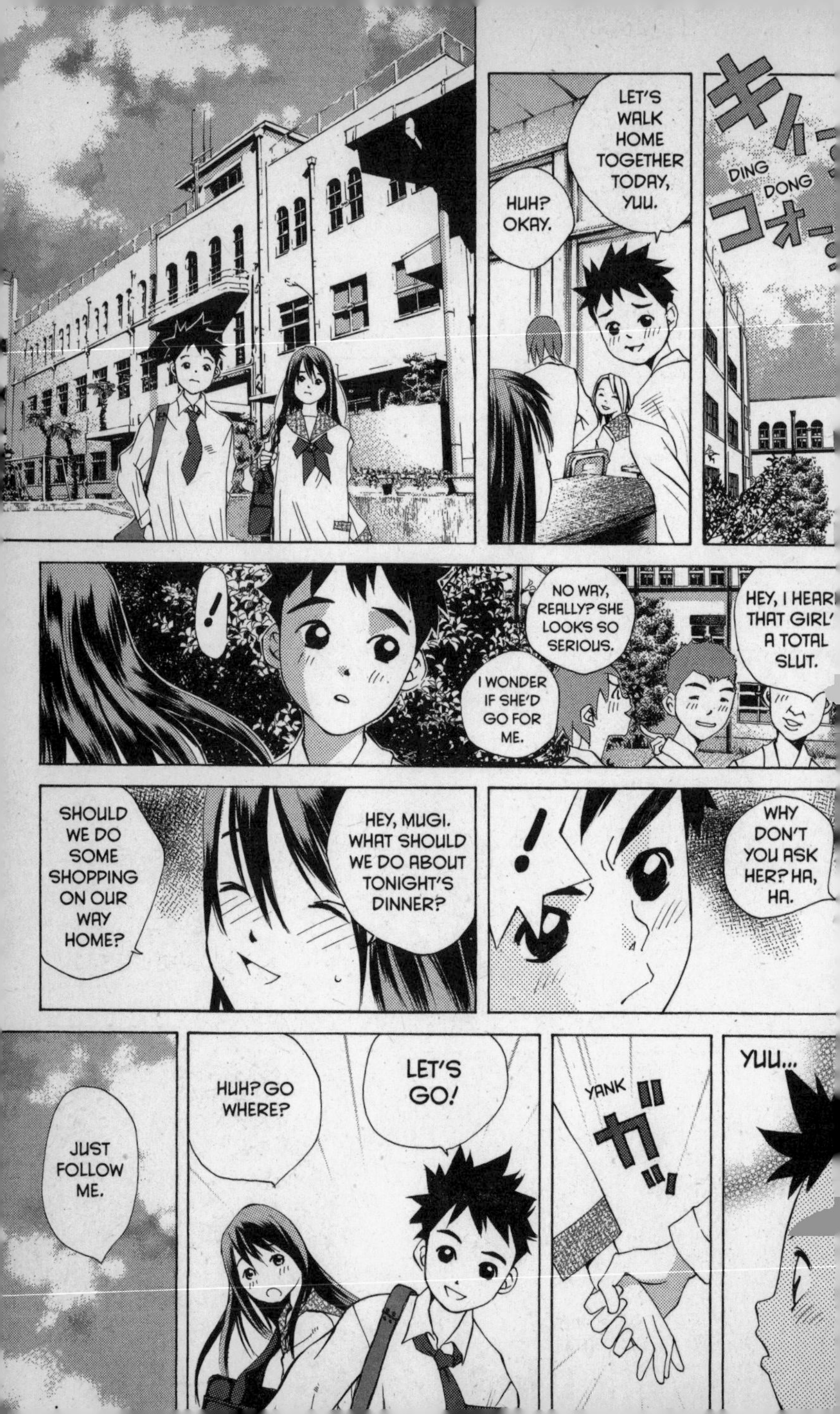

DING
DONG
LET'S WALK HOME TOGETHER TODAY, YUU.
HUH? OKAY.
HEY, I HEAR THAT GIRL' A TOTAL SLUT.
NO WAY, REALLY? SHE LOOKS SO SERIOUS.
I WONDER IF SHE'D GO FOR ME.
!
WHY DON'T YOU ASK HER? HA, HA.
!
HEY, MUGI. WHAT SHOULD WE DO ABOUT TONIGHT'S DINNER?
SHOULD WE DO SOME SHOPPING ON OUR WAY HOME?
YUU...
YANK
LET'S GO!
HUH? GO WHERE?
JUST FOLLOW ME.

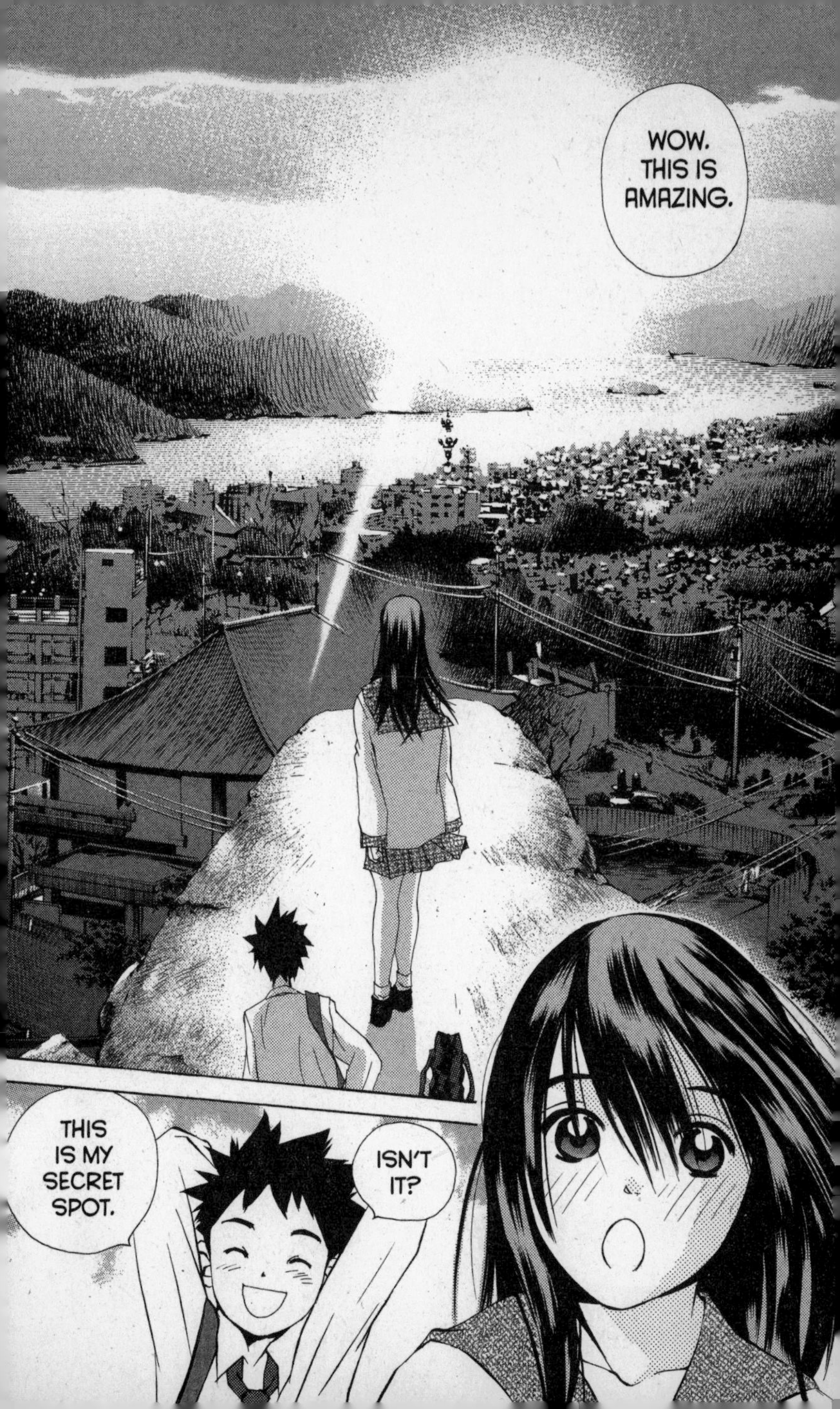
WOW. THIS IS AMAZING.
ISN'T IT?
THIS IS MY SECRET SPOT.

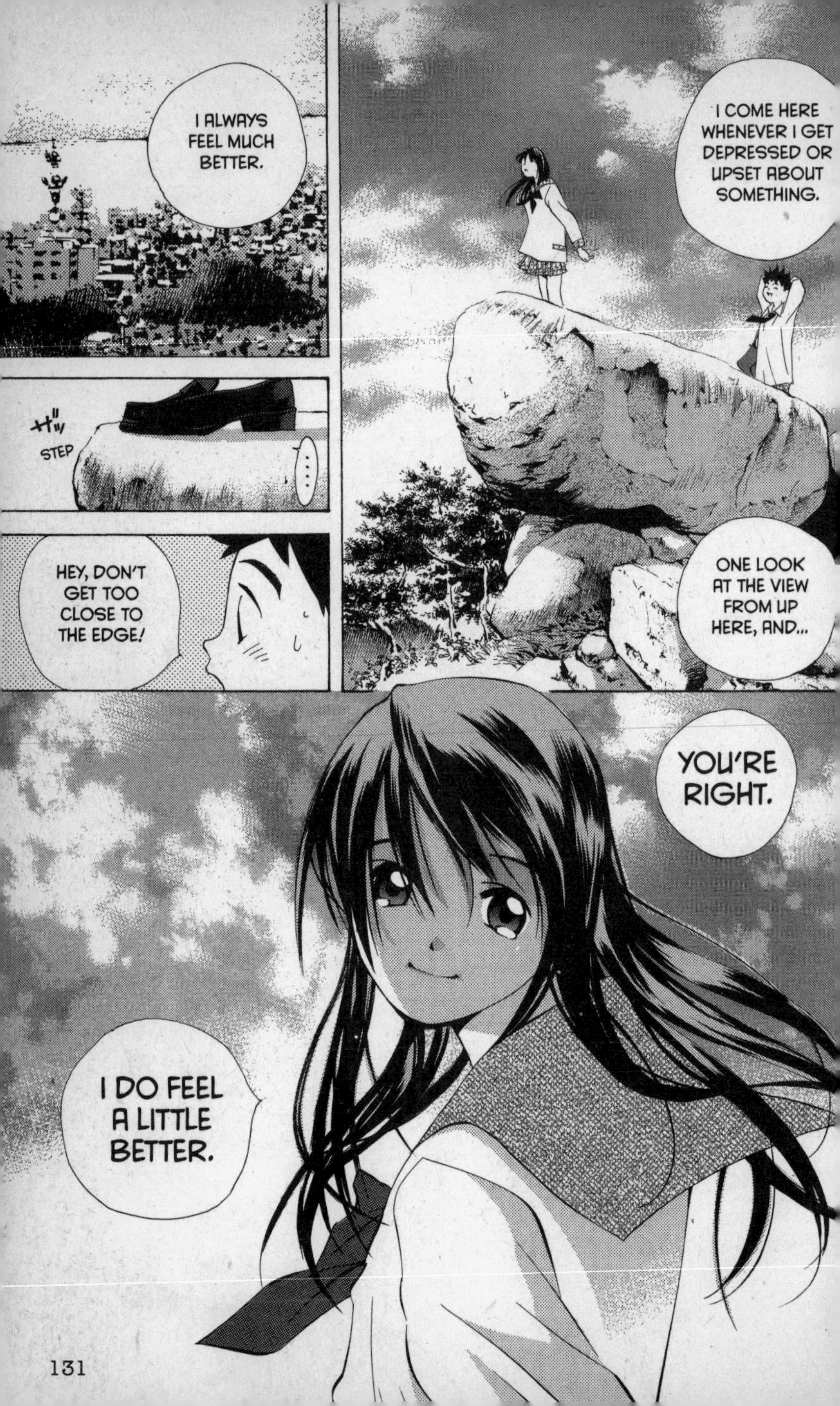
I COME HERE WHENEVER I GET DEPRESSED OR UPSET ABOUT SOMETHING.
ONE LOOK AT THE VIEW FROM UP HERE, AND...
I ALWAYS FEEL MUCH BETTER.
STEP
.....
HEY, DON'T GET TOO CLOSE TO THE EDGE!
YOU'RE RIGHT.
I DO FEEL A LITTLE BETTER.

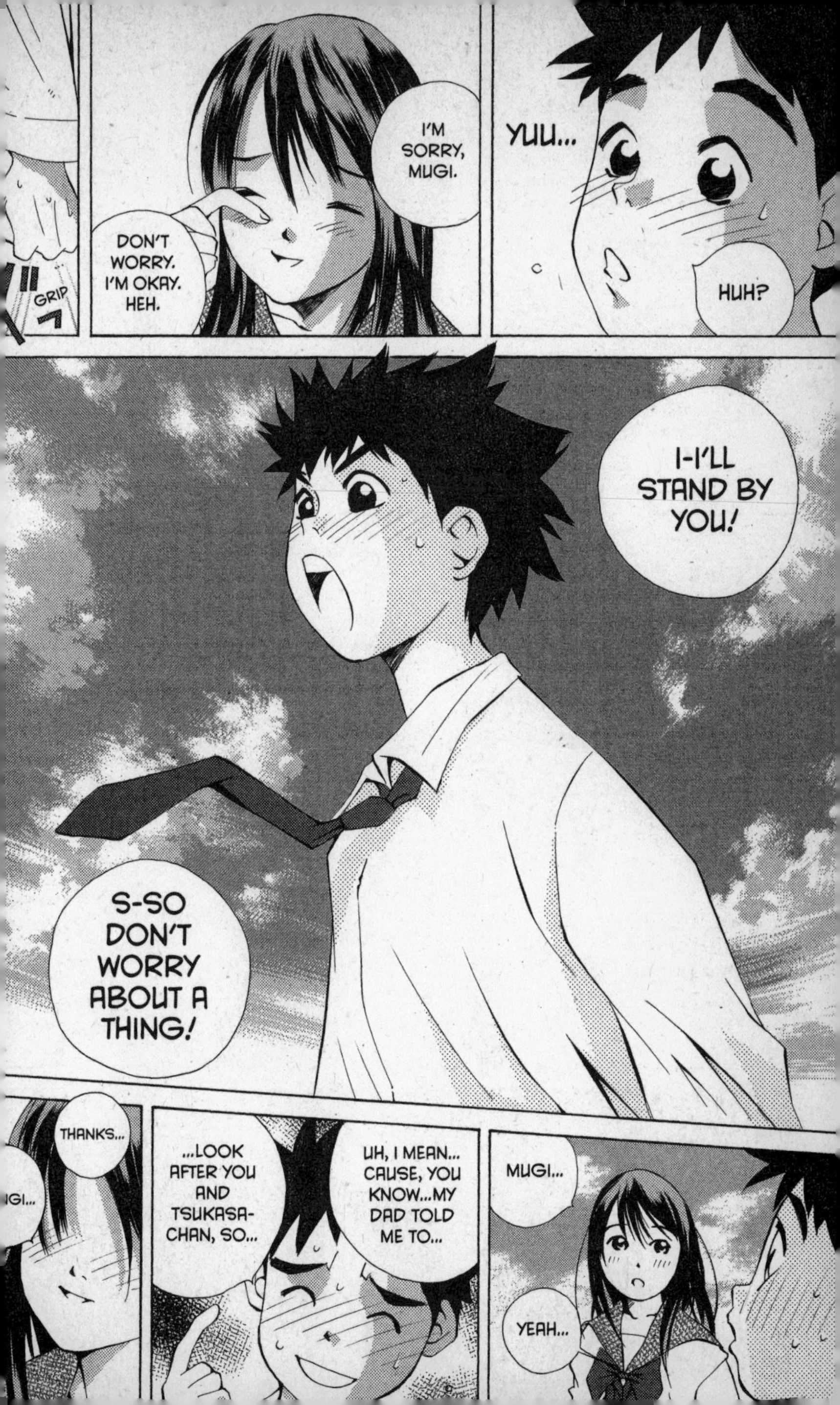
YUU...
HUH?
I'M SORRY, MUGI.
DON'T WORRY. I'M OKAY. HEH.
GRIP
I-I'LL STAND BY YOU!
S-SO DON'T WORRY ABOUT A THING!
MUGI...
YEAH...
UH, I MEAN... CAUSE, YOU KNOW...MY DAD TOLD ME TO...
...LOOK AFTER YOU AND TSUKASA-CHAN, SO...
THANKS...

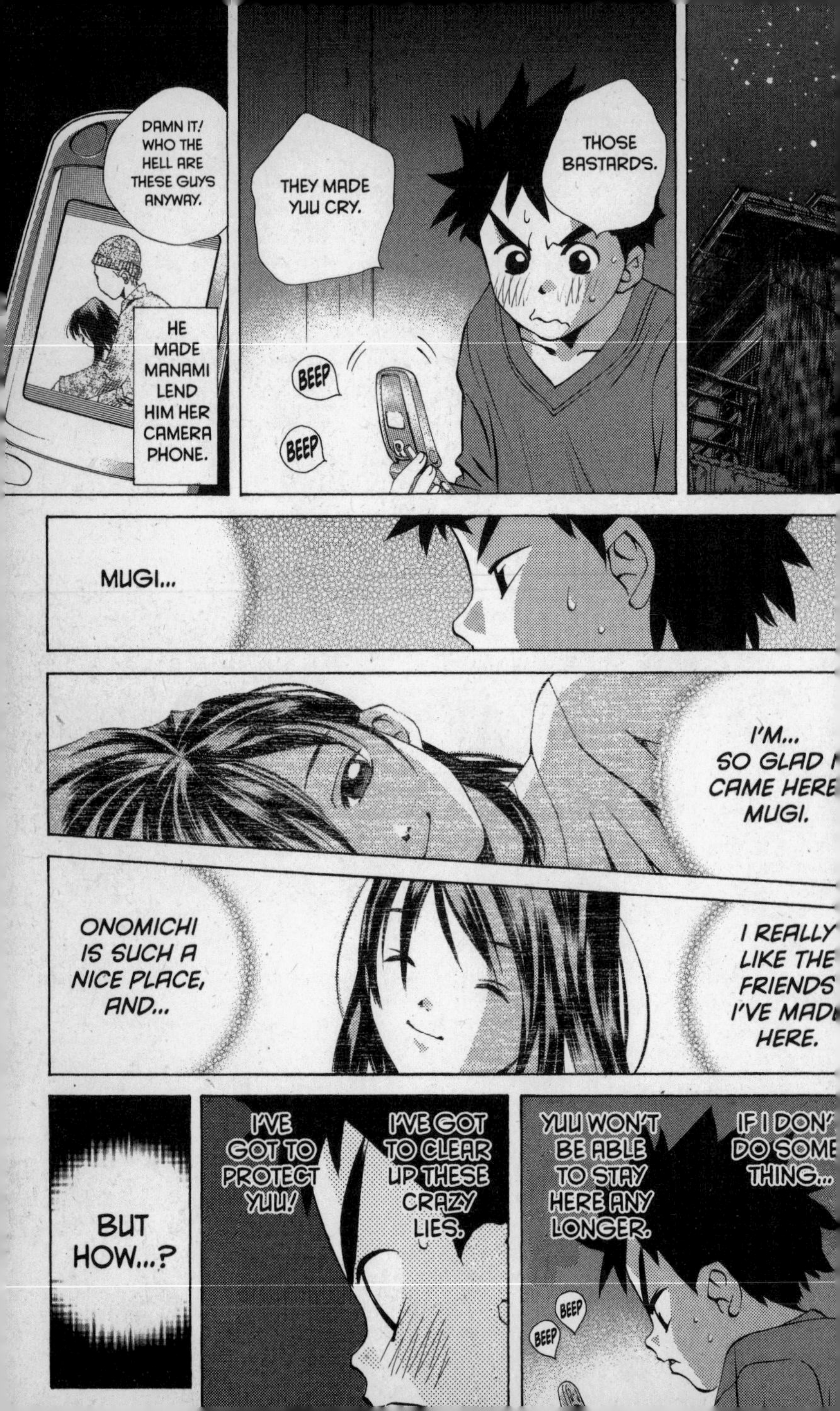
THOSE BASTARDS.
THEY MADE YUU CRY.
BEEP
BEEP
DAMN IT! WHO THE HELL ARE THESE GUYS ANYWAY.
HE MADE MANAMI LEND HIM HER CAMERA PHONE.
MUGI...
I'M... SO GLAD I CAME HERE MUGI.
I REALLY LIKE THE FRIENDS I'VE MADE HERE.
ONOMICHI IS SUCH A NICE PLACE, AND...
IF I DON'T DO SOMETHING...
YUU WON'T BE ABLE TO STAY HERE ANY LONGER.
BEEP
BEEP
I'VE GOT TO CLEAR UP THESE CRAZY LIES.
I'VE GOT TO PROTECT YUU!
BUT HOW...?

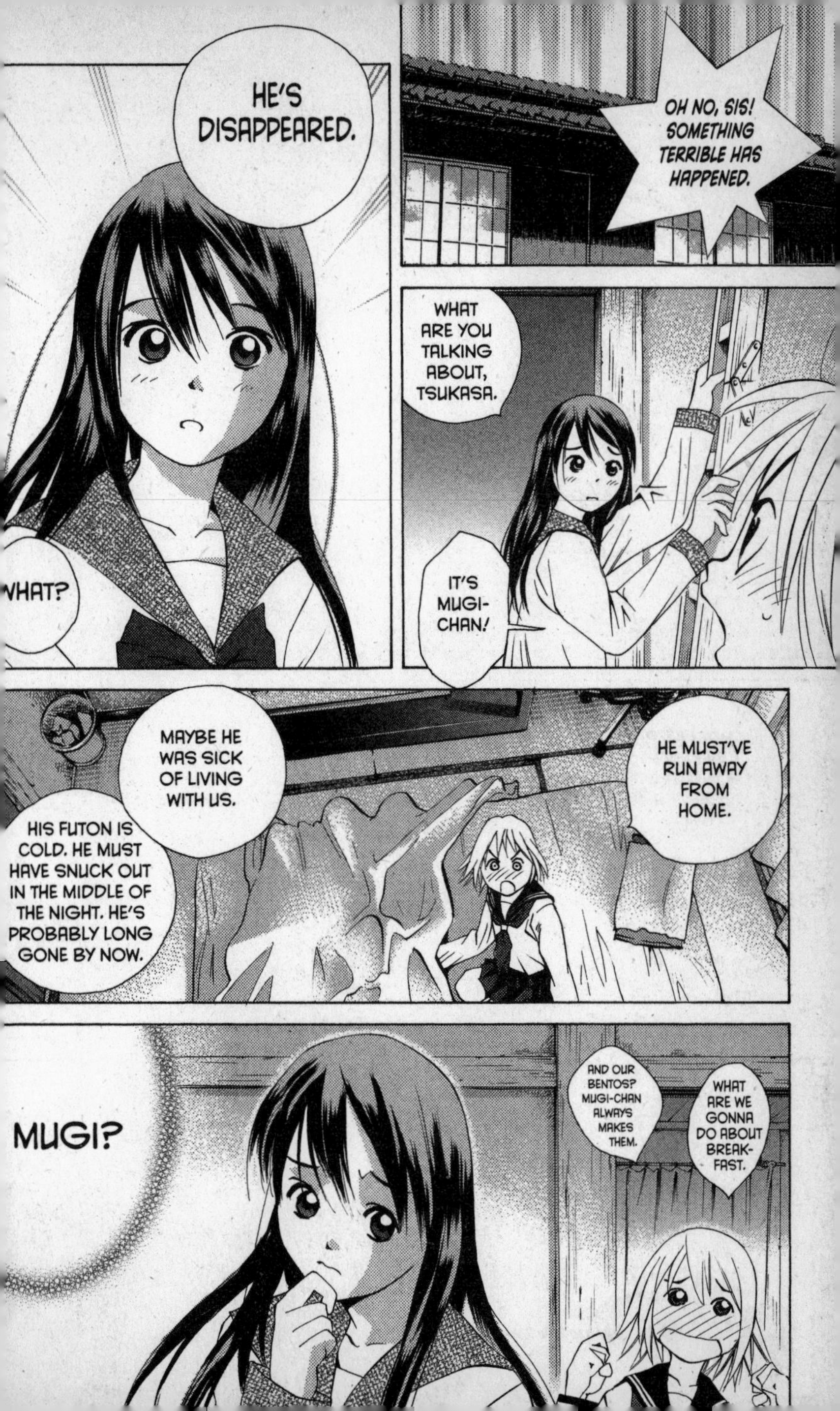
OH NO, SIS! SOMETHING TERRIBLE HAS HAPPENED.
WHAT ARE YOU TALKING ABOUT, TSUKASA.
IT'S MUGI-CHAN!
HE'S DISAPPEARED.
WHAT?
HE MUST'VE RUN AWAY FROM HOME.
MAYBE HE WAS SICK OF LIVING WITH US.
HIS FUTON IS COLD. HE MUST HAVE SNUCK OUT IN THE MIDDLE OF THE NIGHT. HE'S PROBABLY LONG GONE BY NOW.
WHAT ARE WE GONNA DO ABOUT BREAK-FAST.
AND OUR BENTOS? MUGI-CHAN ALWAYS MAKES THEM.
MUGI?

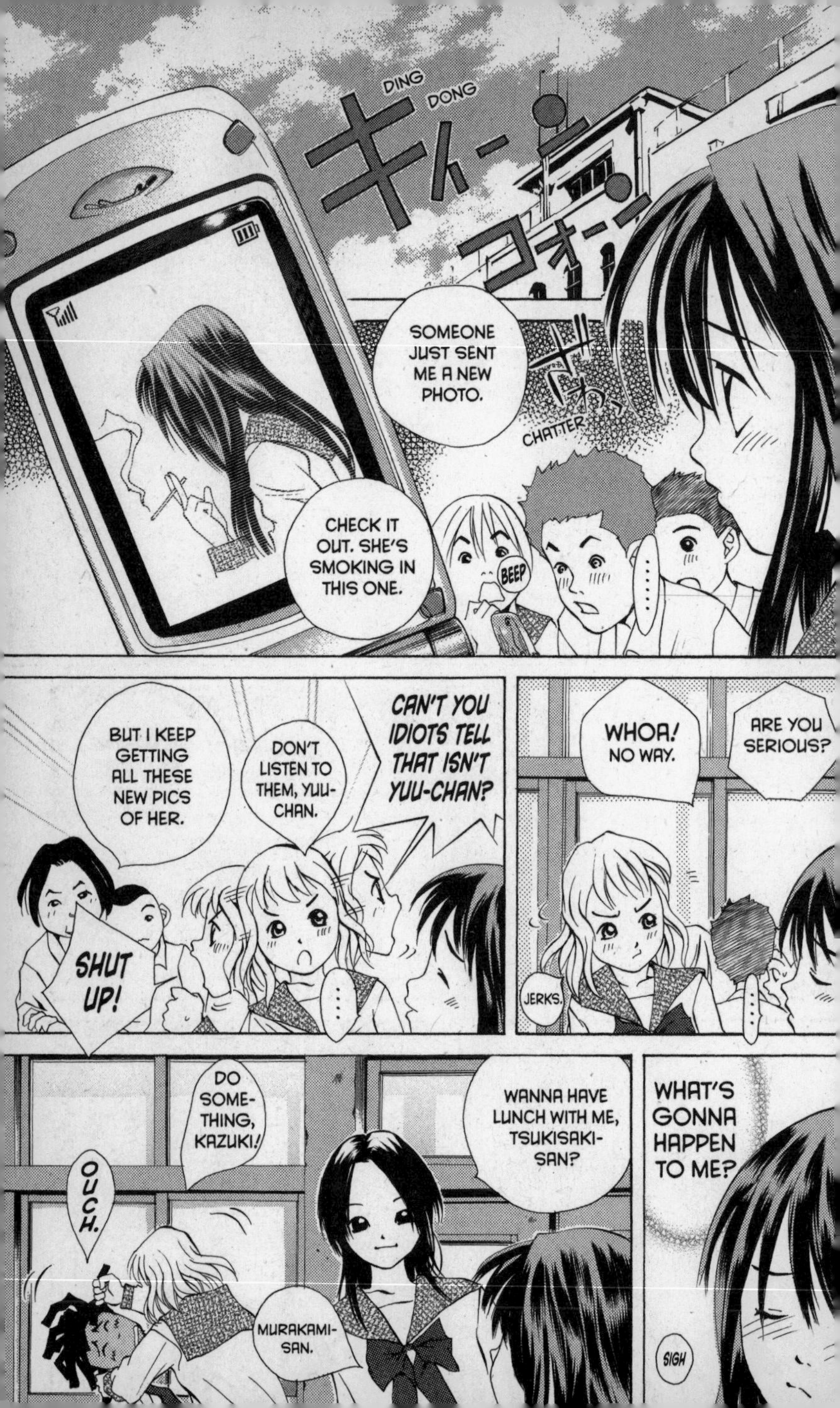
DING
DONG
SOMEONE JUST SENT ME A NEW PHOTO.
CHATTER
.....
CHECK IT OUT. SHE'S SMOKING IN THIS ONE.
BEEP
ARE YOU SERIOUS?
WHOA! NO WAY.
JERKS.
.....
CAN'T YOU IDIOTS TELL THAT ISN'T YUU-CHAN?
DON'T LISTEN TO THEM, YUU-CHAN.
BUT I KEEP GETTING ALL THESE NEW PICS OF HER.
.....
SHUT UP!
WHAT'S GONNA HAPPEN TO ME?
SIGH
WANNA HAVE LUNCH WITH ME, TSUKISAKI-SAN?
DO SOMETHING, KAZUKI!
OUCH.
MURAKAMI-SAN.

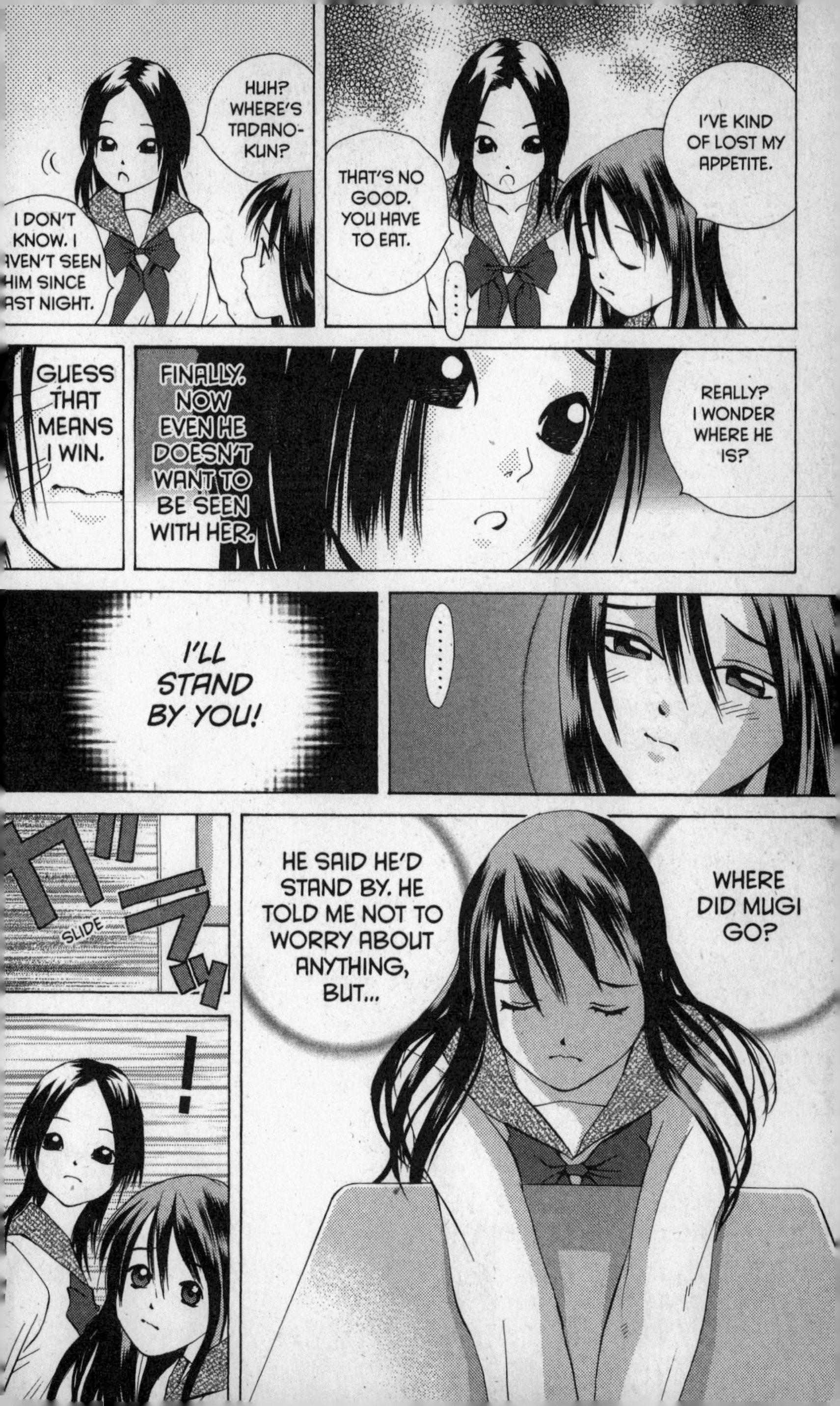
I'VE KIND OF LOST MY APPETITE.
THAT'S NO GOOD. YOU HAVE TO EAT.
......
HUH? WHERE'S TADANO-KUN?
I DON'T KNOW. I AVEN'T SEEN HIM SINCE AST NIGHT.
REALLY? I WONDER WHERE HE IS?
FINALLY. NOW EVEN HE DOESN'T WANT TO BE SEEN WITH HER.
GUESS THAT MEANS I WIN.
......
I'LL STAND BY YOU!
WHERE DID MUGI GO?
HE SAID HE'D STAND BY. HE TOLD ME NOT TO WORRY ABOUT ANYTHING, BUT...
SLIDE
!

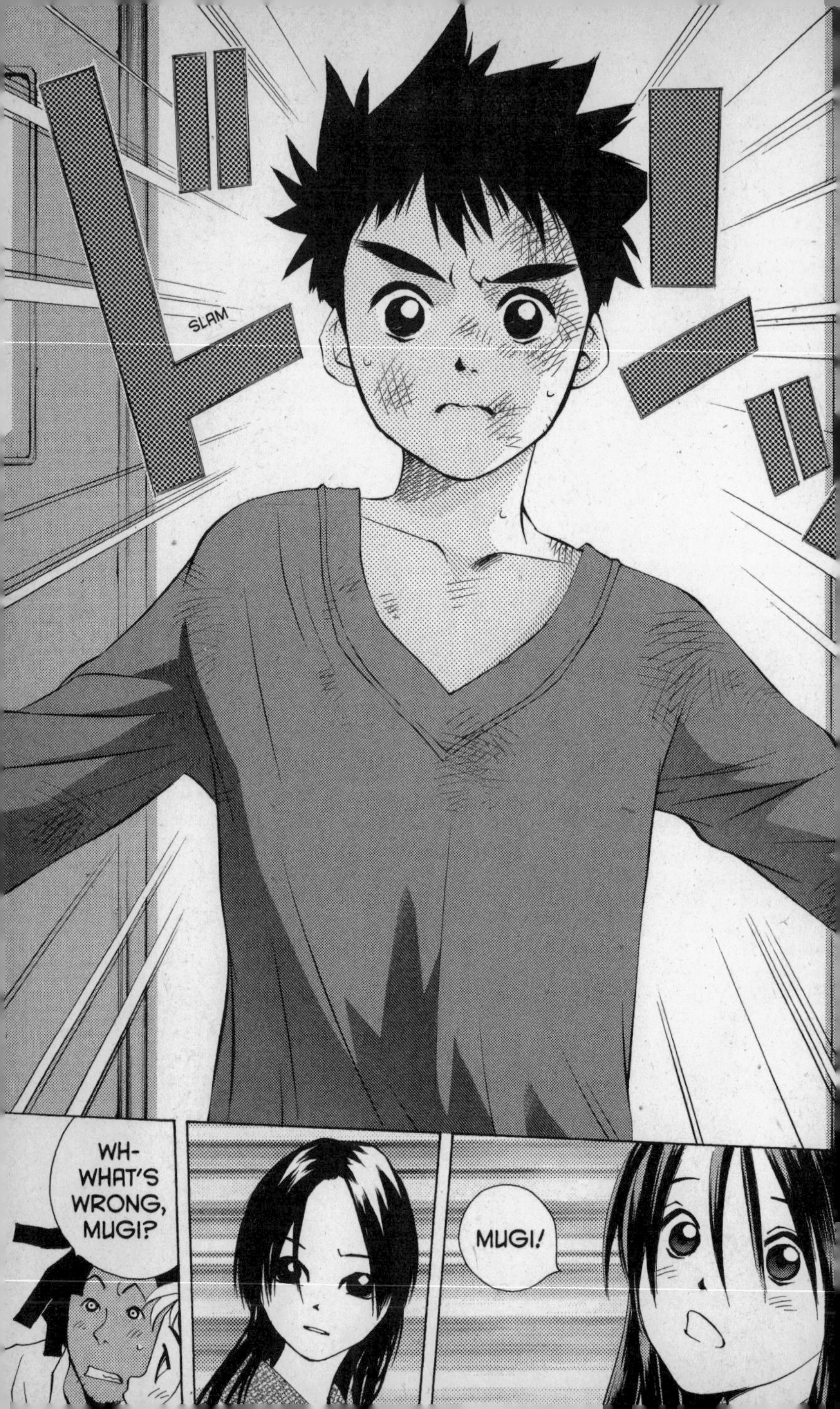
SLAM
MUGI!
WH-
WHAT'S
WRONG,
MUGI?

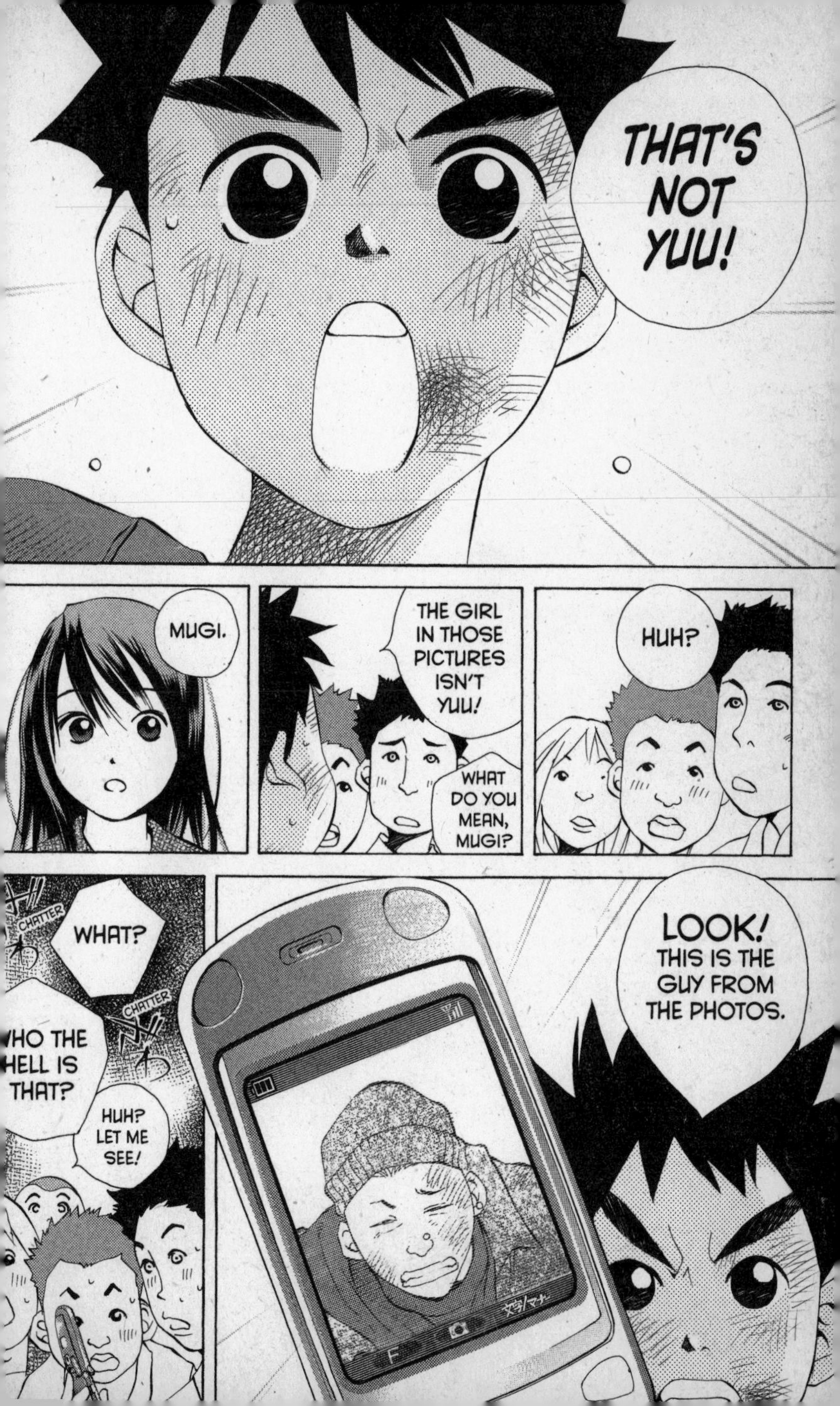
THAT'S NOT YUU!
HUH?
THE GIRL IN THOSE PICTURES ISN'T YUU!
WHAT DO YOU MEAN, MUGI?
MUGI.
LOOK! THIS IS THE GUY FROM THE PHOTOS.
CHATTER
WHAT?
CHATTER
HO THE HELL IS THAT?
HUH? LET ME SEE!

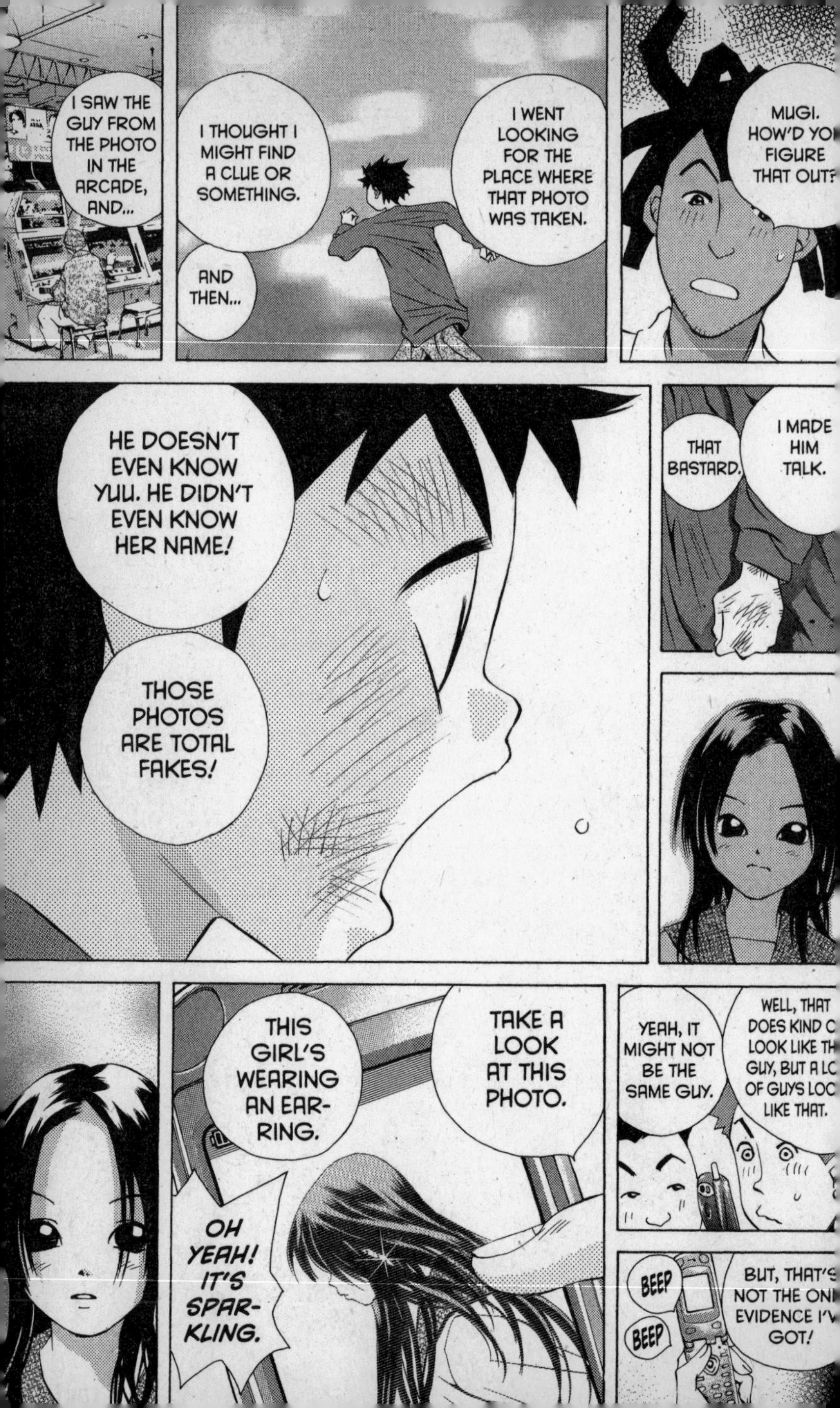
MUGI. HOW'D YO FIGURE THAT OUT?
I WENT LOOKING FOR THE PLACE WHERE THAT PHOTO WAS TAKEN.
I THOUGHT I MIGHT FIND A CLUE OR SOMETHING.
AND THEN...
I SAW THE GUY FROM THE PHOTO IN THE ARCADE, AND...
I MADE HIM TALK.
THAT BASTARD.
HE DOESN'T EVEN KNOW YUU. HE DIDN'T EVEN KNOW HER NAME!
THOSE PHOTOS ARE TOTAL FAKES!
WELL, THAT DOES KIND O LOOK LIKE TH GUY, BUT A LO OF GUYS LOO LIKE THAT.
YEAH, IT MIGHT NOT BE THE SAME GUY.
BUT, THAT'S NOT THE ONL EVIDENCE I'V GOT!
BEEP
BEEP
TAKE A LOOK AT THIS PHOTO.
THIS GIRL'S WEARING AN EAR-RING.
OH YEAH! IT'S SPAR-KLING.

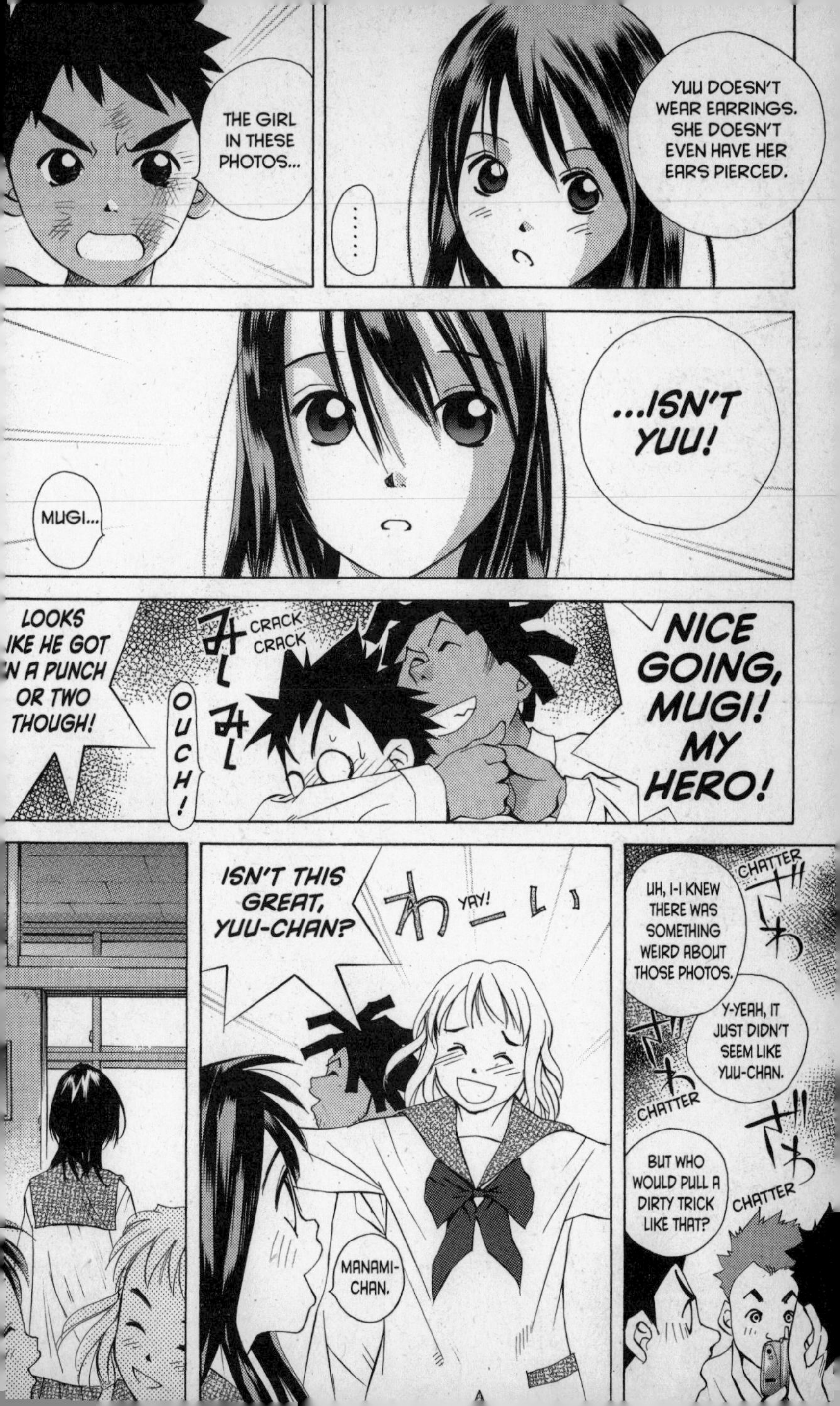

YUU DOESN'T WEAR EARRINGS. SHE DOESN'T EVEN HAVE HER EARS PIERCED.
……
THE GIRL IN THESE PHOTOS...
...ISN'T YUU!
MUGI...
NICE GOING, MUGI! MY HERO!
みしみし
CRACK CRACK
OUCH!
LOOKS
IKE HE GOT
N A PUNCH
OR TWO
THOUGH!
ざわざわ
CHATTER
UH, I-I KNEW THERE WAS SOMETHING WEIRD ABOUT THOSE PHOTOS.
Y-YEAH, IT JUST DIDN'T SEEM LIKE YUU-CHAN.
ざわざわ
CHATTER
ざわざわ
CHATTER
BUT WHO WOULD PULL A DIRTY TRICK LIKE THAT?
わーい
YAY!
ISN'T THIS GREAT, YUU-CHAN?
MANAMI-CHAN.

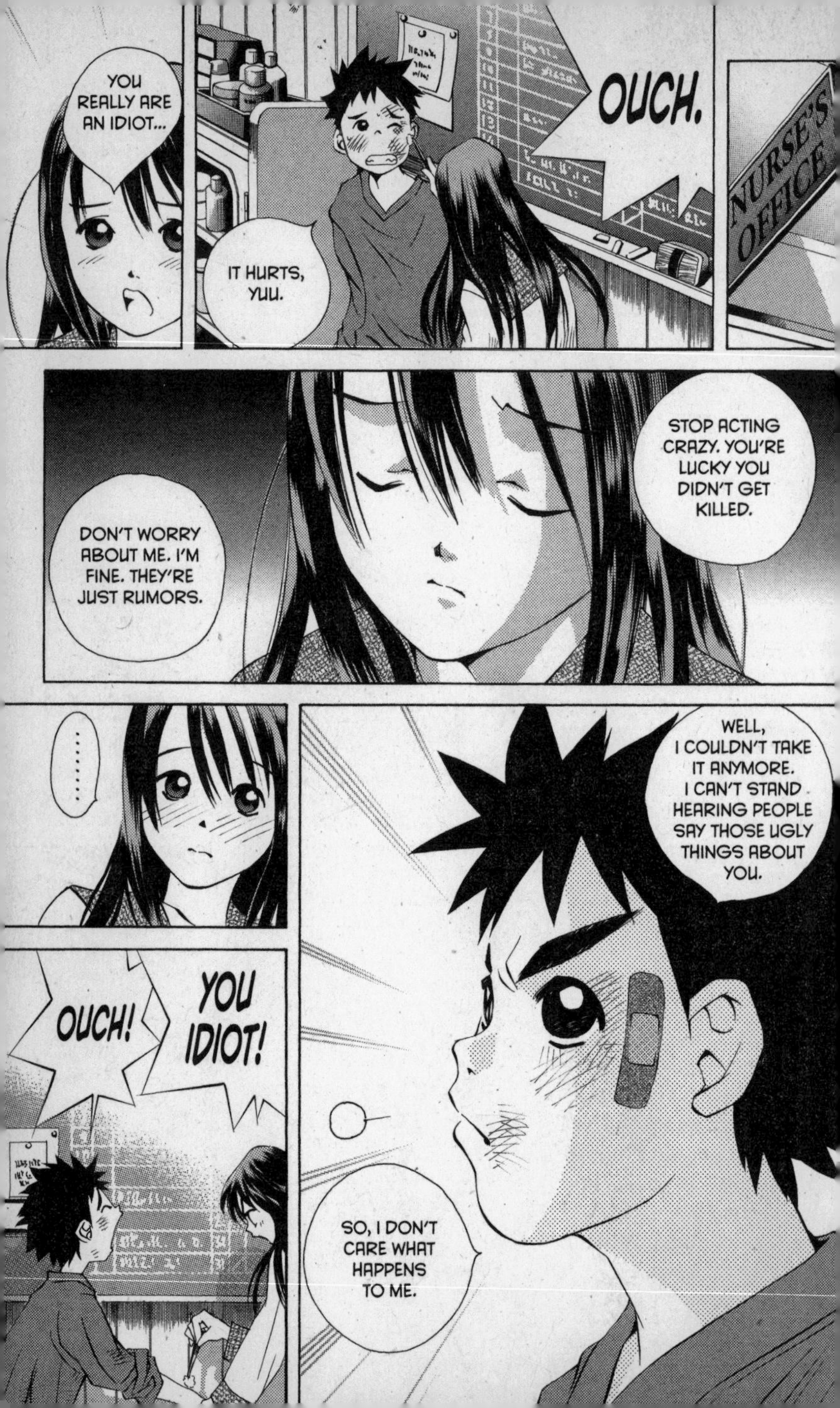
NURSE'S OFFICE
OUCH.
IT HURTS, YUU.
YOU REALLY ARE AN IDIOT...
STOP ACTING CRAZY. YOU'RE LUCKY YOU DIDN'T GET KILLED.
DON'T WORRY ABOUT ME. I'M FINE. THEY'RE JUST RUMORS.
WELL, I COULDN'T TAKE IT ANYMORE. I CAN'T STAND HEARING PEOPLE SAY THOSE UGLY THINGS ABOUT YOU.
SO, I DON'T CARE WHAT HAPPENS TO ME.
......
YOU IDIOT!
OUCH!

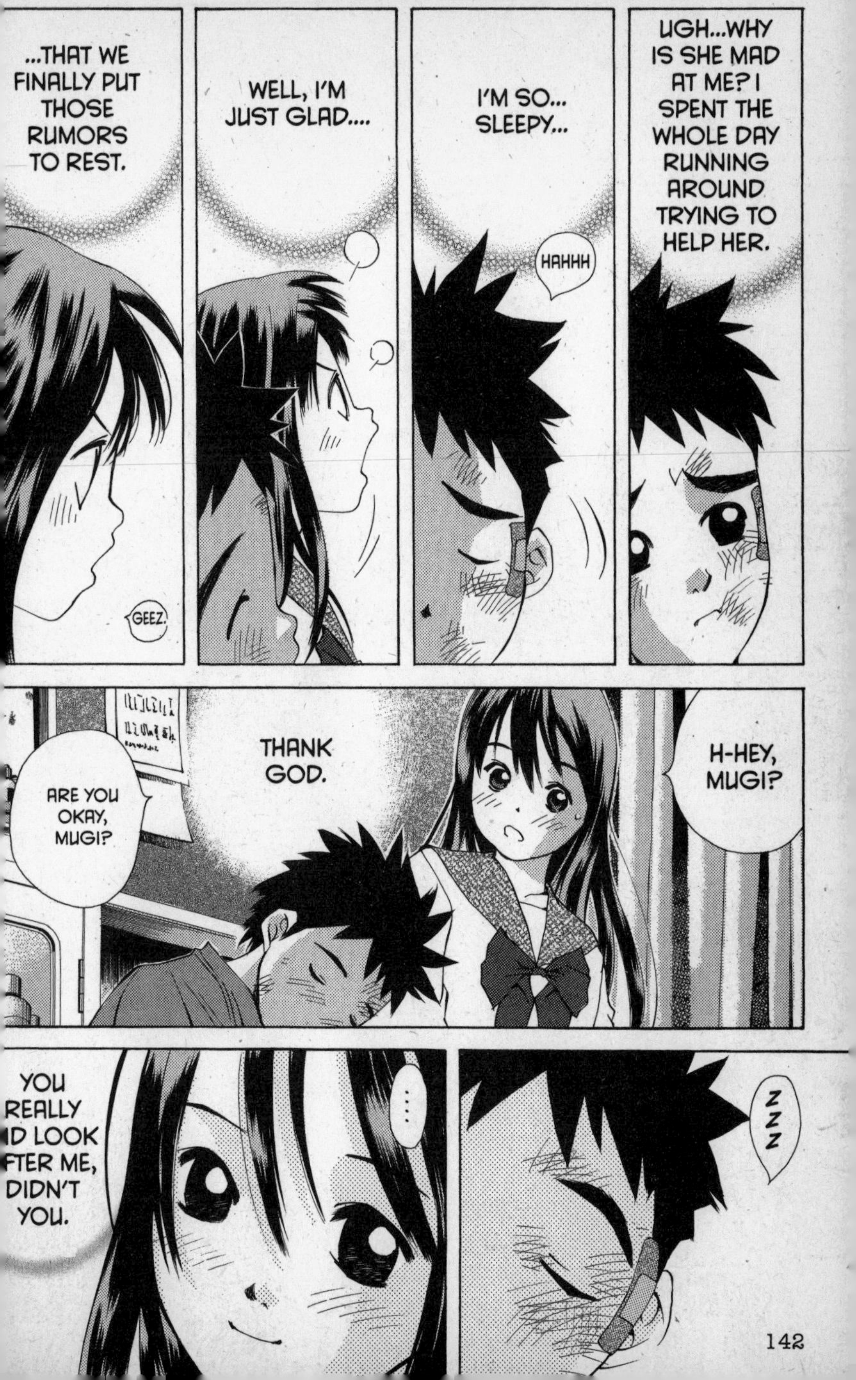
UGH...WHY IS SHE MAD AT ME? I SPENT THE WHOLE DAY RUNNING AROUND TRYING TO HELP HER.
I'M SO... SLEEPY...
HAHHH
WELL, I'M JUST GLAD....
...THAT WE FINALLY PUT THOSE RUMORS TO REST.
GEEZ.
H-HEY, MUGI?
THANK GOD.
ARE YOU OKAY, MUGI?
ZZZ
....
YOU REALLY ID LOOK FTER ME, DIDN'T YOU.

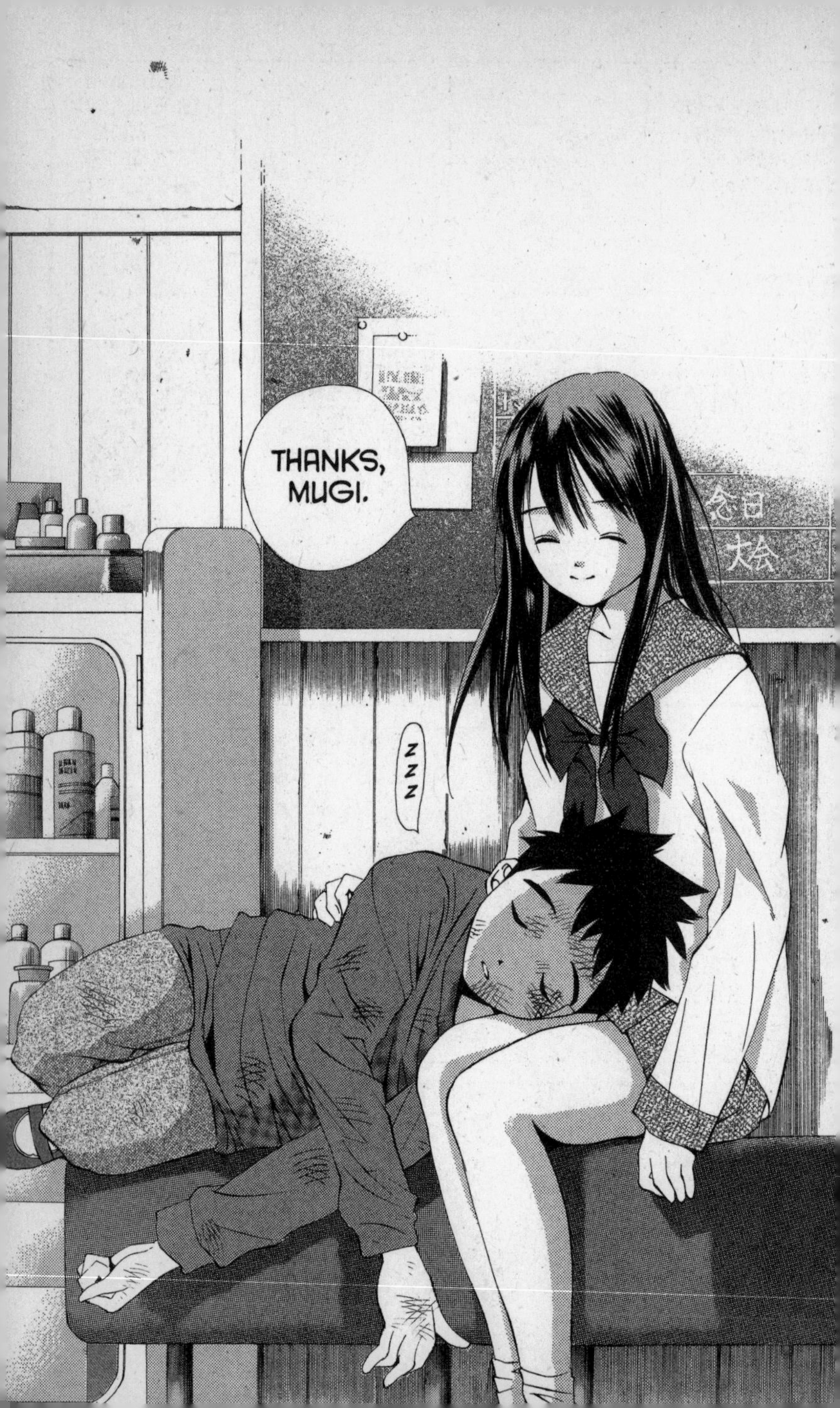
THANKS, MUGI.
ZZZ
念日
大会

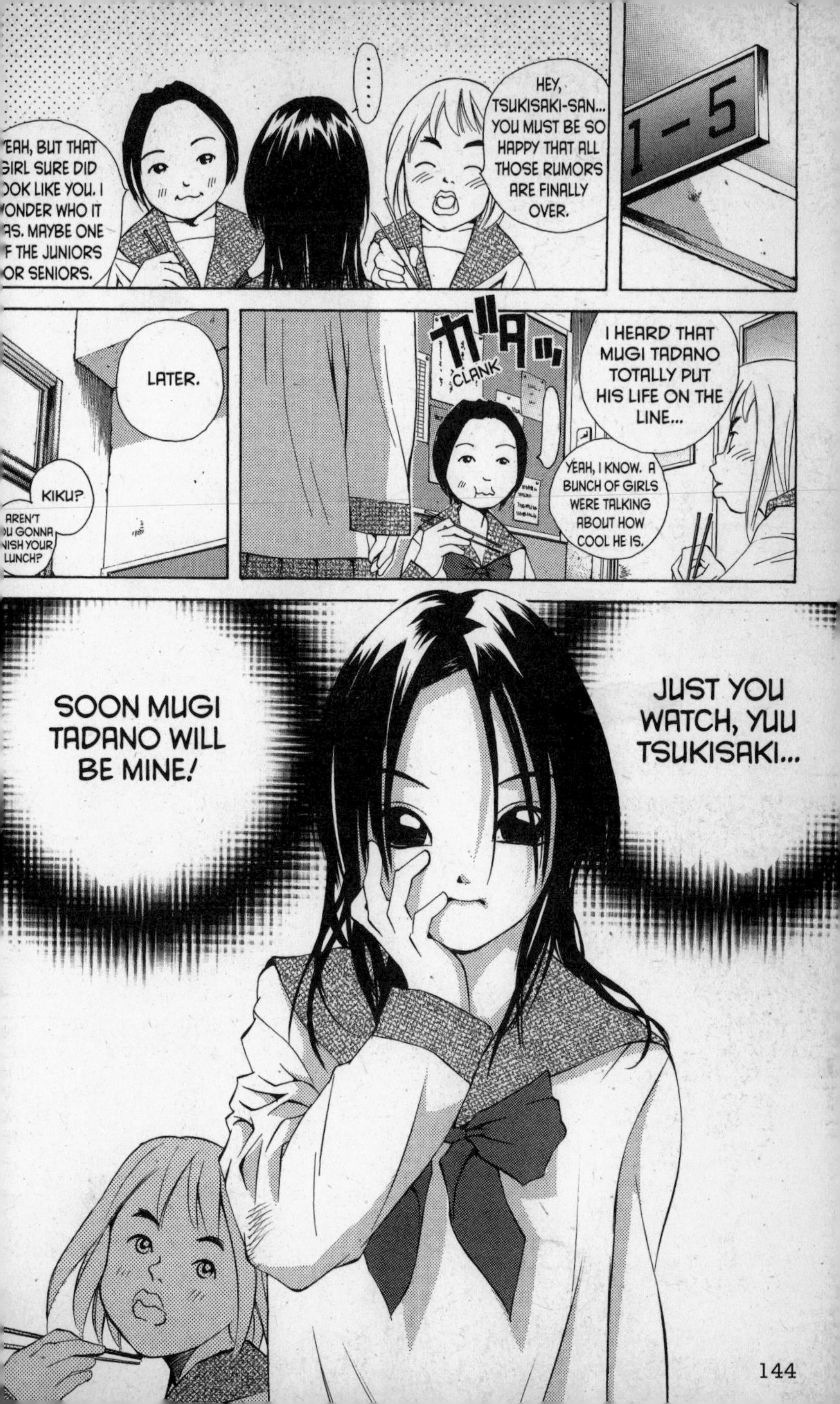
...
HEY, TSUKISAKI-SAN... YOU MUST BE SO HAPPY THAT ALL THOSE RUMORS ARE FINALLY OVER.
EAH, BUT THAT GIRL SURE DID OOK LIKE YOU. I ONDER WHO IT AS. MAYBE ONE F THE JUNIORS OR SENIORS.
I HEARD THAT MUGI TADANO TOTALLY PUT HIS LIFE ON THE LINE...
YEAH, I KNOW. A BUNCH OF GIRLS WERE TALKING ABOUT HOW COOL HE IS.
CLANK
LATER.
KIKU?
AREN'T OU GONNA NISH YOUR LUNCH?
JUST YOU WATCH, YUU TSUKISAKI...
SOON MUGI TADANO WILL BE MINE!

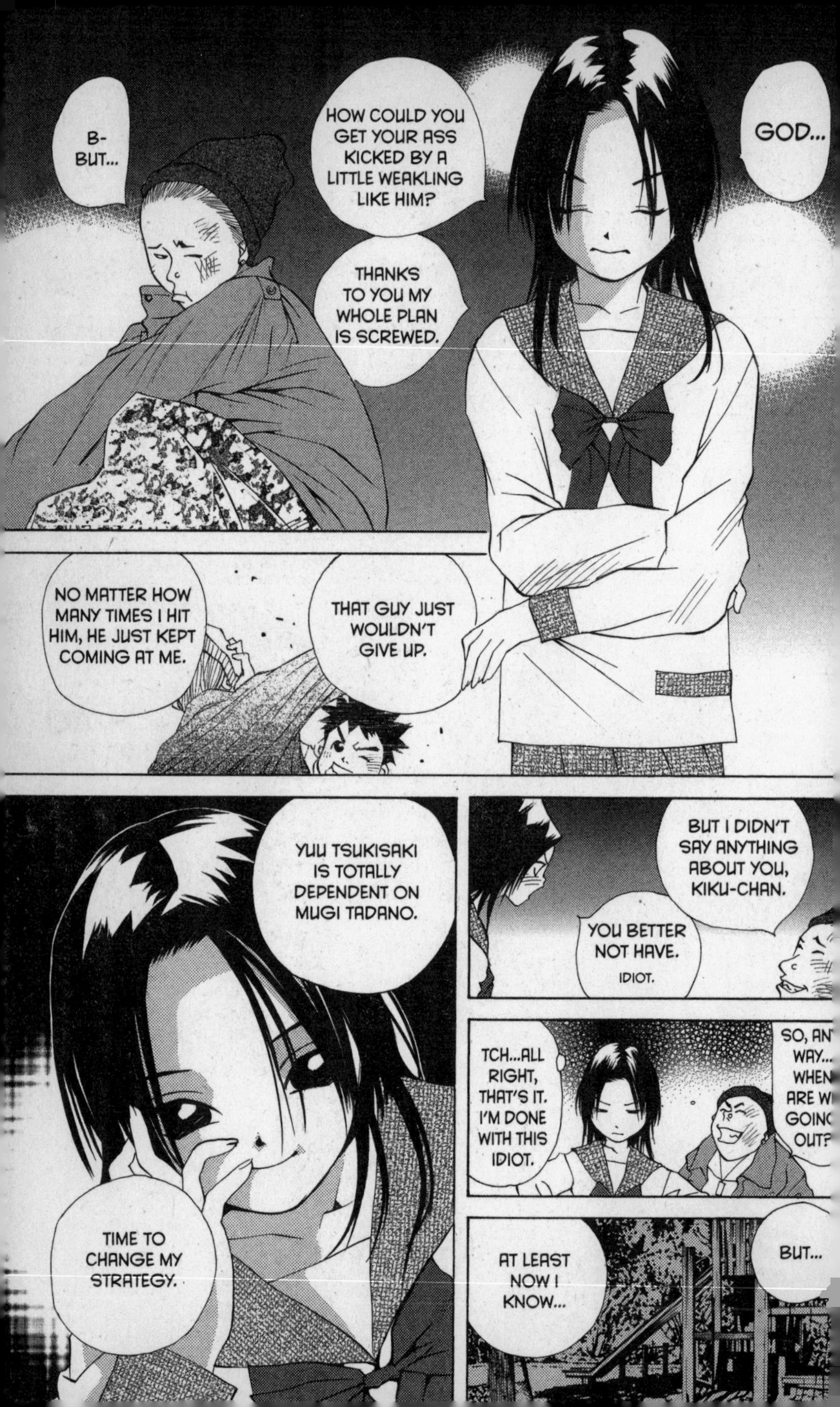
GOD...
HOW COULD YOU GET YOUR ASS KICKED BY A LITTLE WEAKLING LIKE HIM?
THANKS TO YOU MY WHOLE PLAN IS SCREWED.
B-BUT...
THAT GUY JUST WOULDN'T GIVE UP.
NO MATTER HOW MANY TIMES I HIT HIM, HE JUST KEPT COMING AT ME.
BUT I DIDN'T SAY ANYTHING ABOUT YOU, KIKU-CHAN.
YOU BETTER NOT HAVE.
IDIOT.
SO, AN WAY... WHEN ARE W GOIN OUT?
TCH...ALL RIGHT, THAT'S IT. I'M DONE WITH THIS IDIOT.
BUT...
AT LEAST NOW I KNOW...
YUU TSUKISAKI IS TOTALLY DEPENDENT ON MUGI TADANO.
TIME TO CHANGE MY STRATEGY.

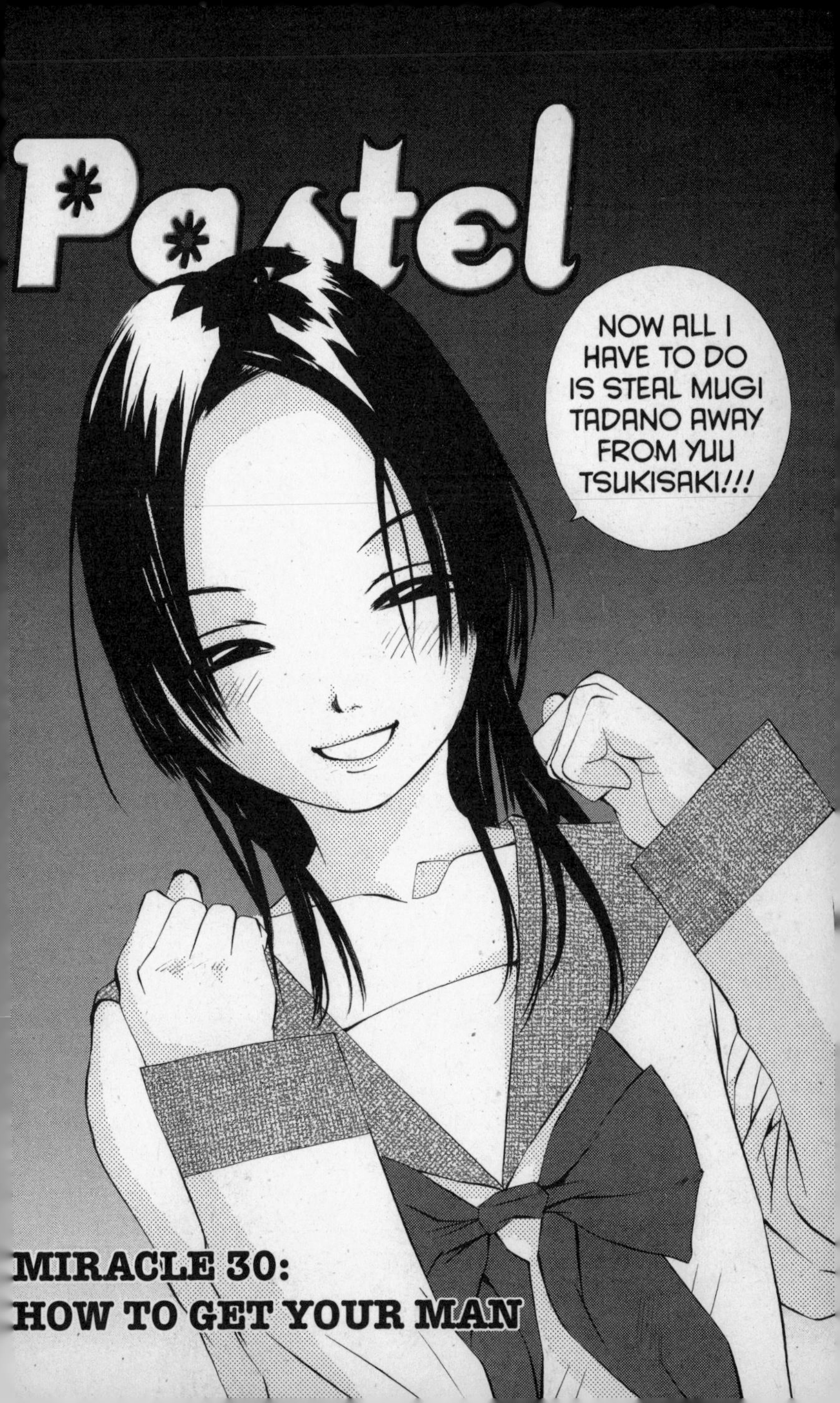
Pastel
NOW ALL I HAVE TO DO IS STEAL MUGI TADANO AWAY FROM YUU TSUKISAKI!!!
MIRACLE 30:
HOW TO GET YOUR MAN

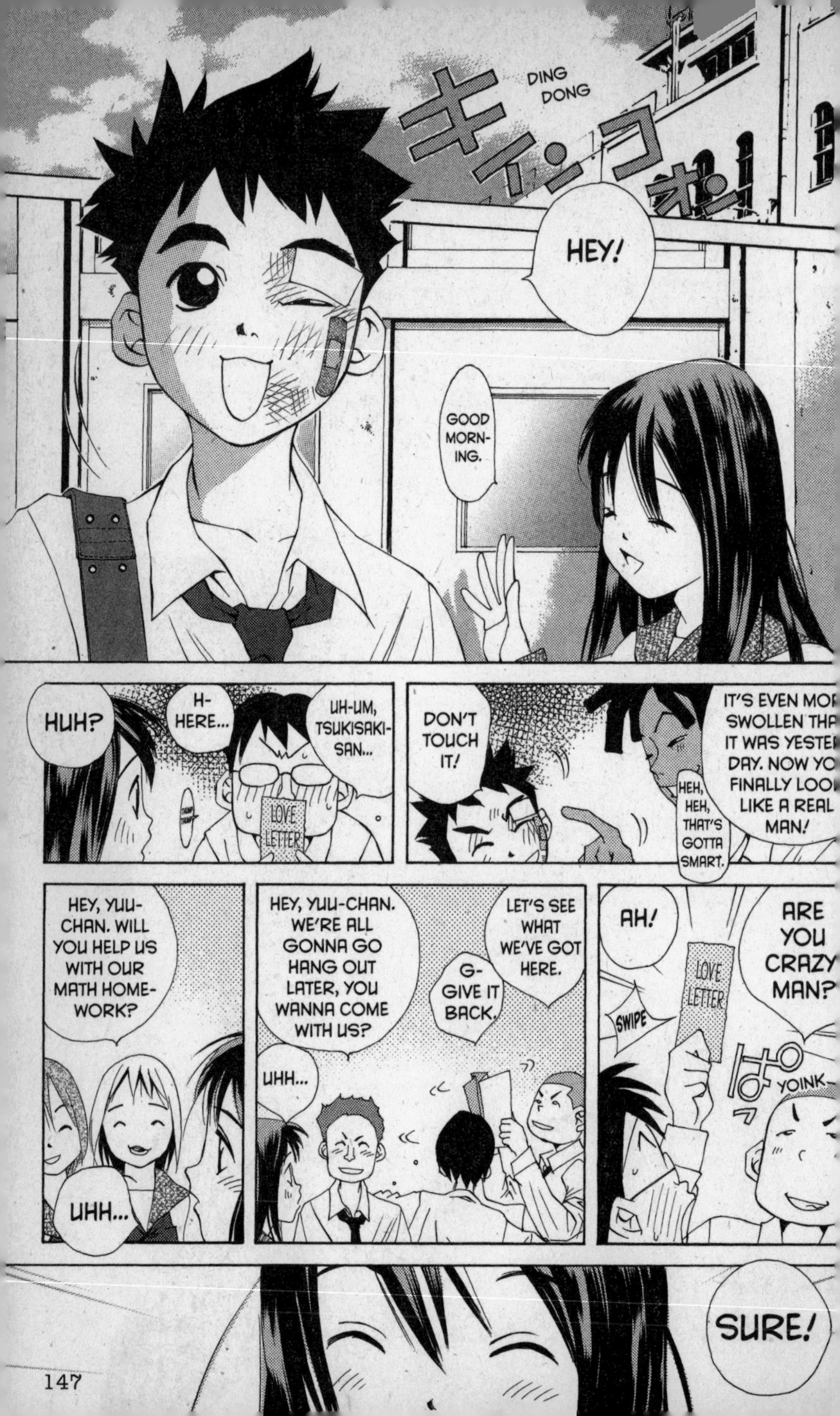
DING DONG
HEY!
GOOD MORNING.
IT'S EVEN MOR SWOLLEN THA IT WAS YESTER DAY. NOW YO FINALLY LOO LIKE A REAL MAN!
HEH, HEH, THAT'S GOTTA SMART.
DON'T TOUCH IT!
UH-UM, TSUKISAKI-SAN...
H-HERE...
LOVE LETTER
HUH?
ARE YOU CRAZY MAN?
AH!
LOVE LETTER
SWIPE
YOINK-
LET'S SEE WHAT WE'VE GOT HERE.
G-GIVE IT BACK.
HEY, YUU-CHAN. WE'RE ALL GONNA GO HANG OUT LATER, YOU WANNA COME WITH US?
UHH...
HEY, YUU-CHAN. WILL YOU HELP US WITH OUR MATH HOMEWORK?
UHH...
SURE!

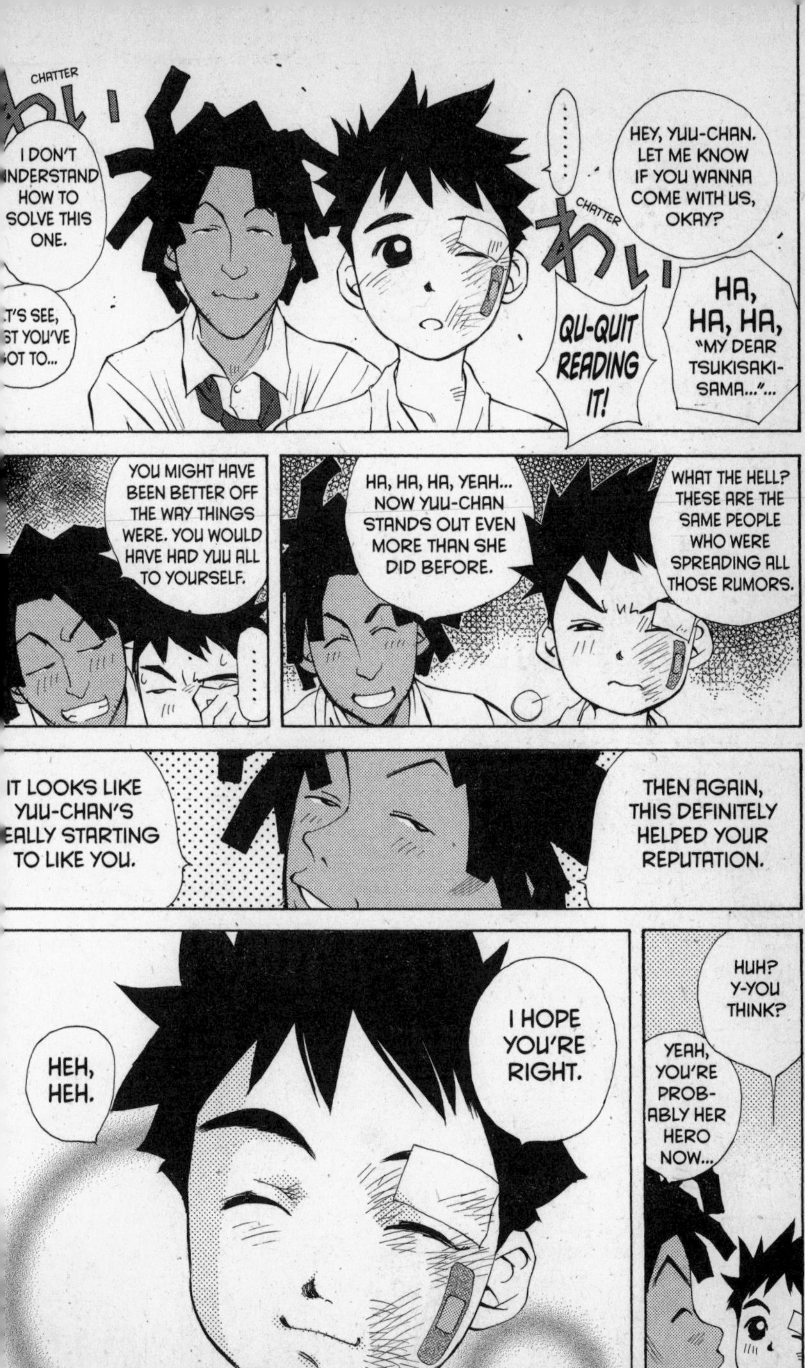
HEY, YUU-CHAN. LET ME KNOW IF YOU WANNA COME WITH US, OKAY?
CHATTER
わい
HA, HA, HA, "MY DEAR TSUKISAKI-SAMA..."...
QU-QUIT READING IT!
......
CHATTER
わい
I DON'T NDERSTAND HOW TO SOLVE THIS ONE.
T'S SEE, ST YOU'VE OT TO...
WHAT THE HELL? THESE ARE THE SAME PEOPLE WHO WERE SPREADING ALL THOSE RUMORS.
HA, HA, HA, YEAH... NOW YUU-CHAN STANDS OUT EVEN MORE THAN SHE DID BEFORE.
YOU MIGHT HAVE BEEN BETTER OFF THE WAY THINGS WERE. YOU WOULD HAVE HAD YUU ALL TO YOURSELF.
......
THEN AGAIN, THIS DEFINITELY HELPED YOUR REPUTATION.
IT LOOKS LIKE YUU-CHAN'S EALLY STARTING TO LIKE YOU.
HUH? Y-YOU THINK?
YEAH, YOU'RE PROB-ABLY HER HERO NOW...
I HOPE YOU'RE RIGHT.
HEH, HEH.

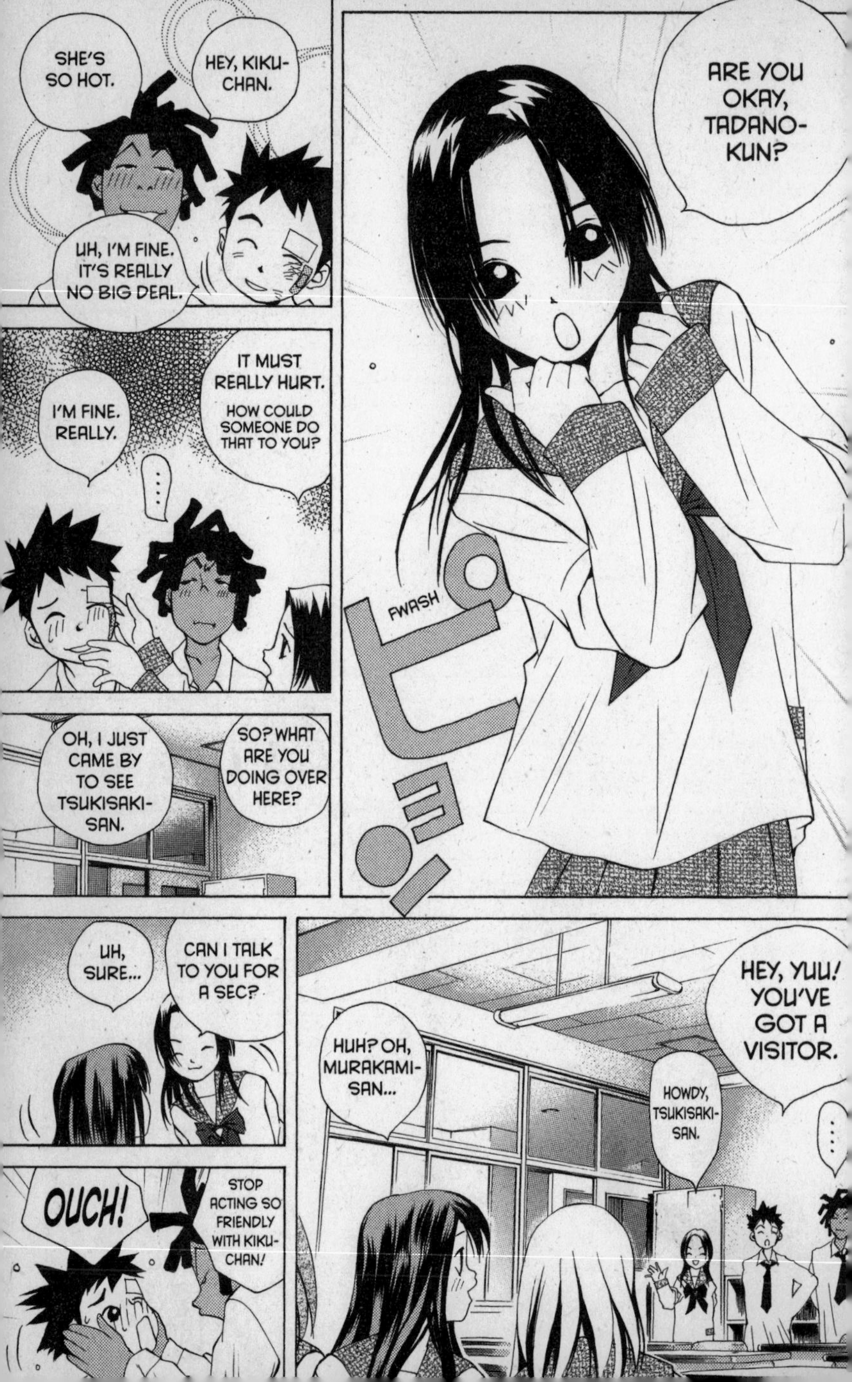
ARE YOU OKAY, TADANO-KUN?
FWASH
HEY, KIKU-CHAN.
SHE'S SO HOT.
UH, I'M FINE. IT'S REALLY NO BIG DEAL.
IT MUST REALLY HURT.
HOW COULD SOMEONE DO THAT TO YOU?
I'M FINE. REALLY.
...!
SO? WHAT ARE YOU DOING OVER HERE?
OH, I JUST CAME BY TO SEE TSUKISAKI-SAN.
HEY, YUU! YOU'VE GOT A VISITOR.
....
HOWDY, TSUKISAKI-SAN.
HUH? OH, MURAKAMI-SAN...
CAN I TALK TO YOU FOR A SEC?
UH, SURE...
STOP ACTING SO FRIENDLY WITH KIKU-CHAN!
OUCH!

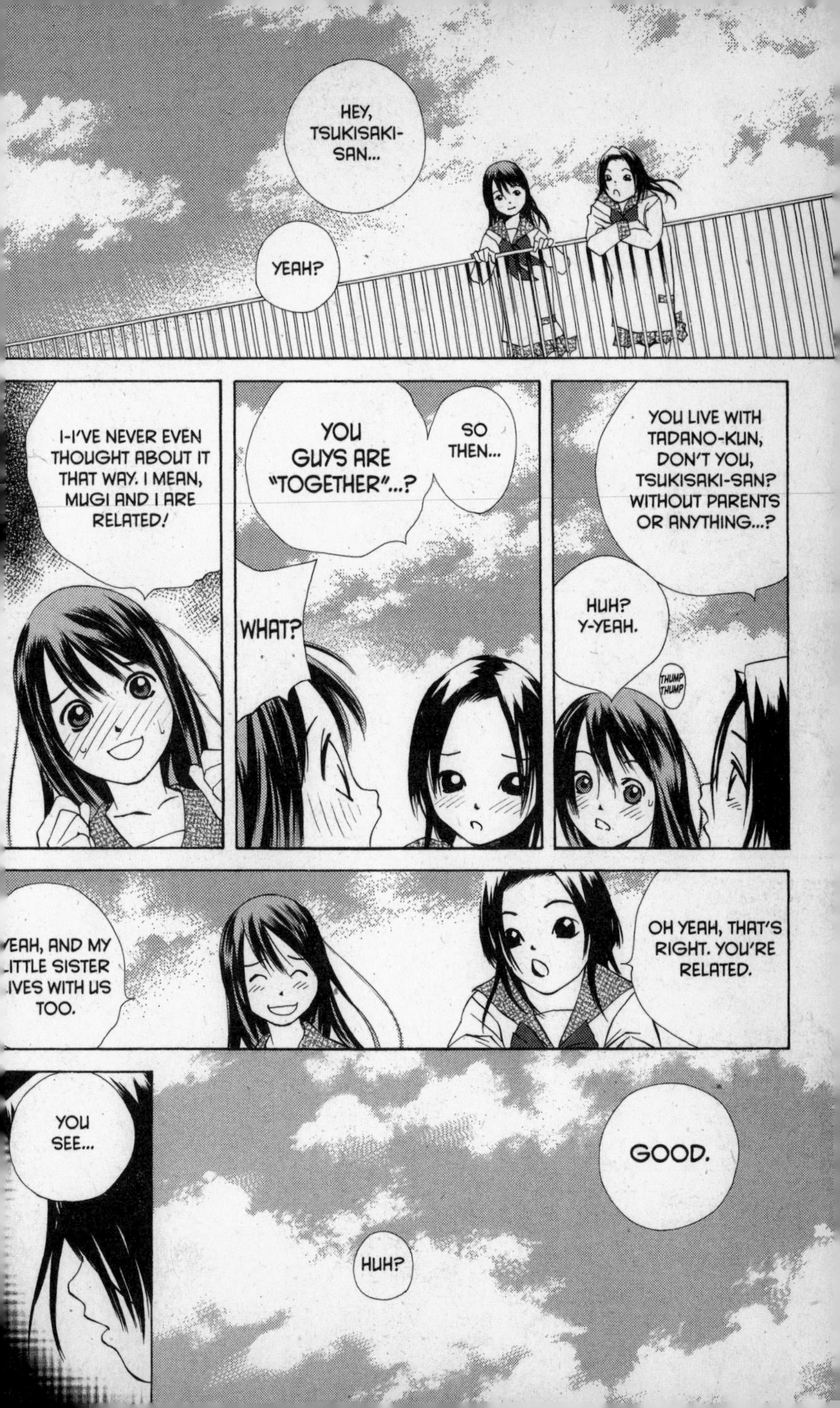
HEY, TSUKISAKI-SAN...
YEAH?
YOU LIVE WITH TADANO-KUN, DON'T YOU, TSUKISAKI-SAN? WITHOUT PARENTS OR ANYTHING...?
HUH? Y-YEAH.
THUMP THUMP
SO THEN...
YOU GUYS ARE "TOGETHER"...?
WHAT?
I-I'VE NEVER EVEN THOUGHT ABOUT IT THAT WAY. I MEAN, MUGI AND I ARE RELATED!
OH YEAH, THAT'S RIGHT. YOU'RE RELATED.
EAH, AND MY LITTLE SISTER IVES WITH US TOO.
GOOD.
HUH?
YOU SEE...

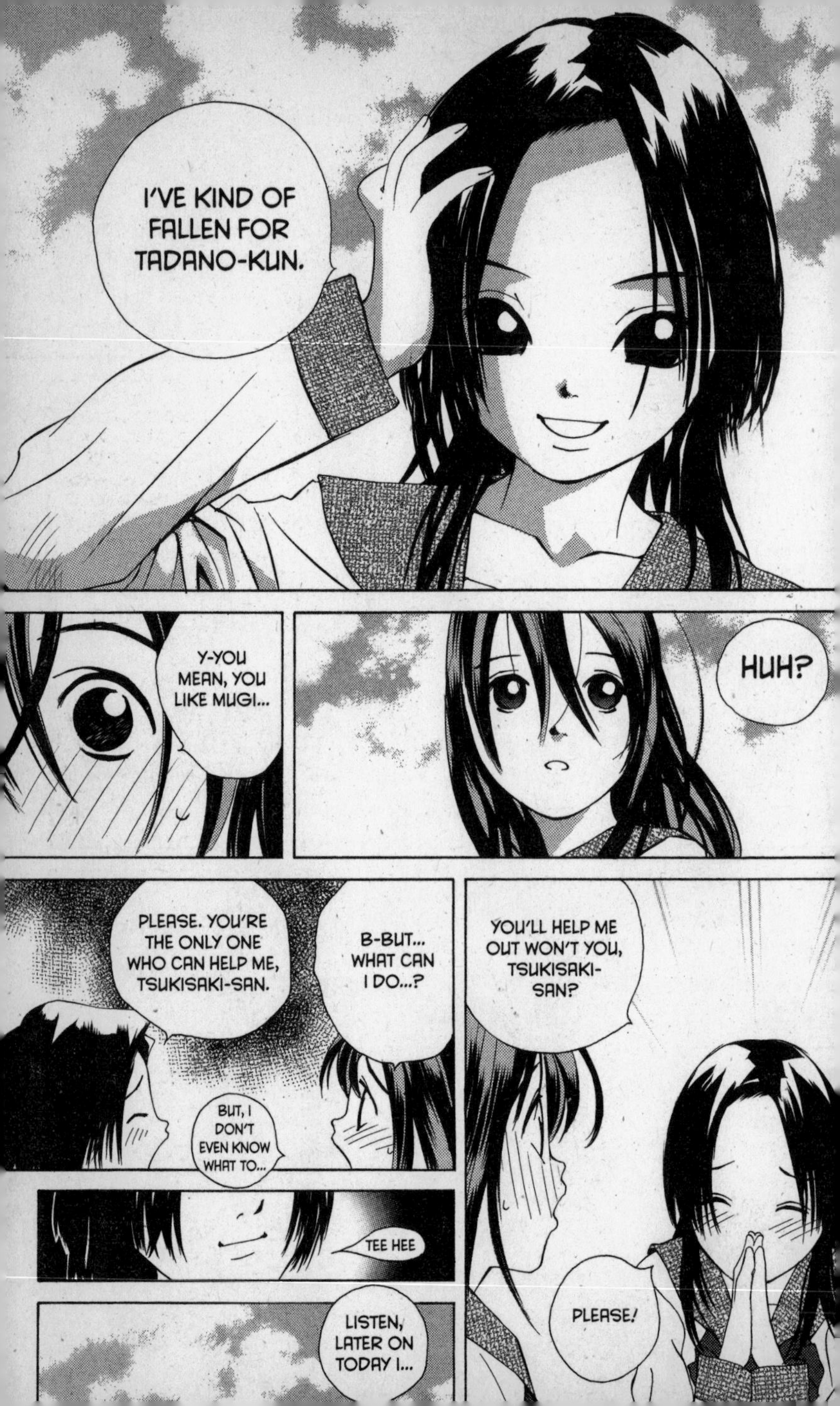
I'VE KIND OF FALLEN FOR TADANO-KUN.
HUH?
Y-YOU MEAN, YOU LIKE MUGI...
YOU'LL HELP ME OUT WON'T YOU, TSUKISAKI-SAN?
PLEASE!
B-BUT... WHAT CAN I DO...?
PLEASE. YOU'RE THE ONLY ONE WHO CAN HELP ME, TSUKISAKI-SAN.
BUT, I DON'T EVEN KNOW WHAT TO...
TEE HEE
LISTEN, LATER ON TODAY I...

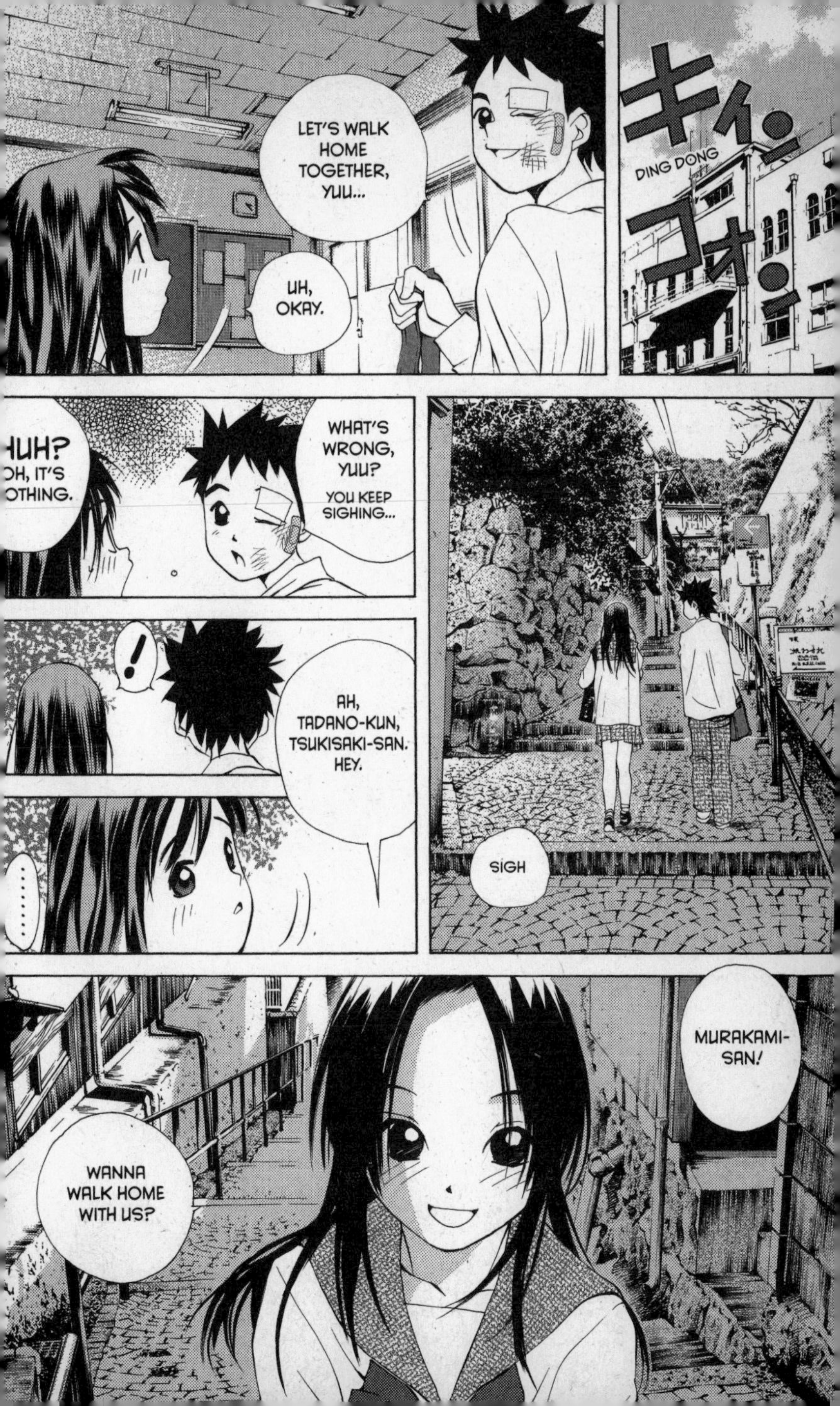
DING DONG
LET'S WALK HOME TOGETHER, YUU...
UH, OKAY.
SIGH
WHAT'S WRONG, YUU?
YOU KEEP SIGHING...
HUH? OH, IT'S OTHING.
!
AH, TADANO-KUN, TSUKISAKI-SAN. HEY.
......
MURAKAMI-SAN!
WANNA WALK HOME WITH US?

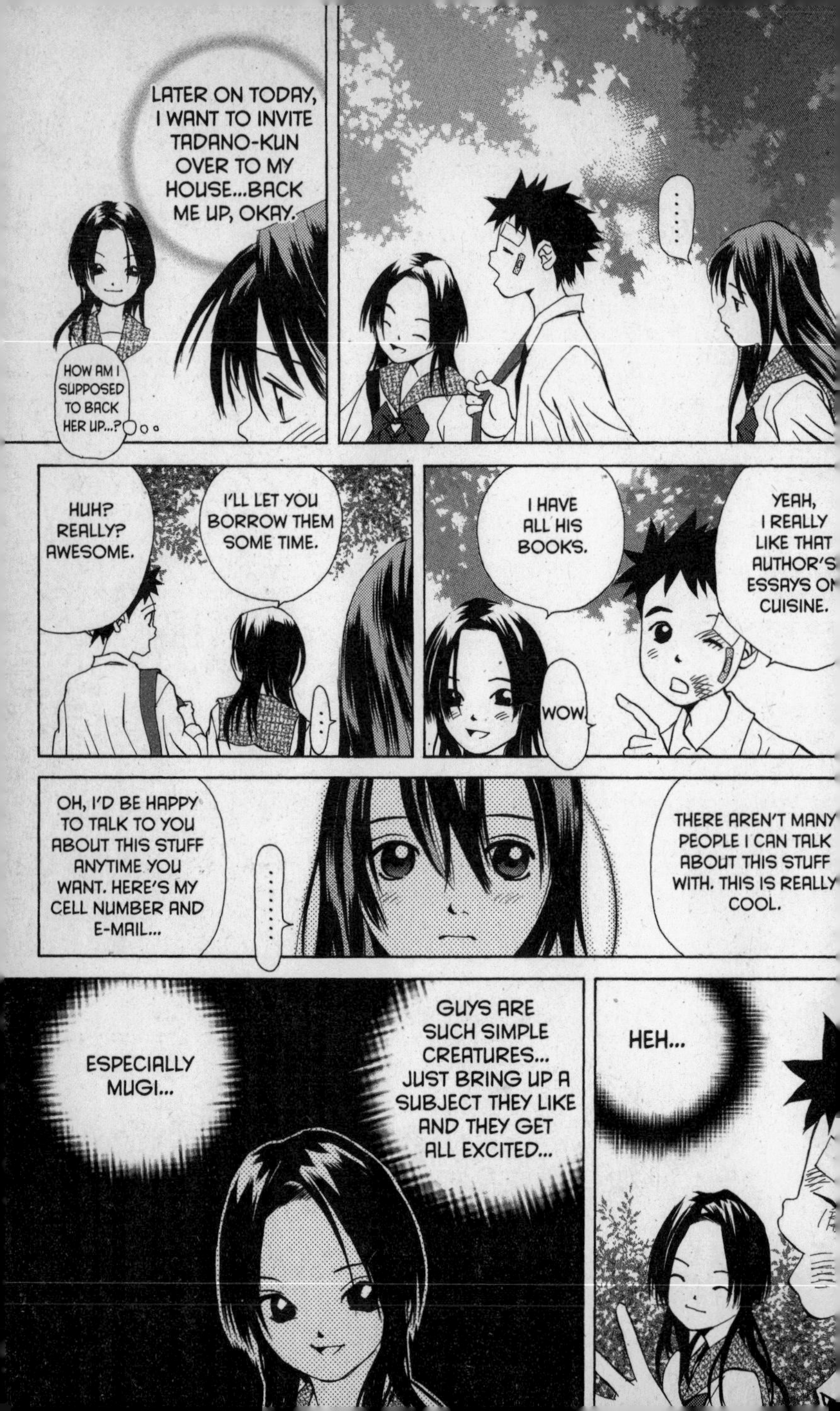
......
LATER ON TODAY, I WANT TO INVITE TADANO-KUN OVER TO MY HOUSE...BACK ME UP, OKAY.
HOW AM I SUPPOSED TO BACK HER UP...?
YEAH, I REALLY LIKE THAT AUTHOR'S ESSAYS ON CUISINE.
I HAVE ALL HIS BOOKS.
WOW
I'LL LET YOU BORROW THEM SOME TIME.
HUH? REALLY? AWESOME.
...
THERE AREN'T MANY PEOPLE I CAN TALK ABOUT THIS STUFF WITH. THIS IS REALLY COOL.
......
OH, I'D BE HAPPY TO TALK TO YOU ABOUT THIS STUFF ANYTIME YOU WANT. HERE'S MY CELL NUMBER AND E-MAIL...
HEH...
GUYS ARE SUCH SIMPLE CREATURES... JUST BRING UP A SUBJECT THEY LIKE AND THEY GET ALL EXCITED...
ESPECIALLY MUGI...

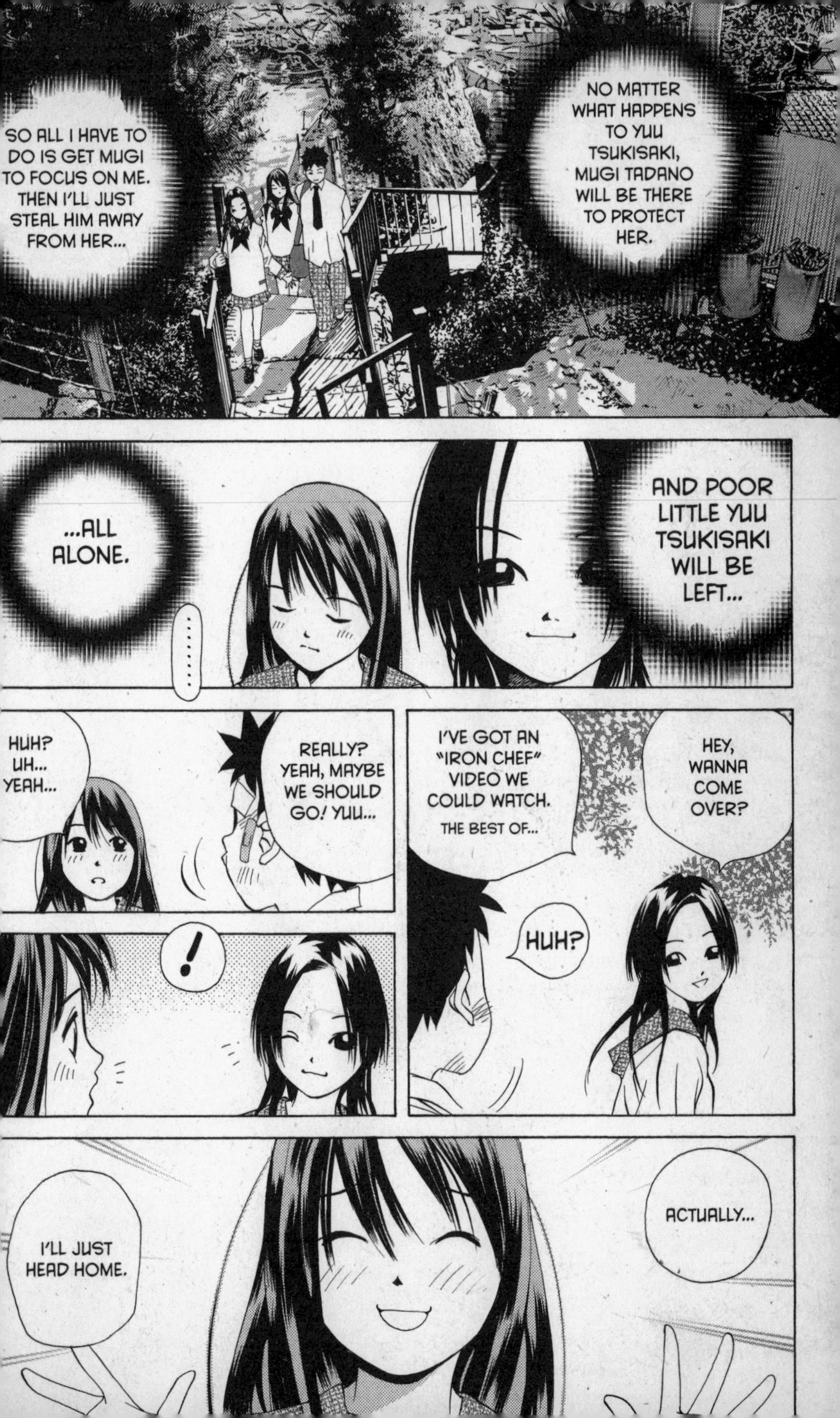
NO MATTER WHAT HAPPENS TO YUU TSUKISAKI, MUGI TADANO WILL BE THERE TO PROTECT HER.
SO ALL I HAVE TO DO IS GET MUGI TO FOCUS ON ME. THEN I'LL JUST STEAL HIM AWAY FROM HER...
AND POOR LITTLE YUU TSUKISAKI WILL BE LEFT...
...ALL ALONE.
......
HEY, WANNA COME OVER?
I'VE GOT AN "IRON CHEF" VIDEO WE COULD WATCH. THE BEST OF...
HUH?
REALLY? YEAH, MAYBE WE SHOULD GO! YUU...
HUH? UH... YEAH...
!
ACTUALLY...
I'LL JUST HEAD HOME.

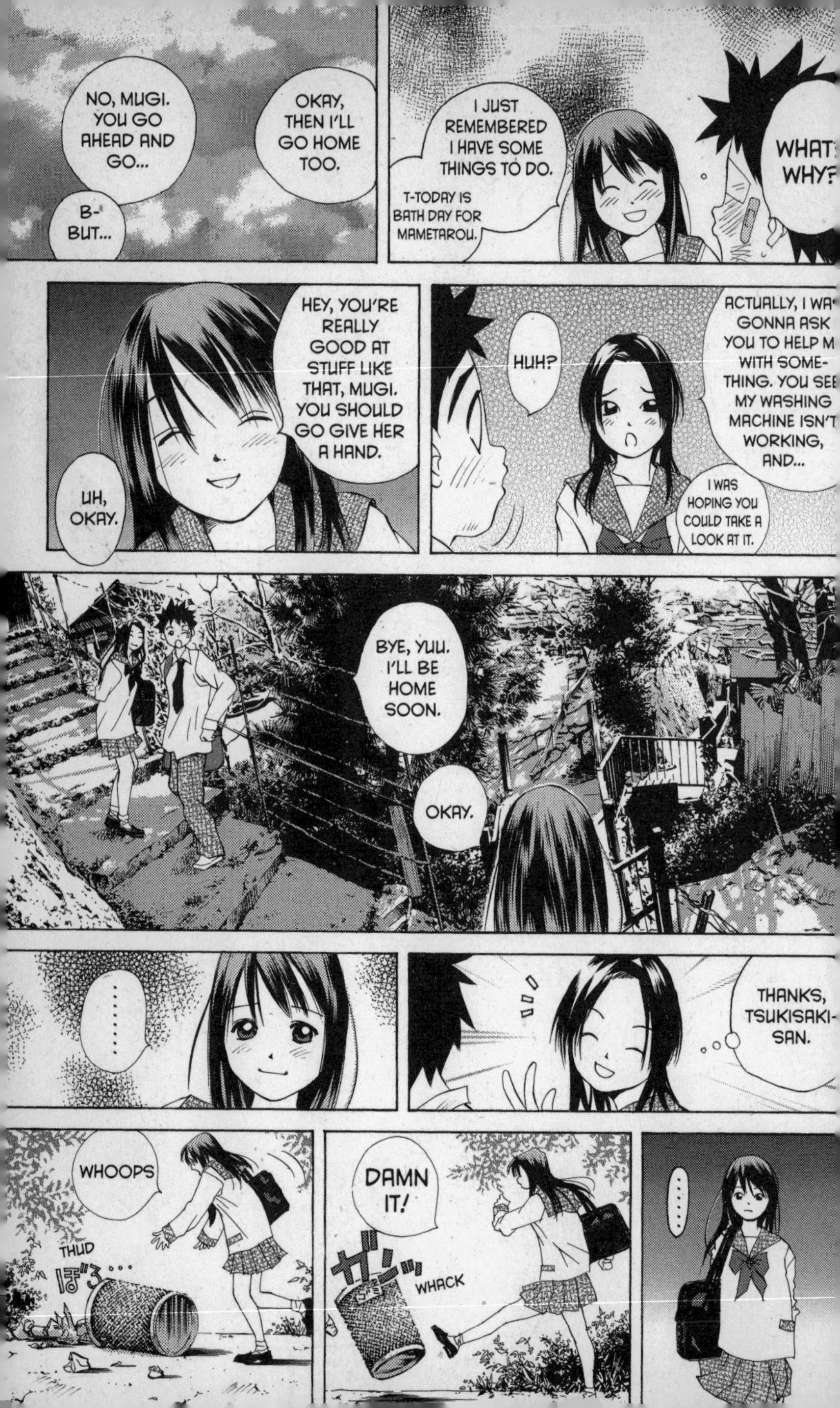
WHAT WHY?
I JUST REMEMBERED I HAVE SOME THINGS TO DO.
T-TODAY IS BATH DAY FOR MAMETAROU.
OKAY, THEN I'LL GO HOME TOO.
NO, MUGI. YOU GO AHEAD AND GO...
B-BUT...
ACTUALLY, I WA GONNA ASK YOU TO HELP M WITH SOME-THING. YOU SEE MY WASHING MACHINE ISN'T WORKING, AND...
HUH?
I WAS HOPING YOU COULD TAKE A LOOK AT IT.
HEY, YOU'RE REALLY GOOD AT STUFF LIKE THAT, MUGI. YOU SHOULD GO GIVE HER A HAND.
UH, OKAY.
BYE, YUU. I'LL BE HOME SOON.
OKAY.
THANKS, TSUKISAKI-SAN.
......
......
DAMN IT!
WHACK
WHOOPS
THUD

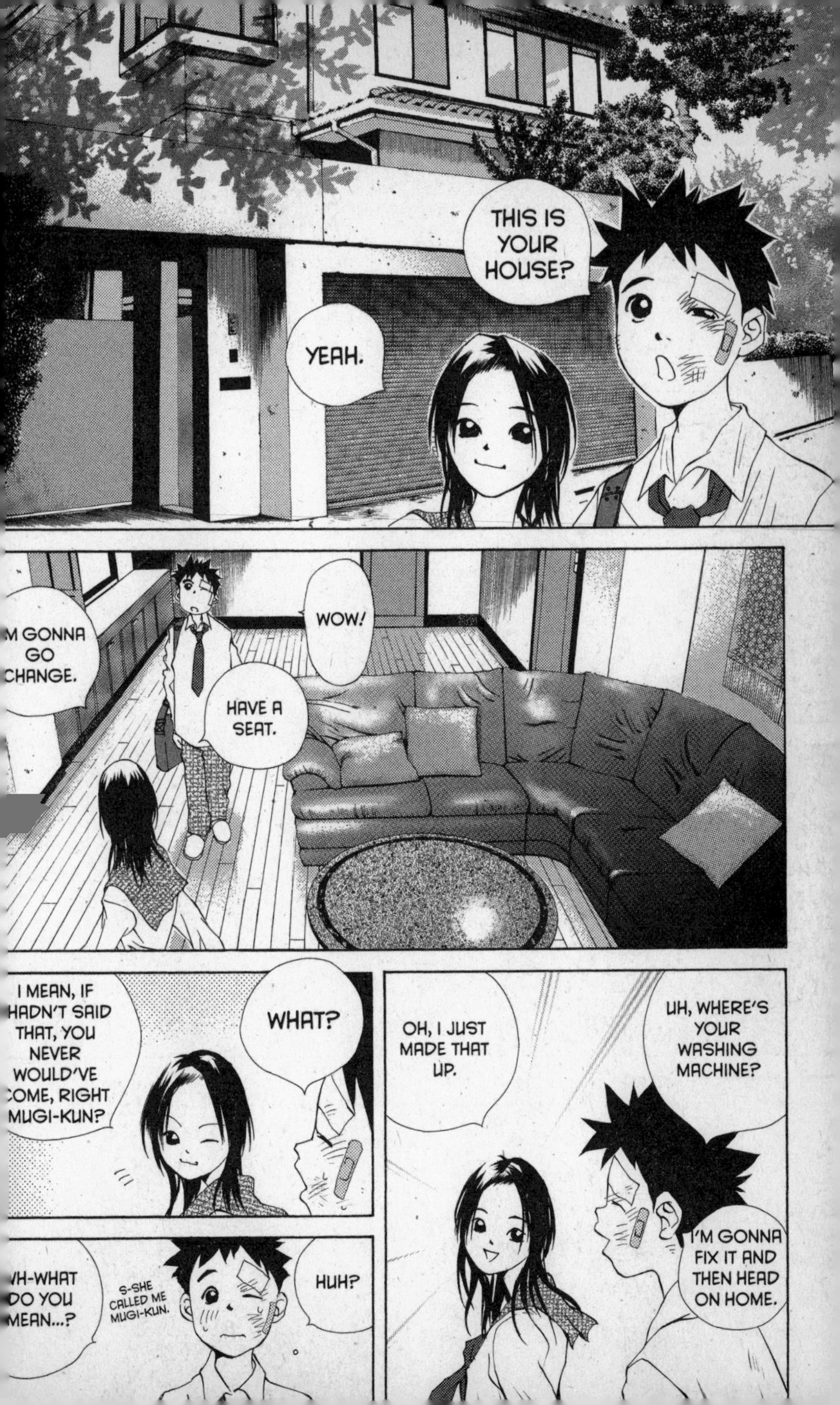
THIS IS YOUR HOUSE?
YEAH.
WOW!
HAVE A SEAT.
M GONNA GO CHANGE.
UH, WHERE'S YOUR WASHING MACHINE?
OH, I JUST MADE THAT UP.
I'M GONNA FIX IT AND THEN HEAD ON HOME.
WHAT?
I MEAN, IF HADN'T SAID THAT, YOU NEVER WOULD'VE COME, RIGHT MUGI-KUN?
HUH?
S-SHE CALLED ME MUGI-KUN.
H-WHAT DO YOU MEAN...?

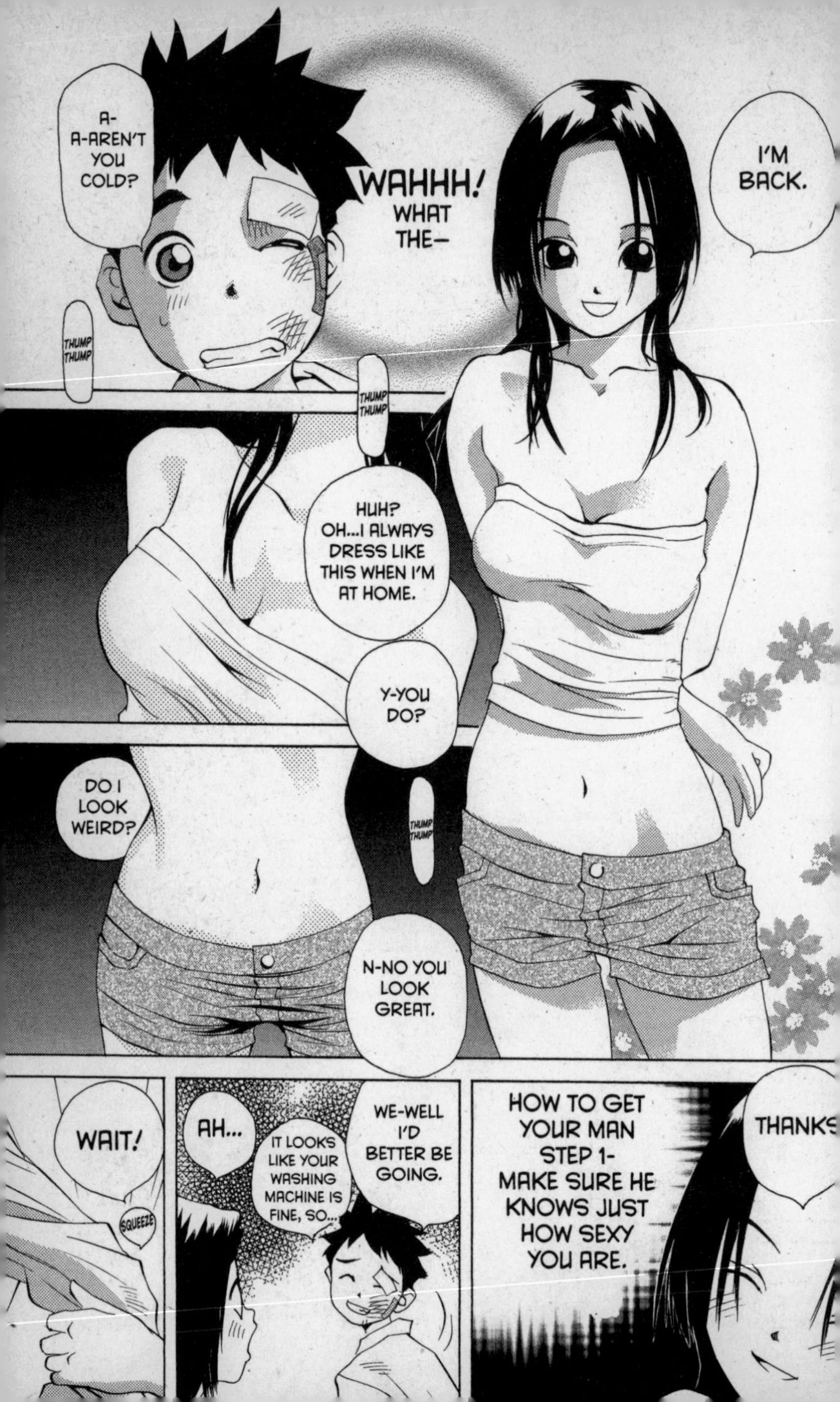
I'M BACK.
WAHHH! WHAT THE—
A- A-AREN'T YOU COLD?
THUMP THUMP
THUMP THUMP
HUH? OH...I ALWAYS DRESS LIKE THIS WHEN I'M AT HOME.
Y-YOU DO?
DO I LOOK WEIRD?
THUMP THUMP
N-NO YOU LOOK GREAT.
THANKS
HOW TO GET YOUR MAN STEP 1- MAKE SURE HE KNOWS JUST HOW SEXY YOU ARE.
WE-WELL I'D BETTER BE GOING.
IT LOOKS LIKE YOUR WASHING MACHINE IS FINE, SO...
AH...
WAIT!
SQUEEZE

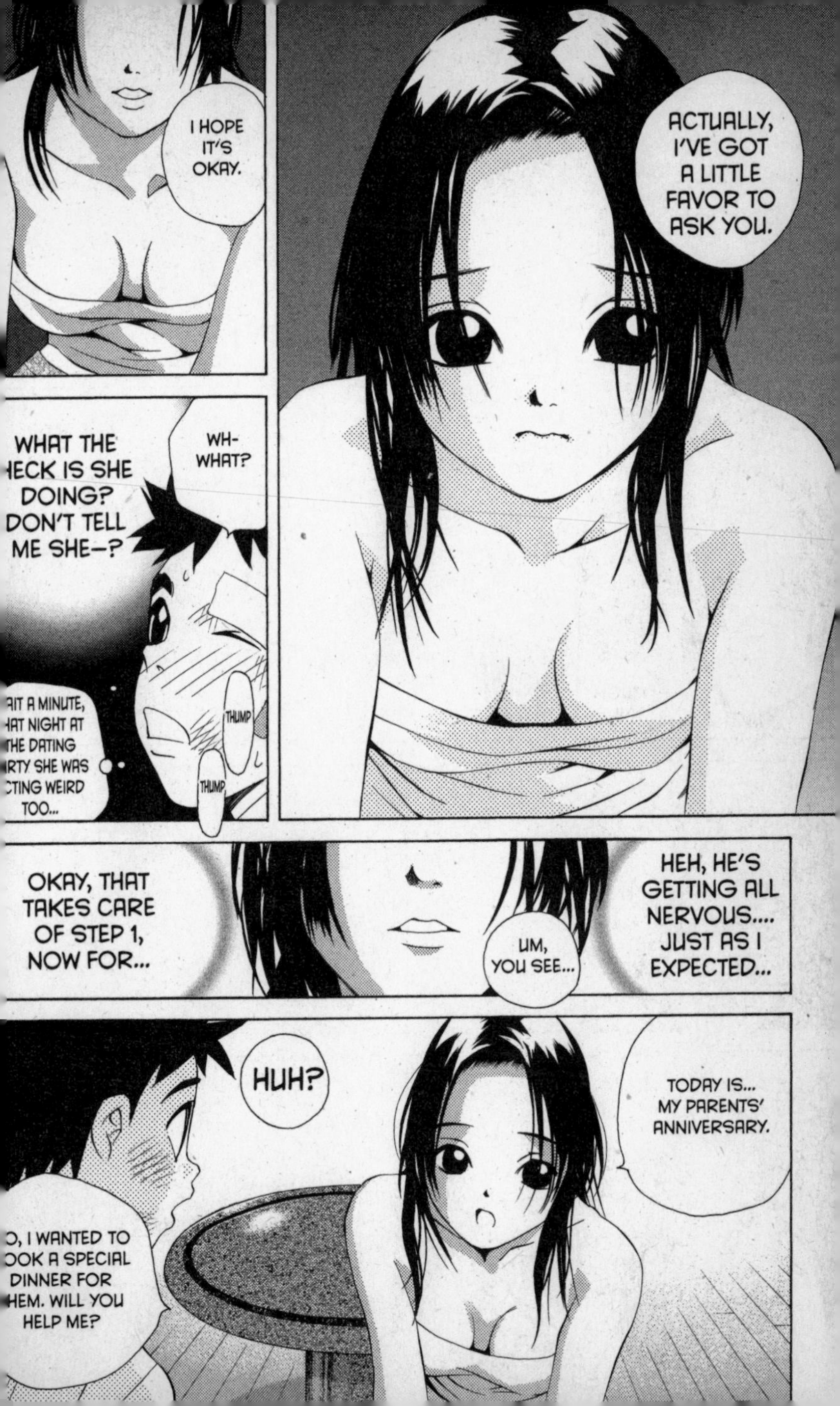

ACTUALLY, I'VE GOT A LITTLE FAVOR TO ASK YOU.
I HOPE IT'S OKAY.
WH- WHAT?
WHAT THE HECK IS SHE DOING? DON'T TELL ME SHE—?
THUMP
THUMP
AIT A MINUTE, HAT NIGHT AT THE DATING RTY SHE WAS CTING WEIRD TOO...
HEH, HE'S GETTING ALL NERVOUS.... JUST AS I EXPECTED...
UM, YOU SEE...
OKAY, THAT TAKES CARE OF STEP 1, NOW FOR...
TODAY IS... MY PARENTS' ANNIVERSARY.
HUH?
O, I WANTED TO OOK A SPECIAL DINNER FOR HEM. WILL YOU HELP ME?

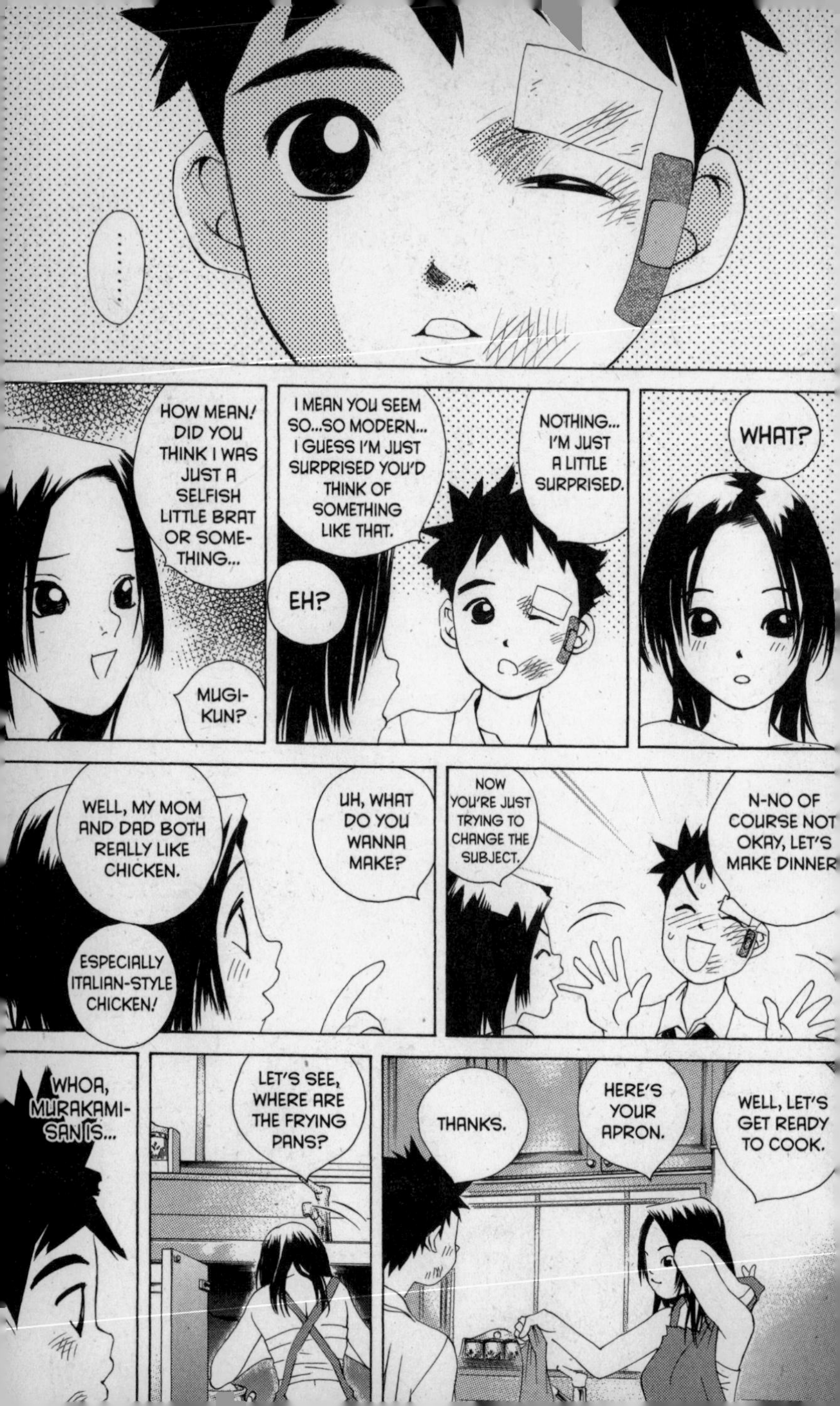
……
WHAT?
NOTHING... I'M JUST A LITTLE SURPRISED.
I MEAN YOU SEEM SO...SO MODERN... I GUESS I'M JUST SURPRISED YOU'D THINK OF SOMETHING LIKE THAT.
EH?
HOW MEAN! DID YOU THINK I WAS JUST A SELFISH LITTLE BRAT OR SOME-THING...
MUGI-KUN?
N-NO OF COURSE NOT OKAY, LET'S MAKE DINNER
NOW YOU'RE JUST TRYING TO CHANGE THE SUBJECT.
UH, WHAT DO YOU WANNA MAKE?
WELL, MY MOM AND DAD BOTH REALLY LIKE CHICKEN.
ESPECIALLY ITALIAN-STYLE CHICKEN!
WELL, LET'S GET READY TO COOK.
HERE'S YOUR APRON.
THANKS.
LET'S SEE, WHERE ARE THE FRYING PANS?
WHOA, MURAKAMI-SAN IS...

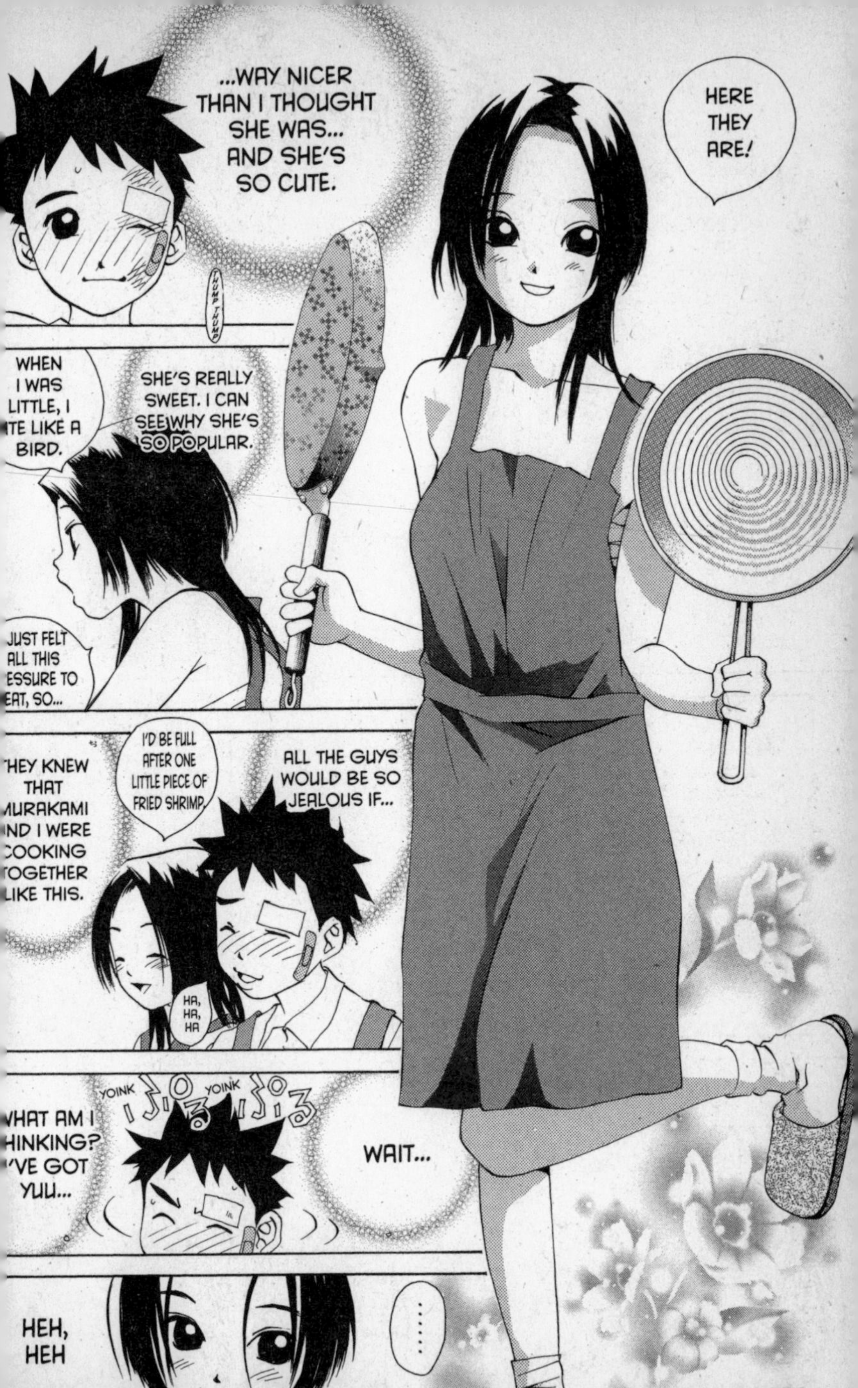
HERE THEY ARE!
...WAY NICER THAN I THOUGHT SHE WAS... AND SHE'S SO CUTE.
THUMP THUMP
SHE'S REALLY SWEET. I CAN SEE WHY SHE'S SO POPULAR.
WHEN I WAS LITTLE, I TE LIKE A BIRD.
JUST FELT ALL THIS ESSURE TO EAT, SO...
ALL THE GUYS WOULD BE SO JEALOUS IF...
I'D BE FULL AFTER ONE LITTLE PIECE OF FRIED SHRIMP.
HEY KNEW THAT URAKAMI ND I WERE COOKING OGETHER LIKE THIS.
HA, HA, HA
WAIT...
YOINK
YOINK
HAT AM I HINKING? 'VE GOT YUU...
......
HEH, HEH

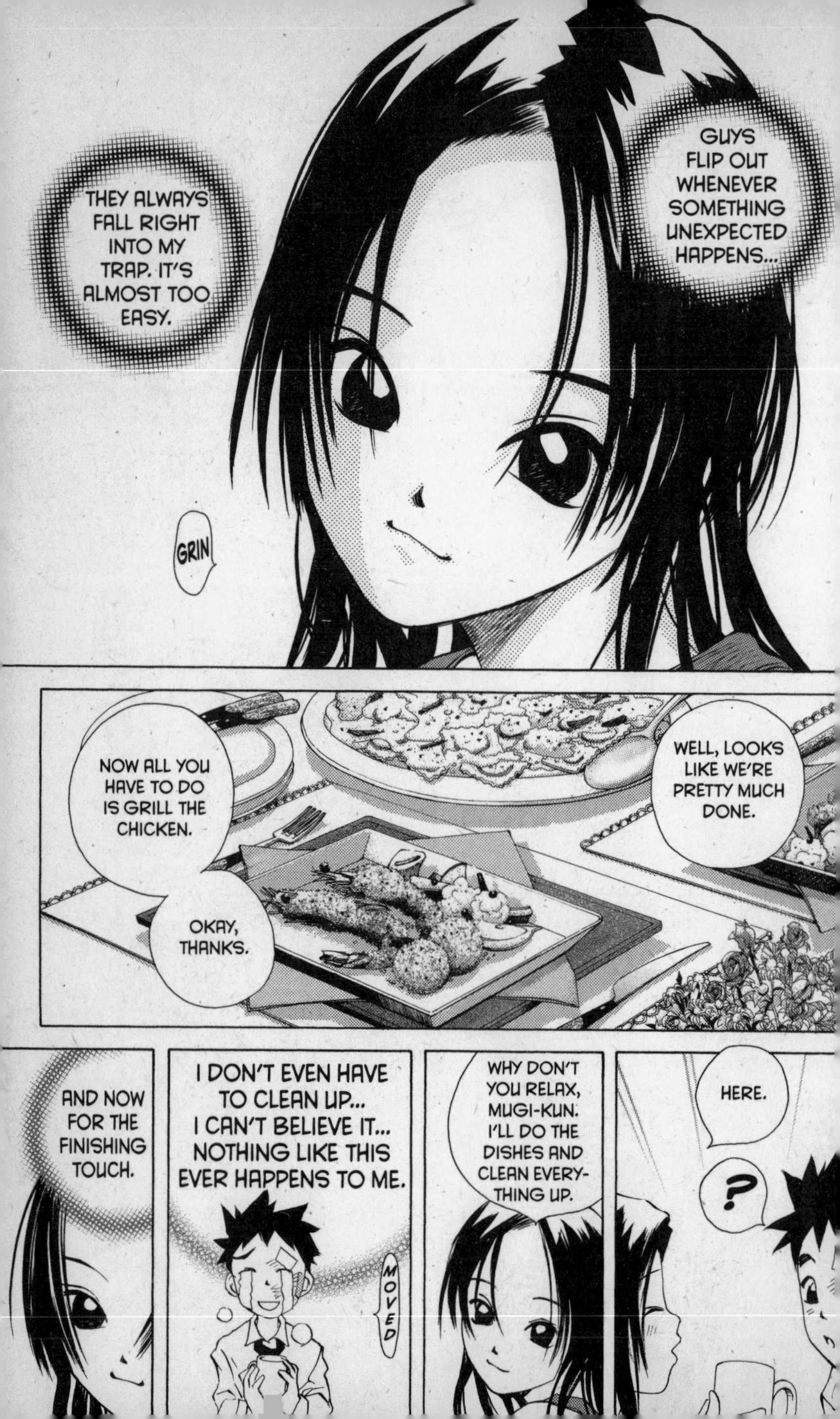
GUYS FLIP OUT WHENEVER SOMETHING UNEXPECTED HAPPENS...
THEY ALWAYS FALL RIGHT INTO MY TRAP. IT'S ALMOST TOO EASY.
GRIN
WELL, LOOKS LIKE WE'RE PRETTY MUCH DONE.
NOW ALL YOU HAVE TO DO IS GRILL THE CHICKEN.
OKAY, THANKS.
HERE.
?
WHY DON'T YOU RELAX, MUGI-KUN. I'LL DO THE DISHES AND CLEAN EVERY-THING UP.
I DON'T EVEN HAVE TO CLEAN UP... I CAN'T BELIEVE IT... NOTHING LIKE THIS EVER HAPPENS TO ME.
MOVED
AND NOW FOR THE FINISHING TOUCH.

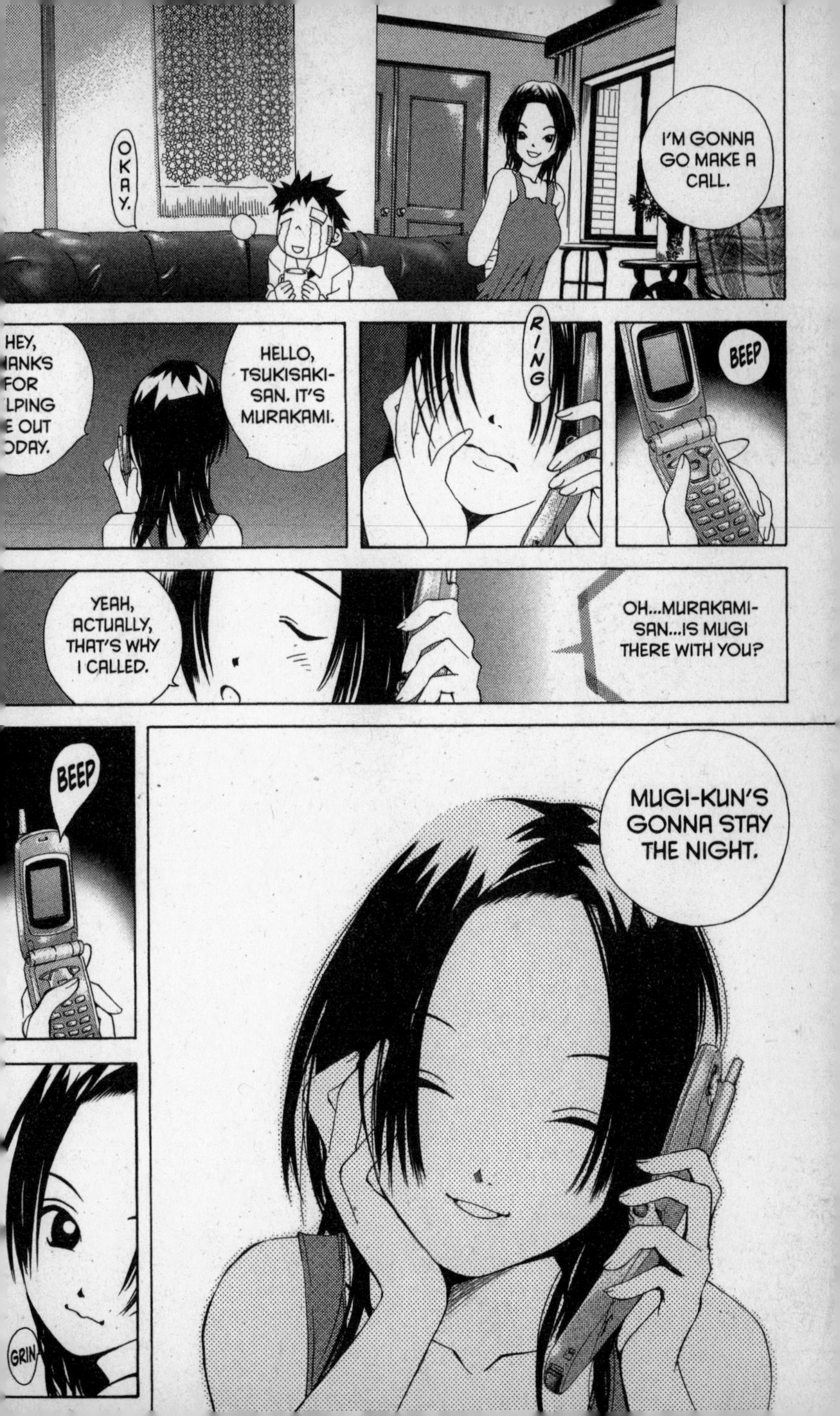
I'M GONNA GO MAKE A CALL.
OKAY.
BEEP
RING
HELLO, TSUKISAKI-SAN. IT'S MURAKAMI.
HEY, ANKS FOR LPING E OUT ODAY.
OH...MURAKAMI-SAN...IS MUGI THERE WITH YOU?
YEAH, ACTUALLY, THAT'S WHY I CALLED.
MUGI-KUN'S GONNA STAY THE NIGHT.
BEEP
GRIN

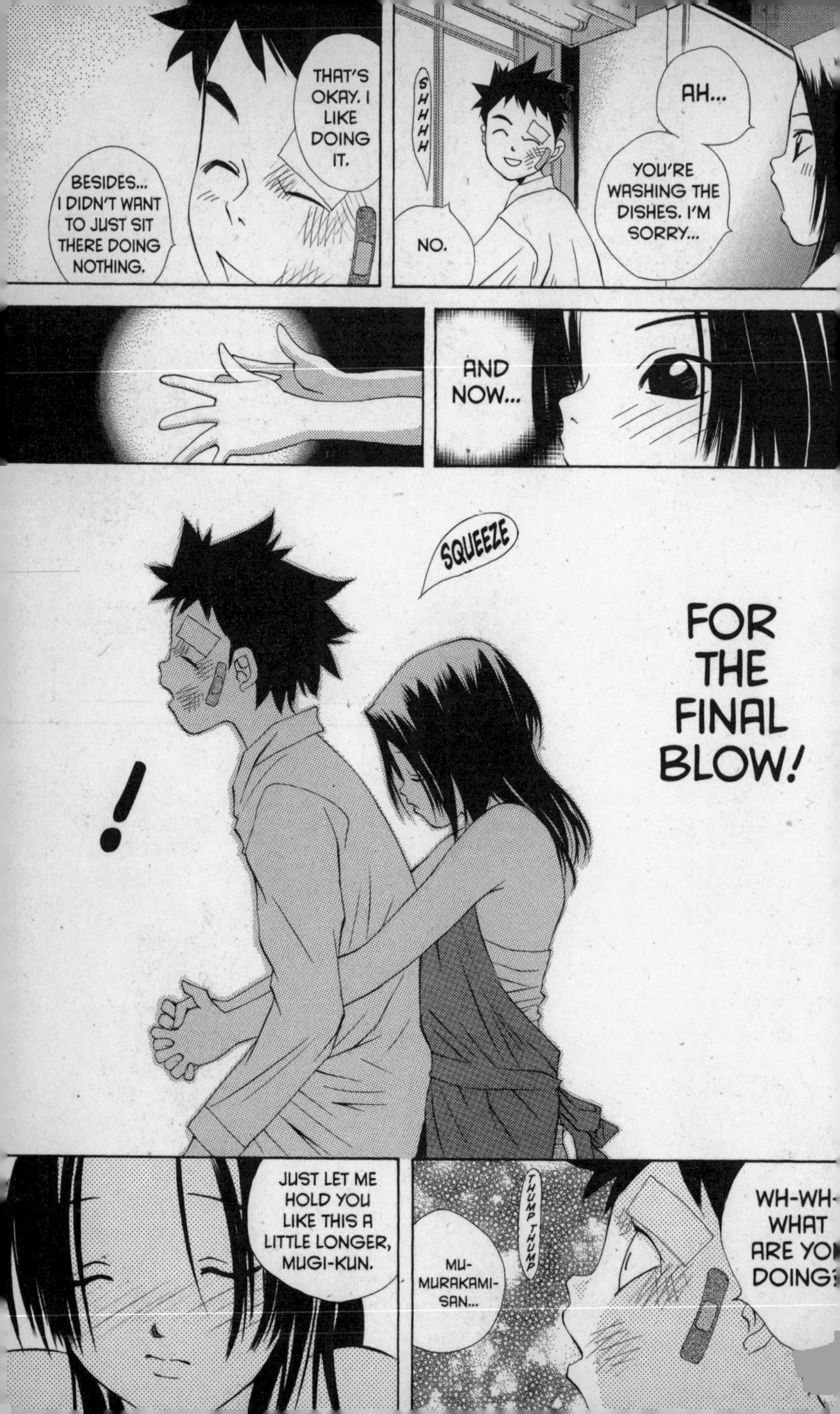
AH...
YOU'RE WASHING THE DISHES. I'M SORRY...
SHHHH
NO.
THAT'S OKAY. I LIKE DOING IT.
BESIDES... I DIDN'T WANT TO JUST SIT THERE DOING NOTHING.
AND NOW...
SQUEEZE
FOR THE FINAL BLOW!
!
WH-WH-WHAT ARE YO DOING
THUMP THUMP
MU-MURAKAMI-SAN...
JUST LET ME HOLD YOU LIKE THIS A LITTLE LONGER, MUGI-KUN.

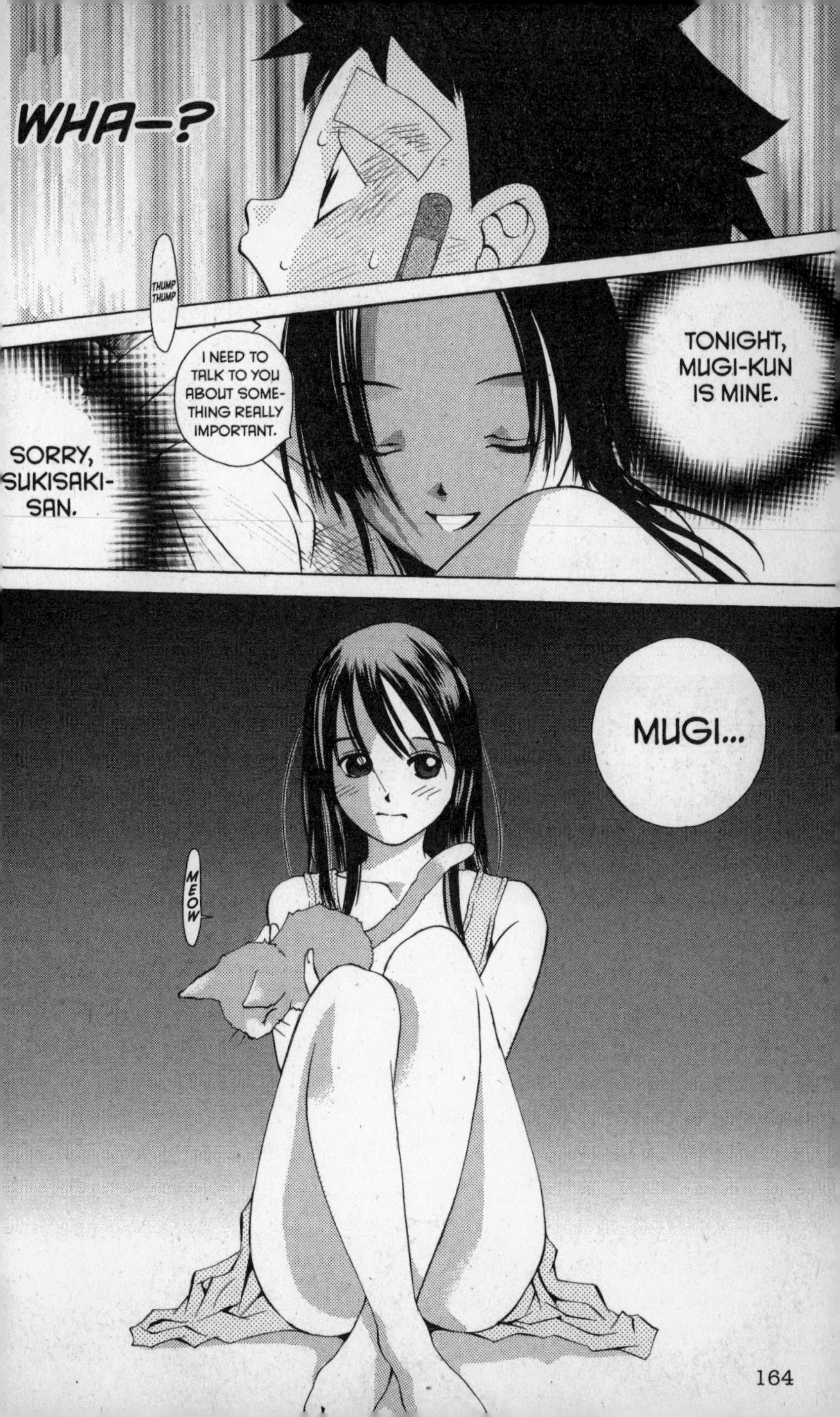
WHA—?
THUMP THUMP
TONIGHT, MUGI-KUN IS MINE.
I NEED TO TALK TO YOU ABOUT SOMETHING REALLY IMPORTANT.
SORRY, SUKISAKI-SAN.
MUGI...
MEOW

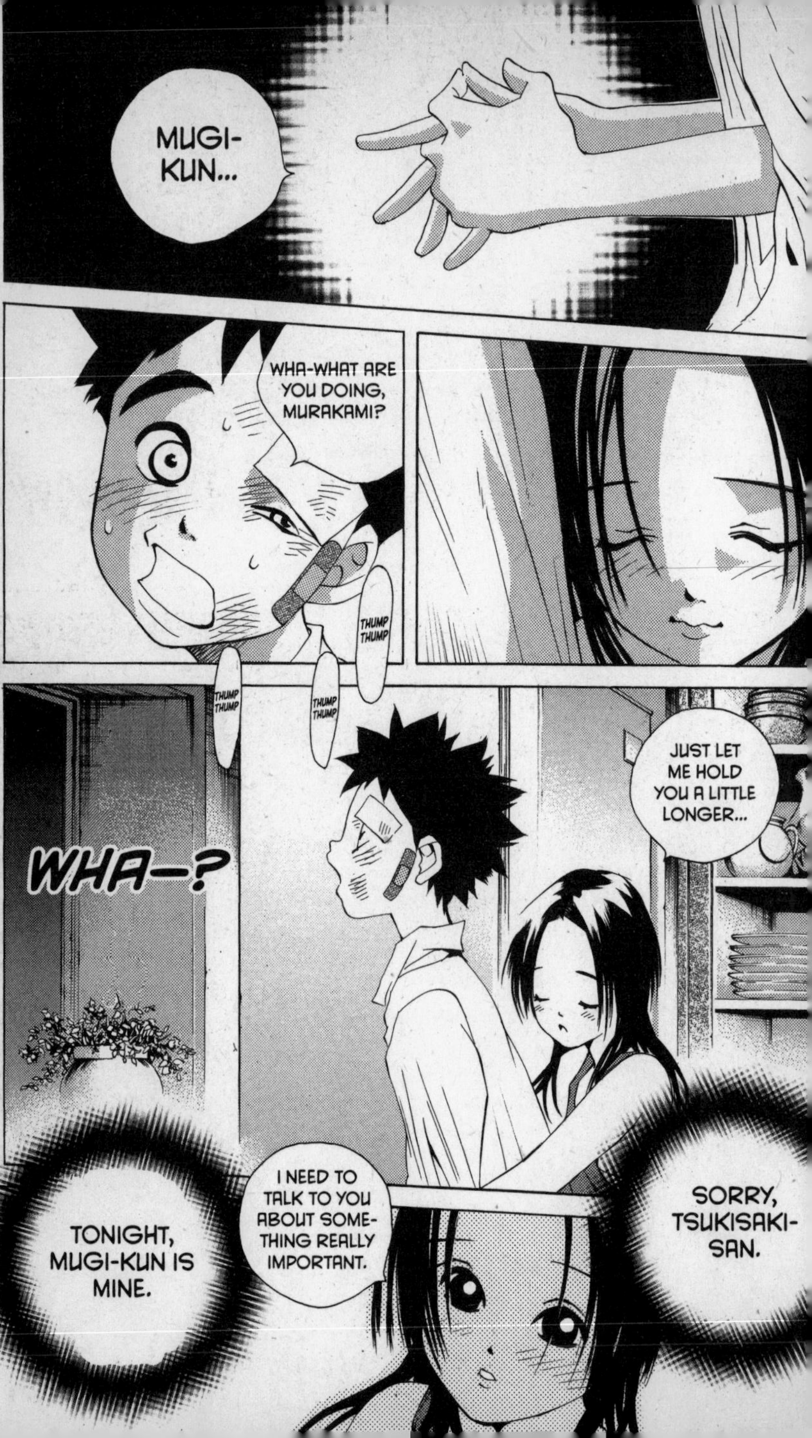
MUGI-KUN...
WHA-WHAT ARE YOU DOING, MURAKAMI?
THUMP THUMP
THUMP THUMP
THUMP THUMP
JUST LET ME HOLD YOU A LITTLE LONGER...
WHA—?
SORRY, TSUKISAKI-SAN.
I NEED TO TALK TO YOU ABOUT SOME-THING REALLY IMPORTANT.
TONIGHT, MUGI-KUN IS MINE.

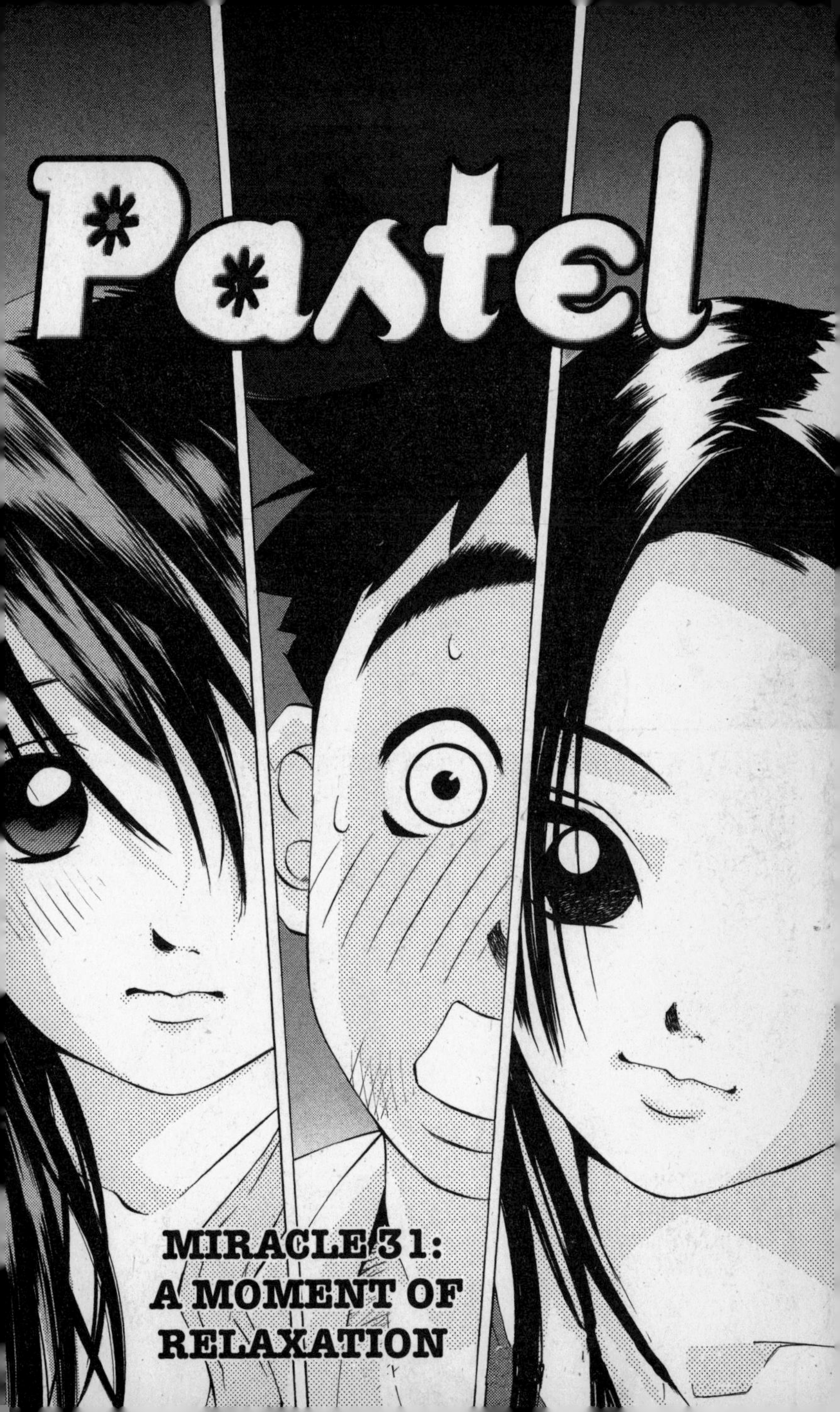
Pastel
MIRACLE 31:
A MOMENT OF
RELAXATION

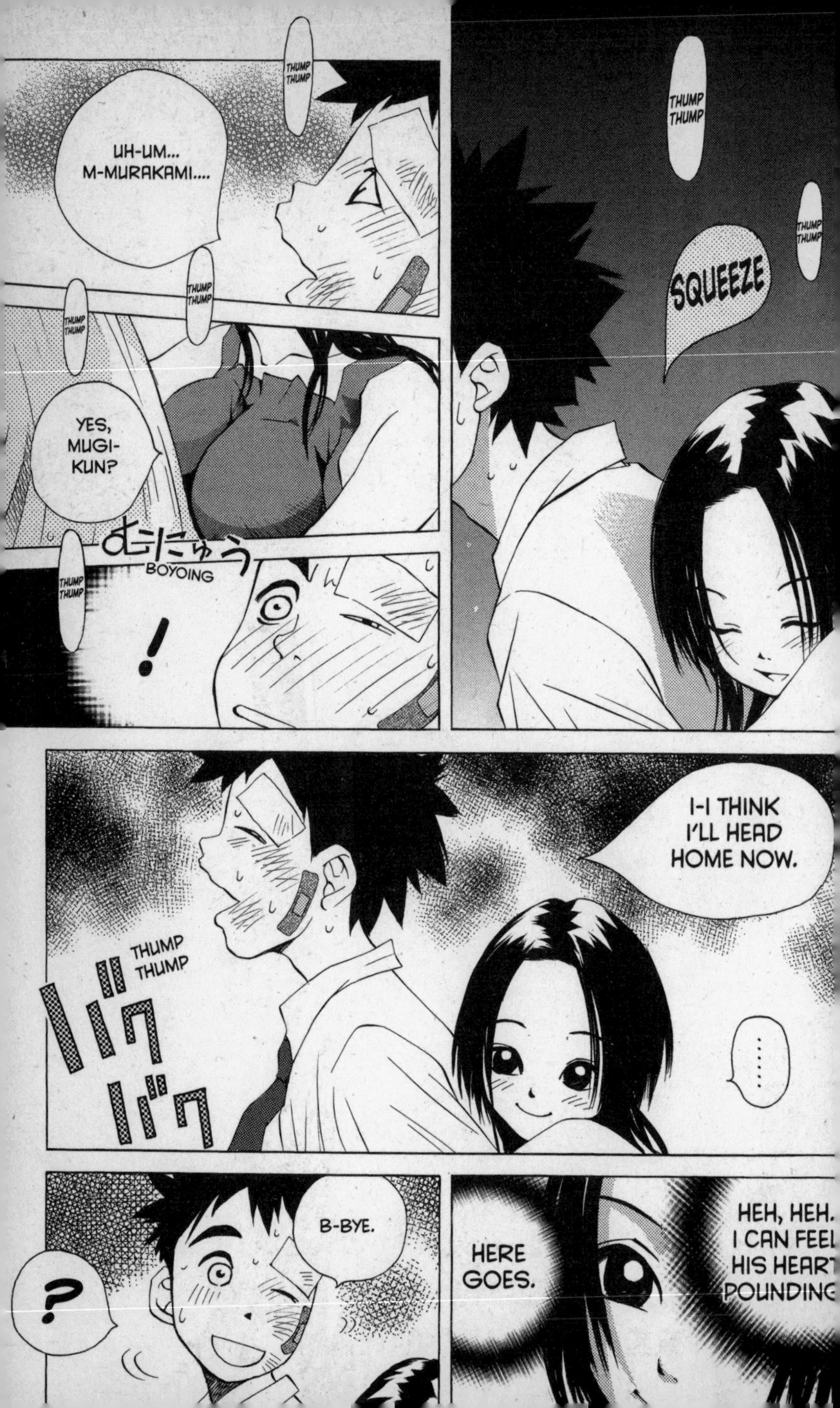
THUMP THUMP
THUMP THUMP
SQUEEZE
THUMP THUMP
UH-UM... M-MURAKAMI....
THUMP THUMP
THUMP THUMP
YES, MUGI-KUN?
むにゅう
BOYOING
THUMP THUMP
!
I-I THINK I'LL HEAD HOME NOW.
......
THUMP THUMP
HEH, HEH. I CAN FEEL HIS HEART POUNDING
HERE GOES.
B-BYE.
?

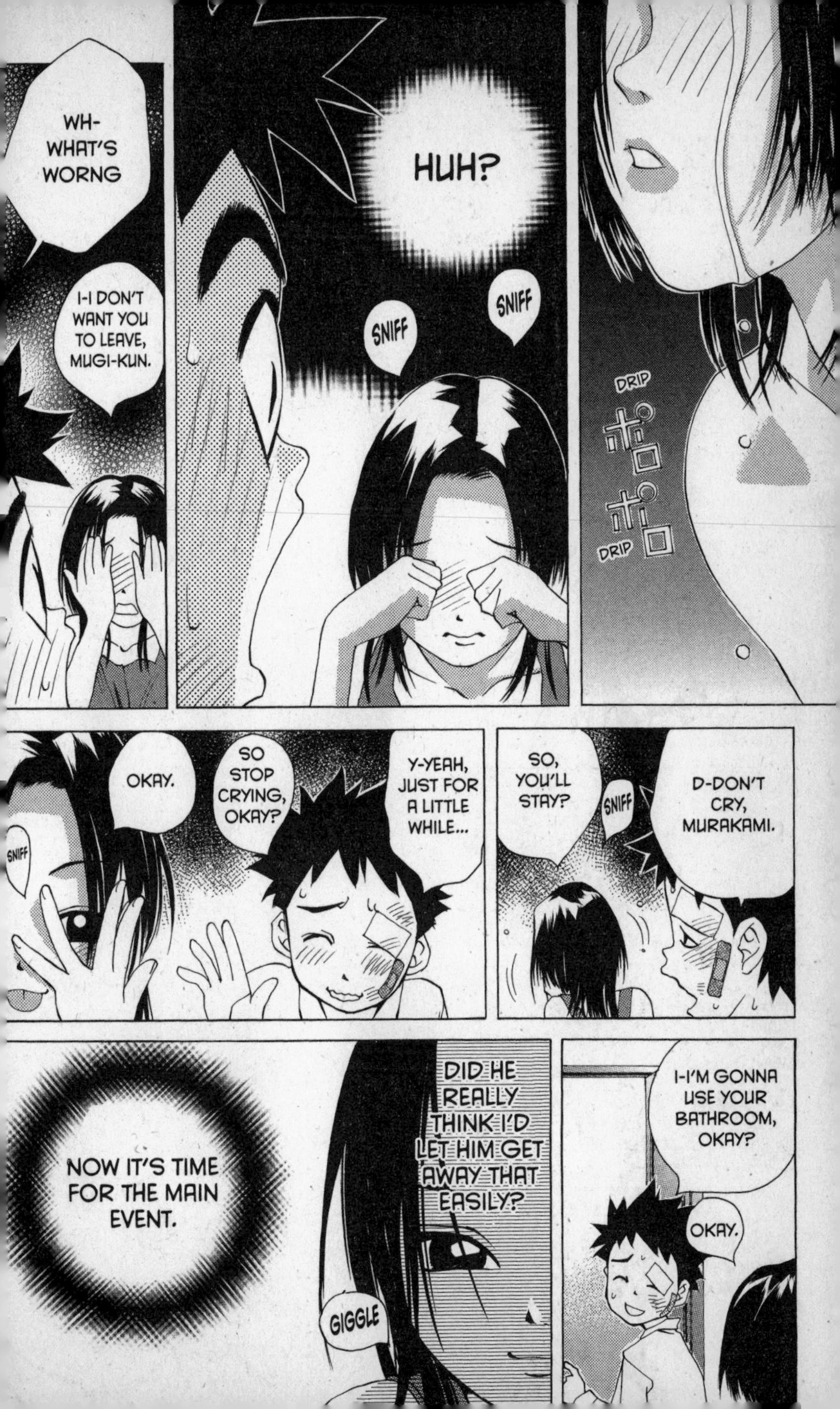
DRIP
ポロポロ
DRIP
HUH?
SNIFF
SNIFF
WH- WHAT'S WORNG
I-I DON'T WANT YOU TO LEAVE, MUGI-KUN.
D-DON'T CRY, MURAKAMI.
SNIFF
SO, YOU'LL STAY?
Y-YEAH, JUST FOR A LITTLE WHILE...
SO STOP CRYING, OKAY?
OKAY.
SNIFF
I-I'M GONNA USE YOUR BATHROOM, OKAY?
OKAY.
DID HE REALLY THINK I'D LET HIM GET AWAY THAT EASILY?
GIGGLE
NOW IT'S TIME FOR THE MAIN EVENT.

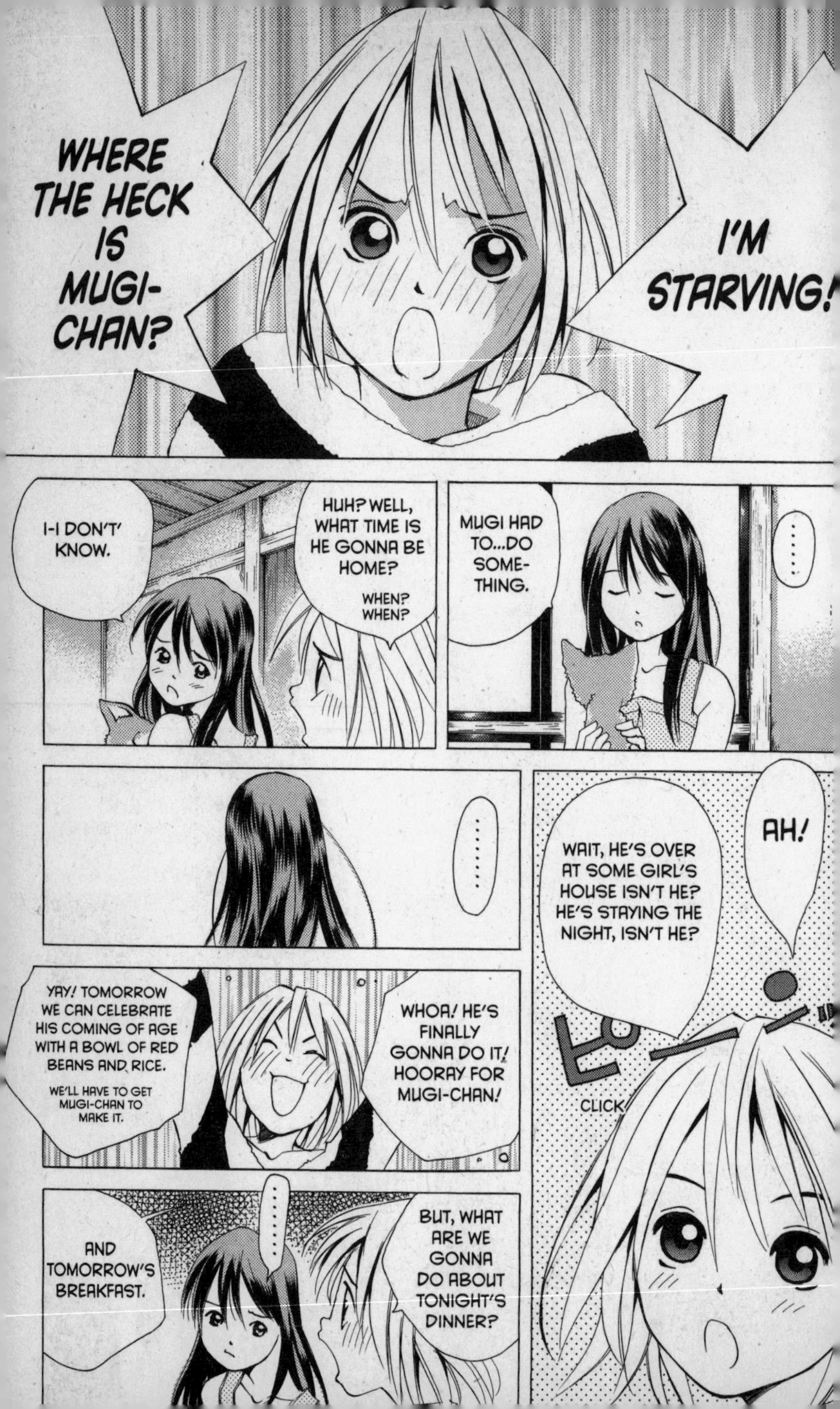
WHERE THE HECK IS MUGI-CHAN?
I'M STARVING!
......
MUGI HAD TO...DO SOME-THING.
HUH? WELL, WHAT TIME IS HE GONNA BE HOME?
WHEN? WHEN?
I-I DON'T' KNOW.
AH!
WAIT, HE'S OVER AT SOME GIRL'S HOUSE ISN'T HE? HE'S STAYING THE NIGHT, ISN'T HE?
CLICK
......
WHOA! HE'S FINALLY GONNA DO IT! HOORAY FOR MUGI-CHAN!
YAY! TOMORROW WE CAN CELEBRATE HIS COMING OF AGE WITH A BOWL OF RED BEANS AND RICE.
WE'LL HAVE TO GET MUGI-CHAN TO MAKE IT.
BUT, WHAT ARE WE GONNA DO ABOUT TONIGHT'S DINNER?
......
AND TOMORROW'S BREAKFAST.

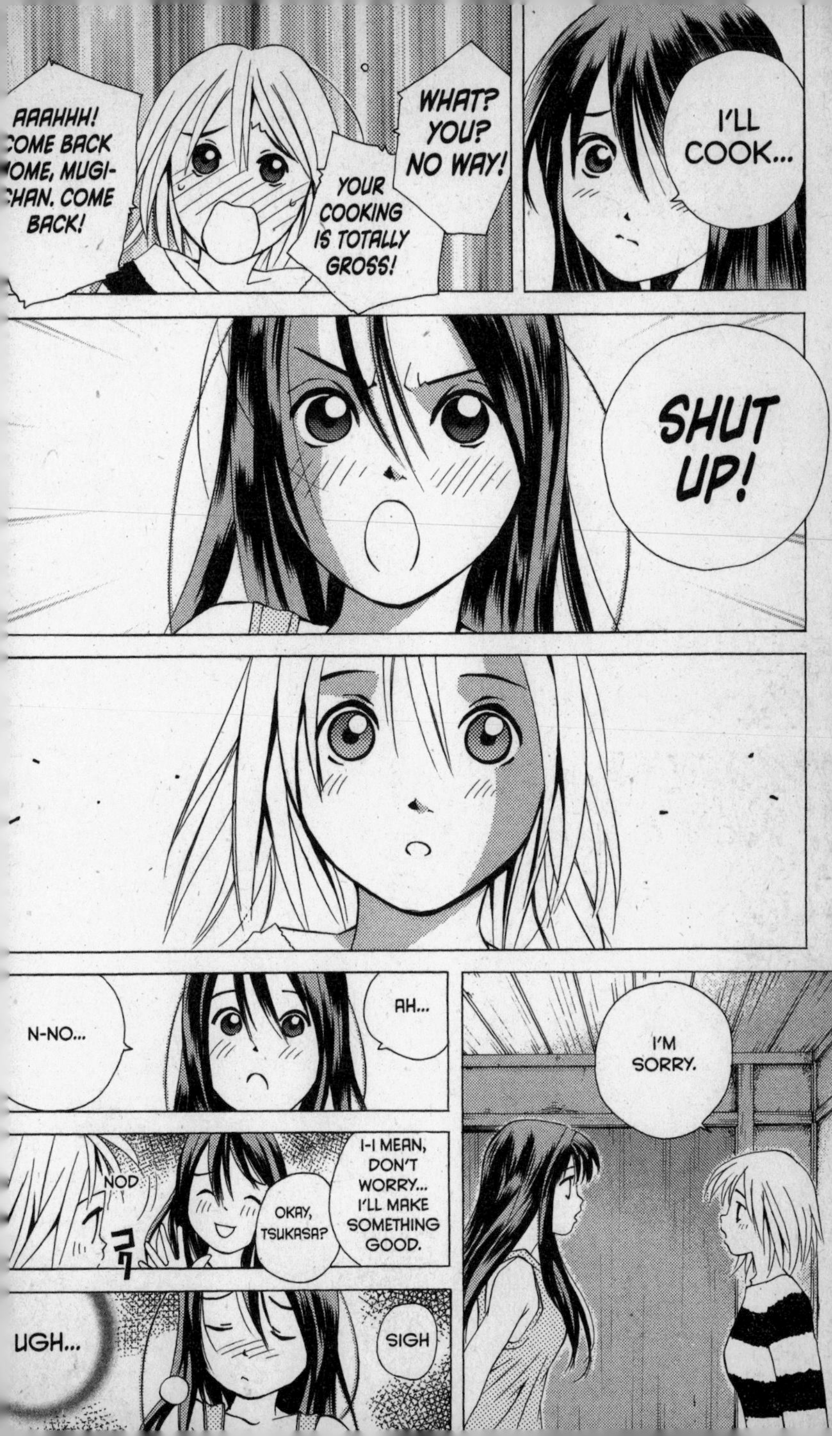

I'LL COOK...
WHAT? YOU? NO WAY!
YOUR COOKING IS TOTALLY GROSS!
AAAHHH! COME BACK HOME, MUGI-CHAN. COME BACK!
SHUT UP!
I'M SORRY.
AH...
N-NO...
I-I MEAN, DON'T WORRY... I'LL MAKE SOMETHING GOOD.
OKAY, TSUKASA?
NOD
コク
SIGH
UGH...

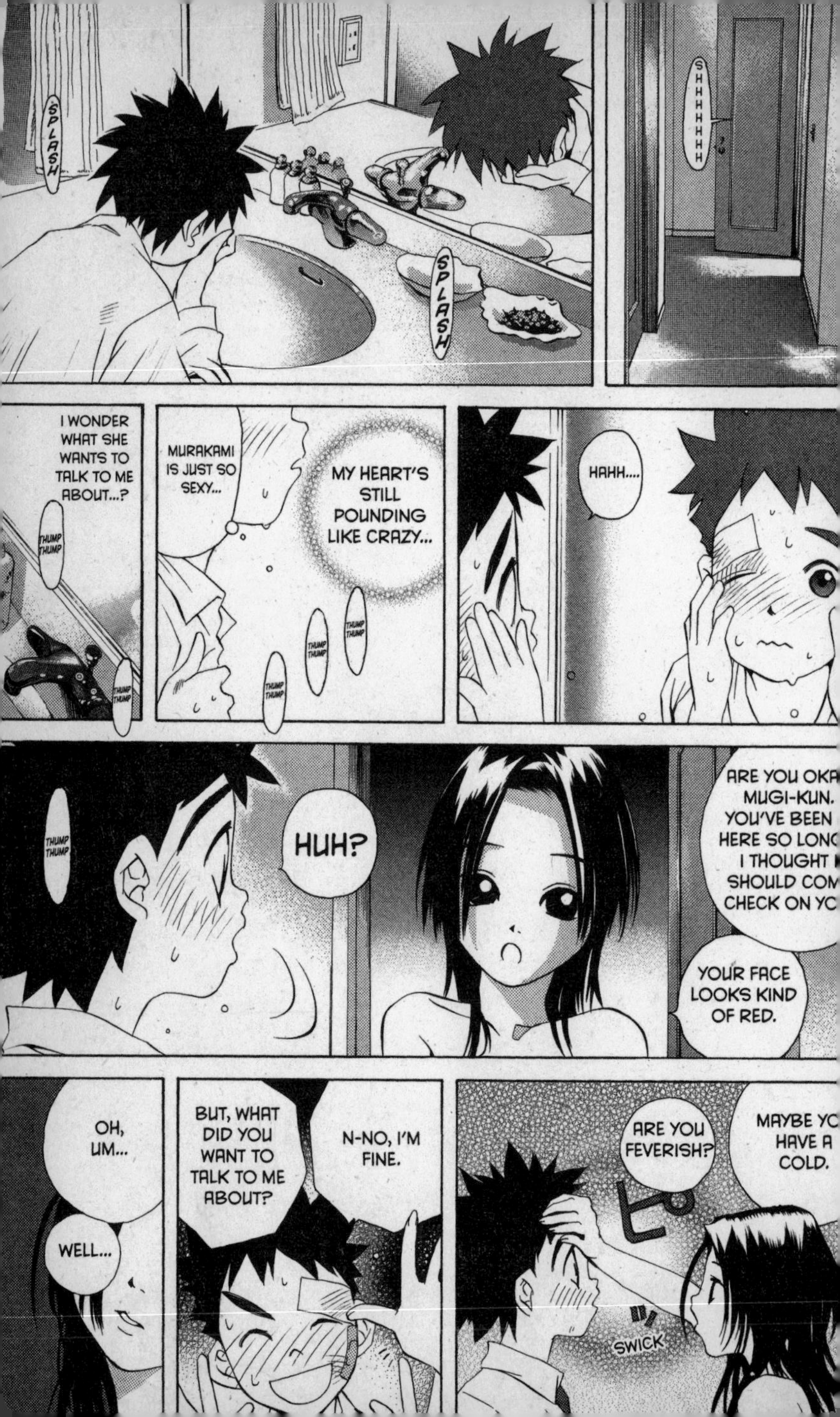
SHHHHHHH
SPLASH
SPLASH
HAHH....
MY HEART'S STILL POUNDING LIKE CRAZY...
MURAKAMI IS JUST SO SEXY...
THUMP THUMP
THUMP THUMP
THUMP THUMP
I WONDER WHAT SHE WANTS TO TALK TO ME ABOUT...?
THUMP THUMP
THUMP THUMP
ARE YOU OKA MUGI-KUN. YOU'VE BEEN HERE SO LONG I THOUGHT I SHOULD COM CHECK ON YO
YOUR FACE LOOKS KIND OF RED.
HUH?
THUMP THUMP
MAYBE YO HAVE A COLD.
ARE YOU FEVERISH?
SWICK
N-NO, I'M FINE.
BUT, WHAT DID YOU WANT TO TALK TO ME ABOUT?
OH, UM...
WELL...

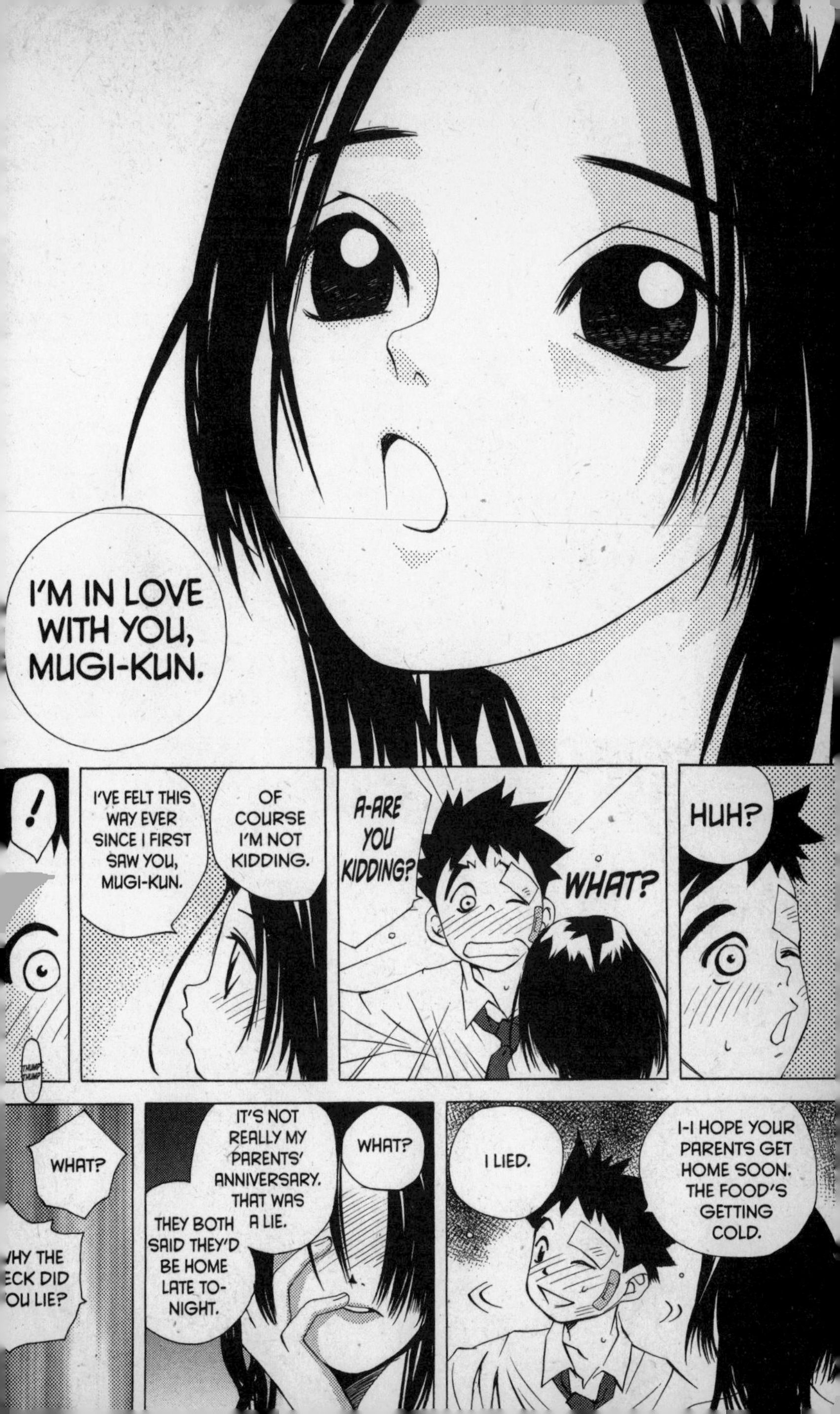
I'M IN LOVE WITH YOU, MUGI-KUN.
HUH?
A-ARE YOU KIDDING?
WHAT?
OF COURSE I'M NOT KIDDING.
I'VE FELT THIS WAY EVER SINCE I FIRST SAW YOU, MUGI-KUN.
!
THUMP THUMP
I-I HOPE YOUR PARENTS GET HOME SOON. THE FOOD'S GETTING COLD.
I LIED.
WHAT?
IT'S NOT REALLY MY PARENTS' ANNIVERSARY. THAT WAS A LIE.
THEY BOTH SAID THEY'D BE HOME LATE TO-NIGHT.
WHAT?
HY THE ECK DID OU LIE?

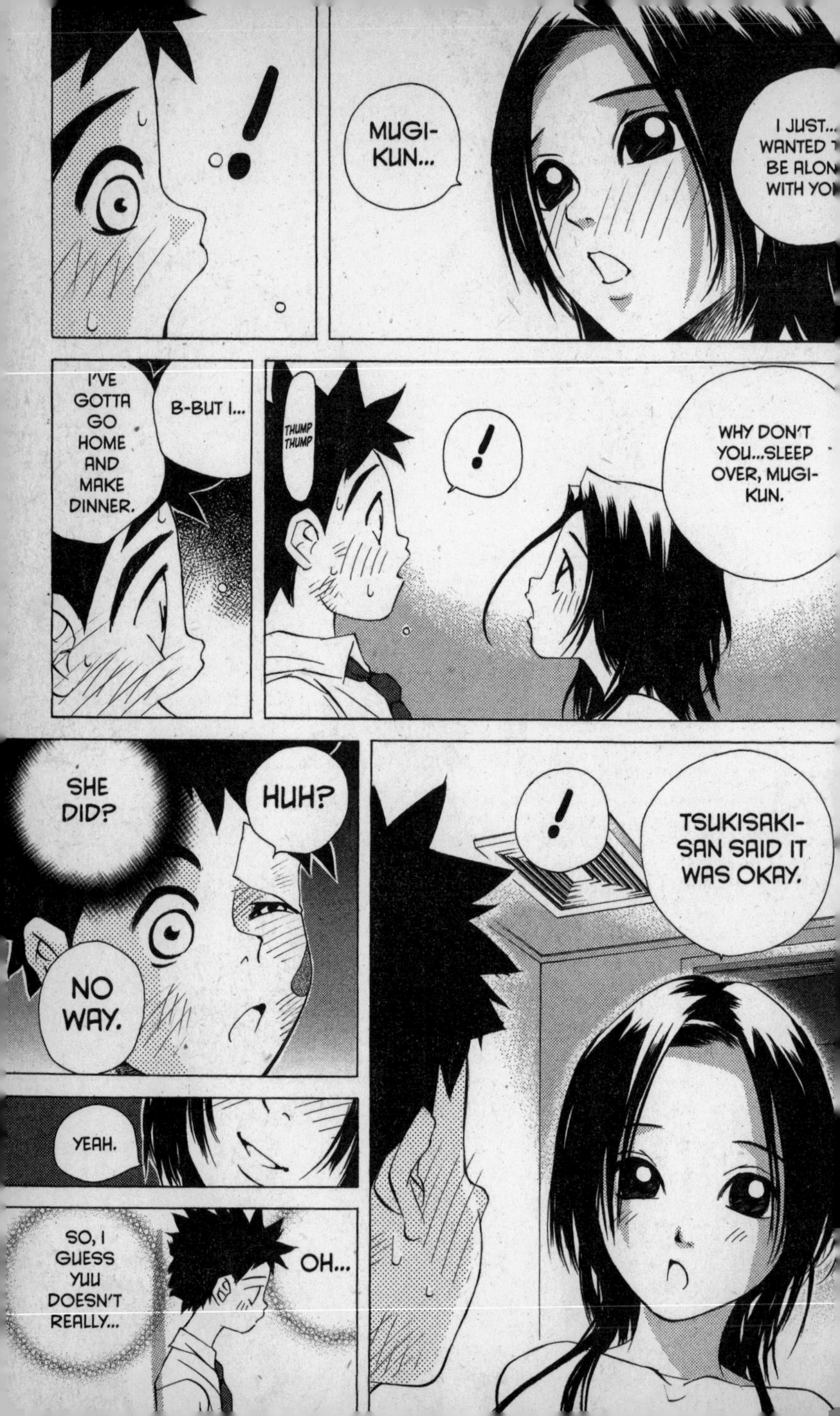
I JUST... WANTED T BE ALON WITH YO
MUGI-KUN...
!
WHY DON'T YOU...SLEEP OVER, MUGI-KUN.
!
THUMP THUMP
B-BUT I...
I'VE GOTTA GO HOME AND MAKE DINNER.
TSUKISAKI-SAN SAID IT WAS OKAY.
!
HUH?
SHE DID?
NO WAY.
YEAH.
OH...
SO, I GUESS YUU DOESN'T REALLY...

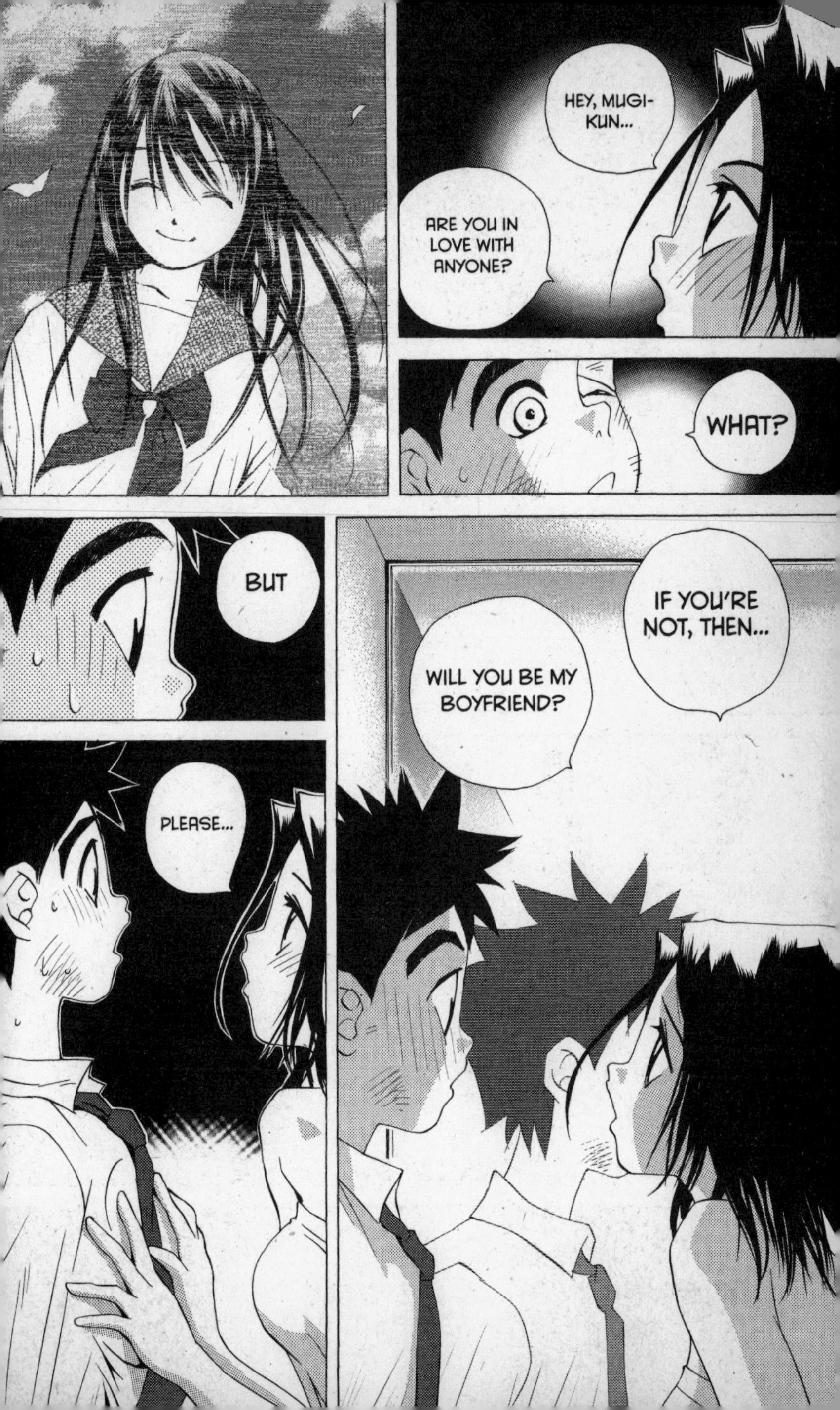
HEY, MUGI-KUN...
ARE YOU IN LOVE WITH ANYONE?
WHAT?
IF YOU'RE NOT, THEN...
WILL YOU BE MY BOYFRIEND?
BUT
PLEASE...

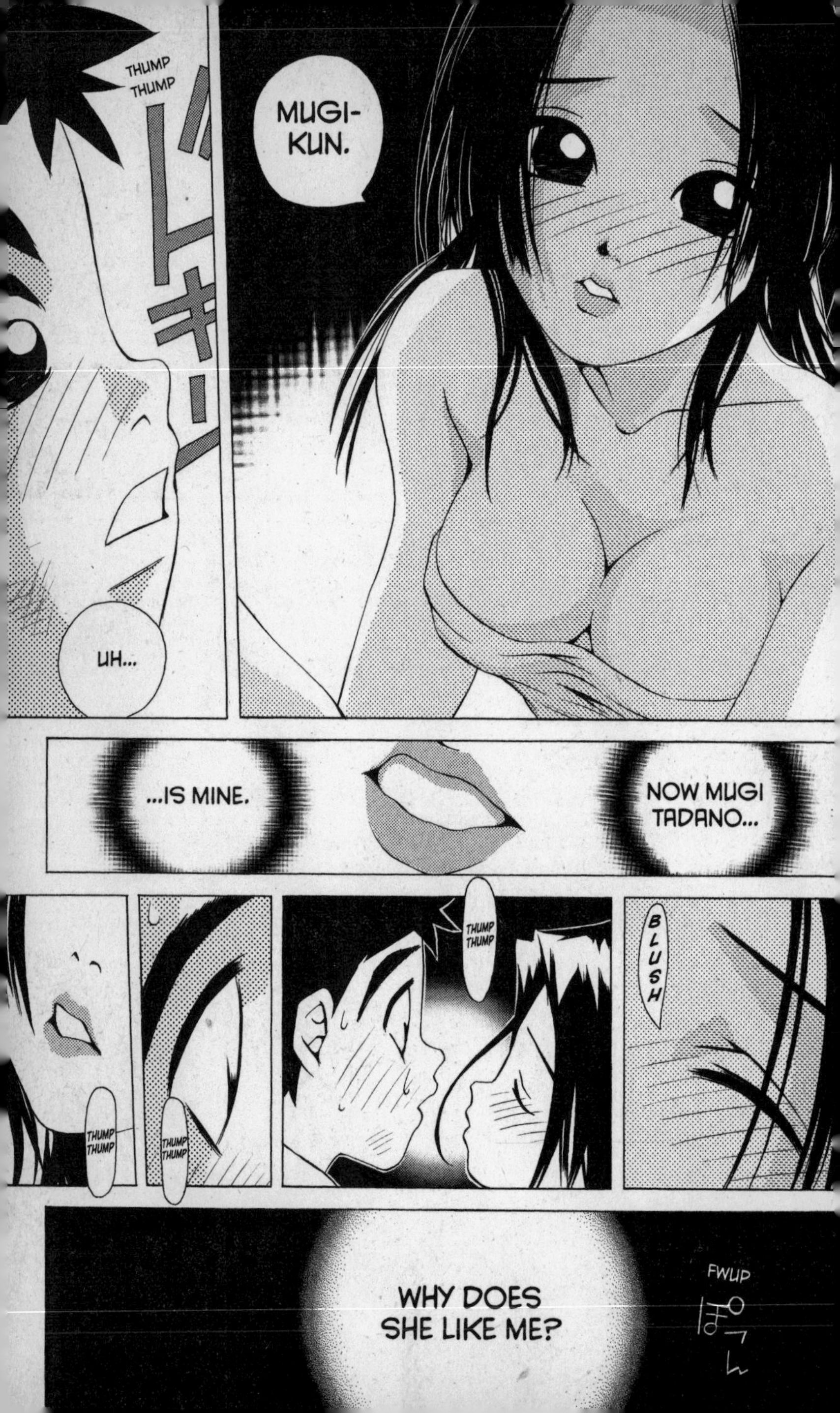
MUGI-KUN.
THUMP THUMP
UH...
NOW MUGI TADANO...
...IS MINE.
BLUSH
THUMP THUMP
THUMP THUMP
THUMP THUMP
FWUP
WHY DOES SHE LIKE ME?

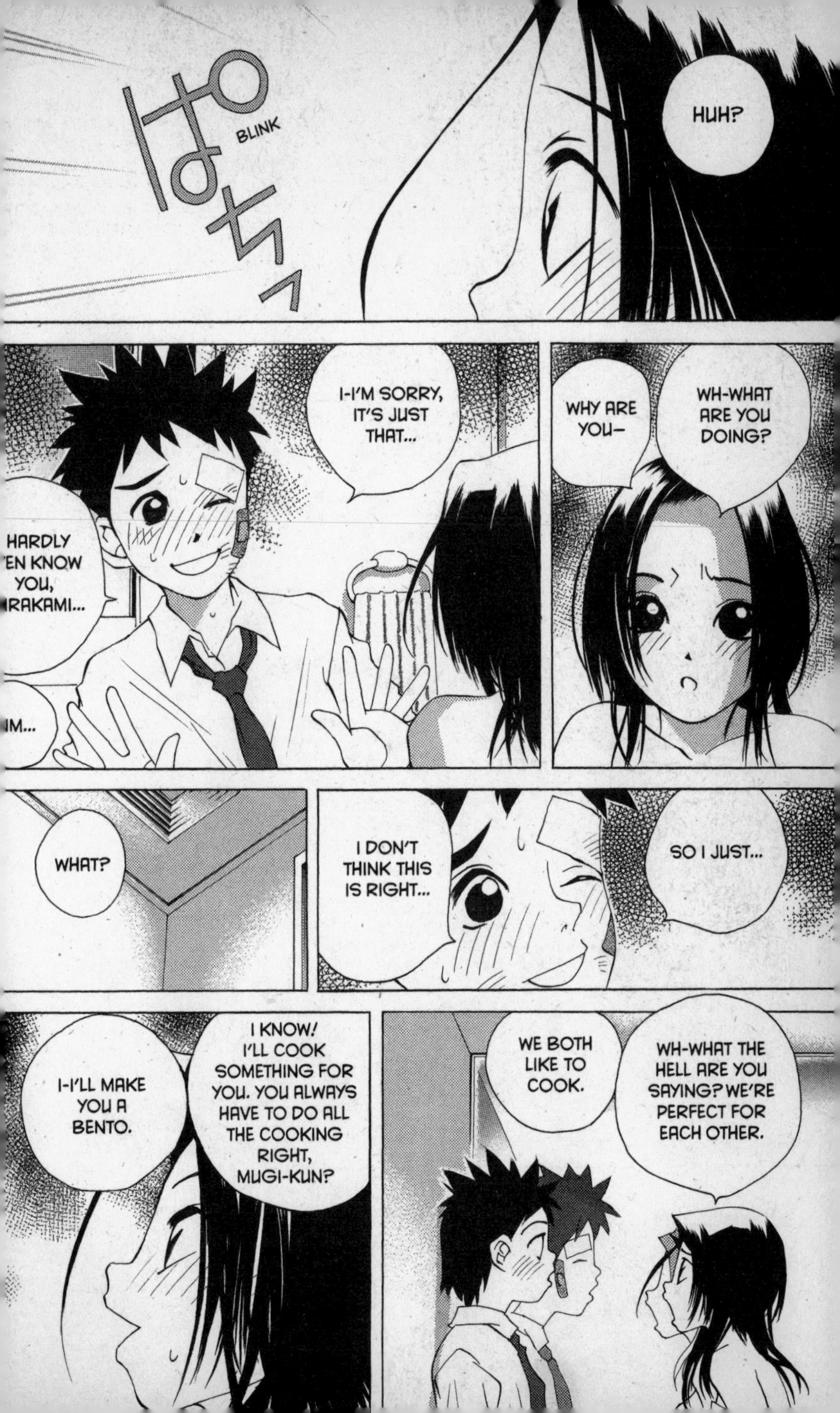
HUH?
BLINK
WH-WHAT ARE YOU DOING?
WHY ARE YOU—
I-I'M SORRY, IT'S JUST THAT...
HARDLY 'EN KNOW YOU, RAKAMI...
IM...
SO I JUST...
I DON'T THINK THIS IS RIGHT...
WHAT?
WH-WHAT THE HELL ARE YOU SAYING? WE'RE PERFECT FOR EACH OTHER.
WE BOTH LIKE TO COOK.
I KNOW! I'LL COOK SOMETHING FOR YOU. YOU ALWAYS HAVE TO DO ALL THE COOKING RIGHT, MUGI-KUN?
I-I'LL MAKE YOU A BENTO.

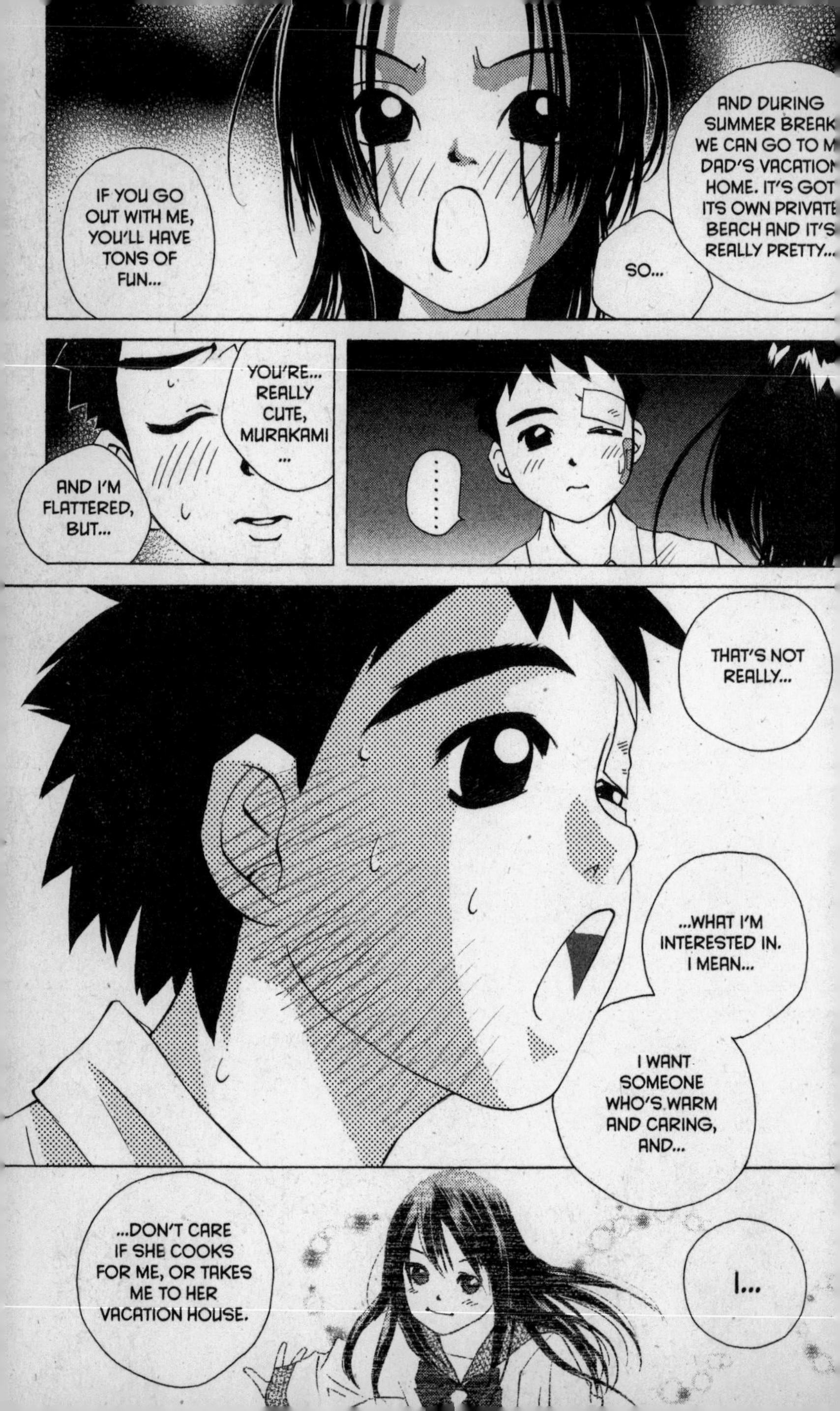
AND DURING SUMMER BREAK WE CAN GO TO MY DAD'S VACATION HOME. IT'S GOT ITS OWN PRIVATE BEACH AND IT'S REALLY PRETTY...
SO...
IF YOU GO OUT WITH ME, YOU'LL HAVE TONS OF FUN...
......
YOU'RE... REALLY CUTE, MURAKAMI...
AND I'M FLATTERED, BUT...
THAT'S NOT REALLY...
...WHAT I'M INTERESTED IN. I MEAN...
I WANT SOMEONE WHO'S WARM AND CARING, AND...
I...
...DON'T CARE IF SHE COOKS FOR ME, OR TAKES ME TO HER VACATION HOUSE.

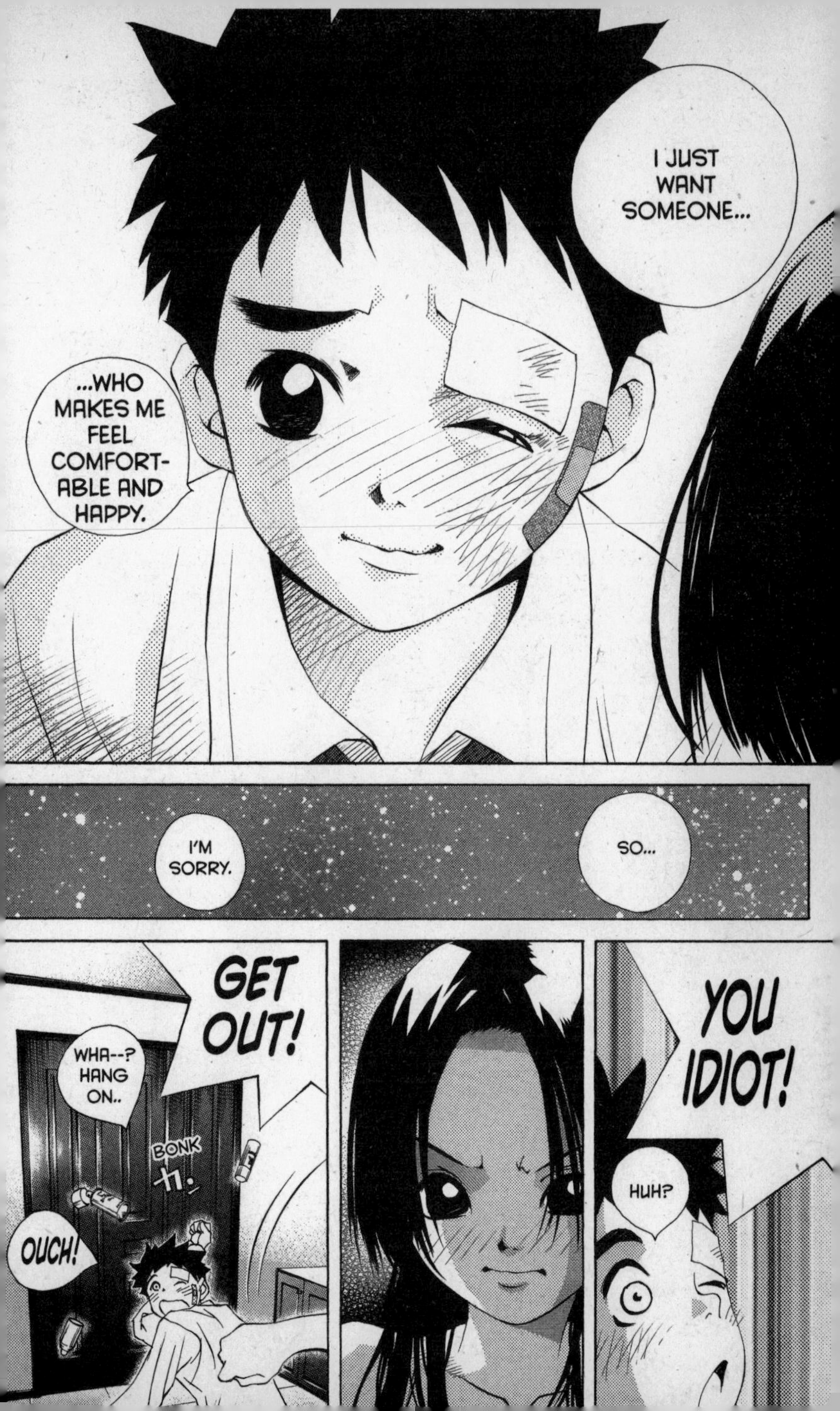
I JUST WANT SOMEONE...
...WHO MAKES ME FEEL COMFORT-ABLE AND HAPPY.
SO...
I'M SORRY.
YOU IDIOT!
HUH?
GET OUT!
WHA--? HANG ON..
BONK
OUCH!

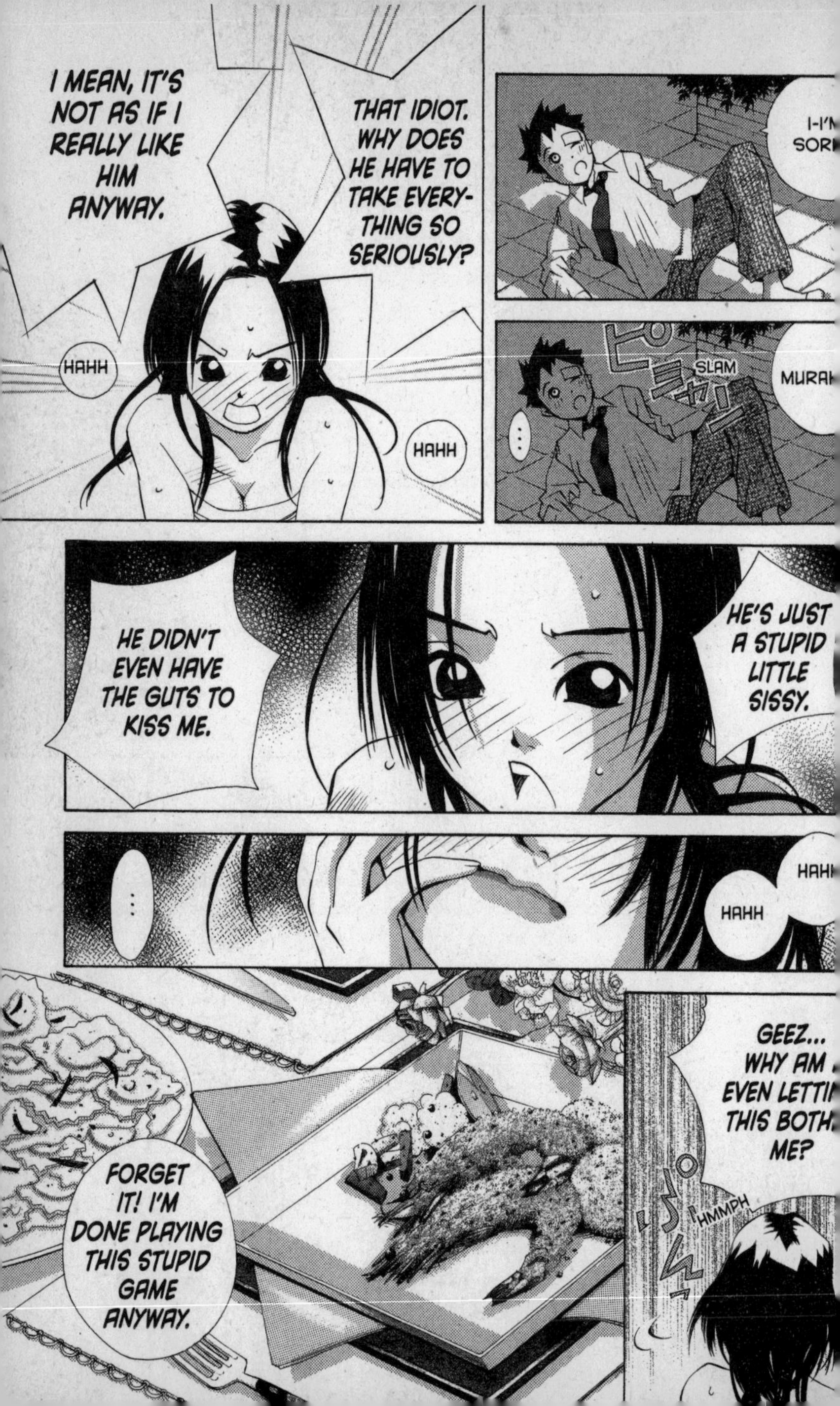
I-I'M
SOR
SLAM
MURAK
...
THAT IDIOT. WHY DOES HE HAVE TO TAKE EVERYTHING SO SERIOUSLY?
I MEAN, IT'S NOT AS IF I REALLY LIKE HIM ANYWAY.
HAHH
HAHH
HE'S JUST A STUPID LITTLE SISSY.
HE DIDN'T EVEN HAVE THE GUTS TO KISS ME.
HAH
HAHH
...
GEEZ... WHY AM EVEN LETTI THIS BOTH ME?
HMMPH
FORGET IT! I'M DONE PLAYING THIS STUPID GAME ANYWAY.

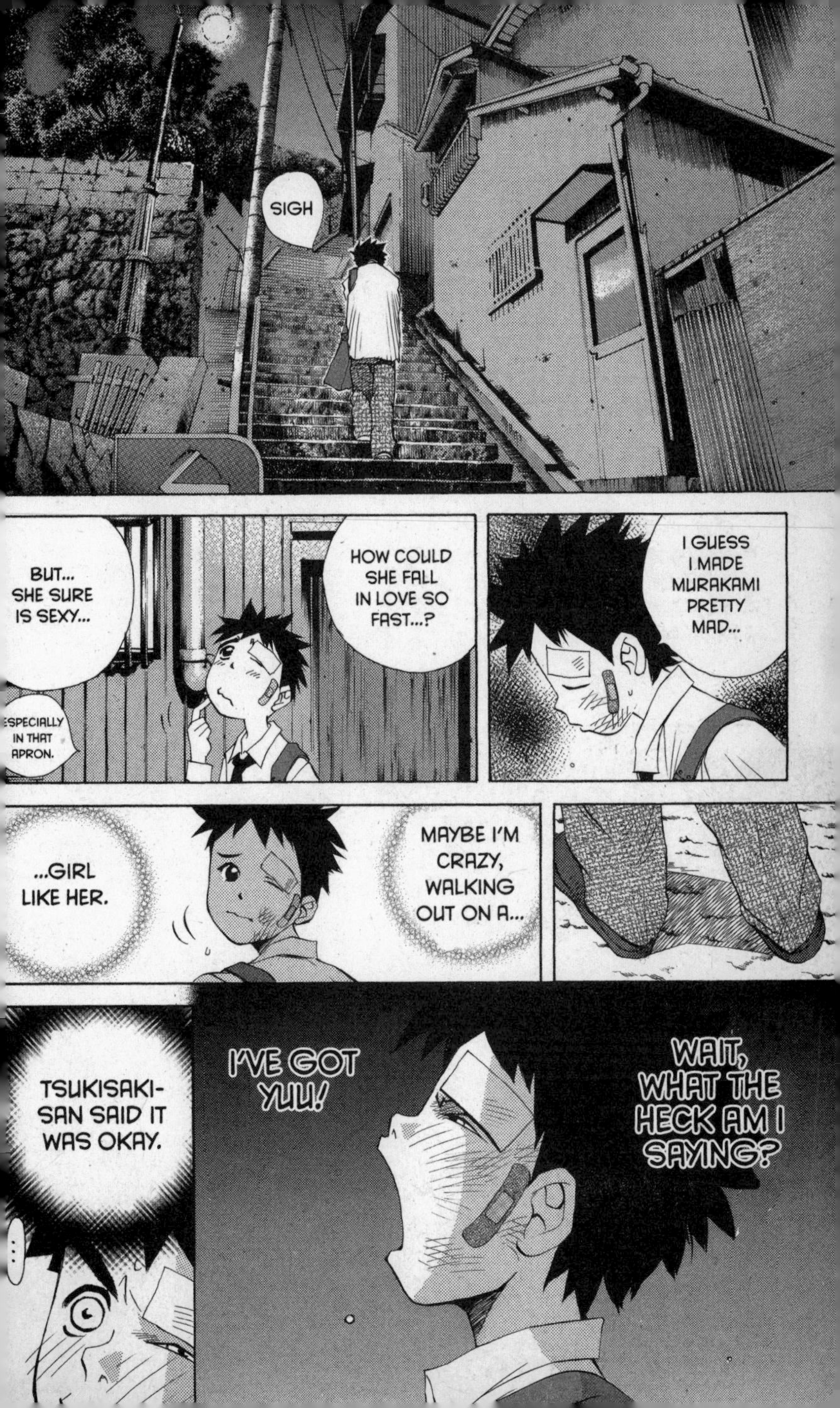

SIGH
I GUESS I MADE MURAKAMI PRETTY MAD...
HOW COULD SHE FALL IN LOVE SO FAST...?
BUT... SHE SURE IS SEXY...
SPECIALLY IN THAT APRON.
MAYBE I'M CRAZY, WALKING OUT ON A...
...GIRL LIKE HER.
WAIT, WHAT THE HECK AM I SAYING?
I'VE GOT YUU!
TSUKISAKI-SAN SAID IT WAS OKAY.
...

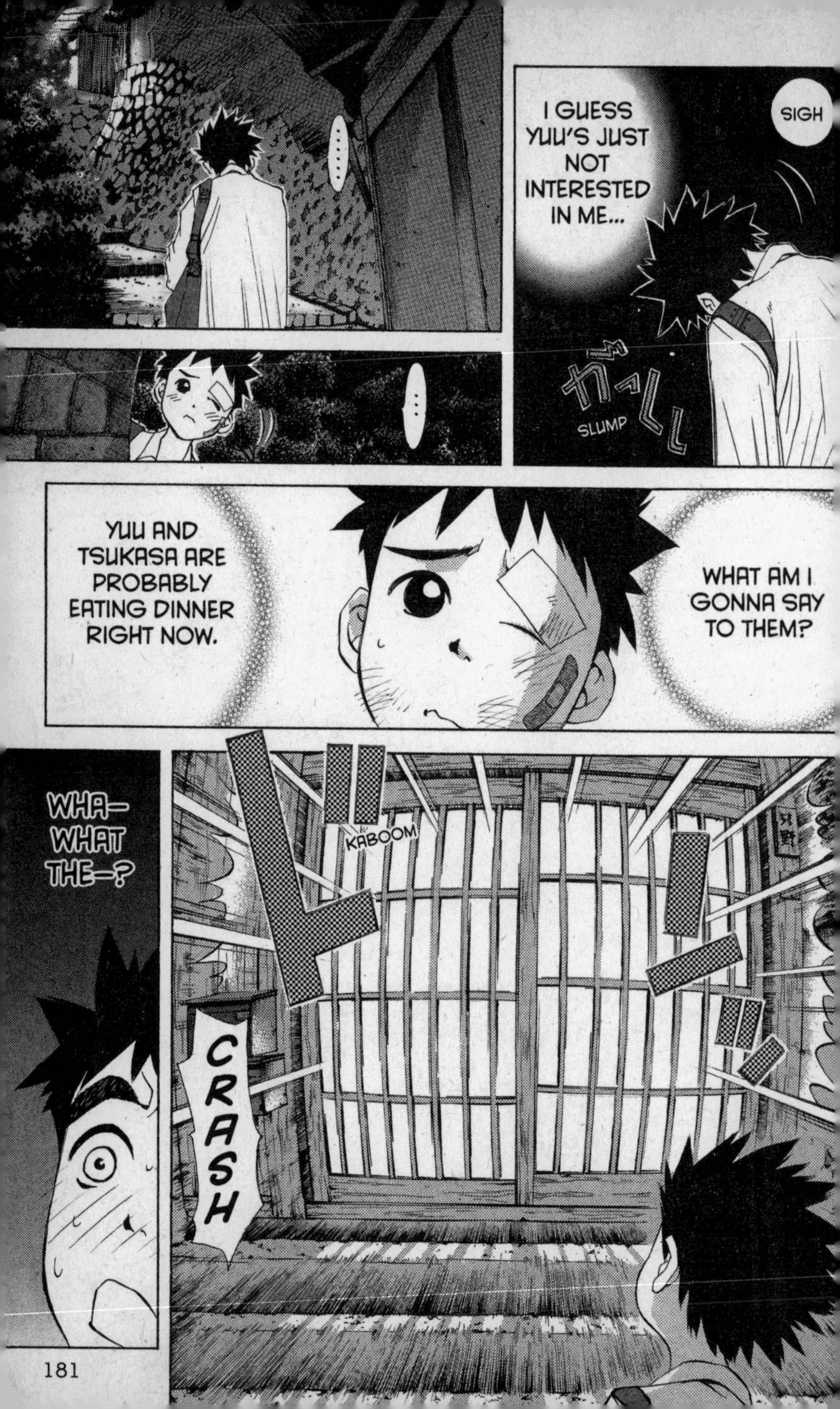
SIGH
I GUESS YUU'S JUST NOT INTERESTED IN ME...
SLUMP
......
...
WHAT AM I GONNA SAY TO THEM?
YUU AND TSUKASA ARE PROBABLY EATING DINNER RIGHT NOW.
KABOOM
CRASH
WHA- WHAT THE--?

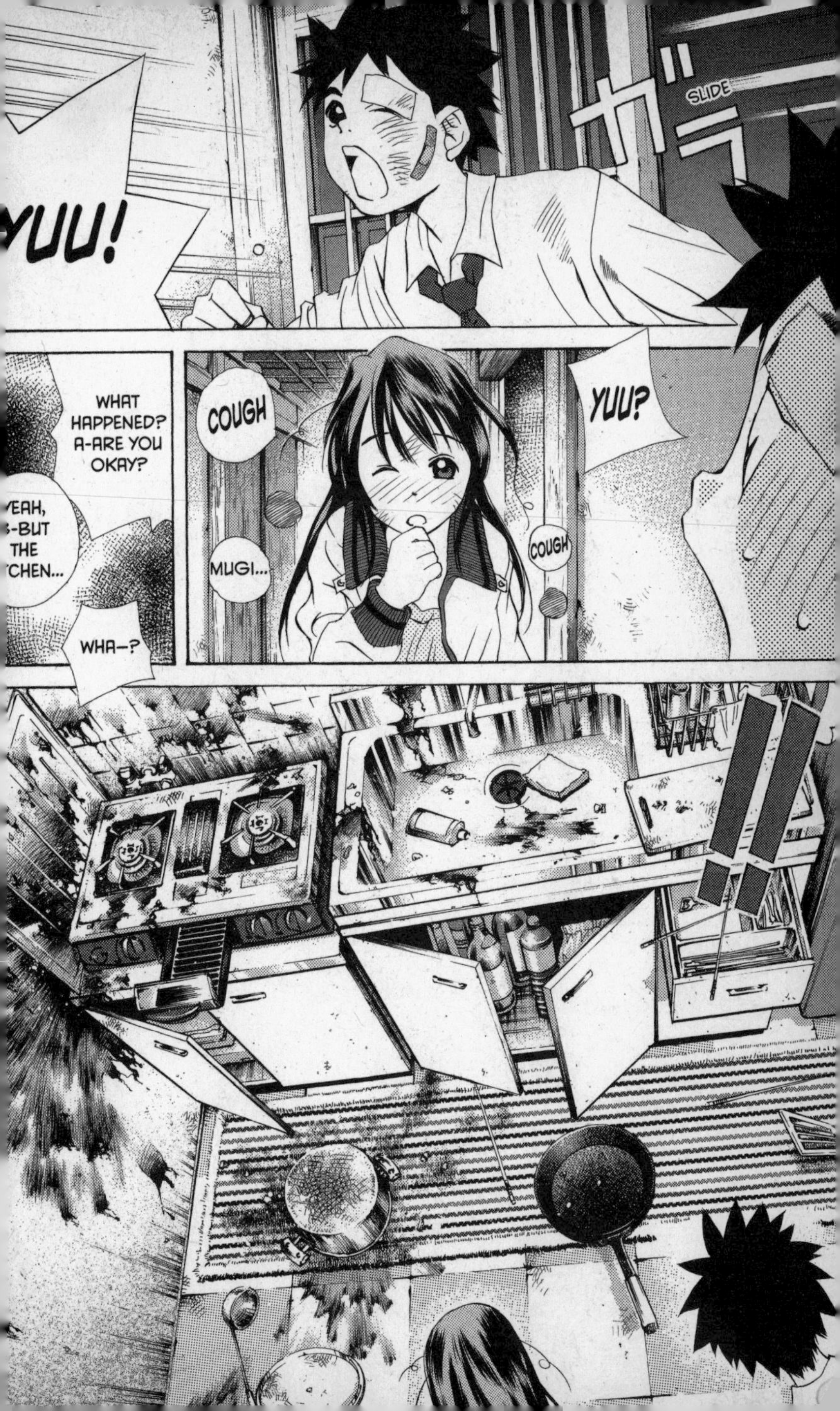
SLIDE
YUU!
YUU?
COUGH
COUGH
MUGI...
WHAT HAPPENED? A-ARE YOU OKAY?
YEAH, -BUT THE TCHEN...
WHA-?

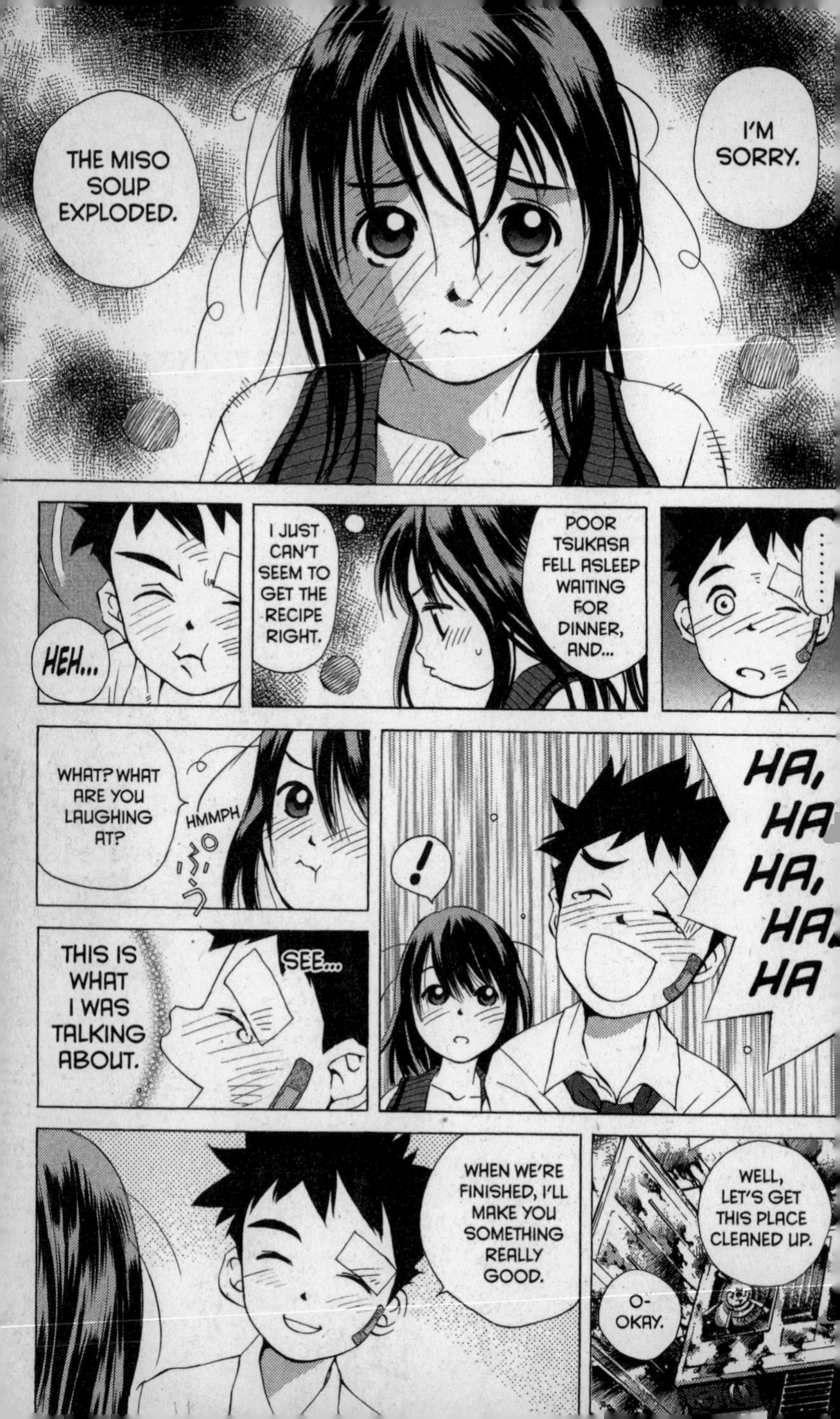

I'M SORRY.
THE MISO SOUP EXPLODED.
......
POOR TSUKASA FELL ASLEEP WAITING FOR DINNER, AND...
I JUST CAN'T SEEM TO GET THE RECIPE RIGHT.
HEH...
HA, HA HA, HA, HA
!
WHAT? WHAT ARE YOU LAUGHING AT?
HMMPH
SEE...
THIS IS WHAT I WAS TALKING ABOUT.
WELL, LET'S GET THIS PLACE CLEANED UP.
O-OKAY.
WHEN WE'RE FINISHED, I'LL MAKE YOU SOMETHING REALLY GOOD.

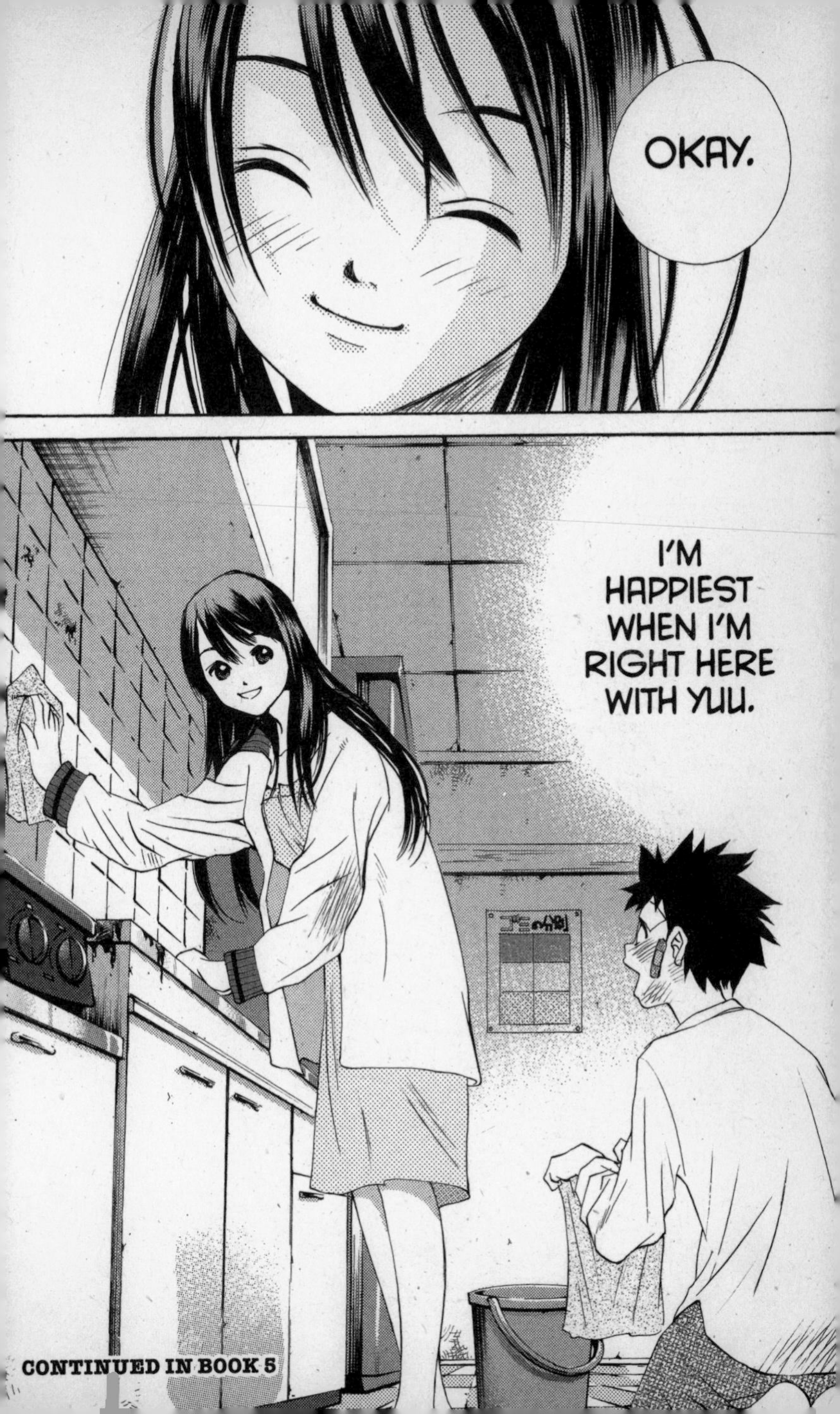
OKAY.
I'M HAPPIEST WHEN I'M RIGHT HERE WITH YUU.

CONTINUED IN BOOK 5

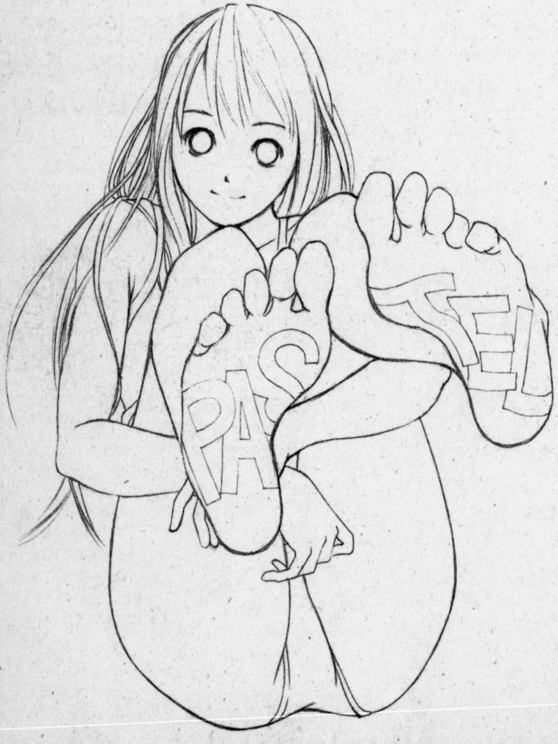
PAS
TEL

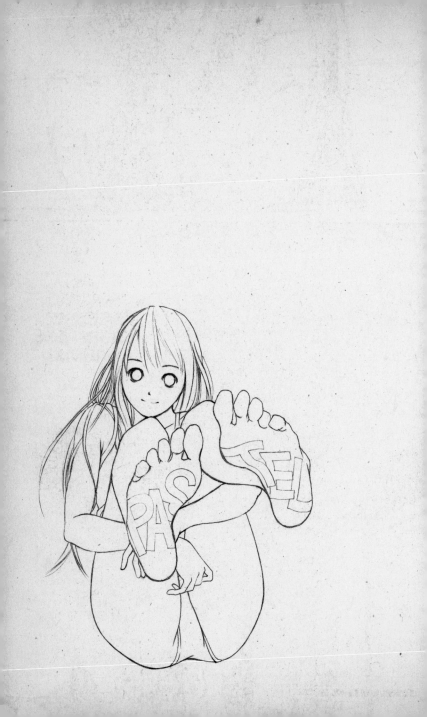

AT WORK ON PASTEL

THE TALE OF THE NINJA

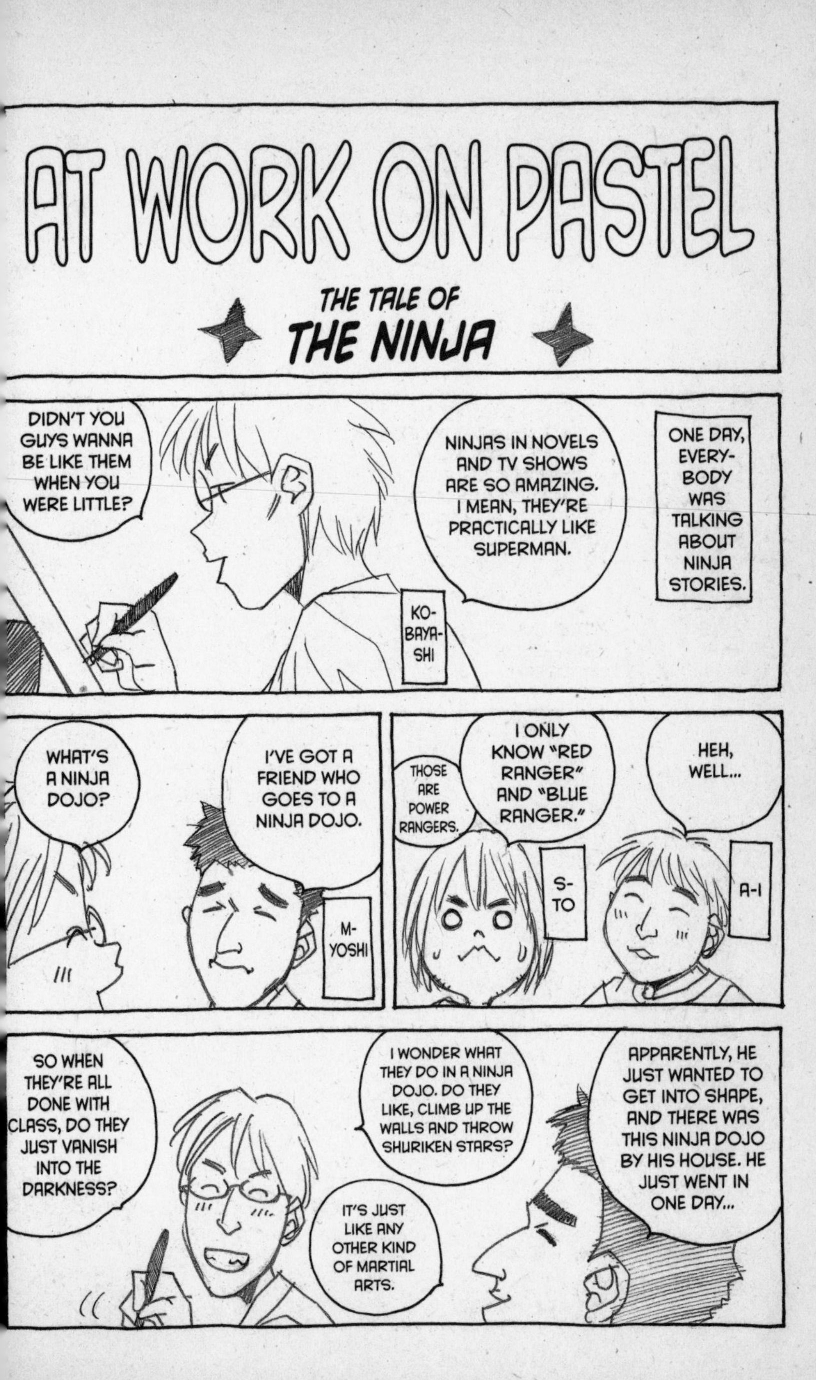
ONE DAY, EVERYBODY WAS TALKING ABOUT NINJA STORIES.
NINJAS IN NOVELS AND TV SHOWS ARE SO AMAZING. I MEAN, THEY'RE PRACTICALLY LIKE SUPERMAN.
KO-BAYA-SHI
DIDN'T YOU GUYS WANNA BE LIKE THEM WHEN YOU WERE LITTLE?
HEH, WELL...
A-I
I ONLY KNOW "RED RANGER" AND "BLUE RANGER."
S-TO
THOSE ARE POWER RANGERS.
I'VE GOT A FRIEND WHO GOES TO A NINJA DOJO.
M-YOSHI
WHAT'S A NINJA DOJO?
APPARENTLY, HE JUST WANTED TO GET INTO SHAPE, AND THERE WAS THIS NINJA DOJO BY HIS HOUSE. HE JUST WENT IN ONE DAY...
I WONDER WHAT THEY DO IN A NINJA DOJO. DO THEY LIKE, CLIMB UP THE WALLS AND THROW SHURIKEN STARS?
IT'S JUST LIKE ANY OTHER KIND OF MARTIAL ARTS.
SO WHEN THEY'RE ALL DONE WITH CLASS, DO THEY JUST VANISH INTO THE DARKNESS?

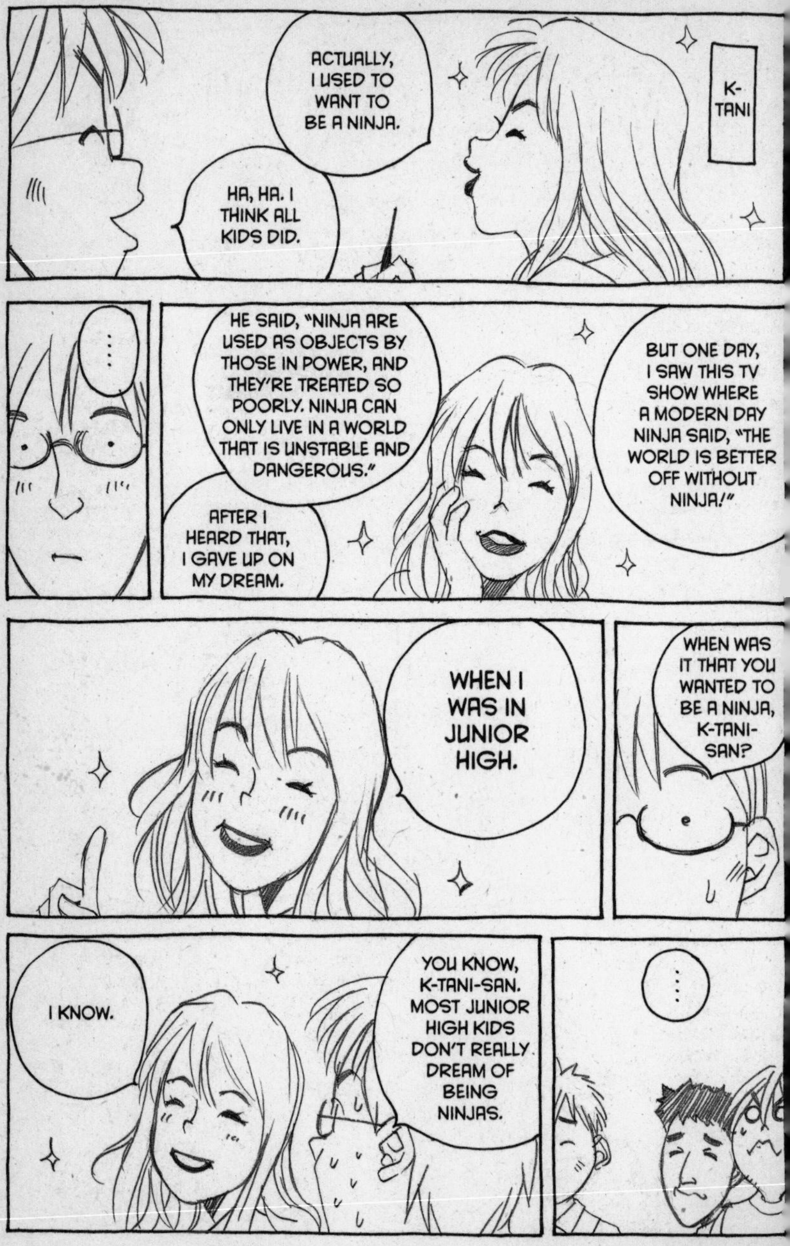
K-TANI
ACTUALLY, I USED TO WANT TO BE A NINJA.
HA, HA. I THINK ALL KIDS DID.
BUT ONE DAY, I SAW THIS TV SHOW WHERE A MODERN DAY NINJA SAID, "THE WORLD IS BETTER OFF WITHOUT NINJA!"
HE SAID, "NINJA ARE USED AS OBJECTS BY THOSE IN POWER, AND THEY'RE TREATED SO POORLY. NINJA CAN ONLY LIVE IN A WORLD THAT IS UNSTABLE AND DANGEROUS."
AFTER I HEARD THAT, I GAVE UP ON MY DREAM.
.....
WHEN WAS IT THAT YOU WANTED TO BE A NINJA, K-TANI-SAN?
WHEN I WAS IN JUNIOR HIGH.
.....
YOU KNOW, K-TANI-SAN. MOST JUNIOR HIGH KIDS DON'T REALLY DREAM OF BEING NINJAS.
I KNOW.

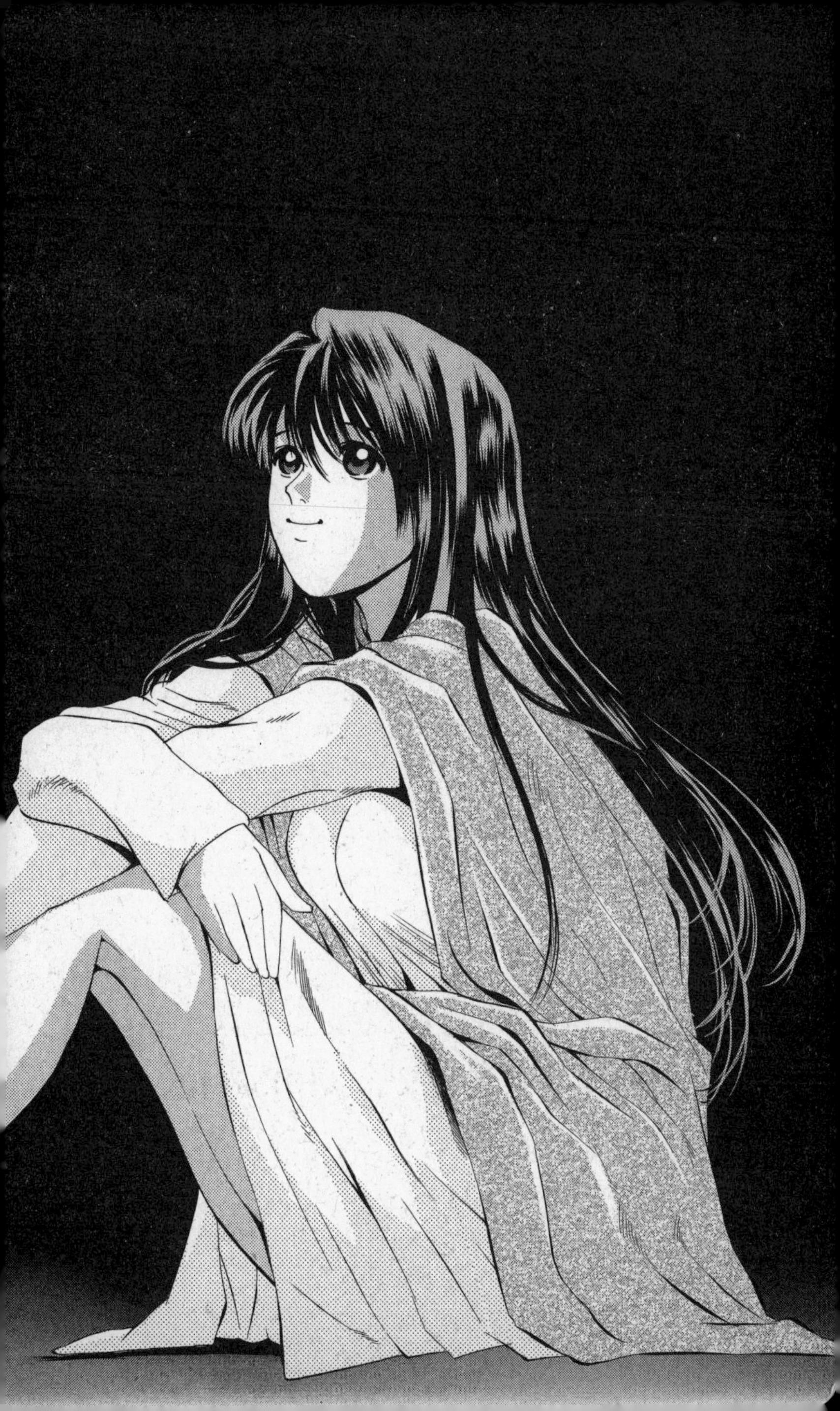

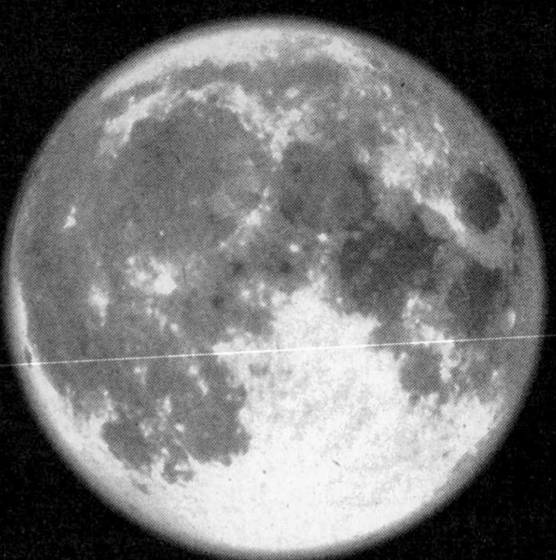

THERE ARE AS MANY COMICS OUT THERE AS THERE ARE STARS IN THE SKY, SO I'D LIKE TO THANK YOU FOR CHOOSING PASTEL. THANKS TO YOU GUYS, I CAN PUT FOOD ON THE TABLE EVERY DAY. AND YOU GUYS EVEN SEND ME LETTERS. THANK YOU SO MUCH. THEY GIVE ME THE COURAGE TO KEEP ON GOING. I GET SO BUSY THAT IT'S HARD FOR ME TO REPLY, BUT I READ EACH ONE. THANK YOU ALL SO MUCH!

TOSHIHIKO KOBAYASHI

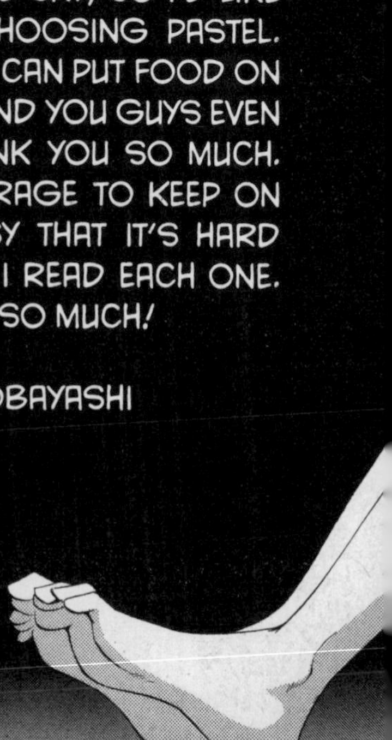

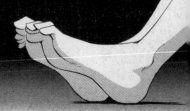

TOSHIHIKO KOBAYASHI

Born in Mihara city in Hiroshima. Birthday is February 25.
In 1995, "Half Coat" was serialized in "Magazine Special" from No.1 to
No.11. After the serial publication of "Parallel" in "Magazine Special"
from No.8 in 2000 to No.1 in 2002, "Pastel" was serialized in "Weekly
Shonen Magazine" from the 32nd issue in 2002 to the 33rd issue in
2003. And now "Pastel" has been running as a serial ever since
"Magazine Special" No.10 in 2003.

Favorites
Fruits
Sleeping
Hot green tea

Dislikes
Being scolded
Excessive expectations
Cigarette smoke

Translation Notes

Japanese is a tricky language for most Westerners, and translation is often more art than science. For your edification and reading pleasure, here are notes on some of the places where we could have gon in a different direction in our translation of the work, or where a Japanese cultural reference is used.

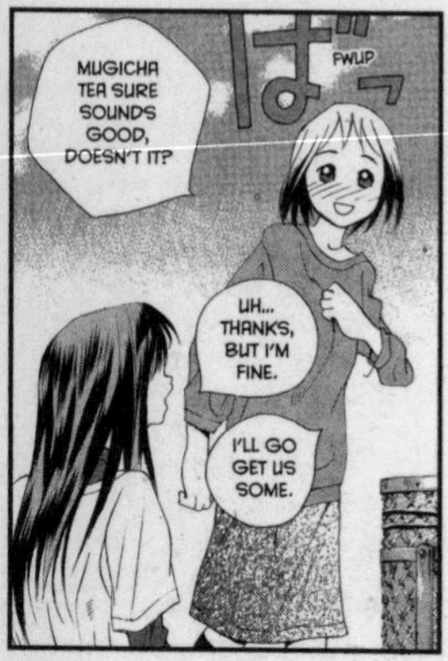
FWUP
MUGICHA TEA SURE SOUNDS GOOD, DOESN'T IT?
UH... THANKS, BUT I'M FINE.
I'LL GO GET US SOME.

Mugicha, page 28

Mugicha is barley tea. It's a popular summer beverage.

Tamagozake, page 57

Tamagozake is a folk remedy used for colds. It's a mixture of raw eggs and Japanese sake

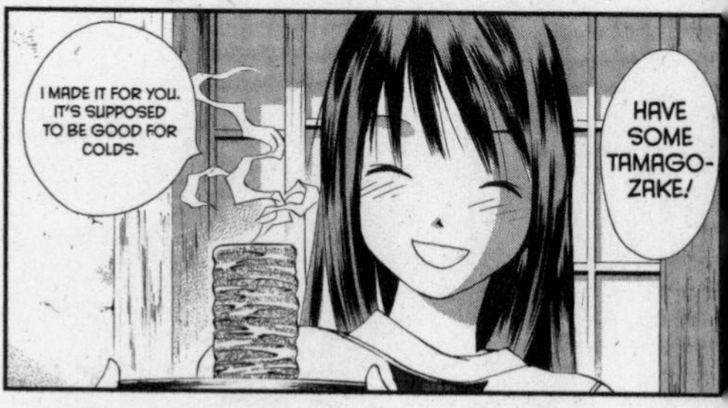
HAVE SOME TAMAGO-ZAKE!
I MADE IT FOR YOU. IT'S SUPPOSED TO BE GOOD FOR COLDS.

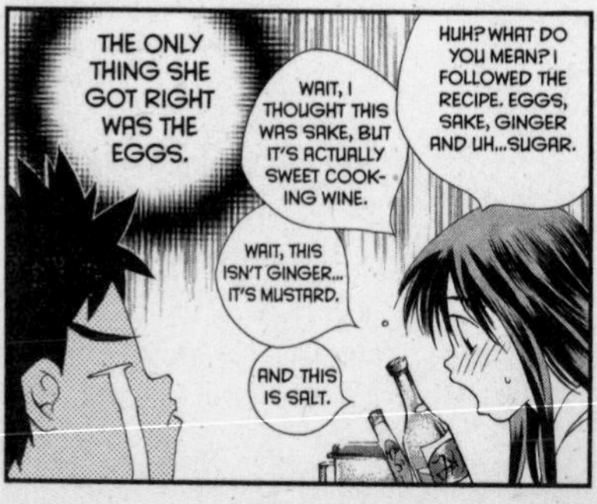
HUH? WHAT DO YOU MEAN? I FOLLOWED THE RECIPE. EGGS, SAKE, GINGER AND UH...SUGAR.
WAIT, I THOUGHT THIS WAS SAKE, BUT IT'S ACTUALLY SWEET COOK-ING WINE.
THE ONLY THING SHE GOT RIGHT WAS THE EGGS.
WAIT, THIS ISN'T GINGER... IT'S MUSTARD.
AND THIS IS SALT.

Mirin, page 57

The sweet cooking wine that Yuu refers to is called *mirin*. It's an essential ingredient in Japanese cooking.

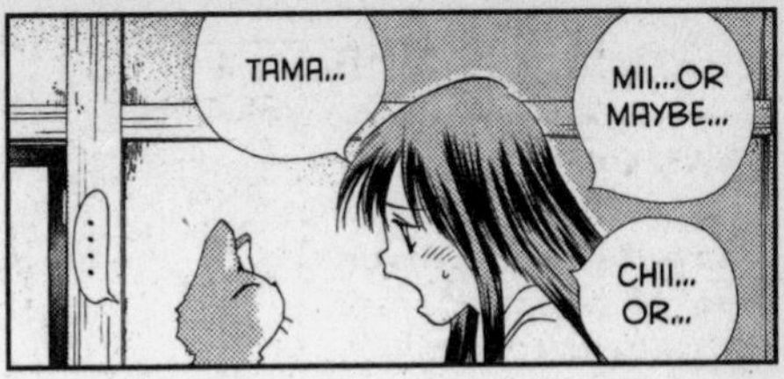
MII...OR MAYBE...
CHII... OR...
TAMA...
....

Mii, Chii, and Tama, page 64

Mii, Chii, and Tama are all popular cat names in Japan.

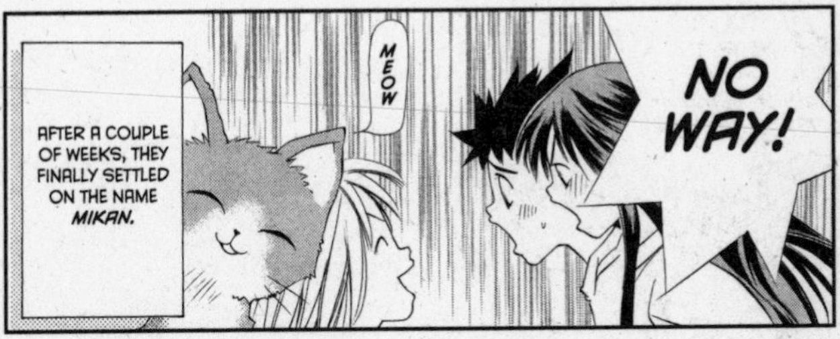
NO WAY!
MEOW
AFTER A COUPLE OF WEEKS, THEY FINALLY SETTLED ON THE NAME *MIKAN.*

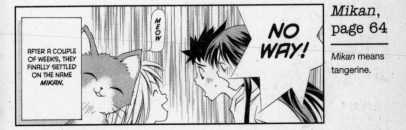

Mikan, page 64

Mikan means tangerine.

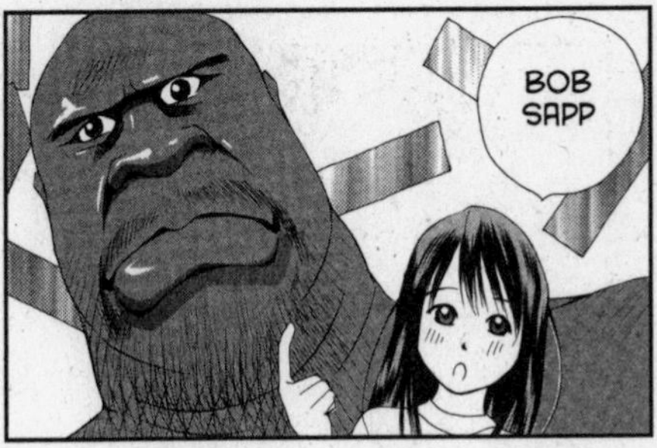
BOB SAPP

Bob Sapp, page 84

Bob Sapp is a former American football player who became a celebrity in Japan.

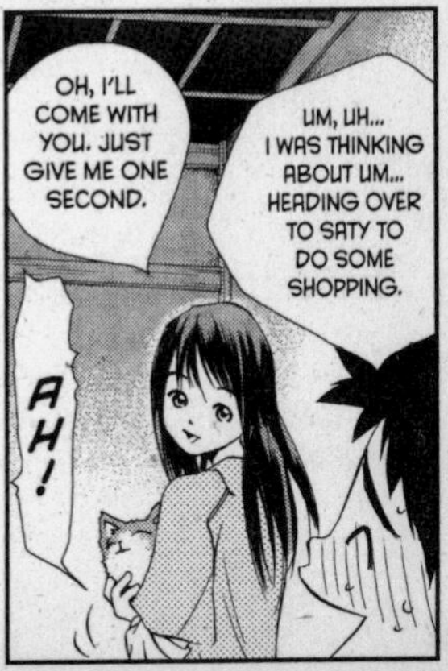
UM, UH... I WAS THINKING ABOUT UM... HEADING OVER TO SATY TO DO SOME SHOPPING.
OH, I'LL COME WITH YOU. JUST GIVE ME ONE SECOND.
AH!

Saty, page 87

Saty is a department store/supermarket.

Gokon, page 88

Mugi and Kazuki are having a *gokon*. This is a Japanese dating ritual in which an even number of guys and girls go out together on a date. It's sort of like a Japanese version of speed dating.

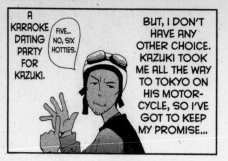

BUT, I DON'T HAVE ANY OTHER CHOICE. KAZUKI TOOK ME ALL THE WAY TO TOKYO ON HIS MOTOR-CYCLE, SO I'VE GOT TO KEEP MY PROMISE...
FIVE... NO, SIX HOTTIES.
A KARAOKE DATING PARTY FOR KAZUKI.

UH, YOU GUYS, AREN'T WE A LITTLE YOUNG TO BE DRINKING...?
SHUT UP! YOU CAN'T SHOW UP LATE AND THEN START LECTURING US.
BESIDES, KAZUKI LOOKS AT LEAST 20.

Drinking age, page 89

The drinking age in Japan is 20 years old.

Ponzu sauce, page 100

Ponzu sauce is a type of flavored soy sauce. A *nabe* is literally a large pot, but the term is used generically to describe any kind of soup, stew, or boiled dish made in a hot pot.

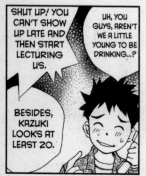

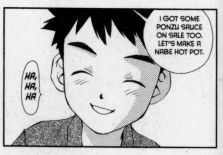

I GOT SOME PONZU SAUCE ON SALE TOO. LET'S MAKE A NABE HOT POT.
HA, HA, HA

Blood type, page 109

Japanese people often interpret people's personalities based on blood type, much like some Americans use astrological signs.

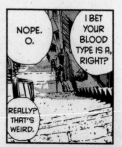

I BET YOUR BLOOD TYPE IS A, RIGHT?
NOPE. O.
REALLY? THAT'S WEIRD.

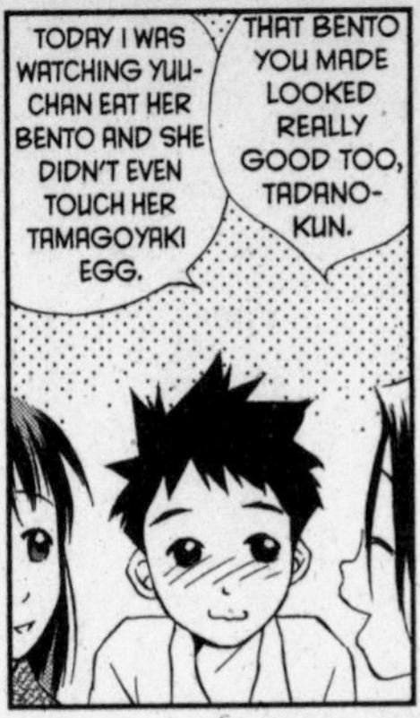
THAT BENTO YOU MADE LOOKED REALLY GOOD TOO, TADANO-KUN.
TODAY I WAS WATCHING YUU-CHAN EAT HER BENTO AND SHE DIDN'T EVEN TOUCH HER TAMAGOYAKI EGG.

Tamagoyaki, page 113

Tamagoyaki is sort of like an egg omelet. It's a common fixture in bento boxes and at sushi restaruants.

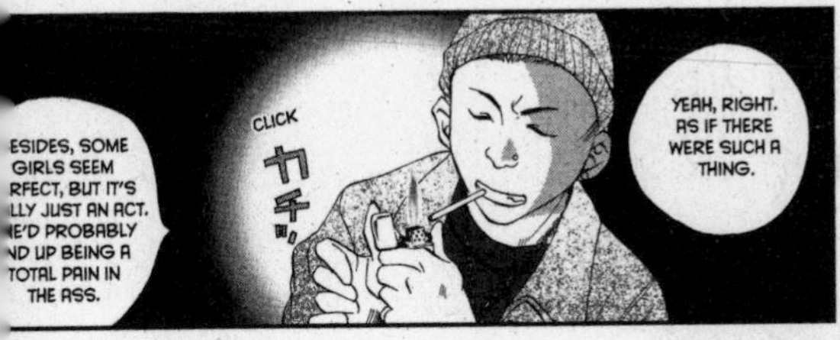
YEAH, RIGHT. AS IF THERE WERE SUCH A THING.
CLICK
ESIDES, SOME GIRLS SEEM RFECT, BUT IT'S LLY JUST AN ACT. E'D PROBABLY ND UP BEING A TOTAL PAIN IN THE ASS.

Burikko, page 118

A *burikko* is a girl who tries to act really childish and dumb in order to seem cute.

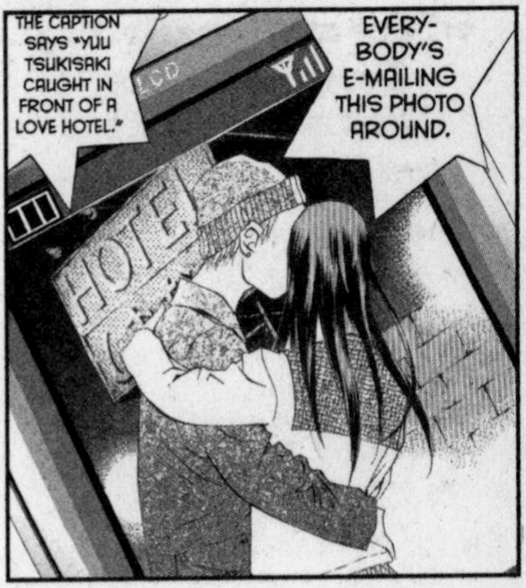
EVERY-BODY'S E-MAILING THIS PHOTO AROUND.
THE CAPTION SAYS "YUU TSUKISAKI CAUGHT IN FRONT OF A LOVE HOTEL."
HOTEL

Love hotels, page 122

Love hotels are specifically designed for couples seeking privacy. They can be rented by the night or by the hour during the daytime. They often have gaudy, Las Vegas–style designs and themed rooms.

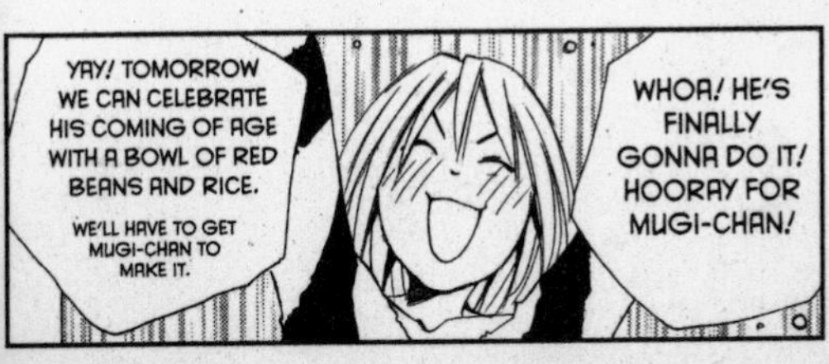
WHOA! HE'S FINALLY GONNA DO IT! HOORAY FOR MUGI-CHAN!
YAY! TOMORROW WE CAN CELEBRATE HIS COMING OF AGE WITH A BOWL OF RED BEANS AND RICE.
WE'LL HAVE TO GET MUGI-CHAN TO MAKE IT.

Sekihan, page 169

Red beans and rice, or *sekihan*, is made with a special kind of rice, called *mochikome*, cooked with azuki beans. It is traditionally eaten during celebrations.

Preview of Volume 5

We are pleased to present you with a preview of Volume 5. This volume will be available in English December 26, 2006. For now you'll have to make do with Japanese!

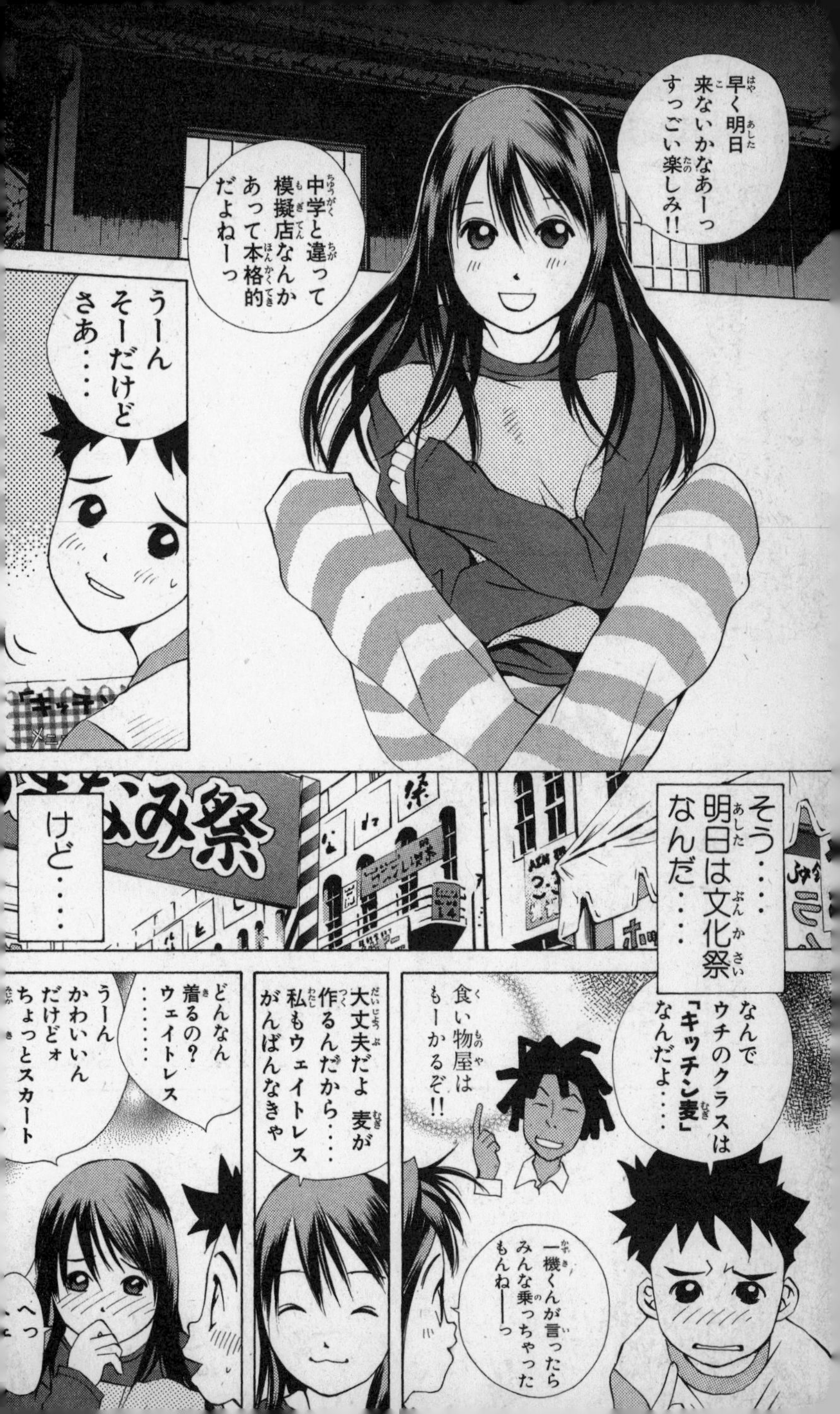
早く明日来ないかなあーっ すっごい楽しみ!!
中学と違って模擬店なんかあって本格的だよねーっ
うーん そーだけどさあ・・・・
そう・・・・明日は文化祭なんだ・・・・
けど・・・・
なんでウチのクラスは「キッチン麦」なんだよ・・・・
食い物屋はもーかるぞ!!
一機くんが言ったらみんな乗っちゃったもんねーーっ
大丈夫だよ 麦が作るんだから・・・・ 私もウェイトレスがんばんなきゃ
どんなん着るの? ウェイトレス・・・・・・
うーん かわいいんだけどォ ちょっとスカート
へっ

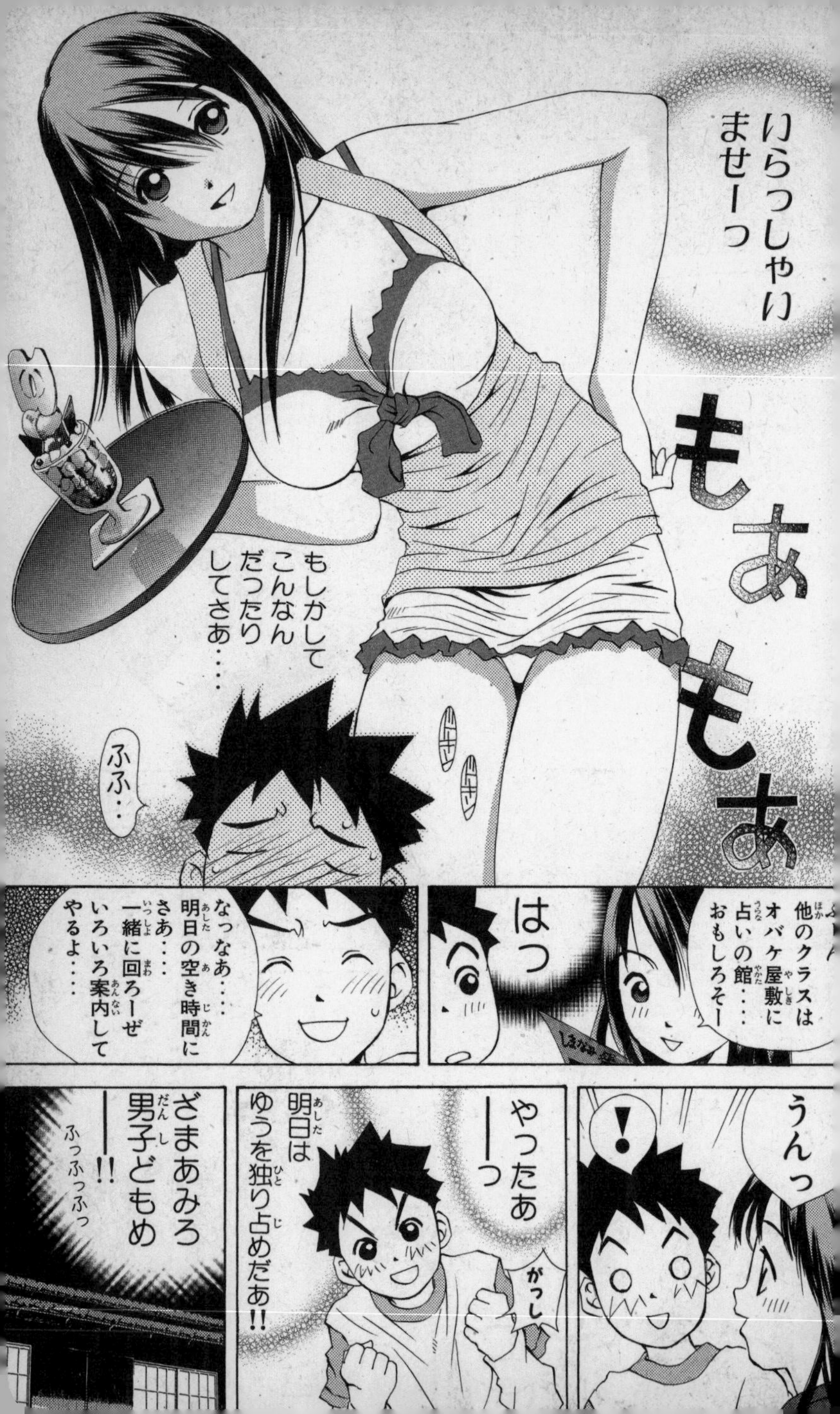

いらっしゃいませーっ
もあもあ
もしかしてこんなんだったりしてさあ・・・・
ふふ・・・
他のクラスはオバケ屋敷に占いの館・・・・おもしろそー
はっ
なっなあ・・・・明日の空き時間にさあ・・・一緒に回ろーぜいろいろ案内してやるよ・・・・
うんっ
!
やったぁーっ
明日はゆうを独り占めだぁ!!
がっし
ざまあみろ男子どもめ——!!
ふっふっふっ

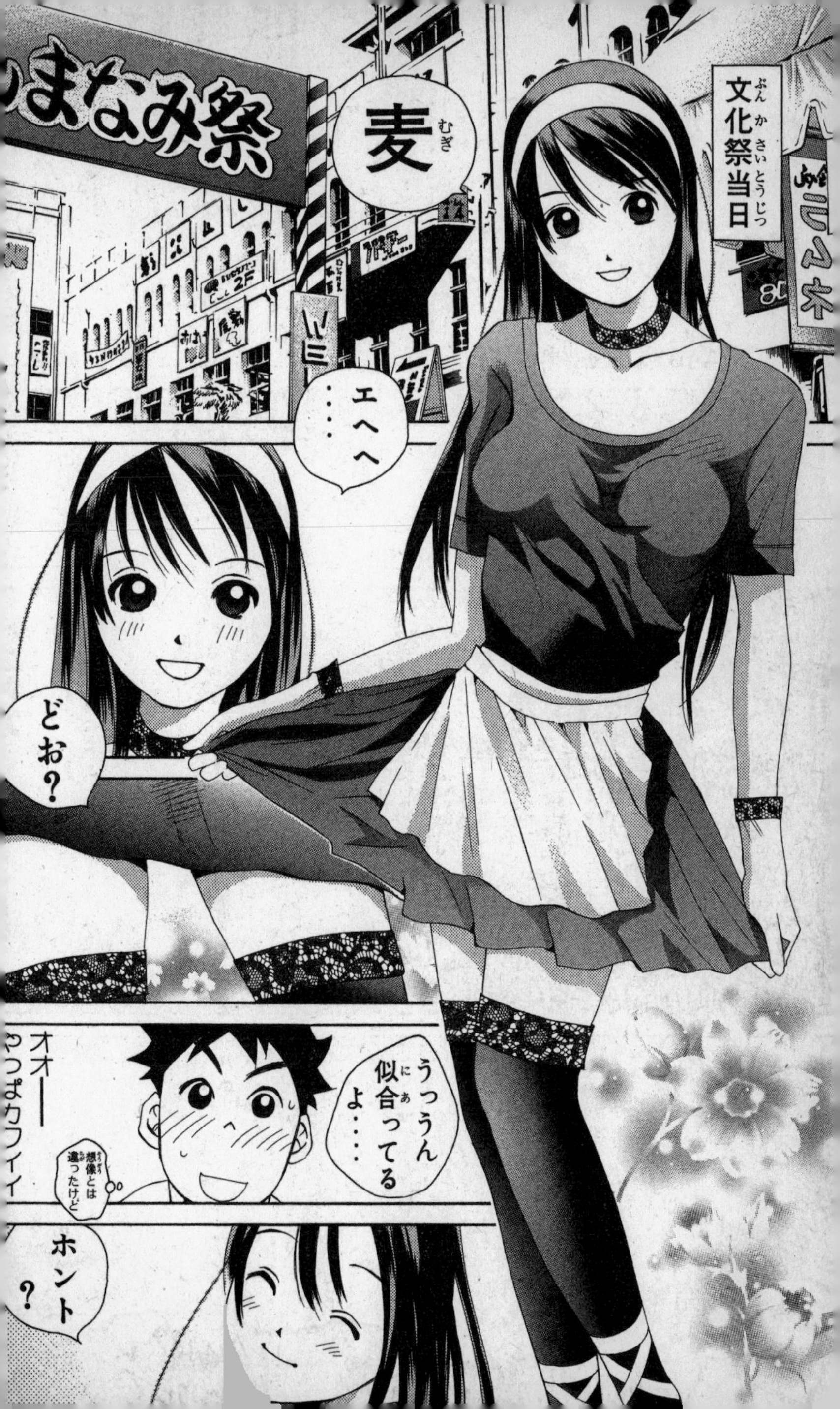
文化祭当日
麦
まなみ祭
エヘヘ・・・・
どお？
うっうん 似合ってる よ・・・・
想像とは違ったけど
オオーー やっぱカワイイ
ホント？

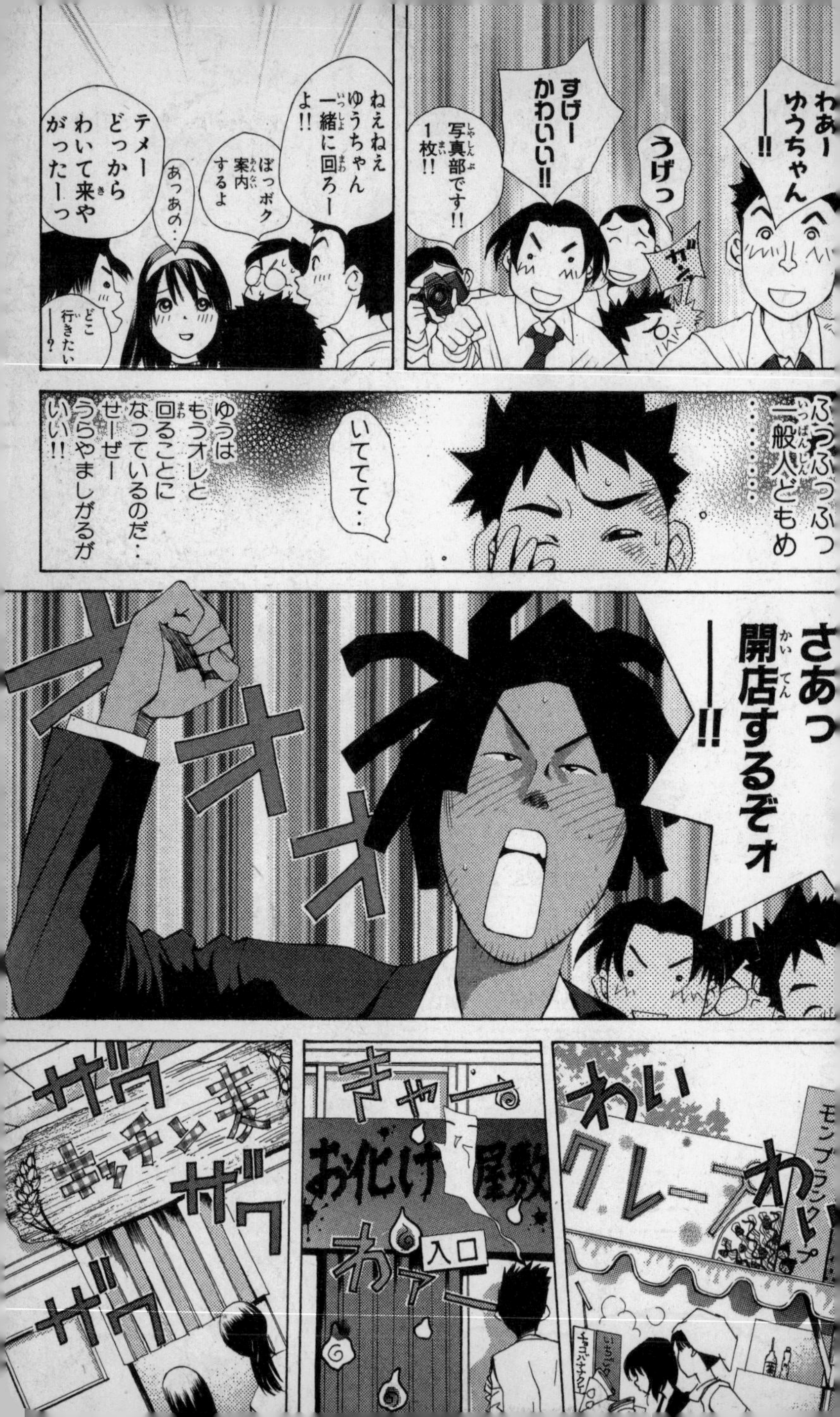
わあーゆうちゃん——!!
うげっ
すげーかわいい!!
写真部です!!1枚!!
ねえねえゆうちゃん一緒に回ろーよ!!
ぼっボク案内するよ
あっあの・・
テメーどっからわいて来やがったーっ
どこ行きたい——?
ふっふっふっ一般人どもめ・・・・・・・・
いててて・・
ゆうはもうオレと回ることになっているのだ・・せーぜーうらやましがるがいい!!
さあっ開店するぞォ——!!
わい
クレープ
わい
モンブランクレープ
きゃー
お化け屋敷
わァー
入口
ザワ
キャッキャッ
ザワ
ザワ

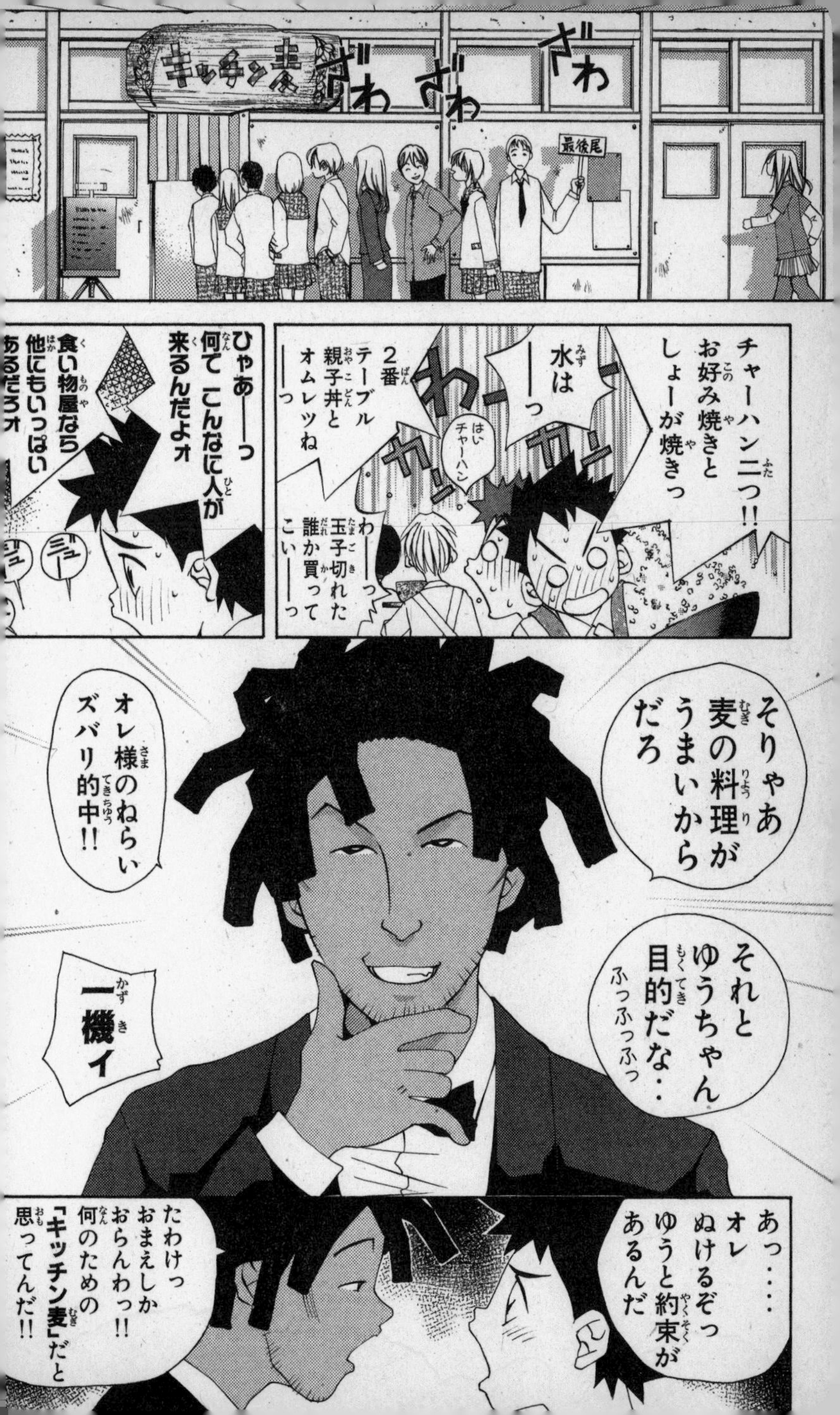
キッチン麦
ざわざわざわ
最後尾
チャーハン二つ!! お好み焼きとしょーが焼きっ
水はーーっ
わーーー
カンカン
はいチャーハン
2番テーブル親子丼とオムレツねーーっ
わーーっ玉子切れた誰か買ってこいーーっ
ひゃあーーっ何て こんなに人が来るんだよォ
食い物屋なら他にもいっぱいあるだろォ
ミュー
ミュ
そりゃあ麦の料理がうまいからだろ
それとゆうちゃん目的だな‥ふっふっふっ
オレ様のねらいズバリ的中!!
一機ィ
あっ‥‥オレぬけるぞっゆうと約束があるんだ
たわけっおまえしかおらんわっ!! 何のための「キッチン麦」だと思ってんだ!!

TOMARE! TOMARE!
TOMARE!

STOP!

YOU'RE GOING THE WRONG WAY!

MANGA IS A COMPLETELY DIFFERENT TYPE
OF READING EXPERIENCE.

TO START AT THE BEGINNING,
GO TO THE END!

THAT'S RIGHT!

AUTHENTIC MANGA IS READ THE TRADITIONAL
JAPANESE WAY—FROM RIGHT TO LEFT. EXACTLY THE OPPOSITE
OF HOW AMERICAN BOOKS ARE READ. IT'S EASY TO FOLLOW:
JUST GO TO THE OTHER END OF THE BOOK, AND READ EACH
PAGE—AND EACH PANEL—FROM RIGHT SIDE TO LEFT SIDE,
STARTING AT THE TOP RIGHT. NOW YOU'RE EXPERIENCING
MANGA AS IT WAS MEANT TO BE.